LONE STAR

JUSTICE

LONE STAR

JUSTICE

A COMPREHENSIVE OVERVIEW OF THE TEXAS CRIMINAL JUSTICE SYSTEM

BY

DAVID M. HORTON AND RYAN KELLUS TURNER

EAKIN PRESS ★ Austin, Texas

Library of Congress Catologing-in-Publication Data

Horton, David M.
    Lone Star Justice: a comprehensive overview of the Texas criminal justice
system / by David M. Horton and Ryan Kellus Turner.—1st ed.
        p.   cm.
    Includes bibliographical references.
    ISBN 1-57168-268-6
    1. Criminal justice, Administration of—Texas.   2. Law enforcement—Texas.
I. Turner, Ryan Kellus.   II. Title.
KFT1762.H67   1998
345.764'05--dc21   98-28970
[B]   CIP

This book is for my mother and the memory of my father, Millie and James Conrad Horton.

—DMH

To my late grandfathers, Garland Turner and Bill Hutchinson, for eternalizing character into my soul and imparting an appreciation for life into my heart. To my grandmothers, Louise Turner and Beth Hutchinson, for providing me with the foundation for a remarkable life (proud, loving, and supportive parents, wonderful families). You both continue to move and inspire me with the joy and comfort you bring, not only to the lives of loved ones, but to everyone you know.

—RKT

★ CONTENTS

ACKNOWLEDGMENTS

A large number of individuals were instrumental in the writing of this book. I would like to acknowledge the assistance and support of those people who took time from their busy schedules to assist in securing library materials and providing current statistics, including Julie Worthen, Connie Cabezas, Alison Carpenter, and Armando Garcia of the Scarborough-Phillips Library at St. Edward's University, Austin, Texas; Donaly E. Brice, Penelope Dukes-Williams, and Diana Boardman Houston, of the Texas State Library and Archives Commission; Pam Nickel, of the Texas Department of Public Safety's Crime Records Service; Mary Kay Bolton and Jayne Tune, of the Texas Commission on Law Enforcement Officer Standards and Education; Debbie J. Fillmore, assistant deputy director, Texas Commission on Jail Standards; Detective Jon Ford, Austin Police Department; Dr. Charles R. Jeffords, director of research and planning, Texas Youth Commission; Wynde L. Brisbin, research specialist with the Community Justice Assistance Division of the Texas Department of Criminal Justice; and Mary B. Karl, of the State Jail Division of the Texas Department of Criminal Justice.

I am especially indebted to a number of people who made valuable contributions to this book by carefully reading and editing the chapter drafts or providing insightful substantive comments, including my wife, Bridget Anne Horton, for her critical editing skills in the area of grammar and syntax; Dr. Maryanne Hopper, dean of the School of Behavioral and Social

Sciences, St. Edward's University, for proofreading chapters; Drs. Terry Newton and James E. Payne, St. Edward's University faculty, for insights on Texas history; Bennie Ray, criminal defense attorney, Austin, Texas, for his assistance with the processes of parole and probation in Texas; and Ashley Nellis, a senior criminal justice major and Honors Program student at St. Edward's University, as well as Private Prison Project coordinator for the Texas chapter of the American Civil Liberties Union, for her insight into private prisons in Texas. A special note of thanks is due to Elsa S. Velasquez for her technical assistance and support with respect to word processing and file conversions.

I would like to express my gratitude to Mary Frances Kucera, my undergraduate research assistant, for her work on the Texas criminal justice internet sites, her consistently cheerful mood, and for the many little production tasks she performed for me during the course of writing this book.

In keeping with my long held belief that there are few things in the academic world more valuable than a good copy editor, I would like to thank Melissa Roberts of Eakin Press for her work in preparing the manuscript for the printer.

Finally, I would like to thank my friend Ed Eakin for his encouragement of and support for this writing project.

DAVID M. HORTON, Ph.D.
Austin, Texas
November 1998

Thanks to the following faculty, visiting faculty, and staff at Southern Methodist University School of Law: Joseph W. McKnight, Elizabeth G. Thornburg, Ernest B. White III for their critiques and comments; Timothy Davis, Lackland H. Bloom, Jr., Roy R. Anderson, Gerry W. Beyer, Laura G. Amberson, Bruce E. Muck, and David P. Whelan for their helpful assistance and advice.

Thanks to Ronald E. Jones at Prairie View A&M University for providing information on HB 1550, Thomas O. Massoll for Mac support (and supporting the Mac), Ginger Ester for her assistance in editing Chapter 4, and David Hall and Wesley Stidham for assistance with visuals.

Recognizing that pictures are truly worth a thousand words, we also greatly appreciate the assistance of Mike Cox at the Texas Department of Public Safety Public Information Office, David Nunley, historian for the Texas Department of Criminal Justice, Kelly George at the State Preservation Board, and Eakin Press for their assistance in collecting the book's photographs.

Special thanks to Frederick C. Moss at Southern Methodist University School of Law for his dedicated effort and supervision; Stephanie Becan for style and syntax editing (plus abundant generosity and enthusiasm); John Rowland for the time, talent, and energy he spent on this and other projects in the works; and Judge Sharon Keller of the Texas Court of Criminal Appeals for the opportunity to serve the Court and take my understanding of criminal justice to a whole new level.

I am personally grateful to the following: J. Randall Price, Will Pryor, Martha McCabe, Marjorie Keele, Ron Hughes, Amina Memon, Nolan and Nancy Jones, Charles Levin, Ed Goodman, Gerald Garoutte, Jitendra N. Bhatt, Donna Kelton, Gina Tackett, Alison Cooper, Presbyterian Hospital of Dallas, Cathy Day, and Robert Vernon Housley.

Finally, I would like to thank my parents and family for helping me get off to a good start. I am also grateful to the friends I have made over the years while living in Vernon, Austin, and Dallas.

RYAN KELLUS TURNER, J.D.
Austin, Texas
November 1998

 **PREFACE**

The phrase "criminal justice system" is a broad, overarching term commonly used to denote a wide range of activities carried out by the legislative, executive, and judicial branches of government in the interests of promoting a safe and orderly society. Included within the range of these governmental activities are the formulation and definition of behaviors that are considered unacceptable and the creation of the organizations for investigating, apprehending, prosecuting, and punishing criminals. It is important to understand, however, that the criminal justice process is not merely about legislators, law enforcement officers, and prison personnel operating as isolated entities. Rather, the term "criminal justice system" connotes the interrelationship of a host of philosophies, professions, and practices. As such, *Lone Star Justice* is written from an interdisciplinary and integrated systems perspective that we believe readers will find beneficial in their pursuit of a comprehensive and well-rounded understanding of the historical, legal, and operational aspects of the Texas criminal justice system.

Until now, anyone interested in understanding how the system of criminal justice is organized and operated in the state of Texas has had to consult a great number of diverse types of documents, each of which tend to treat upon only a small aspect or segment of the system. *Lone Star Justice* represents the first comprehensive overview of the historical development and contemporary organization and operation of all the various governmental activities which, considered in their totality, comprise the system of criminal justice administration in Texas. The information contained in *Lone Star Justice* has been drawn from a very wide range of historical, political, and statutory sources, including past and present Texas state government publications, journal articles, historical as well as contemporary Texas statutes and relevant appellate court decisions, obscure, out-of-print, and otherwise difficult to locate books, doctoral dissertations, and master's theses, and rare archival documents in the possession of the Texas State Library and Archives Commission, the Library of the Center for American History at the University of Texas at Austin, and the Underwood Law Library at Southern Methodist University.

The information compiled from these sources has been used to craft a concise descriptive overview of the Texas criminal justice system that is written in general terms, and we believe it will be of value to a wide range of readers, including students, educators, legal and criminal justice professionals, pedants extraordinaire, proud Texans, and anyone generally interested in Texana. For some readers, *Lone Star Justice* may very well be their first introduction to the subject of criminal justice in Texas. While some of the concepts discussed are complex and involved, such as the structure and operation of the Texas court system, certain aspects of the substantive and procedural criminal law, and parole eligibility requirements, every effort has been made to convey the information in as straightforward a fashion as possible, and make the book user-friendly. Diagrams and organizational charts have been included to supplement the discussions where appropriate, and the appendix contains an extensive glossary as well as a description of important and valuable Internet sites on the World Wide Web for those readers who are interested in further exploring specific aspects of the Texas criminal justice system. For readers who are already somewhat familiar with or have an extensive background in the Texas criminal justice system, *Lone Star Justice* will round out their understanding by providing them with the composite "big picture" of the Texas criminal justice system, both past and present. Additionally, we hope the concise and comprehensive nature of the text makes *Lone Star Justice* an ideal general reference source.

Discussions about the administration of criminal justice are traditionally grounded in one of three approaches: the ideal, the theoretical, or the reality approach. The ideal approach focuses on how the process of criminal justice administration should, under virtually unconstrained and utopian circumstances, be organized and operated. The theoretical approach addresses how the system of criminal justice administration could be improved, given the existing and limited economic, personnel, and material resources available to agents of the legislative, executive, and judicial branches of government. The reality approach describes how the laws and organizational structures created for the administration of criminal justice have evolved and actually operate. *Lone Star Justice* is written from the perspective of the reality approach, and examines the evolution and operation of the Texas criminal justice system from historical, political, and statutory perspectives.

From its inception, we envisioned *Lone Star Justice* providing a solid foundation for further discussions about criminal justice in Texas. We look forward to building relationships with educators, students, and other readers interested in Texas criminal justice. To achieve these goals, we welcome your questions, comments, and suggestions.

DAVID M. HORTON, Ph.D.
RYAN KELLUS TURNER, J.D.

Correspondence

e-mail: lonestarjustice@mailcity.com

mail: Lone Star Justice
c/o Eakin Press
P.O. Box 90159
Austin, Texas 78709

1.
CRIME AND THE ADMINISTRATION OF JUSTICE IN TEXAS

INTRODUCTION

The problem of crime in Texas has been of paramount concern to its residents since the time of Austin's Colony in the early 1820s. Even today, public opinion polls consistently suggest that crime is a major concern of Texans. Texans, both past and present, have always looked to their state, county, and municipal governments to both insure an orderly and well-functioning society and to protect them from criminal depredations. To discharge this responsibility, the state, county, and municipal governmental entities in Texas have created a large and specialized bureaucracy to deal with the problem of crime and social control. Considered collectively, this bureaucracy is referred to as the Texas criminal justice system. The crime prevention and crime control functions that constitute the criminal justice system in Texas include the state legislature which creates the laws and regulates the processes for the administration of criminal justice; state law enforcement agencies, county sheriff departments, and municipal police departments, which enforce the law through routine patrol, investigation, and apprehension of criminal wrongdoers; the criminal court system, which litigates questions of liability associated with accusations of criminal wrongdoing; and the prison and parole

1

systems, which are responsible for the punishment of criminal offenders and their reintegration into mainstream society.

Before proceeding with an examination of the historical, political, and statutory development and current organization and operation of the criminal justice system in Texas, it will be useful to briefly examine crime and the administration of criminal justice in Anglo-American Texas prior to the Texas Revolution of 1836, the nineteenth-century legacy of crime and violence in Texas, and the present state of affairs in Texas with respect to crime.

PART 1:
CRIME AND THE ADMINISTRATION OF CRIMINAL JUSTICE IN ANGLO-AMERICAN TEXAS PRIOR TO THE TEXAS REVOLUTION

The Alcalde System of Criminal Justice Administration under Mexican Colonial Rule: 1821-1836

In the first two decades of the nineteenth century, the geographical area that today comprises the state of Texas was part of Spain's colonial empire in the New World. The mechanisms for the enforcement of law and the administration of criminal justice in Spanish colonial provinces in the Americas were derived from Spain's centuries-old reliance upon the Roman law based tradition as an instrument of national and local government. One feature of the Spanish system of governance, both at home and abroad, was the policy of delegating the principal responsibilities for maintaining law and order and the administration of criminal justice to the municipal level.

Following Mexico's independence from Spain in 1821, what is today Texas became part of the northern Mexican state of Coahuila y Tejas, and Mexico continued to use Spain's Roman law based system as the principal mechanism for the general governance of the northern state. Like Spain, the Mexican oversight of its territory was accomplished through a system of delegating responsibility and authority. The power to govern and administer criminal justice emanated from the president's office in Mexico City, and ran to the governor of the state of Coahuila y Tejas, and thence to the municipal level. In turn, the maintenance of public order and the administration of criminal justice at the municipal level during period of Mexican rule from 1821 to 1836 was accomplished by the use of a number of well-defined institutions that evolved over the centuries in Spain, which, considered collectively, has been referred to as the *alcalde* system. An understanding of the Mexican *alcalde* system is important because it was the basis of Stephen Fuller Austin's first Anglo-American system of criminal justice administration in Texas from 1821 to 1836.

The principal governing body of Mexican colonial municipalities and the surrounding rural areas was the *ayuntamiento*. This body functioned much like a modern-day city council or board of county commissioners, and was responsible for the management of all affairs, both civil and criminal, relating to the general well-being and prosperity of the municipality. As the chief conservator of the public morals and the general welfare of the community, the *ayuntamiento* was responsible for a variety of functions, including promulgating ordinances promoting public safety, the enforcement of law, and the administration of civil as well as criminal justice. The size of the *ayuntamiento* often varied from municipality to municipality, as did the manner in which its composition was determined. In some instances the *ayuntamiento* was elected; in other instances membership was achieved through inheritance, purchase, or appointment. Regardless of the means by which membership on the *ayuntamiento* was achieved, its composition included the most wealthy, learned, and respected members of the municipality who, acting collectively, represented the collective conscience of the community.

The chief members of the *ayuntamiento* were the *alcalde mayor* (or president), the *alcalde de crimen* (the executive officer of the *alcalde mayor* who functioned in the dual capacity of law enforcer and judge), the *alguacil mayor* (the chief law enforcement officer), the *alcalde ordinare* (the officer responsible for matters relating to the administration of civil law), and *reigidors* (the principal administrative officers of city government who functioned much like county commissioners or city council members). The most important office in the Mexican colonial scheme of municipal governance and justice administration was the *alcalde mayor*, a position sometimes referred to in the historical records as the *justicia mayor*. As president of the *ayuntamiento*, the *alcalde mayor* was a powerful position invested with the responsibility and authority to promote the general welfare and safety of the citizenry and preservation of peace and public order. The *alcalde mayor* was answerable to the governor of the Mexican state. In addition to civil responsibilities that included carrying out a yearly census and maintaining the record of all births and deaths, the *alcalde mayor* had very broad powers associated with the administration of criminal justice. This was the municipal officer in whom the overall responsibility was vested for order and the prevention of crime. In discharging this responsibility, the *alcalde mayor* had the power to issue municipal ordinances consistent with promoting and preserving the peace, to cause the arrest of criminal wrongdoers, to ensure that they were prosecuted to the full extent of the law in a just and summary fashion, and to see that convicted criminals received sentences commensurate with their crimes. Additionally, the *alcalde mayor* was responsible for the oversight of the municipal *carcel*, or house of detention.

Most, but not all, of the laws which governed Mexican municipalities after 1821 were derived from the 1680 document titled *Recopilacion de Leyes de los Reynos de las Indias*. This document set forth the minimum behavioral expectations necessary for an orderly and progressive society, and made punishable as state offenses such crimes as murder, robbery, larceny, arson, and treason. As mentioned earlier, however, the *alcalde mayor* was vested with the authority to issue ordinances and prescribe punishments for any behaviors which he deemed disruptive to the public peace of the municipality. Typical of such municipal ordinances were prohibitions against the discharging of firearms within the limits of the municipality without good cause (punishable by a fine of two *pesos*), and public drunkenness (which was punishable by a fine of 25 *pesos* and hard labor on public works for 15 days). Additionally, *alcalde mayors* frequently issued ordinances directed toward merchants who deceived the public with false advertisements and unfair sales practices, shorting customers by false weights and measures, and product adulteration. In instances where a municipality experienced problems with able-bodied, idle vagrants and beggars, the *alcalde mayor* was empowered to issue an ordinance calling for them to secure employment or face either forcible banishment or forced hard labor for a period of time on public works.

While the *alcalde mayor* was vested with the responsibility and authority for a wide range of legislative, executive (i.e., law enforcement), and judicial functions associated with the administration of criminal justice, he was directly active only in the issuing of ordinances whose object was to promote the public peace and safety of the municipality. The actual discharge of the law enforcement and judicial functions was delegated to an *alcalde de crimen*, who was appointed by the *alcalde mayor*. As the chief law enforcement officer of the municipality, the *alcalde de crimen* was empowered by the *alcalde mayor* to enforce all laws and ordinances by organizing patrols, investigating allegations of criminal wrongdoing, and ordering and directing the apprehension of miscreants. The *alcalde de crimen* in turn delegated the responsibility and authority for these functions to an *alguacil mayor*. Functioning in the capacity of an executive officer of the *alcalde de crimen*, the *alguacil mayor* was responsible for carrying out the orders of the *alcalde de crimen* by policing the municipality with the organization of street patrols, physically arresting wrongdoers on the order of the *alcalde de crimen* or on their own initiative, and taking charge of convicted criminals and superintending the discharge of their sentence.

All arrested persons were brought forthwith before the *alcalde de crimen* and tried summarily without benefit of jury. Summary convictions were appealable to the *alcalde mayor* and the *ayuntamiento*. In rural areas outside the confines of the municipality, the responsibility for overseeing the maintenance of law and order was given to a *jueces de campo*, or rural judge, who was appointed by the *alcalde mayor*. As needed, the *jueces de campo* could call upon the authority and services of the *alguacil mayor* to enforce the law and restore order.

The *alcalde* system of criminal justice administration continued to function in Texas, albeit in a modified form, until Texas achieved its independence from Mexico in 1836.

Law and the Administration of Criminal Justice in Anglo-American Texas Prior to the Texas Revolution

Stephen F. Austin is unquestionably the founding father of the Texas criminal justice system. In January 1821 Moses Austin received permission from the government in Mexico City to found the first Anglo-American settlement in what is today the state of Texas, but died that spring before the plan could be realized. In August 1821 Mexican Governor Antonio Maria Martinez granted Stephen F. Austin the authority to continue the colonization enterprise begun by his father.

Austin was allowed to settle 300 families on land whose northern border roughly ran in a line from the present-day Texas towns of Brenham, Navasota, and La Grange south to the Gulf of Mexico. In exchange for the land grant to the "Old Three Hundred" (as the first settlers are referred to today), Austin was expected to establish a system for the general governance of the colony. Included within this expectation was the understanding that Austin would be responsible for establishing law, preserving order, and implementing a system for the administration of criminal justice. From 1821 to 1836 the governance of Austin's Colony was patterned on the *ayuntamiento* system, with Austin holding the position of *alcalde mayor*. It is important to understand, however, that while Austin based his scheme for general governance and the administration of criminal justice on the *ayuntamiento*, the character and operation of Austin's version was greatly influenced by American and English common law traditions. Austin infused into the *ayuntamiento* system common law traditions which he had been exposed to during two years of study at Transylvania University in Lexington, Kentucky, a short tenure as a circuit court judge in the first judicial district of the Arkansas territory, and during the time he devoted to reading law while in New Orleans, Louisiana, in 1820.

In August 1822 the geographical area comprising the Austin land grant was divided into two districts for governance purposes. These were the Brazos and Colorado districts. In establishing a system of governance based upon the *alcalde* system, Austin departed from the Mexican tradition in two significant ways. First, he combined the criminal justice responsibilities of the *alcalde de crimen* and the civil law responsibilities of the *alcalde ordinare* into one position with subject matter jurisdiction over both criminal and civil matters. Under Austin's *ayuntamiento* system, this agent was simply referred to as an *alcalde*. Second, instead of appointing *alcaldes*, Austin allowed the Anglo-American colonists from each of the two districts to elect their own *alcalde*. The first two Anglo-American *alcaldes* were John Jackson Tumlinson, the *alcalde* for the Colorado District, and Josiah Hughes Bell, the *alcalde* for the Brazos District. Tumlinson and Bell had substantially the same authority and responsibilities as their Spanish and Mexican counterparts. Austin empowered Tumlinson and Bell to each appoint a constable to aid them in enforcing the law.

Given the Anglo-American's general unfamiliarity with the law and procedures of the Roman law based system of criminal justice administration, Tumlinson and Bell did not discharge their law enforcement and adjudicatory functions in exactly the same manner as their Spanish and Mexican counterparts. Rather, the discharge of criminal justice under Austin's *alcalde* system was guided by the unique experiences of Anglo-Americans on the Texas frontier and the traditions of law and justice consistent with their American and English common law heritage. This resulted in a lack of uniformity in enforcing the law and administering justice. In the first two years of the Anglo-American *alcalde* system, Tumlinson and Bell were, in effect, almost making up procedure as they went along. This lack of consistency caused resentment and confusion among some of the Anglo-American colonists, and became an issue of concern for Austin. He rectified the problem in early 1824 by promulgating what is the first Anglo-American law code in Texas.

Instructions and Regulations for the Alcaldes

To impress some semblance of uniformity onto the Anglo-American version of the Mexican *alcalde* system of law and criminal justice administration, Austin on 22 January 1824 issued by decree a document titled *Instructions and Regulations for the Alcaldes*. This first Anglo-American law code in Texas was a combination of penal code, code of criminal procedure, and code of civil procedure. The document defined crimes and specified punishments, authorized the creation of the offices of sheriff and constable, established a rudimentary system of courts of justice, and delineated the processes for the adjudication of criminal as well as civil liability.

Crimes and Punishments

Austin's *Instructions and Regulations for the Alcaldes* relied upon English common law concepts for delineating and defining criminal behavior. For example, crimes against the person included murder, punishable by hanging, and battery, abuse, or ill treatment of another, which Austin made punishable by a fine not to exceed $100 and incarceration at hard labor on public works for three months. Additionally, those found guilty of battery, abuse, or ill treatment were required to post a bond to ensure their future good behavior and were made liable for monetary damages in a civil suit brought by the injured party. Crimes against property such as robbery, larceny, and knowingly being in possession of stolen property were punishable by a fine three times the fair market value of the stolen property and incarceration at hard labor on public works. Austin's *Instructions and Regulations for the Alcaldes* also prohibited and made punishable vices and immoral behaviors which he deemed disruptive and threatening to the general peace, tranquility, and dignity of the community of colonists. Typical of this category of prohibited behavior was gambling, which was punishable by a fine of not less than $20 nor more than $200. It is interesting to note that horse racing was not included within the meaning of gambling. Horse racing was permitted in the interests of promoting breeding practices that placed a premium on swiftness and stamina. The placing of wagers on the outcome of horse races, however, was prohibited. Profane swearing and public drunkenness were punishable by a fine of not less than $1.00 nor more than $10. Habitual inebriety was punishable by incarceration for not more than two days. Cohabitation and fornication without benefit of marriage was deemed a serious affront to the dignity of the colony, and was made punishable by a fine of not less than $100 nor more than $500 and incarceration at hard labor on public works. Sturdy beggars, vagabonds, and vagrants were subject to banishment. Respect for the laws and processes of Austin's *alcalde* system was impressed upon the colonists by making those who resisted the administration of justice or verbally abused an officer of the *alcalde* system liable for a fine not to exceed $50 and incarceration at hard labor for a term not to exceed one month.

Law Enforcement

The first Anglo-American law enforcement body in Texas was created by Austin in 1823, and consisted of a volunteer corps of rangers to guard the colony from Indian attack. Because the ranging companies were created before the drafting of Austin's *Instructions and Regulations for the Alcaldes*, the history and evolution of the Texas Rangers will be discussed in Chapter 3.

Austin's *Instructions and Regulations for the Alcaldes* contained a number of provisions for the creation and maintenance of the law enforcement function. The document made clear that the *alcalde* was the chief officer responsible for the enforcement of criminal as well as civil law, but authorized citizen arrest by giving to any person the right to use force for the purpose of physically apprehending criminal wrongdoers and delivering them into the custody of the *alcalde*. In the discharge of his law enforcement functions the *alcalde* was empowered to invoke the common law tradition of *posse commitatus* and raise a body of armed men to pursue fugitive criminals. Additionally, Austin's *Instructions and Regulations for the Alcaldes* not only gave *alcaldes* the power to appoint constables to aid them in the execution of their law enforcement functions, but also gave to Austin the power to appoint a sheriff to aid him in the execution of civil processes connected with his position as *alcalde mayor*. The use of the English common law term "sheriff" in his *Instructions and Regulations for the Alcaldes* represents the first time in Texas history that the term is used in an official document.

It is uncertain whether constables and the sheriff were compensated by salary. What is known is that Article 30 of Austin's *Instructions and Regulations* includes a fee schedule for specific services rendered. For example, constables and the sheriff were to be paid eight bits ($1.00) for serving a criminal arrest warrant, three bits (37.5 cents) for summoning a jury, and two bits (25 cents) for serving a summons. In discharging their legal obligations, constables and the sheriff were authorized to be reimbursed for round-trip mileage at the rate of five cents per mile. Additionally, when the sheriff was directed to sell property to satisfy a civil judgment, he was entitled to receive four percent on amounts less than $200 and one percent on every $100 of property valuation thereafter.

The Judicial System

The Anglo-American *alcaldes*, like their Spanish and Mexican counterparts, had both law enforcement as well as judicial powers. Under Austin's *Instructions and Regulations* they were responsible for not only maintaining order and causing the arrest of criminal wrongdoers, but also for presiding over the adjudication of their criminal liability by empaneling a jury of six men, summoning witnesses, examining evidence, and keeping a written record of the proceedings. A person convicted in the *alcalde* courts of a noncapital offense had the right under Austin's *Instructions and Regulations* to appeal the conviction

by attaching a written statement to the record of the trial proceedings which was then forwarded to Austin for his review.
In all capital convictions, Austin was required to submit the
record of the trial to the governor of the state of Coahuila y
Tejas prior to hanging the condemned. If a convict was not
able to raise the money to satisfy a fine imposed upon him by
the *alcalde* court, he was incarcerated and forced to labor on
public works until the fair market value of his labor equaled
the amount of the imposed fine.

In a situation similar to that of constables and the sheriff,
it is unclear whether *alcaldes* received a fixed salary. Again,
what is known is that Article 30 of Austin's *Instructions and
Regulations for the Alcaldes* stipulates a schedule of fees payable
to *alcaldes* for specific services rendered. For example, *alcaldes*
were paid eight bits ($1.00) for writing the respondent's argu-
ment in instances where the judgment of the court was being
appealed to Austin, four bits (50 cents) for the issuance of a
criminal arrest warrant, and two bits (25 cents) each for issuance of either a summons or a subpoena.

Additionally, *alcaldes* had responsibilities and powers
associated with the discharge of civil law and acted as nota-
ries during the drawing up of contracts, presided over the
adjudication of civil law disputes, and performed civil marriage ceremonies. It is interesting to note that Austin's *Instructions and Regulations for the Alcaldes* required *alcaldes* in
all matters of dispute arising from the civil law to first
attempt resolution by "conciliation" rather than resorting to
formal litigation. This requirement may rightly be said to be
the forerunner of the modern-day concept of mediation, or
alternative dispute resolution.

The evolutionary development and subsequent organization and operation of the Texas criminal justice system from
the period of the Republic of Texas to the present day is dealt
with in the succeeding chapters of this book. Discussed in
detail are the foundations of Texas law and the evolution of
the Texas Constitution, the enforcement of law in Texas, the
Texas court system, criminal procedure in Texas from arrest
through appeal, the historical development of the Texas
prison system and its current organization and operation,

parole and probation in Texas, and the administration of the juvenile justice system.

PART 2:
THE NINETEENTH-CENTURY LEGACY OF CRIME AND VIOLENCE IN TEXAS

Foundations of the Texas Legacy of Crime and Violence

The land, the people, and the social system of Texas, it seems, have always inspired in the public images connected with matters of crime and the administration of justice. Mention the Lone Star State in connection with either crime or justice in the same breath, and many people will immediately think of the archetypal Western outlaw engaged in cattle rustling and train and bank robberies, the Texas Rangers, county sheriffs and town marshals tirelessly working to restore law and maintain order, Judge Roy Bean summarily dispensing frontier justice, and convicted murderers hanged with certainty and celerity. While there is some truth to the reputation Texas earned during the nineteenth century as a state where violence and bloodshed were part of the social fabric, some of the images associated with crime and the administration of justice in the Lone Star State are founded more in myth than in fact.

While a comprehensive and definitive history of crime in Texas remains to be written and is beyond the intended scope of this book, it will be instructive, nonetheless, to briefly touch upon some highlights of crime that seem to have contributed to the view that Texas was a "paradise" of sorts for criminals. The foundation from which this view springs may be appreciated by examining the legacy of crime in Texas from the practice of dueling, the odious practice of vigilantism and lynching, the incidents of feuding among rival groups of cattle ranchers, and some of the major outlaws connected with Texas.

Dueling

From the time of Austin's Colony in 1821 to the close of the nineteenth century, it was not uncommon for men in Texas to go about armed with handguns, rifles, and knives. In the sparsely populated frontier areas of Texas, where law officers were few and the courts of law distant, responsibility for protecting oneself, one's family, and one's property fell principally to each individual. Thus, it is from this circumstance and tradition that the reputation of Texas as a place where rugged individualism prevailed was founded. Men of sober and industrious reputation were considered by their fellow citizens as justified in killing those who threatened their life, their family, or their property.

While the men of nineteenth-century Texas routinely armed themselves for the primary purpose of protection, the ready access to weapons frequently resulted in their being used to settle civil disputes, respond to taunting provocations, or avenge slights to one's reputation and manhood. The term "duel" is today used to describe an incident where death or injury resulted where weapons were used in resolving these types of situations. Especially in instances where insults were directed toward a man or his family, failure to respond with gunplay to defend the honor of one's name or family was often looked upon as a mark of cowardice. The duel took many forms, but few of them in Texas were either conducted with the formality and civility associated with the French *Code Duello*, or in the manner depicted in Hollywood Westerns where the combatants met at high noon on Main Street. Most duels in Texas occurred without the gentlemanly formalities of proffering an invitation, offering a choice of weapons, selecting seconds, selecting a dueling ground, and mutual agreement on the date and time of meeting that are typical of the European tradition of dueling. Rather, the typical Texas duel occurred almost spontaneously, after one of the participants provoked the other by word or deed, guns were drawn, and one or both parties lay dead or wounded. An interesting variant on the practice of dueling in Texas is referred to as the Helena Duel, after the town in South Texas where the form is said to have originated. In this variation of the duel, two combatants would have their left hands tied together, a knife would be placed in their free right hands, and they would then fight to the death.

It is important to understand that Texans drew a distinction between a criminal killing and what was referred to as "a difficulty," or justifiable killing from a duel. A difficulty resulted when a man of poor reputation and character was killed in a gunfight after provoking, threatening, or insulting an otherwise law-abiding and upstanding member of the community. The popular view of such killings was that the instigator deserved what he got, and the actions of the killer were justified on the grounds that he was merely defending his good name and reputation.

The practice of dueling was so well accepted and pervasive in Texas prior to the Revolution that one of the first items of business undertaken by the Congress of the Republic of Texas in 1836 was the passage of a law which made the survivor of a duel that resulted in a killing liable for prosecution for first-degree murder and subject to hanging upon conviction. The 1836 dueling statute also made punishable the act of aiding and abetting a duel by incarceration and fine. The law, however, proved to be ineffective in stopping dueling. The practice of dueling had already become an established custom in Texas, and juries rarely returned convictions for defendants charged under the dueling statute, especially if they were respected members of the community. While records of arrests and convictions were not uniformly kept at this time, archival court records from the period suggest that less than twelve percent of murder prosecutions that resulted from dueling resulted in convictions.

To remedy the reluctance of Texas juries to convict duelists who were perceived to have acted in a socially acceptable manner, the Congress of the Republic of Texas in 1840 reduced the classification of death resulting from a duel from first-degree murder to manslaughter, with the attendant result that a conviction for manslaughter resulting from a duel would be punishable by incarceration rather than death. Extant records from the period 1840 to 1845 indicate that the revised

"Deacon" Jim Miller of Pecos, Texas, killed more than 40 men before a vigilante mob hanged him along with three others in an Oklahoma barn.

dueling law had little effect on the willingness of juries to convict. The Texas Constitution of 1845, drawn up in the year that the state joined the Union, expressly forbade duelists from holding public office, and it is interesting to note that until 1 January 1939 all state officials were required, prior to assuming office, to publicly swear under oath that they had never participated in a duel.

Vigilantism and Lynching

While dueling may be viewed as the act of an individual to secure justice for himself rather than resorting to the court system for relief, vigilantism was a form of extralegal law enforcement carried out by a group of citizens who seized persons suspected of or charged with crimes, or took them from the custody of the law, and inflicted summary punishment upon them without benefit of legal trial and without the warrant or authority of law. From 1840 to 1942 vigilante groups were an almost constant presence in Texas life. So pervasive was vigilantism and lynch law in Texas that only the states of Mississippi and Georgia have a documented history of being more active in this area.

During the 102-year history of documented vigilantism in Texas, two forms of this common process of extrajudicial administration of justice are distinctly identifiable: the traditional vigilance committee that operated for the purpose of superintending community order, and the racially motivated vigilance group whose principal aim was to maintain the racial status quo order through the promotion of white supremacy.

The vigilance committee created for the purpose of superintending community order was the result of well-intentioned Texans interested in securing for themselves and their families a safe social environment conducive to moral stability and economic growth. Outside of the growing metropolitan areas, the sparsely populated ranching and agricultural areas of Texas presented serious problems for promoting the interests of safety and security by means of relying upon the orderly administration of criminal justice established by the state legislature. The normal machinery of law enforcement was many times not adequate to protect Texans from criminal depredations, and courts were often viewed as superfluous and ineffectual in insuring that justice was speedily and equitably meted out to those who deserved it. City marshals were at times weak and ineffective, some jails were insecure, and criminal court judges at times did not discharge their functions with an energy, zeal, promptness, or interest that served to inspire public confidence. Hence, community-minded citizen groups were at times tolerated in Texas as a necessary adjunct to the criminal justice system.

A primitive system of law and order coupled with behavior seen as disruptive and threatening to the established social order in Texas resulted in men of wealth, social standing, and political influence banding together to protect lives and property and superintend community order by circumventing the normal legal process. Vigilance groups of this type were especially active in Texas in the decades after the Civil War, when communities were reeling from the economic ravages of a bloody and prolonged war. Unsettled drifters roamed the state, and

reconstruction politics interfered with the efficient administration of criminal justice. Driven by frustration and justified
by a sense of necessity, vigilance committees in predominantly rural areas took the law into their own hands and punished,
usually by death, those suspected or actually accused of murder,
rape, robbery, or horse and cattle theft. The hapless wrong-
doer would be seized by a group of well-intentioned citizens
and summarily hanged from a tree on the outskirts of town.
Often a placard describing the crime was attached to the body
as a warning to others.

A number of well-documented and notable examples of the
work of vigilance committees superintending community order
and justice in Texas have been preserved in state historical
records as well as local newspaper accounts from the period.
Between 1870 and 1890 large and well-organized vigilance
committees intent on superintending the administration of
criminal justice operated in the counties of Blanco, Callahan,
Comal, El Paso, Hays, Mason, and Shackleford. The first well-
documented instance of this type of vigilance activity in Texas
is also the oddest.

What has become known to Texas historians as the
Regulator-Moderator War took place in the deep East Texas
counties of Shelby, Panola, and Harrison from 1840 to 1844.
Since the arrival of the first Anglo settlers in this rural and isolated area around 1809, the inhabitants had become accus-
tomed to administering law and justice in their own speedy
and certain fashion. When the government of the Republic of
Texas attempted to impress upon them the rule of organized
and systematic law in 1836, a group of leading citizens of the
region became progressively more vocal about their dissatisfaction with the Republic's judges and its slow and often
uncertain system of trial by jury. Frustrations about their
inability to continue administering justice in their own conve-
nient and expedient fashion came to a head in 1840, when
Charles W. Jackson was acquitted for the murder of Joseph G.
Goodman in Shelbyville. A group of 30 men, incensed by
the acquittal, banded together under the name "Regulators."
Believing the Republic of Texas was unable and unwilling to
administer justice, the Regulators vowed to step in and sup-

press crime by extrajudicial means. In an effort to curb crimes against the person and property, the Regulators made arbitrary arrests of suspected wrongdoers, burned their property and crops, looted their valuables, and whipped and hanged those whom they deemed culpable. A rival group of citizens called the "Moderators" soon formed in an attempt to counter the excesses wrought by the Regulators. Taking a neutral stance was not looked upon with favor, and the men of the region were forced to align with one group or the other. This state of affairs resulted in portions of East Texas being turned into a battleground of warring vigilante groups, and a reign of terror quickly ensued. Regulators and Moderators, each acting in the name of justice, shot each other from ambuscades, took prisoners, and hanged or shot them without benefit of trial. Crop land went uncultivated, livestock went untended, and many families who sought not to become involved in the vigilante war were displaced and driven from their homes by fear of retaliation from both warring groups. Finally, on 15 August 1844 President Sam Houston, realizing the area had decayed into a state of anarchy, ordered 600 militia to intervene and suppress the violence. By December 1844 the Regulators and Moderators had been disbanded and neutralized, a district court had been reestablished, and life began to return to normal. The number of killings associated with the actions of the Regulators and Moderators will never be fully established, but it has been estimated that between 25 and 50 people were hanged or shot to death, and several hundred people were severely wounded or permanently maimed.

The Regulator-Moderator War, while being an interesting historical curiosity, was certainly not typical of the activities of vigilance committees formed for the purpose of superintending community order and justice. Local Texas newspapers from the late nineteenth century are a fine source of information about typical activities of superintending vigilance committees. On 23 June 1877, for example, a vigilance committee in Fort Griffin (Shackleford County) showed up at the county jail around midnight with the intention of seizing and hanging John M. Larn, a corrupt former sheriff who was being held on charges of cattle theft. When Larn could not be freed from the iron shackles which bound him to the wall of his jail cell, the vigilance committee formed a firing squad and shot him to death in his cell. A few days later, on 27 June, in Blue (Lee County), Wade Alsup, John Kuykendall, Young Floyd, and Beck Scott, all troublesome drifters suspected of horse and cattle theft who had already ignored a previous warning to leave town, were in attendance at a dance when they were suddenly surrounded by a vigilance committee, taken from the dance hall, and promptly hanged from a tree. A final example is an incident that occurred on the evening of 24 December 1883 in McDade (Bastrop County). Three notorious white men, Thaddeus McLemore, his brother Wright McLemore, and Henry Pfeiffer were openly and brazenly defying arrest on warrants charging them with cattle theft and murder. They had bragged that both the Bastrop County sheriff and McDade constable were powerless to impose upon them the will of the law. While they were attending an afternoon Christmas Eve celebration at the Rock Saloon in McDade, a group of approximately 40 masked and armed men rode up, surrounded the trio, and without further fanfare quickly hanged them from a tree outside the bar. So as not to spoil the spirit of Christmas for the law-abiding citizens of McDade, the bodies were cut down and buried before the vigilance group disbanded and went home to their families for the evening.

While most of the people who came to the attention of the superintending vigilante committees were summarily hanged, it is important to note that lesser punishments were sometimes meted out. Itinerant riffraff, drunks and drifters, gamblers and card sharks, peddlers of green whiskey and patent medicines, traveling pimps and their whores, and general nonresident undesirable and rowdy characters were often bull-whipped, tarred and feathered, and run out of town by vigilance committees.

A second type of distinctly identifiable vigilante group which operated in Texas was one which was primarily motivated by racial hatred and prejudices. Widely held stereotypes of blacks, Mexicans, and Indians as racially and culturally inferior and morally corrupt served to inspire some of the most shameful incidents in the history of crime and the administration of criminal justice in Texas.

While there are documented incidents of racially motivated vigilantism in antebellum Texas, this type of vigilante activity began to emerge during the Civil War, and continued in Texas until 1942. During the Civil War years, Texas vigilante mobs lynched suspected slave rebels, white abolitionists, and Union sympathizers in the interests of preserving social and economic order and demonstrating philosophical solidarity with the southern slave-holding states. The lynching of free blacks, Mexicans, and Indians persisted in the years after the Civil War under the guise of maintaining white supremacy. Frequently, victims of racially motivated vigilante mobs suffered torture and mutilation before being hanged, shot, or burned for not only suspected or actual criminal offenses such as murder and rape, but also for bringing a civil suit against a white person in court, using offensive or disrespectful language to a white man, woman, or child, or refusing to honor a debt. Unlike the superintending vigilante committees that were informally organized with no membership roster or rites of initiation, the racially motivated vigilante groups that operated in Texas after the Civil War, such as the Ku Klux Klan and a less widely known East Texas organization called the Knights of the White Camellia, were regimented formal organizations with mission statements and selective membership requirements. What the two shared in common, however, was that they were both composed of people from a diverse cross-section of the white community, including civic and political leaders, bankers, farmers, and merchants.

A number of infamous and well-documented incidents of racially motivated vigilante activity were so horrific and shocking to the conscience that they became the subject of commentary and condemnation not only in the United States, but in Europe as well. What has become known as "The North Texas Troubles" or "The Texas Slave Panic" began in Tarrant and Dallas counties in July 1860 with a series of incendiary fires that were widely believed to have been set by white abolitionists and blacks acting in concert to secure the freedom of slaves through arson and murder. From July through mid-September, proslavery vigilance groups lynched approximately 50 blacks and more than 20 white Methodist ministers and their followers. Two years later, in October 1862, 42 suspected white abolitionists and Union loyalists who were known to be organizing for the purpose of resisting Confederate conscription were hanged at Gainesville, in Cooke County, during a thirteen-day period. The vigilante violence that has come to be known as "The Great Hanging at Gainesville" was not limited to Cooke County. The activity of the vigilantes quickly spilled over into neighboring Grayson, Wise, and Denton counties, where an untold number of blacks suspected of being engaged in treason and plotting insurrection were hanged.

After the Civil War the incidents of racially motivated vigilantism increased at a furious rate, and the actions of the mobs became more brutal. During the years 1890 to 1935, major American and European newspapers, as well as magazines with international circulation, constantly reported on the more horrific incidents of racially motivated mob violence against blacks. During this forty-five-year period Texas earned an international reputation for mob violence and brutality. For example, on 31 January 1893 an angry mob in Paris (Lamar County) seized Henry Smith, a black man accused of sodomizing and then murdering a three-year-old boy. Smith was first burned with hot branding irons then soaked with oil and set on fire. On 29 October 1895 Henry Hilliard, a black sharecropper, was seized by a mob of approximately 300 men after he confessed to the rape and murder of the young wife of a white farmer. Smith was burned alive in the public square in Tyler while a crowd of men, women, and children estimated to be in excess of 2,000 witnessed the incident. On 15 May 1916 Jesse Washington, an 18-year-old black man, was dragged by an infuriated mob from a McLennan County courtroom in Waco after a jury convicted him for the murder of Lucy Fryer, a young white woman. Washington was burned to death outside the courthouse while a crowd of 15,000 people looked on.

What has come to be the most widely reported incident of racially motivated vigilante violence in Texas history occurred on 9 May 1930 in Sherman (Grayson County), and is referred to today by historians as the "Sherman Riot." George Hughes, a black farm hand, was arrested by local authorities on a warrant charging him with the widely publicized rape of a white woman. To protect him from an outraged mob that had begun to gather outside the courthouse after his arrest, local law enforcement officers locked Hughes in the courthouse vault for his own protection. A mob estimated at 5,000 set fire to the courthouse, with the result that the structure burned to the ground and Hughes died from asphyxiation. After the flames subsided, the vigilante mob used dynamite and acetylene torches to cut into the vault. Hughes' body was taken from the vault and dragged behind a car to the black business section of town, where it was suspended from a tree and set on fire. Following this spectacle, the mob proceeded to burn a substantial portion of the black-owned businesses in Sherman, and a spate of lynchings soon followed in the Grayson County area.

The last known case of racially motivated lynching in Texas took place on 13 July 1942 in Texarkana (Bowie County), when William Vinson, a black man accused of rape and murder, was hanged by an outraged mob. It is important to understand that the incidents in Paris, Tyler, Waco, and Sherman were those that were widely reported on in the international press. Many other racially motivated vigilante lynchings took place in Texas after the Civil War that received little if any press coverage. The enormity of the injustice perpetrated against blacks as well as Mexicans and Indians by racially motivated vigilante groups in Texas can best be understood and appreciated by a perusal of the "Chronology of Vigilantism and Lynching in Texas" at the end of this chapter.

The Cattle Ranching Feuds

Perhaps more so than vigilantism, the mutual enmity, violence, and bloodshed that occurred between rival cattle ranching families and their supporters constituted one of the seminal hallmarks of large-scale, organized violence on the American Western frontier during the nineteenth century. This phenomenon, which has contributed greatly to the legacy of crime associated with the American Western frontier, first emerged in the years immediately after the Civil War and faded into history by the close of the century. Famous in the annals of the history of the American Western frontier are the Lincoln

County Range War in New Mexico during the 1870s, the Graham-Tewksbury feud between rival cattlemen and sheep men in Arizona between 1886 and 1892, and the 1892 Johnson County Range War in Wyoming. Texas, however, was the preeminent battleground for warring cattle clans. Lesser known, but no less bloody and prolonged, were the Sutton-Taylor feud, which raged from 1868 to 1876, the Horrell-Higgins feud from 1873 to 1877, and the Mason County War, which lasted from early 1875 until late 1876.

The Sutton-Taylor feud began in DeWitt County in 1868, and by the time it ended in 1876 it had become known as the longest and bloodiest conflict of its type not only in Texas but in the United States as well. What initially began as an altercation over accusations about cattle and horse theft quickly escalated into an outright war that involved rival armed bands of men that numbered about 200 each. One faction, led by William Sutton, hired the services of Texas gunfighters with reputations as cold-blooded killers, such as Joe Tumlinson and Jack Helm. In response, the rival group, led by Jim Taylor, enlisted the services of noted Texas bad man John Wesley Hardin and a group of his cronies, including the Clements brothers (Mannen, Gyp, Jim, and Joe), who had earned reputations as feared gunmen in their own right. Both the Sutton and Taylor factions were in constant pursuit of one another, and brutal outrages and cold-blooded murders were perpetrated on both sides. One-on-one pistol duels, ambuscades, and skir-

John Wesley Hardin

mishes between large groups of mounted and armed men became an all too frequent occurrence in DeWitt County. Over an eight-year period, more than 40 men are documented to have been killed in DeWitt and adjacent Gonzales counties. By early 1876 the killings had subsided, principally owing to the deaths of both Sutton and Taylor, but bad feelings between the Sutton and Taylor families and their supporters persisted for generations.

Another protracted and bloody war over livestock theft that has contributed greatly to the Texas legacy of violence and crime was the Horrell-Higgins feud, which was begun by rival ranching families in the Central Texas town of Lampasas in 1873. The Horrell brothers (Mart, Tom, Merrit, Ben, and Sam) jointly owned a large spread and employed many riders. Mart Horrell had already earned a reputation as a deadly gunfighter who would brook no interference with his personal or property rights. The trouble began when the brothers accused another rancher, John Calhoun Pinckney "Pink" Higgins, of stealing their cattle by running them in with his herd. Pink Higgins was already widely known in Central Texas as an expert rifleman and a brutal and sadistic killer who tolerated neither cattle theft nor verbal assaults on his reputation. Known as the innovator of the "cow-birth treatment," it was his practice to gun down anyone so unfortunate as to be found in the act of butchering one of his cattle. He would then stuff the rustler's corpse inside the disemboweled dead animal, and proceed to inform authorities of a miracle he had stumbled upon on his ranch: a cow giving birth to a man. When these two personalities clashed over claims and counterclaims of cattle theft, the stage was set for a bloody confrontation. For four years each side raided the other's herds, burned silage, and ambushed one another. The town of Lampasas became a regular battleground for the feudists.

The matter finally came to a head on 14 June 1877, when a protracted gunfight between the two rival factions took place for several hours on the streets of Lampasas. Having had enough, a Texas Ranger detachment under Sgt. N. O. Reynolds was dispatched by the governor to the area in late July 1877 to put a stop to the general lawlessness and violence. When

Ranger Maj. John B. Jones arrived on the scene and took charge, he quickly realized that arrests, convictions, and a few prison sentences or hangings would not end the bloodshed. Jones instead ended the violence by having Higgins and Horrell sign a formal treaty of peace, which, to the surprise of almost everyone, both parties abided by, and the hostilities ceased. No convictions were ever returned in connection with the numerous killings that resulted from this four-year feud.

The last major cattle feud in Texas took place between 1875 and 1876 in Mason County. Known as the Mason County War, or the Hoodoo War, the violence grew out of the rustling practice of mixing in stolen cattle with an already established herd. A short-lived but bloody confrontation erupted in late spring 1875 among rival groups of German immigrant and American-born cattlemen in Mason County who accused each other of livestock theft, and murderous confrontations between the two groups quickly erupted. Mason County Sheriff John Clark and his deputies were unable to restore calm, partly because the German immigrant cattlemen believed some of Clark's deputies were colluding with the American-born cattle thieves. The violence lasted for a little more than a year, until a company of Texas Rangers was called in by the governor to stop the wholesale bloodshed. By the late fall of 1876 relative peace had been restored to the county, but not until the feuding had claimed dozens of lives and wounded and maimed many more. No one from either faction was subsequently arrested, tried, or convicted for murder.

General Lawlessness

The legacy of crime in Texas is most clearly evident in the general lawlessness that infested the state during the last quarter of the nineteenth century. Both native-born Texans as well as lawless drifters from other states who came to Texas when they got into trouble (and subsequently continued their ways) contributed to the problem of crime in the state.

Some of the behavior contributing to the legacy was rather innocuous, such as general acts of riotous and disorderly conduct that breached the peace. Bloody brawling was a commonplace occurrence in the streets, saloons, and houses of prostitution. The practice of "hurrahing," or "taking a town," was a noisy and disorderly event dreaded by citizens and merchants of towns in cattle ranching areas. Groups of drunken cowboys, and sometimes bands or drifters and even soldiers from the outlying military frontier posts in West Texas, would ride into town discharging their weapons into the air causing a general commotion and disrupting the general peace and dignity of the community.

More serious and damaging to the reputation of Texas were the growing incidents of gunplay resulting in deliberate murder, and the robbery of stagecoaches, trains, and banks. No state in the Union during the nineteenth century can lay claim to have been the killing ground of more gunfighters and desperadoes than Texas. The roster of nineteenth-century Texas gunfighters and outlaws includes familiar names such as Sam Bass and John Wesley Hardin, as well as no less deadly desperadoes such as Seaborne Barnes, Benjamin Bickerstaff, Eugene Bunch, Emmanuel Clements, Brack Cornett, Jim "Longhair" Courtright, Foster Crawford, John King Fisher, Alphonso Jennings, James McIntire, Bud Newman, and Ed Welch.

During the years 1876 to 1883, an epidemic of stagecoach robberies that were widely reported in the nation's newspapers served to contribute to the lawless reputation of Texas. More stagecoaches were robbed in Texas during this period than at any time before or after. Prior to the westward expansion from Fort Worth of the Texas and Pacific Railroad beginning in 1879, the stagecoach was the principal means of public mass transit. Often traversing long and desolate stretches of countryside, stagecoaches were easy prey for outlaws acting either alone or more frequently in small groups. After a stagecoach was stopped, mail bags would be taken and passengers would be relieved of their property. To prevent the robbery victims from quickly warning authorities, it was often the custom of the stagecoach robbers to either kill or take the horses that pulled the stage. As the railroads pushed farther into West and South Texas, trains became a favorite target of organized bands of outlaws during the 1880s. This species of crime was almost unknown in the states east of the Mississippi River, and to satisfy the public's curiosity and interest, newspapers routinely published detailed accounts of train robberies which occurred in Texas and the frontier West.

By the late 1880s and early 1890s, the growing incidence of bank robberies around the state and their wide publication in newspapers throughout the nation served to contribute to the public's perception that Texas was a land of unceasing and interminable crime and violence.

PART 3:

CRIME AND VIOLENCE IN TEXAS TODAY

Crime affects all Texans, either directly or indirectly, and results in discernible losses in the quality of our lives. The most obvious effect associated with the problem of crime in Texas is the financial burden we all bear for the operation of the Texas criminal justice system. The annual cost of operating the Texas criminal justice system is staggering. Today Texans shoulder a multibillion-dollar burden associated with both the general protection of their liberties, lives, and property, as well as the subsequent investigation, apprehension, prosecution, and punishment of criminal offenders. Consider just one segment of the Texas criminal justice system: county sheriffs' departments and municipal law enforcement agencies. In 1997 it cost approximately $3.4 billion to operate the 254 county sheriffs' departments and approximately 600 municipal police departments in the state. This translates into a cost of about $180 per year for every man, woman, and child in Texas.

Less obvious are the indirect or hidden costs of crime that have an impact on all Texans. These include private security officers and alarm systems at retail establishments, the costs of which are passed on to consumers in the form of higher merchandise prices; alarm and security systems for automobiles and private homes; increased automobile and home insurance premiums needed to offset insurance industry losses due to theft and burglary; increased medical insurance premiums due to the high cost of hospital treatment and home health care for crime victims; loss of economic productivity associated with criminal victimization; and the decline in property values and the loss of viable tax bases associated with urban decay in high crime rate neighborhoods.

Uniform Crime Reporting

The funding and operation of the Texas criminal justice system today is in very great measure dependent on accurate and reliable information about the nature and frequency of crime on a year-to-year basis. Crime statistics are absolutely essential for not only assessing the moral health of society, but they also are invaluable in helping legislators and criminal justice executives gauge the effectiveness of the Texas criminal justice system and plan for the development of new programs for combating crime. Because crime statistics are such an important factor in the organization and operation of the Texas criminal justice system, it is important to briefly explain how they are collected and reported.

Prior to the late 1920s, statistics on the nature and frequency of crime in the United States, as well as Texas, were collected, compiled, and disseminated in a haphazard, nonuniform, and irregular fashion. Furthermore, there existed no centralized authority vested with the responsibility for maintaining such information either on the state or national level. At various times in Texas history, police departments sometimes kept records of crimes that came to their attention and arrests they made, and sometimes they did not. The same was true of sheriffs' departments. Fairly accurate indicators of the number of arrests made by sheriffs' departments in Texas prior to the twentieth century may be found preserved in the quarto-size booking ledgers routinely used to record the names and offenses of people lodged in county jails. But even in this instance, the fashion in which such arrest information was recorded varied widely from county to county.

In 1927 the International Association of Chiefs of Police sought to develop a uniform system of crime reporting, and formed the Committee on Uniform Crime Records. The task of the committee was to create a standard system for recording crime that would overcome the current and confusing variations in the nomenclature, counting method, and summary reporting of crimes known to the police. To do this, the committee created the Uniform Crime Reporting system, or UCR as it is known today. The UCR consists of eight crimes that were chosen by the committee because of their seriousness, frequency of occurrence, and likelihood of being reported to the police. These eight crimes are known as the "index crimes," because they serve to provide a good index, or gauge, as to the nature and frequency of crime in American society. The index crimes consist of four violent crimes against the person (murder, forcible rape, robbery, and aggravated assault), and four crimes against property (burglary, larceny, motor vehicle theft, and, since 1979, arson).

It is important to note that the UCR is a summary-based statistical system that reflects only the number of index crimes reported to the police. All fifty states participate in the UCR program and forward to the United States Department of Justice's Bureau of Justice Statistics monthly or quarterly UCR summaries. This information is used to compile a yearly report about crime in the United States. The information is reported to the public using three principal statistical formats: (1) crime volume, which is the total number of reported crimes, (2) crime rate, which is an expression of the number of crimes per 100,000 population, and (3) clearance, which is the percentage of all reported crimes for which an arrest was made.

On 1 January 1976 Texas adopted the UCR method of counting the nature and frequency of crimes reported to the police. The Texas Legislature gave to the Department of Public Safety the responsibility for collecting, organizing, and reporting crime data. Since 1976 the Texas Legislature, in order to make better and more informed decisions about policies and

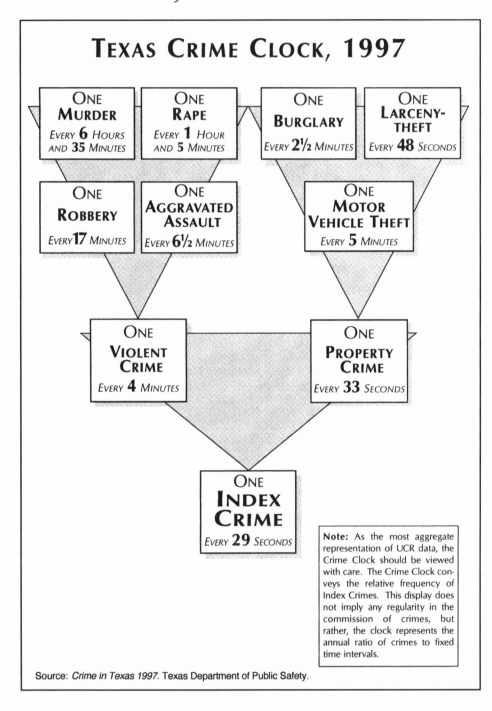

TEXAS CRIME CLOCK, 1997

ONE
MURDER
EVERY **6** HOURS
AND **35** MINUTES

ONE
RAPE
EVERY **1** HOUR
AND **5** MINUTES

ONE
BURGLARY
EVERY **2½** MINUTES

ONE
LARCENY-THEFT
EVERY **48** SECONDS

ONE
ROBBERY
EVERY **17** MINUTES

ONE
AGGRAVATED ASSAULT
EVERY **6½** MINUTES

ONE
MOTOR VEHICLE THEFT
EVERY **5** MINUTES

ONE
VIOLENT CRIME
EVERY **4** MINUTES

ONE
PROPERTY CRIME
EVERY **33** SECONDS

ONE
INDEX CRIME
EVERY **29** SECONDS

Note: As the most aggregate representation of UCR data, the Crime Clock should be viewed with care. The Crime Clock conveys the relative frequency of Index Crimes. This display does not imply any regularity in the commission of crimes, but rather, the clock represents the annual ratio of crimes to fixed time intervals.

Source: *Crime in Texas 1997*. Texas Department of Public Safety.

programs affecting the operation and management of the Texas criminal justice system, has required police to collect and report data on two additional crimes not included in the eight that comprise the traditional index. In 1991 the Texas Legislature required the reporting of incidents of family violence known to the police, and in 1992 the Texas UCR program began collecting statistics on hate crimes that are motivated by prejudice based on the victim's race, ethnicity, religion, or sexual orientation.

In 1998, 926 state, county, and municipal law enforcement agencies in Texas submitted monthly UCR reports to the Department of Public Safety. This represents a crime reporting coverage for 99.9% of Texas. As such, the Texas UCR data provide a highly accurate and reliable picture of the nature and frequency of crime in the state that is heavily relied upon by government crime control policymakers, criminal justice system executives, and the general public.

While a detailed discussion of the historical trends as well as the current problem of crime in Texas is well beyond the scope of this book, a synopsis of the enormity of the situation that the Texas criminal justice system deals with today will suffice. Readers interested in a more detailed statistical overview of crime in Texas should consult the 192-page free publication available from the Texas Department of Public Safety titled *Crime in Texas: 1997.*

A synopsis of crime in Texas for the year 1997 (the most recent year for which a statistical summary is available) is as follows:

- 1,064,914 index crimes were reported to the police
- 22% of the reported index crimes resulted in an arrest
- 1,125,000 arrests were made for non-index crimes, including 98,369 for narcotics, 85,174 for drunk driving, and 14,236 for weapons violations
- 1,328 murders were reported to the police
- 77,239 aggravated assaults were reported to the police
- 181,773 incidents of family violence were reported
- 8,007 reported rapes

- 645,174 reported incidents of theft
- $381 million worth of property was stolen, with an average loss of $589 per victim
- 200,966 reported burglaries, 70% of which were burglaries of homes
- 101,687 reported incidents of automobile theft
- 30,513 reported incidents of robbery
- 331 hate crimes were reported
- 5,072 law enforcement officers were assaulted and 9 were killed while protecting the public

A CHRONOLOGY OF VIGILANTISM AND LYNCHING IN TEXAS

(The following is a record of only the known and documentable vigilante killings that occurred in Texas from 1840 to 1942. If the unverifiable reports and rumors of vigilante lynching in Texas were included, the record would obviously be much longer.)

1840—The beginning of the Regulator-Moderator War in Shelby, Panola, and Harrison counties, which resulted in vigilance committees on both sides dispensing summary justice for alleged criminal wrongdoing.

1841—
9 OCTOBER, in Shelbyville (Shelby County), two white men, "Buckskin Bill" McFaddin and Squire Humphreys, leaders of the Moderators, hanged by a group of approximately 300 Regulator sympathizers from a makeshift gallows erected for the occasion.
LATE OCTOBER, on the banks of the Sabine River (Shelby County), a white Moderator named Boatwright was shot to death by a group of Regulators, cut into pieces, and the dismembered fragments of his body displayed in trees.

1843—In Shelby County, a Regulator named Stanfield was hanged by friends of Samuel Hall, a Moderator who had been shot to death by Stanfield after he alleged Hall stole livestock from his farm. In Shelby County, Henry Runnells, a member

of the Regulators, was lynched by Moderators for his participation in the murder of Samuel Hall. In Shelby County,
James Hall, the brother of Samuel Hall, was hanged and then
shot to death by Regulators in response to the lynching of
Henry Runnels.

1844—In San Augustine (San Augustine County), John M. Bradley,
a Moderator, was ambushed and shot down in cold blood
by Regulator Watt Moorman.

9 AUGUST, in Hilliard Springs (Panola County), a leader of the
Regulators and fifteen others were killed when ambushed by
a large group of Moderators.

1847—In MAY, 23 people die in Shelby County while attending a
wedding reception for a former member of the Regulators,
when a former Moderator poisons the food served to guests.
This is the last documented instance of violence associated
with the Regulator-Moderator vigilante war.

1855—22 NOVEMBER, in Madisonville, an unidentified black man
wrongly lynched for allegedly being the rider of a horse that
trampled a small girl to death. The actual rider escaped.

1860—8 JULY TO MID-SEPTEMBER, in North and East Texas. Known as
the "Texas Troubles," vigilance committees lynched in excess
of 30 blacks alleged to have been involved in a slave insurrection that began with the burning of most of the downtown
section of Dallas. An unknown number of white abolitionist
Methodist ministers and their followers also met their death
at the hands of vigilante mobs.

1862—OCTOBER, in Gainesville (Cooke County). Known as "The Great
Hanging at Gainesville," over 40 white suspected Unionists
and abolitionists were hanged or shot by Confederate sympathizers after being accused of treason and insurrection.

1863—

JULY, in San Antonio (Bexar County), a white man known as
Old Man Franks, hanged from a chinaberry tree outside the
San Antonio jail for allegedly killing two Mexicans who had
come to purchase some of his livestock.

SEPTEMBER, in San Antonio (Bexar County), a white cowhand

and gunman named Robert Augustine is summarily lynched by an angry mob after he was acquitted by a district court judge on a charge of "hurrahing" (disturbing the peace while drunk by discharging his weapons in the street).

1869—26 APRIL, an unidentified white horse thief taken forcibly from the jail at Richmond (Fort Bend County) and hanged from a bridge being built across the Brazos River.

1874—

12 JANUARY, an unidentified white horse thief hanged by vigilantes at Denison (Grayson County).

4 MAY, near McDade (Bastrop County), an unidentified black man lynched for killing a white man.

20 JUNE, in Clinton (DeWitt County), three white men (Kute Tuggle, Jim White, and Scrap Taylor) accused of cattle theft are taken from the county jail by a group of armed and masked men and hanged. This incident occurred in connection with the famous Sutton-Taylor feud.

1875—

In EARLY JANUARY, in McDade (Bastrop County), two white men named Land and Waddell were hanged for being "dangerous characters and desperadoes."

18 FEBRUARY, a group of about 40 men broke into the Mason County jail, seized five white men (Lige Baccus and his cousin, Tom Turley, and two others named Johnson and Wiggins) being held on charges of cattle theft, and hanged and shot them near Hick Springs. This incident occurred in connection with the famous Mason County War.

13 MAY, near Castell (Mason County), Tim Williamson, a white man suspected of cattle theft, is liberated from the custody of Deputy Sheriff John Worley by a group of masked men and shot to death.

In EARLY NOVEMBER, in Bastrop County, a mob lynched a white man named Cordell for being "a hereditary horse thief."

1876—

22 MARCH, near McDade (Bastrop County), two white men named Turk Turner and James H. Crow are shot to death by a group of men lying in wait for them to return to the site to remove two head of stolen cattle which they had recently killed and skinned. As a warning to others, their bodies were

left in the open, wrapped in the green hides they had just removed.

14 APRIL, near Fort Griffin (Shackleford County), four white men (Joe Watson, Charles McBride, a man known only as "Reddy" and another man known only as Dan) were captured, shot, and then hanged by the Shackleford vigilance committee for cattle theft.

9 APRIL, an unidentified man caught in the act of stealing a horse was summarily hanged from a pecan tree in Fort Griffin (Shackleford County). A shovel was left leaning against the tree for the use of any passerby who saw fit to bury the thief.

MAY, on Clear Fork Creek, outside of Fort Griffin (Shackleford County), a white man named Hought Taught was hanged after being caught with stolen horses. A placard was affixed to his body which read: "Horse Thief No. 5 that killed and scalped boy boy [sic] for Indian sign. Shall horse-thieves rule this country? He will have company soon."

MID-MAY, about three miles outside of Fort Griffin (Shackleford County), a white horse thief is found hanging from a tree.

22 MAY, in Williamson County, two unidentified white men suspected of cattle theft were hanged.

2 JUNE, in Albany (Shackleford County), approximately 50 armed men overpower jailers and forcibly take from their custody two white men accused of cattle theft named Henderson and Floyd. The next morning the two men were found hanging from a tree.

JULY, outside of Fort Griffin (Shackleford County), eleven unidentified whites and Mexicans are summarily hanged after a vigilance committee finds them in possession of 27 head of stolen stock.

LATE SUMMER, near Taylor (Williamson County), an unidentified white man suspected of livestock theft was hanged naked.

1877—

23 JUNE, in Fort Griffin (Shackleford County), John M. Larn, a corrupt white sheriff who rustled cattle, was arrested and taken to jail. When a vigilance committee showed up around midnight, Larn could not be freed from the iron shackles which bound him to the wall of his cell. The vigilance committee formed a firing squad and shot him to death in his cell.

27 JUNE, in Blue (Lee County), four white men (Wade Alsup, John Kuykendall, Young Floyd, and Beck Scott) were surrounded by a vigilance committee while attending a dance and hanged from a tree for horse and cattle theft.

1878—

15 DECEMBER, in Meridian (Bosque County), two white brothers, Mart and Tom Horrell, were shot to death in their cell by a mob that stormed the jail where they were confined on charges of complicity in the robbery and murder of a storekeeper. The Horrell brothers were members of the Horrell cattle ranching family that played a part in the Horrell-Higgins feud. Their lynching occurred one year after the Horrell-Higgins violence concluded, and is not considered to be related to the feud.

1883—24 DECEMBER, in McDade (Bastrop County), three white men (Thad McLemore, Wright McLemore, and Henry Pfeiffer) were escorted from the Rock Saloon by more than 40 armed men and hanged for murder and cattle theft.

1889—

19 FEBRUARY, in Liberty (Liberty County), two black men accused of murder lynched.

20 FEBRUARY, in San Saba County, two white men, Asa Brown and W. L. Smith, lynched for unknown reason.

15 APRIL, in Hempstead (Waller County), George Driggs, a black man accused of rape, lynched by an angry mob.

17 MAY, in Millican (Brazos County), an unidentified black man suspected of rape lynched.

14 JULY, in Waco (McLennan County), Henry Davis, a black man, lynched for unknown reason.

26 JULY, in Belen (El Paso County), George Lewis, a black man, lynched after being accused of poisoning well water.

28 JULY, in Greenville (Hunt County), George Lindley, a black man, lynched for unknown reason.

14 AUGUST, in Orange (Orange County), James Brooks, a black man, lynched after being accused of rape.

14 DECEMBER, in White Rock (San Augustine County), two unidentified white outlaws lynched for unknown reason.

28 DECEMBER, in Uvalde (Uvalde County), two white outlaw brothers named O'Dell lynched for unknown reason.

1890—

27 MARCH, in Headsville (Robertson County), an unidentified black man accused of murder.

5 APRIL, in Kosse (Limestone County), a black man named Williams lynched after being accused of rape.

5 APRIL, in Thornton (Limestone County), an unidentified black man lynched after being accused of rape.

20 APRIL, in San Augustine (San Augustine County), Simeon Garrette, a black man, accused of attempted murder.

20 APRIL, in Fays Corner (Hidalgo County), Stephen Jacobs, a black man, accused of arson.

24 APRIL, in San Augustine (San Augustine County), Jerry Teel, a black man, accused of attempted murder.

24 APRIL, in Cameron Station (Milam County), an unidentified black man, hanged for rape.

12 MAY, in Hearne (Robertson County), Edward Bennett, a black man, accused of rape.

1 JUNE, in Hooks Ferry (Bowie County), Thomas Brown, a black man, accused of murder.

20 JUNE, in Livingston (Polk County), an unidentified black man accused of murder.

28 JUNE, in Antelope (Jack County), an unidentified black man lynched for an unknown reason.

3 JULY, in Neches (Anderson County), Patrick Henry, a black man, accused of gambling.

22 JULY, in Red River County, Andy Young, a black man, accused of racial prejudice.

30 JULY, in Cypress (Harris County), William Hawkins, a black man, accused of larceny.

4 AUGUST, in Navasota (Grimes County), John Brown, a black man, accused of rape.

8 AUGUST, in Anderson (Grimes County), an unidentified black man accused of rape.

14 AUGUST, in Mexia (Limestone County), two unidentified black men accused of rape.

1891—

7 FEBRUARY, in Knickerbocker (Tom Green County), Jesus Salceda, a Hispanic, lynched for unknown reasons.

17 FEBRUARY, in Douglas (Nacogdoches County), Thomas Rebin, a black outlaw, hanged for unknown reason.

24 FEBRUARY, in Douglas (Nacogdoches County), Thomas Rowland, a black man accused of robbery.

27 FEBRUARY, in Grimes County, three white men, Jasper Williams and two unidentified partners of Williams, lynched for unknown reasons.

1 APRIL, in Mineola (Wood County), William Field, a white man, accused of attempted rape.

28 MAY, in Belton (Bell County), Monroe Sheppard, a white man, lynched for unknown reason.

8 JULY, in Bell County, Evan E. Shelby, a black man, accused of murder.

28 JUNE, in Cass County, two black men, William Hartfield and Munn Sheppard, accused of being troublesome.

22 JULY, in Henderson (Garfield County), William Johnson, a black man, accused of rape.

26 October, in Linden (Cass County), Leo Green, a black man, accused of murder.

13 NOVEMBER, in Burnet (Burnet County), two unidentified black men lynched for unknown reasons.

22 NOVEMBER, in Moscow (Beaver County), William Black, a black man, hanged for making insulting remarks.

1892—

29 JANUARY, in Thompson (Fort Bend County), Joseph Shields, a white man, lynched for unknown reasons.

26 APRIL, in Riesil (McLennan County), an unidentified black man accused of murder.

10 JUNE, in Bastrop (Bastrop County), Tobe Cook, a black man, accused of rape.

28 JUNE, in Spurger (Tyler County), three black men, Henry Gaines, Thomas Smith, and Prince Wood, all accused of rape.

6 SEPTEMBER, in Paris (Lamar County), three black men, William Armor, John Ransom, and John Walker, all accused of rioting.

19 SEPTEMBER, in Paris (Lamar County), an unidentified black man accused of rape.

23 SEPTEMBER, in Plantersville (Grimes County), William Sullivan, a black man, accused of rape.

1893—

31 JANUARY, in Paris (Lamar County), Henry Smith, a black man accused of sodomizing and then murdering a three-year-old

boy, was seized by an infuriated mob, was first burned with hot irons and then soaked with oil and set on fire. This is the most horrific case of lynching in Texas in the nineteenth century.

17 FEBRUARY, in Hickory Creek (Hunt County), William Butler, a black man, accused of racial prejudice.

14 JUNE, in Waco (McLennan County), George Williams, a black man, accused of rape.

16 JULY, in El Paso (El Paso County), a white man, M. Jazo, accused of murder.

31 AUGUST, in Yarborough (Grimes County), an unidentified black man lynched for unknown reason.

1894—

7 JANUARY, in Shelbyville (Shelby County), Judas Miller, a white man, hanged for unknown reason.

14 APRIL, in Gatesville (Coryell County), Alfred Bren, a black man, hanged for unknown reason.

14 APRIL, in Gainesville (Cook County), Jack Crews, a white man, accused of murder.

9 MAY, in West (McLennan County), an unidentified black man, hanged for writing an amorous letter to a white woman.

17 MAY, in Jefferson (Marion County), Henry Scott, a black man, accused of murder.

13 JUNE, in Sweet Home (Lavaca County), two black men, Bascom Cook and Lon Hall, both accused of murder.

29 JUNE, in Sulphur Springs (Hopkins County), John Williams, a black man, accused of murder.

20 JULY, in Woodville (Tyler County), William Griffith, a black man, accused of rape.

8 OCTOBER, in Fairfield (Freestone County), Henry Gibson, a black man, accused of attempted rape.

20 DECEMBER, in Brownsville (Cameron County), James Allen, a black man, accused of arson.

1895—

9 JANUARY, in Bowie (Montague County), Thomas Boyd, a white man, suspected of murder.

11 MARCH, in Athens (Henderson County), Isaac Manion, a black man, accused of murder.

12 APRIL, in Corsicana (Navarro County), Nelson Calhoun, a black man, accused of rape.

30 APRIL, in Devers (Liberty County), George Jones, a Native American, accused of assault.

25 MAY, in Wharton (Wharton County), three whites, John Crocker, his wife, and his son, all lynched for murder.

11 JUNE, in Lufkin (Angelina County), William Johnson, a black man, accused of rape.

20 JULY, in Mant (Sanpete County), six blacks (Benjamin Johnson, Abe Phillips, Jr., Mrs. Abe Phillips, Edward Phillips, Hannah E. Phillips, and K. D. Taylor) were all hanged after being accused of racial prejudice.

23 JULY, in Brenham (Washington County), an unidentified black woman accused of racial prejudice.

29 JULY, in Lexington (Lee County), Squire Loftin, a black man, accused of rape.

2 AUGUST, in Daingerfield (Morris County), a black man, James Mason, and his wife, both hanged for unknown reasons.

12 AUGUST, in Delta County, an unidentified black man accused of racial prejudice.

22 AUGUST, in Wharton (Wharton County), an unidentified black man accused of murder.

26 AUGUST, in Paris (Lamar County), Jefferson Cole, a black man, accused of racial prejudice.

14 OCTOBER, in Cotulla (La Salle County), Floantina Suitta, a Hispanic woman, accused of murder.

29 OCTOBER, in Tyler (Smith County), Henry Hilliard, a black man who confessed to the rape and murder of the young wife of a white farmer, was seized by a mob of 300 men and burned to death in the public square. A crowd of men, women, and children estimated to be in excess of 2,000 witnessed the incident.

21 NOVEMBER, in Madison County, an unidentified black man lynched for unknown reason.

1896—

20 FEBRUARY, in Wichita Falls (Wichita County), T. Lewis, a white man, accused of robbery and murder.

27 FEBRUARY, in El Paso County, Foster Crawford and Elmer "The Slaughter Kid" Lewis, two white outlaws who robbed and murdered, were captured by the Texas Rangers, jailed, and then hanged by an angry mob that stormed the jail.

29 FEBRUARY, in Wichita Falls (Wichita County), Foster Crawford, a white man, accused of robbery and murder.

3 MAY, in Beaumont (Jefferson County), William Benby, a black man, accused of murder.

10 JUNE, in Bryan (Brazos County), George J. Johnson and Louis Whitehead, two black men, accused of rape.

13 AUGUST, in Hopkins County, Benjamin Gay, a black man, accused of arson.

1897—

25 JANUARY, in Bryan (Brazos County), Eugene Washington, a black man, accused of rape.

5 MARCH, in Elgin (Bastrop County), an unidentified black man accused of burglary.

27 APRIL, in Harrison County, three black men, Rob Brown, and brothers Hal and Russell Wright, all lynched following accusations of their involvement in a robbery and arson.

30 APRIL, in Sunny Side (Waller County), seven black men accused of murder, William Gates, Fayette Rhone, Aaron Thomas, Benjamin Thomas, James Thomas, Lewis Thomas, and William Williams, all hanged following accusations of murder.

14 MAY, in Rosebud (Falls County), three black men, David Cotton, Sabe Stewart, and Henry Williams, lynched after being accused of attempted rape.

18 MAY, in San Augustine (San Augustine County), three black men named White accused of murder.

21 MAY, in Brown County, a white man named Peter lynched for unknown reason.

23 MAY, in Tyler (Smith County), William Jones, a black man, accused of murder.

6 AUGUST, in Nacogdoches (Nacogdoches County), Esseck White, a black man, accused of rape.

10 AUGUST, in Paris (Lamar County), a white man named Rev. Captain Jones, hanged for elopement.

26 AUGUST, in Bellville (Austin County), a black man named Bonner, accused of rape.

26 AUGUST, in Mooresville (Falls County), Wesley Johnson, a white man, accused of attempted rape.

11 OCTOBER, in Brenham (Washington County), Robert Carter, a black man, accused of murder.

18 NOVEMBER, in Bryan (Brazos County), Thomas Sweat, a black man, accused of murder.

1898—

5 April, in Brownsville (Cameron County), Carlos Guilen, a black man, accused of murder.

6 June, in Weimar (Colorado County), George Washington, a black man, accused of murder.

8 August, in Palestine (Anderson County), Dan Ogg, a black man, accused of rape.

1899—

23 May, in Alley (Hale County), a white man named Humphrey and his two sons hanged for aiding and abetting the escape from jail of an accused murderer.

1 July, in Waskom (Harrison County), Allie Thompson, a black man, accused of rape.

14 July, in Goliad (Goliad County), Abe Brown, a black man accused of rape and murder.

14 July, in Iola (Grimes County), an unidentified black man accused of murder.

16 July, in Navasota (Grimes County), Henry McGee, a black man, accused of murder.

25 JULY, in Navasota (Grimes County), Henry Hamilton, a black man, accused of arson.

1900—

11 FEBRUARY, in Port Arthur (Jefferson County), James Sweeney, a white man, accused of murder.

15 NOVEMBER, in Jefferson (Marion County), three unidentified black men accused of attempted murder.

1901—

11 FEBRUARY, in Paris (Lamar County), George Carter, a black man, accused of rape.

13 MARCH, in Corsicana (Navarro County), John Henderson, a black man convicted of rape, was dragged from jail and burned at the stake before a crowd of 5,000 spectators.

1 AUGUST, in Mobile (Tyler County), an unidentified black man accused of verbally insulting a white woman.

20 AUGUST, in Dexter (Cooke County), Abe Wilder, a black man, accused of murder.

25 AUGUST, in Kenedy (Karnes County), Felix Martinez, a Hispanic, lynched for unknown reasons.

3 OCTOBER, in Harrison (McLennan County), five unidentified black men lynched after quarreling over a profit-sharing arrangement.

25 OCTOBER, in Quitman (Wood County), Galner Gordon, a black man, accused of murder.

25 DECEMBER, in Paris (Lamar County), J. H. McClinton, a black man, was lynched for unknown reason.

1902—

11 MARCH, in Luling (Caldwell County), Nathan Bird, a black man, and his son both lynched for unknown reason.

22 MAY, in Longview (Gregg County), Dudley Morgan, a black man, accused of physically assaulting a white woman, was taken by force from the sheriff by a mob of 4,000, tortured, and then burned at the stake.

4 SEPTEMBER, in Hempstead (Waller County), Jesse Walker, a black man, accused of rape.

4 OCTOBER, in Columbus (Colorado County), Utt Duncan, a black man, accused of attempted rape.

21 OCTOBER, in Hempstead (Waller County), Reddish Barton and Joseph Wesley, two black men, accused of rape.

1903—

14 JANUARY, in Angleton (Brazoria County), Ransom O'Neal and Charles Tunstall, two black men, accused of murder.

26 APRIL, in Carthage (Panola County), Hensley Johnson, a black man, accused of attempted rape.

27 MAY, in Kemp (Kaufman County), an unidentified black man accused of rape.

23 JULY, in Beaumont (Jefferson County), Moony Allen, a black man, accused of murder.

31 JULY, in Alto (Cherokee County), an unidentified black man accused of assault.

12 AUGUST, in Whitesboro (Grayson County), eight unidentified black men were arrested for an attack on a white woman. Seven of the men were subsequently released, but the eighth was hanged from a tree, and the mob went on a terror spree in the black community.

1 OCTOBER, in Marshall (Harrison County), Walker Davis, a black man, accused of murder.

1904—

30 JULY, in Lockhart (Caldwell County), John Larremore, a black man, accused of racial prejudice.

31 AUGUST, in Weimer (Colorado County), Oscar Turner, a black man, accused of attempted rape.

1 SEPTEMBER, in Weimer (Colorado County), Oscar Tucker, a black man, accused of rape.

1905—

16 FEBRUARY, in Dale (Caldwell County), Carlos Munoz, a Hispanic, accused of rape.

17 FEBRUARY, in Smithville (Bastrop County), William Johnson, a black man, accused of rape.

14 MARCH, in Longview (Gregg County), Julius Stevens, a black man, accused of assault with intent to commit murder.

20 JUNE, in Riverside (Walker County), Ford Simon, a black man, accused of rape.

14 JULY, in Golinda (Goliad County), Frank Mason, a black man, accused of rape.

20 JULY, in New Braunfels (Comal County), Sam Green, a black man, accused of rape.

29 JULY, in Avery (Avalon County), an unidentified black man accused of rape.

 8 AUGUST, in Waco (McLennan County), Sank Majors, a black man, accused of rape.

11 AUGUST, in Sulphur Springs (Hopkins County), Thomas Williams, a white man, accused of attempted rape.

14 AUGUST, in Sulphur Springs (Hopkins County), another Thomas Williams, this one a black man, accused of attempted rape.

 7 SEPTEMBER, in Italy (Ellis County), Stephen Davis, a black man, accused of rape.

11 NOVEMBER, in Henderson (Rusk County), three black men, Robert Askew, John Reese, and a third unidentified man, all accused of murder.

1906—

10 JANUARY, in Moscow (Polk County), Benjamin Harris, a black man, accused of murder.

24 APRIL, in Groesbech (Limestone County), an unidentified black man accused of rape.

25 APRIL, in Oakwood (Leon County), an unidentified black man accused of rape.

15 SEPTEMBER, in Rosebud (Falls County), Mitchell Frazier, a black man, accused of assault with intent to commit murder.

26 OCTOBER, in Toyah (Reeves County), Slab Pitts, a black man, lynched by an angry mob after he married a white woman.

1907—

14 JULY, in Del Rio (Val Verde County), Fred Wilson, a black man, accused of murder.

6 AUGUST, in Goliad (Goliad County), Thomas Hall, a black man, accused of attempted assault.

4 NOVEMBER, in Brownsville (Cameron County), Alex Johnson, a black man, accused of attempted rape.

26 DECEMBER, in La Marque (Galveston County), Anderson Callaway, a black man, accused of attempted rape.

1908—

28 FEBRUARY, in Conroe (Montgomery County), Clem Scott, a black man, accused of attempted rape.

10 MARCH, in Navasota (Grimes County), John Campbell, a black man, accused of assault with intent to commit murder.

24 MARCH, in Conroe (Montgomery County), an unidentified black man accused of attempted rape.

24 MARCH, in Magnolia (Montgomery County), two unidentified black men accused of attempted rape.

9 APRIL, in Longview (Gregg County), Albert Fields, a black man, accused of rape.

19 APRIL, in Atlanta (Cass County), Jasper Douglas, a black man, accused of rape.

7 MAY, in Naples (Morris County), John Williams, a black man, accused of murder.

22 JUNE, in Hemphill (Sabine County), nine black men (Jerry Evans, William Johnson, William Manuel, "Rabbit Bill" McCoy, Moses Spellman, Cleveland Williams, Frank Williams, and two others whose names are not known), were all lynched after being accused of murder.

15 JULY, in Beaumont (Jefferson County), an unidentified black man, hanged for an unknown reason. His seizure and unfortunate hanging were later found to be attributed to a case of mistaken identity.

15 AUGUST, in Bellville (Austin County), Moses Jackson, a black man, hanged for an unknown reason.

1909—

7 MARCH, in Rockwall (Rockwall County), Anderson Ellis, a black man, accused of rape.

27 APRIL, in Marshall (Harrison County), James Hodges, a black man, accused of rape.

30 APRIL, in Marshall (Harrison County), Mose Creole, Pie Hill, and Matthew Chase, three black men, accused of murder.

28 MAY, in Abilene (Taylor County), Thomas Burnett, a white man, accused of murder.

13 SEPTEMBER, in Sandy Point (Brazoria County), two unidentified black men accused of murder.

20 DECEMBER, in Rosebud (Falls County), Cope Mills, a black man, accused of murder.

1910—

2 FEBRUARY, in Beaumont (Jefferson County), an unidentified black man accused of rape.

3 MARCH, in Dallas (Dallas County), Holland Brooks, a black man, accused of rape.

5 APRIL, in Centerville (Leon County), Frank Bates, a black man, accused of murder.

26 JUNE, in Rusk (Cherokee County), Leonard Johnson, a black man, accused of murder.

5 JULY, in Rodney (Navarro County), an unidentified black man, accused of attempted rape.

12 July, in Belton (Bell County), Henry Gentry, a white man, suspected of rape and murder.

8 NOVEMBER, in Rock Springs (Edwards County), Antonio Rodriguez, a Hispanic man, accused of murder.

1911—

20 JUNE, in Thorndale (Milam County), an unidentified Hispanic boy accused of murder.

12 AUGUST, in Farmersville (Collin County), Commodore Jones, a black man, accused of verbally insulting white women.

29 OCTOBER, in Marshall (Harrison County), an unidentified black man accused of attempted rape.

8 NOVEMBER, in Clarksville (Red River County), Riley Johnson, a black man, accused of attempted rape.

1912—

13 FEBRUARY, in Marshall (Harrison County), George Saunders, a black man, accused of aiding and abetting a murder.

14 FEBRUARY, in Marshall (Harrison County), Mary Jackson, a black woman, accused of aiding and abetting a murder.

25 MAY, in Tyler (Smith County), Dan Davis, a black man, accused of rape was burned at the stake.

1913—

17 JANUARY, in Paris (Lamar County), Henry Monson, a black man, accused of murder.

23 JANUARY, in Fullbright (Red River County), Richard Stanley, a black man, accused of rape.

25 FEBRUARY, in Marshall (Harrison County), a black man named Anderson was hanged for an alleged murder.

25 FEBRUARY, in Karnach (Harrison County), Robert Perry was lynched for horse theft.

4 JUNE, in Beaumont (Jefferson County), an unidentified black man accused of assault with intent to commit murder.

5 JUNE, in Newton County, Richard Galloway, a black man accused of racial prejudice.

6 JUNE, in Beaumont (Jefferson County), an unidentified black man was shot to death by a mob after being released from jail on bail, where he and two others were being held after they were arrested for attacking a group of white men.

21 SEPTEMBER, in Franklin (Robertson County), William Davis, a black man accused of murder.

1914—

8 JANUARY, in Jefferson (Marion County), David Lee, a black man, accused of assault with intent to commit murder.

13 MARCH, in Hearne (Robertson County), William Williams, a black man, accused of murder.

29 APRIL, in Marshall (Harrison County), Charles Fisher, a black youth, is severely mutilated by a mob after it was reported that he kissed the white daughter of a local farmer.

7 JUNE, in Navasota (Grimes County), William Robertson, a black man, accused of murder.

14 OCTOBER, in Angleton (Brazoria County), Joseph Durfee, a black man, was dragged from the jail and hanged by a mob angry at Governor Colquitt's having commuted his sentence of death to life imprisonment.

1915—

9 MAY, in Big Sandy (Upshur County), an unidentified black man accused of murder.

29 JULY, in Brownsville (Cameron County), Adolfo Munoz, a Hispanic man, accused of murder.

20 AUGUST, in San Benito (Cameron County), six unidentified Hispanic men accused of pillage and murder.

24 AUGUST, in Shiner (Lavaca County), John Slovak, a white man, accused of beating his wife.

29 AUGUST, in Sulphur Springs (Hopkins County), King Richmond, a black man, hanged for murder.

14 SEPTEMBER, in San Benito (Cameron County), six unidentified Hispanic men accused of banditry.

10 OCTOBER, in Brownsville (Cameron County), ten unidentified Hispanic men accused of train wrecking and murder.

1916—

24 JANUARY, in Boston (Bowie County), W. J. Maxfield, a white man, accused of murder.

5 MAY, in Hempstead (Waller County), Thomas Dixon, a black man, accused of rape.

15 MAY, in Waco (McLennan County), Jesse Washington, an 18-year-old black man, was dragged from the courtroom after the jury returned a verdict of guilty for the murder of Lucy Fryer, and burned to death while a crowd estimated to be 15,000 looked on. This was one of the largest lynch mobs ever assembled in the United States.

20 JUNE, in Brownsville (Cameron County), Jeronimo Lerma, a black man, accused of assault with intent to commit murder.

7 AUGUST, in Seymour (Baylor County), Stephen Brown, a black man, accused of murder.

19 AUGUST, in Rice (Navarro County), Edward Lang, a black man, accused of murder.

5 OCTOBER, in Graceton (Upshur County), William Spencer, a black man, accused of murder.

5 NOVEMBER, in Bay City (Matagorda County), Joseph Johnson, a black man, accused of murder.

29 NOVEMBER, in Clarksville (Red River County), Buck Thomas, a black man, accused of assault with intent to commit murder.

1917—

22 JUNE, in Courtney (Grimes County), Benjamin Harper, a black man, accused of murder.

23 JUNE, in Riesel (McLennan County), Elijah Hays, a black man, accused of striking a white woman.

25 JUNE, in Galveston (Galveston County), Charles Sawyer, a black man, accused of rape.

29 JUNE, in Temple (Bell County), Robert Jefferson, a black man, hanged for unknown reason.

3 JULY, in Orange (Orange County), Gilbert Guidry, a black man, accused of attempted rape.

22 AUGUST, in Marshall (Harrison County), Charles Jones, a black man, accused of attempted rape.

3 SEPTEMBER, in Beaumont (Jefferson County), Charles Jennings, a black man, hanged for unknown reason.

21 SEPTEMBER, in Goose Creek (Harris County), Bert Smith, a black cook for an oilfield work crew, was accused of assaulting a white woman. He was seized by an estimated 800 oilfield workers and hanged. His body was then riddled with bullets and mutilated with sledgehammers and knives.

1918—

27 MAY, in Beaumont (Jefferson County), Kirby Goolsie, a black man, accused of attacking a white girl.

4 JUNE, in Huntsville (Walker County), six members of the black Cabaniss family, Bessie, Cute, Pete, Sarah, Tenola, and Thomas, were all lynched by a mob for George Cabaniss' allegedly threatening a white man.

4 JUNE, in Sanderson (Terrell County), Edward Valentine, a white man, accused of murder.

27 JULY, in Benhur (Terrell County), Gene Brown, a black man, accused of assaulting a white woman.

18 SEPTEMBER, in Buff Lake (Terrell County), Abe O'Neal, a black man, accused of shooting and wounding a white man.

14 NOVEMBER, in Fort Bend (Fort Bend County) Charles Shipman, a black man, was hanged by a mob after a disagreement with a white man.

1920—6 JULY, in Paris (Lamar County), the Arthur brothers, Herman, 28, and Irving, 19, were burned at the stake by a mob of 3,000 angered by reports that they had murdered their landlord and his son.

1921—

15 AUGUST, in Datura (Limestone County), Alexander Winn, a black man accused of assaulting a 7-year-old girl, was hanged by an enraged mob. After Winn's death, another mob

stormed the funeral home, dragged his body out of its coffin, and burned it in the street.

11 OCTOBER, in Leesburg (Camp County), Wylie McNeely, a 19-year-old black man, was burned at the stake by a mob of 500 after being suspected of assaulting an 18-year-old girl.

11 DECEMBER, in Fort Worth (Tarrant County), Fred Rouse, a black packing house worker who was in the hospital with a fractured skull following a fight in which he had wounded two white colleagues, was taken from his hospital bed and hanged from a tree near the hospital.

1922—

6 MAY, in Kirvin (Freestone County), three black men, Shap Curry, 26, Mose Jones, 44, and John Cornish, 19, were all tied together and burned alive in the city square after being accused of murdering a 17-year-old girl, Eula Ausley. Two white men were later arrested for the crime.

27 MAY, in Waco (McLennan County), Jesse Thomas, a wrongly accused black man, was burned alive in the public square after being identified by a woman he allegedly attacked.

24 JUNE, in Dacus (Montgomery County), Warren Lewis, an 18-year-old black man, was hanged by a mob of 300 after he confessed to having attacked a white woman.

11 DECEMBER, in Streetman (Freestone County), the unidentified uncle of a black man wanted for an attack on the county sheriff was lynched after a posse was unable to locate his nephew.

14 DECEMBER, in Huntsville (Walker County), a 25-year-old unidentified black man accused of attacking a white woman was abducted from the Texas State Penitentiary by a mob estimated to be 1,500 strong and shot to death in the street.

29 DECEMBER, in Pilot Point (Denton County), two unidentified black men accused of stealing two horses were found to be missing from their jail cell and presumed to have been lynched.

1930—

9 MAY, in Sherman (Grayson County), George Hughes, a black man waiting to stand trial for the rape of a white woman, was burned alive when a mob set fire to the courthouse where he was being held. After the fire was extinguished his body was retrieved by a mob of 5,000 people, dragged

behind a car to the front of a store in the black business section of Sherman, hanged from a tree, doused with gasoline, and set on fire. Following this incident, the mob went on a rampage through the black section of town, setting fire to most of the town's black businesses and homes. This incident has become known as "The Sherman Riot of 1930."

18 MAY, in Honey Grove (Fannin County), George Johnson, a black man, accused of murdering his landlord.

17 JUNE, in Bryan (Brazos County), William Roane, a black man, accused of attempted rape.

1933—8 DECEMBER, in Kountze, David Gregory, a black man accused of killing a white woman, was mutilated and burned by a mob after he resisted arrest by a posse.

1934—21 JUNE, in Newton (Newton County), John Criggs, a black man accused of associating with a white woman, was seized from two deputy sheriffs by a mob of 200 armed men, hanged, and then shot.

1935—In Colorado County, two young black men (ages 15 and 16) accused of murdering a white woman, Miss Kollman, were seized by a mob of 700 and hanged.

1936—18 JUNE, in El Campo (Wharton County), a mob of 300 attempted the lynching of five black men and four black women accused of committing a murder in a cafe. After the Texas Rangers prevented the lynching, the mob burned the cafe.

1942—13 JULY, in Texarkana (Bowie County), William Vinson, a black man accused of rape and murder, was hanged by an outraged mob. This is the last known case of vigilante mob lynching in Texas.

WORKS CONSULTED AND SUGGESTIONS FOR FURTHER READING

Austin, Mattie Alice. "The Municipal Government of San Fernando de Bexar." *Quarterly of the Texas State Historical Association*, vol. 8 (1905), pp. 73-98.

Bancroft, Hubert Howe. *The Works of Hubert Howe Bancroft: Volume*

XI, History of Mexico. San Francisco, California: A. L. Bancroft &
Company, 1883, pp. 517-552.

————. *The Works of Hubert Howe Bancroft: Volume XVI, History of
the Northern Mexican States and Texas*. San Francisco, California:
The History Company, 1889, pp. 94-95, 390-393, 530-533.

Barker, Eugene C. "The Government of Austin's Colony, 1821-1831."
Southwestern Historical Quarterly, vol. 21 (1918), pp. 17-34.

————. "Minutes of the Ayuntamiento of San Felipe de Austin,
1828-1832: Parts 1-12." *Southwestern Historical Quarterly*,
vols. 22-24 (July 1918-October 1920).

Boner, Marian. *A Reference Guide to Texas Law and Legal History:
Sources and Documentation*. Austin, Texas: University of Texas
Press, 1976, pp. 1-12.

Brown, Richard Maxwell. "Western Violence: Structure, Values,
Myth." *Western Historical Quarterly*, vol. 24 (1993), pp. 5-20.

Chapman, David. "Lynching in Texas." Lubbock, Texas: M.A. thesis,
Texas Tech University, 1973.

"Crime in Texas." *Illustrated American*, vol. 8 (1891), p. 244.

Cruz, Gilbert. "The City Ordinances of San Antonio of Bejar, 1829."
Texana, 7 (1969), pp. 3-11.

Fenton, James I. "Tom Ross: Ranger Nemesis." *Quarterly of the
National Association and Center for Outlaw and Lawman History*,
vol. 14 (1990), pp. 1-21.

"Ghastly Horror in Texas: A Negro Tortured to Death." *Review of
Reviews* (London), vol. 7 (1893), p. 520.

Gurr, Ted. *Violence in America: The History of Crime*. Thousand
Oaks, California: Sage, 1989.

Hogan, William Ransom. "Rampant Individualism in the Republic of
Texas." *Southwestern Historical Quarterly*, vol. 44 (1941), pp.
454-480.

Holden, W. C. "Law and Lawlessness on the Texas Frontier, 1875-
1890." *Southwestern Historical Quarterly*, vol. 44 (October
1940), pp. 188-203.

Jones, O. Garfield. "Local Government in the Spanish Colonies as
Provided by the Recopilacion de Leyes de los Reynos de las
Indias." *Southwestern Historical Quarterly*, vol. 19 (1915).

Lack, Paul D. "Slavery and Vigilantism in Austin, Texas: 1840-1860."
Southwestern Historical Quarterly, vol. 85 (1981), pp. 1-20.

"Lynching and Torture of Negroes in Texas." *Public Opinion*, vol. 19
(1895), p. 696.

"Lynching in Texas." *Albany Law Journal*, vol. 47 (1893), p. 141.

McCaslin, Richard B. "Tainted Breeze: The Great Hanging at

Gainesville," Austin, Texas: Ph.D. dissertation, University of Texas, 1988.

McKay, S. S. "Constitution of Coahuila and Texas." *The New Handbook of Texas*. Austin, Texas: The Texas State Historical Association, 1996, vol. 2, p. 287.

Miller, Margaret. "Survey of Civil Government of San Antonio, Texas 1731-1948." San Antonio, Texas: M.A. thesis, St. Mary's University, 1948.

O'Neal, Bill. *Encyclopedia of Western Gunfighters*. Norman, Oklahoma: University of Oklahoma Press, 1979.

————. "Violence in Texas History," in *Texas: A Sesquicentennial Celebration*. Donald W. Whisenhunt, editor. Austin, Texas: Eakin Press, 1984, pp. 353-369.

Priestly, H. I. "Spanish Colonial Municipalities." *California Law Review*, vol. 7 (1919).

Rather, Ethel Z. "De Witts Colony." *Quarterly of the Texas State Historical Association*, vol. 7 (1904).

Ravkind, William. "Comments: Justifiable Homicide in Texas." *Southwestern Law Journal*, vol. 13 (1959), pp. 508-524.

Rister, C. C. "Outlaws and Vigilantes on the Southern Plains, 1865-1885." *Mississippi Valley Historical Review*, vol. 19 (1933), pp. 537-554.

Robbins, Peggy. "Sam Bass: The Texas Robin Hood." *American History Illustrated*, vol. 17 (1982), p. 37.

Roberts, Gary L. "Violence and the Frontier Tradition," in *Kansas and the West: Bicentennial Essays in Honor of Nyle H. Miller*. Forrest R. Blackburn, editor. Topeka, Kansas: Kansas State Historical Society, 1976, pp. 96-111.

Ross, John R. "Lynching." *The New Handbook of Texas*. Austin, Texas: Texas State Historical Association, 1996, vol. 3, pp. 346-347.

————. "At the Bar of Judge Lynch: Lynching and Lynch Mobs in America." Lubbock, Texas: Ph.D. dissertation, Texas Tech University, 1983.

Sonnichsen, C. L. *Ten Texas Feuds*. Albuquerque, New Mexico: University of New Mexico Press, 1957.

————. *I'll Die Before I'll Run: The Story of the Great Feuds of Texas*. New York: Devin-Adair Company, 1962.

"Texas and Ashantee." *Illustrated American*, vol. 13 (1893), p. 211.

"The Texas Horror." *Public Opinion*, vol. 14 (1893), p. 448.

Thompson, Nolan. "Sherman Riot of 1930." *The Handbook of Texas*.

2.
FOUNDATIONS OF TEXAS LAW

INTRODUCTION

When broken down into its simplest components, the "law" can be understood as a series of rights, rules, and restrictions created and enforced by a governing authority. The law can be divided into two general categories: *private law* and *public law*. Private law governs relations between citizens (examples include tort and contract law). In contrast, public law governs the relationship between citizens and their government. This chapter is limited to a discussion of the latter.

In the field of criminal justice, there are two types of public law which are of particular importance: constitutional law and criminal law. Constitutional law provides governmental structure and individual rights. Criminal law forbids and punishes particular conduct. Courts are often called upon to construe the constitutionality of statutory criminal laws (i.e., laws created by the Texas Legislature) and to determine how such laws should be applied. Such decisions, referred to as *case law* or *precedent*, act as a third source of law and often affect the criminal justice system.

The goals of this chapter are twofold: Part 1 surveys the historical evolution of the Texas Constitution. It also addresses the portions of the Texas Bill of Rights that are pertinent to criminal justice. Part 2 details the function and structure of the Texas Penal Code. Note that while the Penal Code governs the punishment of many criminal wrongs, it is not an exclusive source of Texas criminal law. State drug laws (the Texas Dangerous Drug Act and the Controlled Substance Act) are located in the Texas Health and Safety Code. Additionally, traffic rules and regulations, including the state's DWI (driving while intoxicated) statutes, are located in the Texas Transportation Code.

PART 1:
THE TEXAS CONSTITUTION

What is a constitution? Scholars have debated the term's meaning. It has been defined as the fundamental law from which governments are built and operate. Other definitions emphasize that while a constitution spells out the structure and functions of government, a constitution's primary purpose is to protect citizens from the powers of the government. While such definitions give us an academic starting point for discussion, they each ignore the human aspect of why people unite to create an ultimate governing doctrine. To understand the meaning of the Texas Constitution in a broader sense, it is important to understand the underlying motivations and circumstances in which it was created.

Constitutional History

Early Texas: Spain and Mexico (1812-1836)

Though Texans have lived under nine constitutions, it should be noted that three were enacted while Texas was still part of the northern frontier of Mexico. Initially, as the farthest northern province of Spain, Texas was governed briefly by the Spanish Constitution of 1812. Spanish rule came to an end in 1821 when Mexico revolted and became independent from Spain. Nearly three years later, under the Mexican Constitution of 1824, the Province of Texas was integrated into the state of Coahuila. In 1827 the Constitution of the State of Coahuila y Tejas provided citizens of the newly integrated territory with limited independence from the central government in Mexico City. While the Constitution of 1827 guaranteed all citizens liberty, security, property, and freedom from slavery, many of the state constitutional promises were not initially implemented. The liberty, security, and property of Texans were threatened by the fact that few Anglo-Texans could understand the laws which, by law, were only at first published in Spanish. Additionally, the constitutional guarantee of trial by jury was not fulfilled until 1834.

Widespread dissatisfaction with government resulted in Anglo-Texans proposing a constitution in 1833 which gave Texas statehood separate from Coahuila. Modeled on the Missouri, Louisiana, and Tennessee constitutions, the proposed constitution of 1833 was a major departure from the earlier constitutions which had been firmly rooted in European governmental principles. Stephen F. Austin was selected to present the constitution to the Congress in Mexico City. Opposed to many of the suggested constitution's Anglo-American ideals and Texas' request for independence from Coahuila, the Mexican Congress rejected the proposal.

During Austin's return he was arrested in the northern Mexico city of Saltillo because of letters he had written to San Antonio political leaders that challenged Mexico's governing authority. Though he was never formally charged and received no trial, Austin was kept in solitary confinement in Mexico City for three months. Some consider Austin's imprisonment as the beginning of the chain of events which culminated in the Texas Revolution.

The Constitution of the Republic of Texas (1836-1845)

The constitution of the Republic of Texas was drafted by 59 delegates who met at Washington-on-the-Brazos on 1 March 1836. The brevity of the document (less than 6,500 words), as well as its similarity to the U.S. Constitution, is attributable to the fact that the framers faced an ever-present threat of attack by Mexican cavalry. Independence from Mexico was not won until 21 April 1836, when Gen. Sam Houston defeated Gen. Antonio Lopez de Santa Anna at the Battle of San Jacinto.

Ideologically, the new constitution of the Republic reflected a blend of influences. It adopted the use of English common law in all criminal cases. Borrowing from principles of Jacksonian democracy, imprisonment for debt was abolished. To assure separation of church and state, ministers and priests were prohibited from holding elected office. Finally, from Spanish-Mexican civil law, the constitution incorporated the concepts of community property (i.e., all property and assets acquired during marriage belong equally to both spouses) and debtor relief (i.e., bankruptcy).

Though most Texans supported the annexation of Texas by the United States, northern states feared admitting another slave state into the Union. For years, the issue of slavery obstructed Texas' efforts to become part of the United States. It was not until the election of President James K. Polk in 1844 that the tide of support in America began turning in favor of annexing Texas. In February 1845, the U.S. Congress passed a joint resolution offering Texas admission into the Union. Eight months later, by an overwhelming vote of 4,254 to 257, the citizens of the Republic of Texas approved annexation. On the same ballot, by a vote of 4,174 to 312, Texans approved the first state constitution. Texas became the 28th state in the Union on 29 December 1845. Two months later, at a ceremony transferring authority to the newly elected state government, Anson Jones, president of the Republic of Texas, announced, "The final act in the great drama is now performed; the Republic of Texas is no more."

Statehood Constitution (1845-1861)

At the Constitutional Convention of 1845, the framers drew heavily on the proposed constitution of 1833 and the newly adopted constitution of Louisiana. Ultimately, however, as a working model the constitution of the Republic was used to plan the structure of government and bill of rights. When completed, the Constitution of 1845 was twice as long as the Constitution of the Republic of Texas and more complex than any of its predecessors. Interestingly, Article VII, the longest article in the Constitution of 1845, contained a limitation on

Sam Houston
(Courtesy Barker Texas History Center)

Anson Jones, last president of the Republic of Texas

Santa Anna

the legislature which forbade participants of duels from holding elected office. Yet, despite its extended length, the Constitution of 1845 was straightforward and simple in comparison to other state constitutions of the era. Even opponents of Texas' admission into the Union, such as U.S. Senator Daniel Webster, called the document the best state constitution of the day.

The Constitution of 1845 was progressive for its time. It added separate property rights for women and greatly expanded the right to a jury trial. Among historians, the Constitution of 1845 remains one of the most popular of all Texas constitutions.

Constitution of 1861

Texas seceded from the Union on 23 February 1861. To mark the state's detachment from the Union and to illustrate its loyalty to the Confederacy, the Constitution of 1845 was amended. Throughout the document the words "United States of America" were changed to the "Confederate States of America." States' rights and slavery were defended, and the freeing of slaves was declared illegal. Today the Constitution of 1861 is considered historically significant, not for any radical substantive changes made in the law, but for the act of rebellion which it ultimately symbolized.

Reconstruction Constitution of 1866

In 1865 President Andrew Johnson appointed a provisional governor to oversee the adoption of Texas' first post-Civil War constitution. During what has come to be known historically as Presidential Reconstruction, the Constitution of 1866 was the first step in restoring normal relations with the Union. The document, which passed by a narrow majority, removed all references to the Confederacy, abolished the state's right to secession, repudiated the state's war debt, and outlawed slavery. Aside from these changes, the Constitution of 1866 essentially reinstated the substantive provisions of the Constitution of 1845.

Reconstruction Constitution of 1869

The second and final step in restoring normal relations with the United States was for Texas to submit a constitution for U.S. Congressional approval (i.e., Congressional Reconstruction). This proved not to be an easy task. Efforts to finalize a constitution at the Constitutional Convention of 1868-1869 were derailed in what proved to be a "long, drawn out raucous affair" (May at 11). At one point during the convention, radical delegates called for the western portion of Texas (where Union sentiment was strong) to be separated from the rest of the state. Though presented to Congress, attempts to create the state of West Texas and approve its own separate constitution were ultimately rejected. The Constitutional Convention broke up without completing a constitution. Five months later, provisions from the Convention's defunct effort were collected in a piecemeal manner. The Constitution of 1869 was ultimately assembled by a committee appointed by the U.S. military and signed by 46 of the Convention's 78 delegates. Though many Texans believed that the Constitution of 1869 was forced upon them by Washington D.C., it nevertheless was ratified by a substantial majority of voters (72,466 to 4,928). To this day, the Constitution of 1869 remains one of the most controversial of all Texas constitutions.

Constitution of 1876 (The Present Constitution)

Despite the controversy and public unrest which surrounded the Constitution of 1869, Reconstruction politics played a limited role in the push for a new state constitution. Rather, Texas' present constitution, the Constitution of 1876, came to exist as a result of an ideological division within the Democratic Party (which at the time controlled the executive and legislative branches of the government) and because of popular support for the Texas Grange (an alliance of agrarians and farmers who were "committed to the cause of economy and limited government"). Convention delegates (predominantly Grange and Republican), dissatisfied with the Constitution of 1869, came to the Constitutional Convention

in Austin zealously determined to rid Texas of what they perceived as corruption at all levels of government. To such delegates, a new constitution was an opportunity not only to
reform the structure of government, but also a chance to
"break state governments' 'unholy' alignment with big business, railroads, and monopolies" (Harrington at 8).

Reflecting a strong national trend among state constitutions, the Constitution of 1876 was drafted to be restrictive
in nature. Due to their distrust of government institutions, the
framers went to great efforts to precisely define the rights,
powers, and prerogatives of all governmental departments and
agencies (a task traditionally reserved for the legislature). The
framers' distrust was not limited merely to institutions of state
government. Distrust of banks, stemming from the Panic of
1869 in which many farmers lost their savings and land,
resulted in a constitutional prohibition of banking institutions.
Distrust of the federal government, stemming from President
Lincoln's suspension of the writ of habeas corpus during the
Civil War, resulted in the writ being incorporated into the state
Bill of Rights as an absolute right that cannot be suspended
under any circumstances. (Habeas corpus is discussed in detail
in Chapters 4 and 5.)

The Constitution of 1876 was ratified by the people of
Texas on 25 February 1876, by a lopsided 2 to 1 margin
(136,606 to 56,652). Unlike earlier Texas constitutions which
were born out of revolution, annexation, secession, and/or
reconstruction, no single event in the last 120 years has neces-
sitated a new constitution. Rather, since 1876 the preferred
method of constitutional reform has been modification by
amendment. More than 550 amendments have been submitted
to voters since 1879. By 1997 the Texas Constitution had been
amended 364 times. In contrast, the U.S. Constitution has been
amended only 27 times.

The Constitution Today

Constant Evolution

Today the Texas Constitution is one of the longest in the nation, exceeding 80,000 words in length (more than eight times the length of the U.S. Constitution) and containing more than 370 sections. In the last 120 years, the Texas Constitution has evolved into an incredibly complex document. In 1995 the Texas secretary of state commented that the difference between the Texas Constitution and the literary classic *War and Peace* is that the latter is not getting any longer. In contrast, the Texas Constitution is constantly undergoing change by amendment and interpretation. Scholars have described it as "hard to nail down" (May at xxxi). One Texas Supreme Court justice has gone so far as to describe it as one of the most confusing and potentially frustrating constitutions in America.

Could a revised constitution be on the horizon? Historically, all revision efforts have failed, lacking the requisite political support. Nevertheless, in late 1997 the League of Women Voters initiated efforts to convince Texas citizens that their constitution needs revision, not constant amendments. If constitutional revision becomes a priority issue in the 1999 legislative session, Texans could ratify their tenth constitution by 2001.

Overview of Constitutional Articles

Vernon's Annotated Constitution of State of Texas consists of three bound volumes which exceed 1,800 pages in length. The constitution's statutory-like provisions address a vast array of subjects, many of which exceed the scope of criminal justice. For reference purposes, the following is an overview of the constitution's present structure (articles which are of importance in the administration of criminal justice have been noted with an asterisk).

Article I.	Bill of Rights*
	(detailed in this chapter)
Article II.	The Powers of Government*
Article III.	Legislative Department*
Article IV.	Executive Department*
Article V.	Judicial Department*
Article VI.	Suffrage

Article VII.	Education
Article VIII.	Taxation and Revenue
Article IX.	Counties
Article X.	Railroads
Article XI.	Municipal Corporations*
Article XII.	Private Corporations
Article XIII.	Spanish and Mexican Land Titles (Repealed August 5, 1969)
Article XIV.	Public Lands and Land Office
Article XV.	Impeachment
Article XVI.	General Provisions*
Article XVII.	Mode of Amending the Constitution of this State

Texas Bill of Rights

While applicable articles of the constitution shall be referred to directly and indirectly throughout this text, Article I (Bill of Rights) is of such importance in understanding Texas' criminal justice system that it deserves special attention. (It is reproduced in its entirety in Appendix A.)

The framers believed the Texas Bill of Rights to be so important to the welfare of Texas' citizens that it has consistently been placed at the beginning of all five constitutions. In contrast, the U.S. Bill of Rights is located at the end of the federal constitution. In outlining the basic rights of all individuals during the 1875 convention, delegates expanded the Texas Bill of Rights in an effort to assure the people that government would neither violate nor fail to defend their rights. Since ratifying the Constitution in 1876, voters have amended the Texas Bill of Rights eight times. Today the provisions of the state's Bill of Rights can be seen as falling into three categories:

- the nature of government and the role of government with respect to individuals (Tex. Const. art. I, §§ 6, 13, 24, 26, 29)
- personal substantive liberty and property rights (Tex. Const. art. I, §§ 3-4, 6-8, 11-14, 16-23, 25, 27)
- procedural rights in criminal and civil proceedings (Tex. Const. art. I, §§ 5, 8-16, 30)

Texas Bill of Rights	Nature of Right	Equivalent Federal Constitutional Provisions	Commentary
Section 3	Equal rights	14th Amendment	While Texas *guarantees* rights, the U.S. *prohibits* denial of equal protection.
Section 3a	Equality under law	None	Texas specifically prohibits denial of equality on the basis of race, sex, color, creed, or national origin.
Section 5	Witnesses not disqualified by religious beliefs or affirmations	1st Amendment	Texas allows witnesses to testify regardless of their beliefs or lack of beliefs.
Section 9	Search and seizures	4th Amendment	While Texas requires warrants to describe persons, places, or things "as near as may be," the U.S. requires warrants "particularly describing" (more specific).
Section 10	Rights of accused in criminal prosecutions	5th Amendment; 6th Amendment	Texas allows legal representation by "both" self and/or attorney.
Section 11	Bail	8th Amendment	While Texas *guarantees* bail (except in capital cases), the U.S. *prohibits* excessive bail.
Section 11a	Multiple convictions; denial of bail	8th Amendment	Texas guarantees preferential appeal to the court of

(*continued on page 65*)

Texas Bill of Rights	Nature of Right	Equivalent Federal Constitutional Provisions	Commentary
Section 11a (*continued*)			appeals in cases where the amount of bail is at issue or in cases where bail is denied.
Section 12	Habeas corpus	Article I, sect. 9	While Texas guarantees the right to habeas corpus, the U.S. allows suspension in the event of invasion or rebellion. In recent years, laws have been passed to limit successive applications.
Section 13	Excessive bail or fines; cruel or unusual punishment; due course of law	5th Amendment, 8th Amendment, 14th Amendment	While Texas prohibits "cruel *or* unusual" punishment, the U.S. prohibits "cruel *and* unusual" punishment. Additionally, Texas guarantees open access to courts to all people.
Section 14	Double jeopardy	5th Amendment	While Texas extends jeopardy protection to "life and liberty," the U.S. provides protection to "life and limb."
Section 15	Right of trial by jury	6th Amendment	Unlike the U.S., Texas addresses the rights of the mentally ill who are temporarily committed after committing criminal acts.

Texas Bill of Rights	Nature of Right	Equivalent Federal Constitutional Provisions	Commentary
Section 16	*Bill of attainder, Ex post facto laws; retroactive laws*; laws impairing contracts	Article I, sections 9, 10	U.S. provisions do not address retroactive laws. While both U.S. and Texas provisions protect the right to enter into contracts, contracts which violate the criminal law are void.
Section 18	Imprisonment for debt	None	The U.S. has no comparable provision.
Section 19	Deprivation of life, liberty, property, privileges, or immunities	5th Amendment, 14th Amendment	Texas protects against deprivations by prohibiting citizens from being "disenfranchized" without due course of law.
Section 20	No outlawry or transportation for offense; confinement of out of state inmates; detention of state inmates in other states	None	This provision prohibits people from being declared an outlaw or being deported for an offense. However, prisoners from other states may be imprisoned in Texas and the State reserves the right to detain inmates in other states.
Section 28	Suspension of law	None	Only the State legislature can suspend the laws of Texas.
Section 30	Rights of criminal victims	None	The U.S. has no comparable provision.

Compared to Federal Constitutions

While all states are obligated to provide their citizens, at a minimum, the rights guaranteed to them under the U.S. Constitution, such "fundamental" rights may be extended by additional rights provided by state constitutions (U.S. Const. Amendment X). The only limitation on states is that any additional protections must not contradict or violate any existing federal law (U.S. Const. Article IV). While the Texas Bill of Rights is similar to the U.S. Bill of Rights, it is important to recognize how they differ in their approach to criminal justice.

PART 2:

THE TEXAS PENAL CODE

After winning independence from Mexico, the founders of the Republic began devising a system of criminal laws (i.e., rules forbidding and punishing certain types of conduct). Since many of the state's founders were educated in the United States and already familiar with Anglo-American common law (stemming from English law), the Republic of Texas in 1836 adopted common law crimes. For 20 years common law crimes were not comprehensively memorialized by statute. Hence, the fate of criminal defendants sometimes rested merely on the perspective of the judge or jury. To remedy this situation, the common law was codified (incorporated into the written law) by the Penal Code of 1856 (effective February 1857). For more than 120 years the criminal law in Texas has evolved as a result of constitutional interpretation (how the constitution has been interpreted by the judiciary at both the state and federal level), statutory interpretation and statutory modifications enacted by the legislature (recent reforms to the Penal Code were made in 1973 and 1993). The Penal Code of 1993 (effective September 1994) features important changes in definitions of crimes, periods of imprisonment, and conditions for parole and community supervision. (Parole and community supervision are discussed in Chapter 8.)

Objectives

The general objectives of the Penal Code are to insure public safety by deterring, rehabilitating, and punishing those who unjustifiably threaten to harm individual or private interests (PC § 1.02). The code's additional stated objectives are to:

- DEFINE to the people what acts are prohibited as well as the consequences of their violation;
- PRESCRIBE penalties that are proportionate to the seriousness of the offense while acknowledging the individual offender's potential for rehabilitation;
- PROTECT conduct which is not criminal from arbitrary or capricious prosecution;
- LIMIT the exercise of official discretion in law enforcement;
- ESTABLISH the scope of state interests in law enforcement as they pertain to specific offenses and the exercise of state criminal jurisdiction.

Interpretation

The Penal Code provides specific instructions as to how it is to be interpreted by its readers. Specifically, the code is to be construed in a manner to "promote justice" and satisfy the code's objectives (PC § 1.05). This is a departure from common law interpretation which construed criminal laws "narrowly" against the government and in favor of the individual accused of criminal wrongdoing. Since words often have more than one meaning, the Penal Code provides specific definitions to insure that key terms are consistently interpreted and applied.

General Principles of Criminal Responsibility

Terms defined in the Penal Code are also of great importance because they often constitute the elements of a crime. In turn, the elements of a crime act as building blocks, which, when assembled, constitute the actual offense. For a person to be convicted of any crime, each and every element must be proved beyond a reasonable doubt (reasonable doubt is discussed in Chapter 5). In other words, the finder of fact (either a judge or a jury) must be convinced that all elements have been adequately proven. (In subsequent chapters the trial process, where crimes are proven, will be addressed.) It is important to first understand the elements of a crime under the Penal Code.

There are generally four components which must be established to hold someone criminally responsible:

1. ACTUS REUS (i.e., the "guilty act")—The prosecution must prove that the accused engaged in certain prohibited conduct;
2. MENS REA (i.e., the "guilty mind")—The prosecution must prove that the accused had a specified state of mind when he engaged in the prohibited conduct;
3. CAUSATION—The accused's conduct must cause a result specified by law. Note, however, that not all crimes require a result (e.g., DWI, 49.04);
4. THE INAPPLICABILITY OF AN EXCEPTION—No general defenses to criminal responsibility are applicable.

Actus Reus: "The Forbidden Conduct"

To commit an offense a person must engage in a specifically forbidden conduct. The Penal Code defines three types of forbidden conduct (PC § 6.01). First, it prohibits individuals from engaging in certain actions (affirmative acts or acts of commission). The definition of what constitutes an affirmative act varies among offenses. Second, in certain instances the Penal Code prohibits individuals from failing to act (i.e., negative acts or omissions). Criminal liability for omissions may exist where certain people with recognized legal duties (e.g., parents, public servants, legal guardians) fail to act accordingly (e.g., failure to pay child-support, failure of law enforcement to report the death of a prisoner). Third, the code forbids possession of prohibited items (e.g., illegal weapons, child pornography, and human body parts).

Regardless of the type of conduct, an offense is not committed unless it is voluntarily. An act is generally considered "voluntary" if it is the result of any conscious thought or movement. The failure to act, or the knowledge that one possesses a prohibited item, is also voluntary conduct.

Mens Rea: The Required Culpability

With respect to each element of the offense, Texas law requires the accused to be criminally culpable (i.e., blameworthy) (PC § 6.02). Even if a prohibited act is committed, no individual is guilty of a crime unless he or she also had a culpable state of mind. Accordingly, as defined by the offense, the accused must act with one of the classified mental states (from highest to lowest):

> INTENTIONALLY—The accused purposely committed the offense;
> KNOWINGLY—The accused was aware that he was committing the offense;
> RECKLESSLY—The accused was aware that his conduct could have dangerous consequences but chose to ignore the risk (i.e., conscious risk taking); OR,
> WITH CRIMINAL NEGLIGENCE—The accused should have been aware that his actions might have dangerous consequences (i.e., inattentive risk taking) (PC § 6.03).

The accused, however, does not need to realize whether the conduct is a crime, nor are the intentions or motivations of the accused necessarily relevant in determining if a punishable offense has occurred. Some crimes do not require a guilty state of mind. These are called absolute liability offenses. The actor's state of mind is irrelevant (e.g., bigamy, PC § 25.01; public intoxication, PC § 49.02).

Causation: "A Required Result"

Assuming that the *actus reus* and *mens rea* can be established as existing concurrently (i.e., they overlap in time), the forbidden conduct must be shown to have caused a particular result. For instance, assume that Tim is accused of murder (PC § 19.02) by means of poisoning Neil's drink. Not only must it be proven that Tim placed the poison in Neil's drink (*actus reus*), and that he did so either "intentionally or knowingly" (*mens rea*), it must also be shown that the poison was the cause of Neil's death (causation). Since death is a "required result" in the offense of murder, the prosecution must prove that Neil died from poison, and not some unrelated intervening cause. Thus, if Neil suffered a fatal stroke or heart attack and died as he was about to place his lips to the cup, Tim may be proven guilty of attempted murder (PC §§ 15.01 & 19.02) but not the specific crime of murder.

The Inapplicability of an Exception: "No Legal Defense"

Even if the prosecution is able to prove the *actus reus*, *mens rea*, and causation, the culprit may not be held criminally responsible if a legal defense is applicable. The Penal Code separates legal defenses into two categories: affirmative defenses and general defenses.

Affirmative defenses either: (1) excuse what would otherwise be criminal conduct or (2) mitigate (i.e., reduce) punishment imposed upon the accused. An affirmative defense admits prohibited conduct (i.e., the *actus reus*) but excuses the accused due to some internal or external condition that was beyond the accused's control or was not the accused's fault. If raised, the accused must prove the affirmative defense by a preponderance of evidence (i.e., 51% probability). Examples of affirmative defenses include:

INSANITY—It is an affirmative defense that at the time of the conduct the accused did not know that his crime was wrong. The inability to differentiate between right and wrong must be the result of severe mental disease or defect (excluding repeated criminal or otherwise socially unacceptable conduct) (PC § 8.01).

MISTAKE OF LAW—The Penal Code embraces the Latin maxim *"ignorantia legis neminem excusat"* (ignorance of the law is no excuse). However, where the accused relied on a "narrow class of official statements or interpretations of the law" (e.g., court opinions, agency regulations), mistake of law may be submitted as an affirmative defense (PC § 8.03; *Hawkins v. State*, 656 S.W.2d 70, 73 (Tex. Crim. App. 1983)).

INTOXICATION—While intoxication (i.e., the disturbance of mental and physical capacity resulting from any substance taken into the body) is no defense to prosecution, it may be used to mitigate the punishment attached to the offense (PC § 8.04).

DURESS—It is an affirmative defense that the accused committed the offense because he was compelled to do so by threat of bodily or serious injury to himself or another. The threat, however, must be of a nature which would compel a "reasonable person" to commit the offense (PC § 8.05).

In contrast, general defenses do not "mitigate" punishment or rely on external or internal conditions to "excuse" prohibited conduct. Rather, general defenses "justify" conduct that would otherwise be illegal (e.g., self-defense). If successful at trial, a general defense entirely insulates the accused from criminal responsibility. It is the burden of the prosecution to disprove general defenses "beyond a reasonable doubt" (see Chapter 5). If the prosecution fails to disprove a general defense, the accused must be acquitted (i.e., found not guilty). Examples of general defenses include:

ENTRAPMENT—It is a general defense that the accused committed the offense because he was induced to do so by a law enforcement agent. However, the persuasion or means used by the agent must be likely to cause other people to commit the offense. Merely presenting the accused with an opportunity to commit the offense does not constitute entrapment (PC § 8.06).

MISTAKE OF FACT—It is a general defense that the accused by mistake formed a reasonable belief about a matter of fact pertinent to the offense. However, the mistaken belief must negate the mental element (*mens rea*) required for committing the crime (PC § 8.02)

THE JUSTIFIED USE OF FORCE—The Penal Code explicitly states situations in which, out of necessity, citizens are justified in using either deadly or non-deadly force:

1. Protection of Persons
   • self-defense (PC § 9.31)
   • defense of other people (PC § 9.33)
2. Protection of Property
   • protecting personal property (PC § 9.41)
   • protecting the property of others (PC § 9.43)
   • the use of devices to protect property (PC § 9.44)

3. Law Enforcement
   - the use of force in arrest and search (PC § 9.51)
   - prevention of escape from custody (PC § 9.52)
   - maintaining security in correctional facilities (PC § 9.53)

Punishments

Classifying Offenses

The Penal Code classifies offenses as either misdemeanors or felonies. Misdemeanors fall into three categories according to the seriousness of the offense (PC §§12.03, 12.21-.23):

CLASS A
> Confinement not to exceed one year in a county jail, or a fine not to exceed $4,000, or both

CLASS B
> Confinement not to exceed 180 days in a county jail or a fine not to exceed $2,000 or both

CLASS C
> No confinement and a fine not to exceed $500

There are five categories of felony offenses (P.C. §§ 12.04, 12.31-.35):

CAPITAL
> Life in prison, or death by lethal injection; only applicable to offense of capital murder (PC § 19.03)

1ST DEGREE
> 5 to 99 years in prison or life in prison; an optional fine not to exceed $10,000

2ND DEGREE
> 2 to 20 years in prison; an optional fine not to exceed $10,000

3RD DEGREE
> 2 to 10 years in prison; an optional fine not to exceed $10,000

STATE JAIL
> 180 days to 2 years in a state jail; an optional fine not to exceed $10,000

"Value Ladder" Offenses

Acquisition offenses, such as theft (PC § 31.03) (referred to by common names such as "shoplifting," "embezzlement," etc.) are punished according to the worth of the property when it is taken (i.e., its fair market value). For such offenses a "value ladder" is used in determining a penalty. The penalty increases with the value of the property stolen (PC §§ 31.01-.13).

Less than $20 (in some cases $50)	Class C misdemeanor
$20 (or $50)–less than $500	Class B misdemeanor
$500–less than $1,500	Class A misdemeanor
$1,500–less than $20,000	State jail felony
$20,000–less than $100,000	3rd degree felony
$100,000–less than $200,000	2nd degree felony
$200,000 or more	1st degree felony

Corporations and Associations

While most crimes are committed by individuals, crimes are also committed by organized entities. The Penal Code provides two classifications of such entities: corporations and associations.

A "corporation" is a business entity formally organized under the laws of the state (PC § 1.07 (a) (13)). An "association" is a partnership or a group of two or more individuals who share a common economic interest (PC § 1.07 (a) (6)). Under the doctrine of vicarious liability, either type of entity may be held criminally responsible if one of its agents (e.g., directors, officers, agents, or employees) commits an offense which was "authorized, requested, commanded, performed, or recklessly tolerated" by the entity (PC §§ 7.21-.22). If convicted of an offense the following fines may be imposed:

FELONIES (all classifications)—
    A fine not to exceed $20,000
CLASS A OR B MISDEMEANORS—
    A fine not to exceed $10,000
CLASS C MISDEMEANORS—
    A fine not to exceed $2,000
CLASS A MISDEMEANORS OR FELONIES
INVOLVING SERIOUS BODILY INJURY OR DEATH—
    A fine not to exceed $50,000

Enhancement of Punishment

When later crimes are committed by the same offender, prior convictions act to heighten the severity of punishment (known as enhancement). Enhancements are intended to discourage offenders from becoming recidivists ("repeat offenders" or "career criminals") and to protect society from its worst criminals. For instance, if the accused has two felony convictions (one being a sex crime), upon conviction for a separate sex offense the offender may be deemed a "habitual sex offender" and automatically sentenced to life in prison (PC §12.42 (a) (2)).

Felony Enhancements (PC §12.42)

If the accused has a prior felony conviction that resulted in a prison sentence and is later convicted of a:

- **1ST DEGREE FELONY**—minimum punishment is increased from 5 to 15 years;
- **2ND DEGREE FELONY**—punishment is enhanced to a 1st degree offense;
- **3RD DEGREE FELONY**—punishment is enhanced to a 2nd degree offense;
- **STATE JAIL FELONY**—punishment is enhanced to a 3rd degree offense if the accused has prior convictions for violent crimes or used or possessed a deadly weapon in committing a prior or present offense.

Misdemeanor Enhancements (PC §12.43)

If the accused has a prior conviction for a:

- **CLASS A MISDEMEANOR (OR ANY FELONY)**—conviction of a separate Class A misdemeanor shall result in punishment ranging from 90 days to 1 year with a maximum optional fine of $4,000;
- **CLASS A AND B MISDEMEANORS (OR ANY FELONY)**—conviction of a separate Class B misdemeanor shall result in punishment ranging from 30 to 180 days with a maximum optional fine of $2,000;
- **CLASS C**—no Class C misdemeanor can be used for enhancement purposes (*Axelrod v. State*, 764 S.W.2d 296, 302 (Tex. App. Houston [1st Dist.] 1988, pet. dism'd)).

Division of Offenses

Crimes addressed in the Penal Code can be broken down into eight categories of offenses:

1. inchoate (i.e., preparatory offenses and incomplete criminal acts stopped short of completion)
2. against the person (e.g., murder, battery, sexual assault)
3. against the family (e.g. bigamy, child custody offenses)
4. against property (e.g., theft, burglary, robbery)
5. against public administration (e.g., perjury, bribery, tampering with government records)
6. against public order and decency (e.g, disorderly conduct, rioting, prostitution)
7. against public health, safety and morals (e.g., DWI, unlawfully carrying a weapon, gambling)
8. organized crime (i.e., business activities directed toward economic gain by unlawful means).

OUTLINE OF TEXAS PENAL CODE OFFENSE

* denotes new offenses created in 1997

Title and Offense	Penal Code	Classification
I. Inchoate Offenses		
A. Preparatory Offenses:		
1. Attempt, Criminal	15.01	One degree lower than offense attempted.
2. Conspiracy, Criminal	15.02	"
3. Solicitation, Criminal	15.03	"
B. Criminal Instruments & Interception of Wire or Oral Communication:		
1. Stored Communications, Unlawful Access	16.04	Class A
2. Public Communications, Illegal Divulgence	16.05	State Jail Felony
• cellular phone	"	Class C
• intent to gain benefit	"	Class A
3. Interception of Communication, Unlawful (wire, oral, or electronic)	16.02	2nd Degree
• interference w/ lawful govt. interception	"	State Jail Felony
• sale or distribution of device	"	State Jail Felony

Title and Offense	Penal Code	Classification
4. Unlawful Use of:		
• Criminal Instrument	16.01	One degree lower than offense attempted.
• Pen Register Trap or Trace Device	16.03	State Jail Felony

II. Offenses Against the Person

A. Criminal Homicide:

1. Negligent Homicide, Criminally	19.05	State Jail Felony
2. Murder	19.02(b)	1st Degree
(caused by sudden passion)	19.02(d)	2nd Degree
3. Capital Murder	19.03	Capital Felony

B. False Imprisonment and Kidnapping:

1. Unlawful Restraint (formerly False Imprisonment)	20.02	Class B
• risk of serious bodily injury	"	3rd Degree
• under 14 years of age	"	Class A
2. Kidnapping	20.03	3rd Degree
• aggravated	20.04	1st Degree
• aggravated (victim safely released)	20.04(d)	2nd Degree

C. Sexual Offenses:

1. Homosexual Conduct	21.06	Class C
2. Indecency with a Child		
• contact	21.11(a)(1)	2nd Degree
• exposure	21.11(a)(2)	3rd Degree
3. Indecent Exposure	21.08	Class B
4. Public Lewdness	21.07	Class A

D. Assaultive Offenses:

1. Abandoning/Endangering a Child	22.041	
• with intent to return	"	State Jail Felony
• without intent to return	"	3rd Degree
• imminent danger	"	2nd Degree
2. Assault	22.01	
• bodily injury	"	Class A
• threat or contact	"	Class C
• aggravated	22.02	2nd Degree
• aggravated (public servant or retaliation)	"	1st Degree

Title and Offense	Penal Code	Classification
3. Assault, Sexual	22.011	2nd Degree
• aggravated	22.021	1st Degree
4. Deadly Conduct	22.05(a)	Class A
• knowing discharge of firearm (at a person, habitation, etc.)	22.05(b)	3rd Degree
5. Injury to Child, Elderly or Disabled	22.04	
• reckless bodily injury	"	State Jail Felony
• negligent bodily injury	"	"
• reckless serious bodily injury	"	2nd Degree
• intentionally or knowingly causing serious bodily injury		1st Degree
6. Leaving a Child in a Vehicle	"	Class C
7. Suicide, Aiding (causing death or serious bodily injury)	22.08	State Jail Felony
8. Tampering with Consumer Product	22.09	2nd Degree
• serious bodily injury	"	1st Degree
• threat	"	3rd Degree
9. Terroristic Threat	22.07	Class B
• interrupting occupation of building	"	Class A
• public utilities & services	"	3rd Degree
• public officials & volunteer agencies	"	Class B

III. Offenses Against the Family

A. Advertisement For Placement of a Child*	25.09	Class A
B. Agreement to Abduct from Custody	25.031	State Jail Felony
C. Bigamy	25.01	Class A
D. Criminal Nonsupport (failure to pay child support)	25.05	State Jail Felony
E. Enticing a Child	25.04	Class B
F. Incest ("Prohibited Sexual Relations")	25.02	3rd Degree
G. Interference with Child Custody	25.03	State Jail Felony
H. Sale or Purchase of Child	25.08	3rd Degree
I. Violation of Protective Order	25.07	Class A or State Jail Felony

Title and Offense	Penal Code	Classification

IV. Offenses Against Property

Title and Offense	Penal Code	Classification
A. Arson	28.02	2nd Degree
(bodily injury or death)	"	1st Degree
B. Burglary:		
• of Building	30.02	State Jail Felony
• of Coin Operated Machine	30.03	Class A
• of Habitation		
(involving theft)	30.02	2nd Degree
(felony other than "theft")	"	1st Degree
• of Vehicle	30.04	Class A
C. Breach of Computer Security	33.02	Class A
(less than $20,000)	"	State Jail Felony
($20,000 or more)	"	3rd Degree
D. Credit Fraud:		
1. Credit Card Transaction Record Laundering Offense	32.35	Value Ladder
2. Credit/Debit Card Abuse	32.31	State Jail Felony
3. False Statement to Obtain Property/Credit	32.32	Class A
4. Fraudulent Transfer of a Motor Vehicle	32.34	
• less than $20,000	"	State Jail Felony
• $20,000 or more	"	3rd Degree
5. Hindering Secured Creditors	32.33	Value Ladder Offense
E. Lien or Claim, Fraudulent*	32.49	Class A
F. Mischief, Criminal	28.03	Value Ladder Offense
G. Simulation, Criminal	32.22	Class A
H. Simulation of Legal Process*	32.48	Class A
I. Telecommunication Crimes*:		
• unauthorized use	33.A02	Class A or B
• unauthorized manufacture, possession or delivery of unlawful device	33.A03	3rd Degree
• theft of service	33.A04	Class B, A or State Jail Felony
• publication of telecommunication device	33.A05	Class A or 3rd Degree
J. Trademark Counterfeiting*	32.23	Value Ladder Offense

Title and Offense	Penal Code	Classification
K. Criminal Trespass:	30.05	Class B
• with a deadly weapon	"	Class A
• into a habitation or "shelter center"	"	"
L. Trespass by Licensed Carrier of Concealed Handgun*	30.06	Class A
M. Forgery	32.21	Class A
N. Graffiti*	28.08	Value Ladder Offense
O. Fraudulently Deceptive Practices:		
1. Bad Check, Issuance	32.41	Class C
2. Commercial Bribery	32.43	State Jail Felony
3. Deceptive Business Practices	32.42	Class A or C
4. Deceptive Preparation/ Marketing of Academic Product*	32.49	Class C
5. Destruction, Removal or Concealment of Writing (will, deed, security agreement)	32.47	Class A or State Jail Felony
6. Endless Chain Scheme	32.48	Class B
7. Illegal Recruitment of an Athlete	32.441	Class A
8. Misapplication of Fiduciary Property or Property of Financial Institution	32.45	Value Ladder Offense
9. Securing Execution of Document by Deception	32.46	Value Ladder Offense
10. Rigging Publicly Exhibited Contest	32.44	Class A
P. Insurance Fraud	35.02	
(less than $20)	"	Class C
($21-$499)	"	Class B
($500-$1,499)	"	Class A
($1,500-$19,999)	"	State Jail Felony
($20,000-$99,999)	"	3rd Degree
($100,000-$199,999)	"	2nd Degree
($200,000 or more)	"	1st Degree
Q. Interference with Rail Road Property	28.07	Value Ladder Offense (with exceptions)

Title and Offense	Penal Code	Classification
R. Money Laundering	34.02	
($3,000-$19,999)	"	3rd Degree
($20,000-$99,999)	"	2nd Degree
($100,000 or more)	"	1st Degree
S. Reckless Damage or Destruction	28.04	Class C
T. Robbery	29.02	2nd Degree
(aggravated)	29.03	1st Degree
U. Tampering with Identification Numbers	31.11	Class A
V. Theft:	31.03	Value Ladder Offense
• of services	31.04	"
• of trade secrets	31.05	3rd Degree
W. Unauthorized Use:		
• of Television Reception Devices	31.12	
(for personal use)	"	Class B
(for profit)	"	Class A
• of a Vehicle	31.07	State Jail Felony

V. Offenses Against Public Administration

A. Abuse of Office:		
1. Abuse of Official Capacity	39.02	
(misapplication of property)	"	Value Ladder Offense
(violation of law)	"	Class A
2. Failure to Report Death of Prisoner	39.05	Class B
3. Misuse of Official Information	39.06	Class C or 3rd Degree
4. Official Oppression	39.03	Class A
5. Violation of Prisoner's Civil Rights	39.04	Class A
B. Bribery and Corrupt Influence:		
1. Acceptance of Honorarium	36.07	Class A
2. Bribery	36.02	2nd Degree
3. Coercion of Public Servant or Voter	36.03	3rd Degree
4. Gift to Public Servant		
• Accepting	36.08	Class A
• Offering	36.09	Class A

Title and Offense	Penal Code	Classification
5. Improper Influence	36.04	Class A
6. Obstruction or Retaliation	36.06	3rd Degree
C. Obstructing Governmental Operation:		
1. Absence from Correctional Facility, Unauthorized	38.113	State Jail Felony
2. Bail Jumping/Failure to Appear	38.10	
(Class C offenses)	"	Class C
(Class B or A offenses)	"	Class A
(Felony offenses)	"	3rd Degree
3. Barratry (seeking unlawful economic benefit)	38.12	Class A or 3rd Degree
4. Escape	38.06	Class A
(bodily injury)	"	2nd Degree
(felony or secure correctional facility)	"	3rd Degree
(serious bodily injury/deadly weapon)	"	1st Degree
5. Evading Arrest or Detention	38.04	Class B
(serious bodily injury)	"	3rd Degree
6. Failure to Identify	38.02	
(fugitive)	"	Class B
(self)	"	Class C
7. Falsely Holding Oneself Out As A Lawyer	38.122	2nd Degree
8. Hindering Apprehension or Prosecution	38.05	Class A
(of a felony)	"	3rd Degree
9. Hindering Proceeding by Disorderly Conduct	38.13	Class A
10. Implements for Escape	38.09	3rd Degree
(provided deadly weapon)	"	2nd Degree
11. Inmate Misuse of Information Gained Through Work Program	38.111	3rd Degree
12. Interference With Public Duties	38.15	Class B
13. Permitting of Facilitating Escape	38.07	Class A
(felony or secure correctional facility)	"	3rd Degree
(deadly weapon/post-felony conviction)	"	2nd Degree
14. Practice of Law, Unauthorized	38.123	Class A or 3rd Degree

Title and Offense	Penal Code	Classification
15. Preventing Execution of Civil Process	38.16	Class C
16. Prohibited Substances in Correctional Facility	38.11	3rd Degree
17. Resisting Arrest, Search, Transportation	38.03	Class A
(with deadly weapon)	"	3rd Degree
18. Taking or Attempting to Take a Weapon from a Peace Officer	38.14	State Jail Felony
D. Perjury, Concealment and Other Falsifications:		
1. False Identification as Peace Officer	37.12	Class B
2. False Report to Peace Officer	37.08	Class B
3. Fraudulent Court Document or Record, Use of*	37.13	Class A or 3rd Degree
4. Fraudulent Filing of Financial Statement*	37.101	Class A, 2nd, or 3rd Degree
5. Knowing Failure to Report Location of Human Remains to Law Enforcement*	37.09	Class A
6. Impersonating a Public Servant	37.11	
(non-peace officer)	"	Class A
(peace officer)	"	3rd Degree
7. Perjury	37.02	Class A
(aggravated)	37.03	3rd Degree
8. Tampering:		
• with Physical Evidence	37.09	3rd Degree
• with Governmental Record	37.10	
(intent to defraud or harm)	"	3rd Degree
(license, certificate, permit, seal, etc.)	"	Class A
• with Witness	36.05	State Jail Felony

VI. Offenses Against Public Order and Decency

Title and Offense	Penal Code	Classification
A. Abuse of Corpse	42.08	Class A
B. Child Pornography, Possession or Promotion	43.26	3rd Degree
C. Cruelty to Animals	42.09	Class A
D. Destruction of Flag	42.11	Class A

Title and Offense	Penal Code	Classification
E. Dog Fighting (profits from,	42.10	Class A
owns property used for)	"	State Jail Felony
(spectator)	"	Class C
F. Disorderly Conduct	42.01	Class C
(display or discharge of firearm)	"	Class B
G. Discharge of Firearm in Certain Metropolitan Areas	42.015	Class A
H. Disrupting Meeting/Procession	42.05	Class B
I. Employment Harmful to Children	43.251	Class A
J. False Alarm or Report	42.06	Class A
(school or public utility)	"	State Jail Felony
K. Obscenity:	43.23	Class A
• Wholesale Promotion	"	State Jail Felony
• Display or Distribution	43.22	Class C
• Display or Distribution to a Minor	43.24	Class A
L. Obstructing Highway/Passageway	42.03	Class B
M. Prostitution:	43.02	Class B
• Aggravated	43.04	3rd Degree
• Compelling	43.05	2nd Degree
• Promoting	43.03	Class A
N. Riot	42.02	Class B
O. Sexual Performance by a Child (Promotion or production)	43.25	2nd Degree
	"	3rd Degree
P. Silent or Abusive Calls to 911 Services	42.061	Class B
Q. Stalking*	42.072	Class A

VII. Offenses Against Public Health, Safety & Morals

A. Gambling:	47.02	Class C
• Communicating Information	47.05	Class A
• Keeping a Place of	47.04	Class A
• Possession of Equipment, Paraphernalia	47.06	Class A
• Promotion	47.03	Class A
B. Human Organ, Sale or Purchase	48.02	Class A
C. Intoxication Offenses:		
1. Consumption/Possession in Motor Vehicle	49.03	Class C

Title and Offense	Penal Code	Classification
2. Operating a Vehicle While Intoxicated:		
• Boating	49.07	Class B with 72 hours confinement
• Driving While Intoxicated	49.04	Class B with 72 hours confinement; 6 days if with open container
• Flying	49.05	Class B with 72 hours confinement
3. Intoxication Assault	49.07	3rd Degree
4. Intoxication Manslaughter	49.08	2nd Degree
5. Public Intoxication	49.02	Class C
D. Smoking Tobacco in Prohibited Place	48.01	Class C
E. Stalking	42.072	Class A or 3rd Degree
F. Weapon Offenses:		
1. Accessible to a Child (Causing death or serious bodily injury)	46.13 "	Class C Class A
2. Explosive Components	46.09	3rd Degree
3. Hoax Bombs	46.08	Class A
4. In Penal Institutions	46.10	3rd Degree
5. Prohibited Weapons	46.05	Class A
6. School Zone, Within	46.11	One degree higher than offense committed
7. Unlawful Carrying:	46.02	Class A
• Licensed Premises (liquor stores etc.)	"	3rd Degree
• By License Holder	46.035	Class A
• By Felon	46.04	3rd Degree
8. Unlawful Transfer	46.06	Class A

VIII. Organized Crime

A. Court Order Violation	71.021	Class A
B. Engaging in Criminal Activity	71.02	One degree higher than most serious offense planned or committed

WORKS CONSULTED AND SUGGESTIONS FOR FURTHER READINGS

*(Note: Unless otherwise stated, all statutory citations noted (PC)
in Part 2 of this chapter are from the Texas Penal Code.)*

Barkan, Maxine. "Renew Efforts to Revise Outdated Constitution."
    Dallas Morning News, 22 October 1997: A15.
Buenger, Walter. "Constitution of 1861." *The New Handbook of
    Texas*, vol. 2. Austin, Texas: Texas State Historical Association,
    1996, p. 288.
Ericson, Joe. "Constitution of the Republic of Texas." *The New
    Handbook of Texas,* vol. 2. Austin, Texas: Texas State Historical
    Association, 1996, p. 292.
Ericson, Joe, and Ernest Wallace. "Constitution of 1876." *The New
    Handbook of Texas*, vol. 2. Austin, Texas: Texas State Historical
    Association, 1996, pp. 289-291.
Harrington, James. *Our Texas Bill of Rights*. Austin, Texas: Texas Civil
    Rights Project, 1991.
Jones, Eugene, et al. *Practicing Texas Politics*, 3rd ed. Geneva, New
    York: Houghton Mifflin, 1977.
———. *Practicing Texas Politics*, II, 9th ed. Geneva, New York:
    Houghton Mifflin, 1995.
Mauer, John. "Constitution Proposed in 1874." *The New Handbook
    of Texas*, vol. 2. Austin, Texas: Texas State Historical Associa-
    tion, 1996, pp. 291-292.
May, Janice. *Texas State Constitution: A Reference Guide*. Westport:
    Greenwood, 1996.
McKay, S. S. "Constitution of Coahuila and Texas"; "Constitution of
    1824"; "Constitution of 1869"; "Constitution Proposed in
    1833." *The New Handbook of Texas*, vol. 2. Austin: Texas State
    Historical Association, 1996, pp. 287-289, 291.
McKnight, Joseph. "Law." *The New Handbook of Texas*, vol. 4. Aus
    tin, Texas: Texas State Historical Association, 1996, pp. 114-
    117.
———. Personal interview, October 1997.
Patterson, Caleb, Sam McAlister, and George Hester. *State and Local
    Government in Texas*. New York: Macmillan, 1940.
Roberson, Cliff. *Texas Criminal Law*. Thousand Oaks: Sage, 1996.
Texas, Our Texas. Austin, Texas: Holt, Rinehart, Winston, 1993.

3.
LAW ENFORCEMENT IN TEXAS

INTRODUCTION

The police power of a state—or the legitimate power of a state to statutorily authorize the creation of law enforcement agencies to promote the public peace and enforce the law—is derived from the 10th Amendment to the United States Constitution. In turn, the police power of a state government allows it to delegate to counties and municipalities the authority to establish law enforcement agencies to promote the public safety and welfare. As a result, the law enforcement function in Texas, as in all other states, is a responsibility that is today shared by a very wide variety of state, county, and municipal law enforcement agencies whose peace officers have different authorities and powers.

Article 2.12 of the *Texas Code of Criminal Procedure* defines the wide range of individuals who are statutorily vested with law enforcement authority. A large number of state agencies have law enforcement functions associated with their operation, and consequently employ commissioned peace officers with statewide investigatory and arrest powers. State agencies with law enforcement functions include the Department of Public Safety and the Texas Rangers, the Texas Alcoholic Beverage Commission, the Parks and Wildlife Commission (game wardens), the Office of the State Attorney General, the Texas State Board of Medical Examiners, the Texas Racing

Since 1823 members of law enforcement have put their personal safety at risk so that the safety of the public may be preserved. Pictured above on the Capitol of Texas Highway in Austin are Troopers Lupe Garza and the late Carlos Warren. Trooper Warren was killed in the line of duty on 5 March 1991.   (Photo courtesy of TDPS)

Commission, the State Board of Pharmacy, the Texas Department of Health, the State Fire Marshal's Office, and the Texas Youth Commission.

Additionally, Article 2.12 of the *Texas Code of Criminal Procedure* also gives the power to enforce law to peace officers associated with the operation of county or municipal governments in the state. County law enforcement officers include county sheriffs and their deputies, investigators attached to criminal district attorneys' or county attorneys' offices, and airport and county park police. Law enforcement at the local level is accomplished by municipal police officers and constables and deputy constables. There are approximately 50,000 full-time state, county, and municipal law enforcement officers in Texas today.

The duties and powers of peace officers are stated generally in Article 2.13 of the *Texas Code of Criminal Procedure*, and from a general standpoint include preserving the peace by using all lawful means to protect the public, prevent or suppress crime, investigate allegations of criminal wrongdoing, and the physical exercise of dominion and control (arrest) of alleged criminal offenders.

PART 1:
PEACE OFFICER TRAINING AND CERTIFICATION IN TEXAS

Prior to the beginning of the twentieth century, there were no uniform standards with respect to qualification for employment as a peace officer, and virtually no formal law enforcement training. In the past, to qualify for an appointment as a peace officer in Texas, the applicant had to be of good moral character and have no record of arrest. But even this requirement could be circumvented if the applicant had the right political connections. Prior to the twentieth century the training of law enforcement officers was exclusively accomplished by means of an apprenticeship, where a new officer with no experience was paired with a veteran officer. Under the guidance of the experienced officer, the new recruit would learn the craft of law enforcement by observation and practice. Even with the advent of the first rudimentary training classes for police in Texas during the second decade of the twentieth century, there was wide variation in both their content and quality, and despite the early experiments with training classes, most Texas law enforcement agencies persisted in relying upon the apprenticeship method. Until the mid-1960s the qualification requirements and training standards for peace officers in Texas were left totally to the discretion of state, county, and municipal law enforcement agencies.

The Texas Commission on Law Enforcement
Officer Standards and Education

In an effort to both improve law enforcement performance and elevate peace officers to the status of professionals, the 59th Texas Legislature in 1965 created the Texas Commission on Law Enforcement Officer Standards and Education. Chapter 415 of the *Texas Government Code* describes the commission as a policy-making body with the statutory responsibility for both creating and enforcing minimum qualifications for the selection, training, and certification of law enforcement officers in Texas. Today the commission discharges its statutory mandate in three ways. First, the commission is responsible for insuring that all Texas law enforcement officers, regardless of whether they are employed at the state, county, or municipal level of government, meet uniform standards of employment eligibility. Second, the commission ensures that all law enforcement officers employed in Texas receive a minimum number of hours of training before they begin to enforce the law. Third, the commission is responsible for creating a standardized statewide training curriculum for peace officers. To accomplish this threefold mandate, the commission sets minimum eligibility standards for the selection of applicants, develops pre-service and in-service curricula, licenses law enforcement training academies and their instructors, and administers the peace officer certification examinations. The Texas Legislature appropriated almost $8 million to the commission in 1997. To help defray the expenses associated with work of the commission, the Texas Legislature also authorized the assessment of a one-dollar fee against all persons convicted of a misdemeanor or felony offense in Texas.

The Texas Commission on Law Enforcement Officer Standards and Education is composed of fourteen members. Nine of the members are appointed by the governor with the advice and consent of the Texas Senate and serve staggered, six-year terms, while the remaining five are ex-officio members. To ensure that the selection, training, and curriculum requirement policies created and enforced by the commission reflect the needs of law enforcement executives, as well as rank and file police officers, and that the policies represent the broad public safety interests of the citizens of Texas, the overall composition of the commission has been specifically defined by the Texas Legislature. Of the nine gubernatorial appointments, three must be either a county sheriff, municipal chief of police, or a constable; three must be law enforcement officers who hold non-supervisory positions in the agency where they are employed; and three must be members of the general public. The five ex-officio members of the commission consist of the Texas attorney general, the commissioner of the Texas Department of Education, the commissioner of the Texas Higher Education Coordinating Board, the director of the Texas Department of Public Safety, and the executive director of the Criminal Justice Division of the governor's office. The chairman of the commission is elected by the commission members. All of the positions are non-salaried, but commission members are reimbursed on a per-diem basis for expenses incurred in the performance of commission duties.

To receive a peace officer certification license in Texas today, an individual must satisfy two requirements: the minimum general eligibility requirement and the minimum training requirement. To satisfy the minimum general eligibility requirement for becoming a law enforcement officer in Texas, one must (1) be a citizen of the United States, (2) be at least 21 years of age, (3) have a high school diploma or general educational development (GED) degree, (4) never have been convicted of a felony or driving while intoxicated offense, (5) not have a conviction for a Class B misdemeanor in the previous six months or a Class A misdemeanor in the previous twelve months, and (6) not currently be on probation.

The minimum training requirements to sit for the commission's full-time peace officer certification examination may be satisfied in one of two ways. A candidate must have either (1) successfully passed a 560-hour basic peace officer certification course offered by a commission-approved law enforcement training academy, or (2) the candidate must have successfully completed a series of 10 college level courses known as the Criminal Justice Transfer Curriculum. The Criminal Justice Transfer Curriculum consists of seven traditional higher education courses (Crime in America, Introduction to Criminal Justice, Fundamentals of Criminal Law, Courts and Criminal Procedure, Police Systems and Practices, Criminal Investigation, and Legal Aspects of Law Enforcement), and three courses that are referred to as the Texas Peace Officer Sequence (Texas Peace Officer Law, Texas Peace Officer Procedures, and Texas Peace Officer Skills).

It is important to point out that the commission's training requirements for certification are minimum requirements only. All of the large metropolitan police departments in Texas today, such as those in Houston, Dallas, and Austin, operate their own commission-approved training academies, and the length of their basic training courses frequently exceeds 1,200 to 1,500 hours. Currently, about 40 municipal police departments, 20 sheriffs' departments, and five state law enforcement agencies in Texas operate their own commission-approved training academies. To accommodate the training certification requirements of smaller county and municipal law enforcement agencies that cannot afford the expense of establishing and maintaining a full-time training academy facility and staff, the commission has established 15 regional training centers around the state, some of which are operated on community college campuses or use the physical facilities on four-year college and university campuses.

The Bill Blackwood Law Enforcement Management Institute of Texas

The philosophy of the Texas Legislature, which recognizes the wisdom and value of mandating minimum basic training standards for the certification of licensed peace officers, has, in a fashion, been extended to include the chief executives and staff of state, county, and municipal law enforcement agencies. To develop and enhance the managerial and leadership skills of law enforcement executives, the Texas Legislature in 1987 created the Law Enforcement Management Institute of Texas. The mission of the institute is to "provide an opportunity for current and future law enforcement leadership to acquire and develop the knowledge, concepts, and skills necessary to

deliver effective law enforcement services in a free society."
In May 1993 the Texas Legislature passed House Bill 977,
which renamed the institute in honor of Representative Bill
Blackwood, a Republican from Mesquite who had earned a
reputation during his many years in the Texas Legislature
as an unwavering supporter of law enforcement officers in
Texas. House Bill 977 also designated the George Beto
Criminal Justice Center at Sam Houston State University in
Huntsville as the institute's permanent home. Furthermore, in
1997 the Texas Legislature passed House Bill 1881, which
created a new executive development program for police
chiefs. Newly appointed chiefs of police in Texas are now
required to complete an 80-hour course before the second
anniversary of their appointment as a first-time police chief.
Incumbent chiefs of police are required by the legislation to
attend a 40-hour in-service course every two years. The operation of the institute is funded in part by a one-dollar fee that
is assessed against every defendant convicted of a criminal
offense in Texas.

The institute, which is operated on an annual budget of
about $2.5 million, provides current police executives, as well
as law enforcement personnel whose futures hold great promise
with respect to leadership potential, with advanced graduate
level seminars designed to enhance their ability to proactively
respond to changing economic, political, and social conditions
that affect the law enforcement function in Texas. To accomplish the mandate, the institute offers one program and three
seminars of advanced study taught by visiting university faculty who are recognized leaders in their fields of expertise. The
institute's core program is called the Graduate Management
Institute. This program focuses on imparting general as well as
advanced management and administration principles to law
enforcement executives. The Graduate Management Institute
program is supplemented by the Executive, Policy Development, and Special Program series of seminars.

The Executive Seminar educates senior law enforcement
managers about how to effectively plan for and deal with the
long-term and persistent problems that are associated with
policing, such as changing economic conditions, social and

demographic trends, the prevalence of drug use, and incarceration rates.

The focus of the Policy Development Seminar is twofold. First, this seminar provides police executives with an overview of current policy problems that directly affect the management of law enforcement organizations, such as budgeting, manpower utilization, and community policing; and second, it provides police executives with the skills necessary to develop meaningful management policy.

Finally, the Special Program series of seminars focuses on a wide variety of recurring or current issues relevant to the effective administration and management of law enforcement organizations, such as racial and ethnic diversity issues, technology utilization, intergovernmental relations and community alliance, and media relations.

PART 2:
LAW ENFORCEMENT IN TEXAS: PAST AND PRESENT

A detailed examination of the history and contemporary organization and operation of all peace-keeping and law enforcement functions in the state of Texas today is beyond the scope of this chapter. Rather, this chapter will focus principally on the development and operation of law enforcement at the state level, through an examination of the Texas Rangers and the Department of Public Safety, and at the county and local levels of government by an examination of the role of county sheriffs, municipal police, and constables.

State Law Enforcement

The Texas Rangers

The oldest state law enforcement organization in the United States, and certainly the most prestigious, celebrated, and legendary law enforcement unit in Texas, is the Texas Rangers. No discussion of law enforcement in Texas would be complete without an overview of their history and contemporary organization and operation. The historical development of the Texas Rangers is best discussed by examining the four distinct eras that the famed law enforcement unit has gone through: the era of the Texas Ranger as Indian fighter and frontier border guardsman (1823-1866); the era of the Texas Ranger as legendary Western lawman (1874-1900); the era of change and political patronage (1900-1935); and the era of the modern Department of Public Safety Texas Ranger (1935-present).

1823-1866: THE ERA OF THE RANGER AS INDIAN FIGHTER AND FRONTIER BORDER GUARDSMAN

In 1823 Stephen Fuller Austin created a company of men whose responsibility it was to patrol Austin's Colony, maintain vigilance against disorder, and protect the colonists from attacks by a wide variety of Indian tribes who inhabited the area, including the Apaches, Comanches, Cherokees, Karankawas, and Tonkawas. Austin created this company of peacekeepers pursuant to the terms of colonization granted to him by Mexico City in 1821 that required him to be responsible for providing public security within the geographical district encompassed by the original land grants. Austin's original company of peacekeepers consisted of only ten men, and in the early years of their inception they were officially referred to by a variety of titles, including Ranging or Ranger Company, Range Riders, Rangers, and Volunteer Rangers. While organized under the legal auspices of a militia, they were not considered members of an army because they were not uniformed in standard attire, nor were they subject to military laws, regulations, or courtesies. They also were distinct from what we would today consider county sheriffs and municipal police because their commission from Austin granted them regionwide authority. Members of the first Ranging Company were paid monthly, but not in money or scrip. Rather, the salary of the first Rangers was paid in land equal in value to $15.

This original company of peacekeepers consisted of armed and mounted civilian volunteers who came from a wide variety of backgrounds. The term of their volunteer enlistment at this time was typically for three to six months. The enlistment papers from the period record that the composition of the early Ranging Companies included men who listed their occupations as blacksmiths, butchers, masons, farmers, sailors, surveyors, and lawyers. A few entries on the early enlistment rosters were signed with an "X," indicating that some of the volunteers could neither read nor write. The job was not originally full time. Rather, members of the Ranging Company were called upon as needed, and they temporarily disbanded to pursue their occupations during periods when Indian depredations were not occurring.

The first Ranging Company remained loosely organized and small in number until the threat of the Texas Revolution began to loom large on the horizon. While an army was being raised by Gen. Sam Houston to fight Mexican rule, an officially designated Corps of Rangers was organized by the fledgling provisional government of the Republic of Texas to secure and protect the border territory from both Indian attack and from incursions by Mexican Irregulars. Article 21 of the provisional government established three Ranger Companies of 56 men each. The three companies were placed under the command of Robert McAlpin Williamson, who was affectionately known as "Three-Legged Willie" Williamson. (Williamson's sobriquet owes its origin to the fact that his right leg from the knee down was severely withered by polio and bent back at the knee. He wore a wooden peg from the knee down to provide support and help him walk.) When the Corps of Rangers first took to the field on 24 November 1835, their salary was $1.25 per day, enlistment was for a period of one year, and they were required to supply their own weapons, horses, and equipment. The beginning of the Ranger legend, and their reputation for bravery and tenacity, may be traced to this period, when the Corps of Rangers took part in some of the most famous Indian battles in Texas history, including the East Texas Cherokee War in July 1839, the Council House Fight at San Antonio on 19 March 1840, and the Battle of Plum Creek, near Lockhart, on 12 August 1840.

It was also during this period that another legend associated with the Texas Rangers was born: the Walker Colt. Ranger

Samuel H. Walker was sent to New York in the early 1840s to meet with firearm maker Samuel Colt and purchase weapons for the Corps of Rangers. While in New York, Walker suggested some design changes to Colt that would make his handgun a more efficient and lethal tool for fighting while mounted on a horse. Colt enthusiastically embraced the suggested changes and incorporated them into the model that subsequently became known as the Walker Colt. This handgun was a .44-caliber, six-shot revolver that sported a nine-inch barrel and weighed a hefty four pounds, nine ounces. The mere act of unholstering the weapon, it has been said, was enough to compel respect for, fear of, and submission to the authority of the Ranger wielding it. The Walker Colt very quickly became the firearm of choice among the Texas Rangers, and remained so well into the twentieth century.

The Corps of Rangers continued to be the principal peace-keepers during the period of the Republic of Texas, and later after Texas joined the Union. It is interesting to note that the only time in the history of the Rangers that they operated as a military unit was during the war against Mexico. From 1846 to 1848 they served as scouts and skirmishers in the forces of Generals Winfield Scott and Zachary Taylor. Following the conclusion of the American Civil War, the 11th Texas Legislature passed a bill in 1866 that for the first time used the term "Texas Ranger." The bill provided for the creation of three companies of Texas Rangers to enforce the laws of the state of Texas and protect and secure the border along the Rio Grande. The bill, however, did not provide for the allocation of funding for the three companies of Texas Rangers, and law enforcement in Texas immediately following the Civil War was disorganized and haphazard.

1874–1900: THE ERA OF THE TEXAS RANGER
AS A LEGENDARY WESTERN LAWMAN

In the decade following the conclusion of the Civil War, crime and social disorder were rampant in Texas. Unlike the period before the Civil War, however, citizens were no longer seriously threatened by marauding Indians. Rather, the threat to public peace and prosperity came principally from lawless Anglos and Mexican bandits.

Lacking a full-time and organized force dedicated to law enforcement and peacekeeping, Governor Richard Coke persuaded the Texas Legislature in 1874 to statutorily authorize and provide funding for two Ranger forces to cope with the lingering post-Civil War lawlessness. The first of these two forces was the Frontier Battalion. The Frontier Battalion consisted of six companies of 75 men each whose primary responsibility was to patrol the border with Mexico along the Rio Grande and prevent incursions by Mexican bandits and freebooters. The second force created by the Texas Legislature was designated the Special Force. Its principal responsibility was the suppression of general lawlessness and banditry within the geopolitical boundaries of the state. The manpower resources

Capt. Leander H. McNelly
(Western History Collections,
University of Oklahoma Library)

of the Special Force were used to track down a wide assortment of malefactors, including garden variety outlaws wanted on charges of murder or robbery, organized groups of cattle rustlers, horse thieves, fence cutters, and private feudists bent on rectifying personal vendettas. The Special Force had a complement of approximately 30 men under the command of Capt. Leander H. McNelly, and for this reason the Special Force is sometimes referred to today by historians as McNelly's Rangers. This piece of 1874 legislation is of particular importance in the history of Texas law

Texas Rangers under the command of Capt. D. W. Roberts camp near Ft. McKavett, Menard County, in 1878.   (Courtesy of TDPS)

enforcement in general and the history of the Texas Rangers in particular because for the first time the Texas Legislature invested members of these two Ranger units with specific law enforcement responsibilities and statewide jurisdictional powers. This was accomplished by the language of the 1874 legislation, which invested a Ranger with "all the powers of a peace officer and the duty to execute all criminal process directed to him, and make arrests of any kind of any and all parties charged with offense against the laws of Texas."

The bulk of the legend and lore traditionally associated with the Texas Rangers and the suppression of lawlessness in the American West is a product of Ranger exploits during this era. The tracking and subsequent arrest (or death by gunfire) of notorious outlaws such as the pistoleer John Wesley Hardin, the train robber Sam Bass, and the gunfighter King Fisher are inextricably linked with the work of the Texas Rangers during

the period 1874-1900. Lacking the sophisticated crime information and retrieval systems for identifying fugitive criminals
that police so heavily rely upon today, the Texas Rangers of
this period depended on a publication issued periodically by
the Texas Adjutant General's Office that was given the official
title "A List of Fugitives From Justice." The publication, which
sometimes ran to 227 pages in length, was a quick reference
guide, organized on a Texas county-by-county basis, of the
names of people wanted by the law, the crimes for which they
were wanted, and a brief physical description of each fugitive.
The publication was frequently annotated by Texas Rangers, and
was known among the Texas Rangers as "The Book of Knaves."

1900-1935: THE ERA OF CHANGE AND POLITICAL PATRONAGE

The first three and a half decades of the twentieth century
were a time of great change for the Texas Rangers. This era in the
history of the Texas Rangers is characterized by two dominant
themes. First, there was a shift in the focus of their law enforcement function away from dealing with the archetypal Western
outlaw (for which they had by this time become famous) to more
mundane aspects of domestic social control. And second, the
reputation of the Texas Rangers was enormously sullied by gubernatorial meddling and political patronage.

With the taming of the West and the demise of the
Western outlaw by the close of the nineteenth century, the
organization, size, and mission of the two Texas Ranger units
created by the Texas Legislature in 1874 had outlived their
usefulness. To cope with changing law enforcement demands,
the Texas Rangers were reorganized by the Texas Legislature in
1900. Four companies of Texas Rangers with twenty men each
were authorized and funded by the legislature and placed
under the control of the Texas adjutant general. The adjutant
general was appointed by the governor and was responsible
for the maintenance and deployment of the Texas National
Guard, a state organization maintained as a reserve for the
United States military.

In the early decades of the twentieth century the law
enforcement role of the Texas Rangers slowly expanded to

In July of 1894 two companies of Texas Rangers were called to Temple, Texas, to monitor heated tempers during an ongoing railroad strike.

(Courtesy of TDPS)

Texas Rangers circa 1920 during oil exploration
of the Red River bed.

(Courtesy of TDPS)

embrace a wide range of peacekeeping activities that were completely new to them, and decidedly unpopular with many of the citizens of Texas. By the 1920s the Texas Rangers were being used to enforce Texas state laws against gambling and prostitution, and to keep order in rough and disorderly oil boom towns like Borger, Mexia, and Wink. From 1920 to 1933 the Texas Rangers were used to enforce prohibition by raiding bootleg stills and interdicting liquor smugglers crossing the Rio Grande from Mexico into Texas. Also, in the early 1920s, Texas experienced for the first time civil disturbances associated with the growing labor union movement. Because local police and county sheriffs were unable to maintain order in places such as the Thurber coal fields, Galveston during labor troubles in 1920, and Denison during the police strike in 1922, the Texas Rangers were dispatched to these areas to restore order. The Rangers were used as strike breakers in an attempt to quell the increasing number of disputes between

Prohibition era liquor and gambling raid.

labor unions and management in Texas that erupted into violence. Additionally, the Rangers were regularly used to protect pretrial detainees as well as convicted criminals waiting to be transferred to the state prison system from vigilante mobs bent upon taking the law into their own hands. It was during this period that the legendary phrase "one riot, one Ranger" was born.

While the new peacekeeping functions assigned to the Texas Rangers during this period resulted in a growing sentiment of resentment and disrespect among some segments of the Texas population, their traditional crime fighting reputation continued to expand nonetheless, especially during the depression years of the early 1930s. While some Texans may not have appreciated the new peacekeeping functions of the Texas Rangers and their heavy-handed tactics, they did support, and were justifiably proud of, the work of the Rangers as traditional crime fighters.

During the depression years, Texas, like other states, was plagued by a rash of bank robberies and cold-blooded murders. The law enforcement work of Texas Ranger Capt. Frank A. Hamer, and his role in ending the criminal careers of Clyde Barrow and Bonnie Parker, greatly served to sustain the traditional image of the Texas Rangers as tenacious crime fighters, and kept alive the dwindling spirit of pride in the force that Texans had slowly cultivated since 1823. The entire nation was at that time captivated by the bloody and violent swath that Texas natives Clyde Barrow and Bonnie Parker were cutting across the American South, and disappointed that local law enforcement had been unable to bring them to justice. Frank Hamer was given the responsibility for apprehending the fugitive couple, and on 10 February 1934 he began his search. His pursuit ended 102 days later, when on 23 May 1934 Hamer and his group of officers ambushed and killed the couple in a hail of gunfire while they were driving on a rural country road. This incident, more than any other between 1900 and 1935, served to capture the rapt and admiring attention of the American public and to give Texas once again a reason to be justifiably proud (and boastful) of the Texas Rangers.

Clyde Barrow
(Courtesy of Sheriff Evans)

*May 23, 1934—Rangers appraise
aftermath of fatal ambush.*
(Courtesy of Sheriff Evans)

Bonnie Parker and Clyde Barrow look over a "haul."
(Courtesy of Sheriff Evans)

While the esteem of the Texas Rangers suffered due to their changing law enforcement role during the period 1900-1935, the greatest damage to their reputation during this period came from political meddling and patronage. As mentioned earlier, the Texas Legislature in 1900 placed the Texas Rangers under the auspices of the Texas adjutant general, a position filled by gubernatorial appointment. As a result, the governor was in a position to politically influence the appointment of Texas Rangers. While a number of governors during this period took an active role in filling the ranks of the Texas Ranger companies with political supporters, none was more notorious for destroying the reputation and esprit de corps of the Rangers than Miriam A. "Ma" Ferguson, who served as governor of Texas from 1933 to 1935. Upon taking office in 1933, Governor Ferguson summarily fired all of the Texas Rangers who supported her political rival during the election campaign, Governor Ross Sterling. Many of those Texas Rangers who were not fired resigned their commissions in disgust. The decimated ranks of the Texas Rangers were then filled by Governor Ferguson, who handed out more than 2,300 "Special Ranger" commissions to political cronies. This newly constituted group of lawmen was derogatorily referred to as "Ferguson's Rangers." Among the ranks of the Ferguson Rangers were many ex-convicts, and during the tenure of her governorship, many of her Ranger appointees were convicted of bribery, murder, theft, embezzlement, abuse of authority, and operating illegal gambling houses. Without a doubt, the nadir in the history of the Texas Rangers occurred during this period, and the organization earned the reputation as the most scandal-ridden law enforcement agency in American history.

1935-PRESENT: THE ERA OF THE MODERN TEXAS RANGER

The credit for saving the Texas Rangers as a legitimate law enforcement organization and restoring its reputation goes to Governor James V. Allred. When he took office in 1935, Governor Allred canceled all of the Special Ranger commissions given by Governor Ferguson, and persuaded the 44th Texas Legislature to pass legislation that would remove the Texas

Rangers from the Adjutant General's Office and reorganize them as a division under the control of the newly created Department of Public Safety.

Today the statutory authority for the Texas Rangers is derived from Chapters 411.021-023 of the *Texas Government Code*, and the Rangers are responsible for a variety of law enforcement functions, including the protection of life and property by enforcing the provisions of the *Texas Penal Code*, the investigation of major felony crimes (including gambling and narcotics), the investigation of public corruption cases, the apprehension of fugitives from justice, and the suppression of riots and insurrections. The Texas Rangers are also responsible today for providing security for the governor and for providing criminal investigation expertise and assistance to municipal and county law enforcement agencies in Texas. The peacekeeping authority of Texas Rangers is governed by the laws which regulate and define the powers and duties of a county sheriff, except that a Texas Ranger may conduct criminal investigations, make arrests, and execute process in criminal cases in any county in Texas, and, if specifically directed by a judge of a court of original jurisdiction, execute process in civil cases.

Since 1991 the Texas Ranger Division has been part of the staff of the director of the Texas Department of Public Safety. The Texas Ranger Division is today divided into six field companies and a headquarters company. Field offices are located in Garland, Houston, Lubbock, Midland, San Antonio, and Waco. The headquarters company is located in Austin. The Texas Ranger Division is commanded by a senior Ranger captain who answers to the director of the Department of Public Safety, and each of the six field companies is commanded by a Ranger captain.

Since the demise of the Ferguson Rangers, the force has been small, usually numbering no more than 100. When the force was reorganized in 1935, there were only 34 Texas Rangers; in 1945 there were 45; in 1947 there were 51; in 1969 there were 62; and in 1975 there were 82 Texas Rangers. In January 1998 the Texas Rangers numbered 106.

From 1935 until the early 1980s, it was customary to

recruit Texas Rangers from county sheriff or municipal police departments. Department of Public Safety Director James Adams changed the tradition in the early 1980s by requiring all Texas Rangers to be recruited from the rank and file of Department of Public Safety troopers. To be eligible for consideration and appointment as a Texas Ranger, a Department of Public Safety trooper must have a minimum of eight years of law enforcement experience with the department, and must pass a battery of extremely rigorous and competitive written and oral examinations.

In the past the membership of the Texas Rangers was almost totally dominated by white males. This, however, is changing. While the Texas Rangers today are still overwhelmingly white males, its membership includes two women as well as a number of Americans of African, Hispanic, and Asian descent. Today the average age of a Texas Ranger is 45, and approximately one-fourth of the Rangers possess baccalaureate degrees, and a small but growing number possess graduate degrees.

The Texas Rangers remain today the most celebrated state law enforcement organization in the United States. Their legend has been preserved and perpetuated in a variety of ways, including pulp fiction accounts of their exploits, the "Lone Ranger" series of films and television programs, and even the Texas Rangers professional baseball team. Additionally, Texas writer Larry McMurtry has done much in recent years to perpetuate their legend in the public's mind through his series of historical novels entitled *Lonesome Dove, Dead Man's Walk,* and *Comanche Moon.* The novels, two of which have been turned into highly acclaimed television miniseries, chronicle the lives and times of fictitious Texas Rangers Augustus McCrae and Woodrow F. Call. Finally, few people realize that the Texas Rangers were lauded in the poetry of Walt Whitman. In section 34, lines 880 to 883, of Whitman's 1892 epic poem *Song of Myself*, he paid tribute to the Texas Rangers when he wrote:

> "They were the glory of the race of rangers,
> Matchless with horse, rifle, song, support, courtship,
> Large, turbulent, generous, handsome, proud, and affectionate,
> Bearded, sunburnt, dressed in the free costume of hunters."

Over the years a number of states attempted, with varying degrees of success and failure, to create law enforcement units modeled on the Texas Ranger tradition. The most successful and enduring of the attempts to create units similar to the Texas Rangers were the Arizona Rangers, established in 1901, and the New Mexico Mounted Police, which began operation in 1905. California, Colorado, Nevada, and Oregon all made efforts to create a mounted, statewide law enforcement unit patterned after the Texas Rangers, but without much success. The most enduring monument to the Texas Rangers is the Texas Ranger Hall of Fame and Museum, located on the Brazos River in Waco, on the site of the 1837 Ranger Company outpost known as Fort Fisher. The public museum was opened in 1968 as the permanent repository for keeping the history and displaying the artifacts associated with the more than 175 years of Texas Ranger legend and lore. The museum is also home to the Moody Texas Ranger Memorial Research Library, the most extensive holding of archival material on the Texas Rangers in the world.

By way of a final word, it is interesting to note that the legendary status and reputation of the Texas Rangers, despite the problems associated with the period 1900-1934, has extended far beyond the confines of Texas and the United States. For example, German military archival records from World War II indicate that when intelligence officers reported to Berlin that United States Army Rangers were part of the allied invasion force landing on the beaches at Normandy, France, the Germany military high command became unusually agitated and concerned. They mistakenly thought that the Texas Rangers were part of the invasion force.

The Department of Public Safety

Historical Development

The origin of a Texas state police force separate and distinct from the Texas Rangers may be traced to the post-Civil War legislation sponsored by Governor Edmund Jackson Davis. In the years immediately following the conclusion of the Civil

War, Texas was in a state of social turmoil and unrest. With the failure of the 11th Texas Legislature in 1866 to appropriate funding for three companies of Texas Rangers, crime in the state became rampant. County and local law enforcement officers were ineffectual, and the public's confidence in the ability of the court system to fairly and equitably administer justice was minimal. For example, during the Texas Constitutional Convention of 1868–1869, the Committee on Lawlessness and Violence reported that during the preceding three-year period from 1865 to 1868 a total of 939 murders had reportedly been committed in Texas. A later amendment to the report updated the total to 1,035.

In 1869 Edmund J. Davis ran for governor on a platform that called for the restoration of law and order and the creation of a state police force with jurisdiction to step in and take control when county sheriffs and municipal police were either unable or unwilling to enforce the law. Following Davis' election, the Texas Legislature passed the Police Act in July 1870. The Police Act authorized and provided funding for a force of four captains, eight lieutenants, twenty sergeants, and 225 privates, and gave to the Texas adjutant general the power to manage, direct, and oversee the operation of the force. As adjutant general, James Davidson became the first head of the Texas State Police. The Texas State Police were indeed effective in helping to bring the post-Civil War crime problem in Texas under some semblance of control. Between 1870 and 1872, for example, the Texas State Police made 6,820 arrests (587 for murder and 760 for attempted murder) and recovered an estimated $200,000 in stolen property.

Despite the inroads the Texas State Police made toward reducing the overall level of violent crime in Texas, the force was fraught from its very inception in 1870 with scandal, and was politically misused as an agency of law enforcement. Many of the men who were appointed to the Texas State Police by Governor Davis and Adjutant General Davidson were said to have been of low character and general ill repute. Most of them were Republicans, and some of the appointees had a record of prior criminal convictions. In addition to fighting crime, the Texas State Police were used between 1870 and

1873 to thwart the aspirations of Democratic politicians and advance the agenda of Reconstructionist Republicans. Conducting operations under the guise of maintaining the public peace and order, the Texas State Police disrupted Democratic political gatherings, intimidated voters of the Democratic persuasion, stuffed ballot boxes, entered and searched private homes without warrants, and made wholesale false arrests. Additionally, members of the Texas State Police were implicated in the murder of prisoners in their charge as well as aiding and abetting the escape of politically connected prisoners from county jails and the Huntsville prison.

The overt political favoritism displayed by the Texas State Police in the discharge of their official duties did not serve to endear them to the civilian population. To compound matters, in 1872 Davidson, the adjutant general and head of the Texas State Police, embezzled $37,434.67 in state funds. Davidson drew warrants on the Texas State Treasury to meet the payroll requirements of the Texas State Police, pocketed the cash, and reportedly fled to Belgium. He was neither seen nor heard from again.

By 1873 Texans had had enough of the Texas State Police. An ever increasing number of Texans had gradually come to view the Texas State Police as armed stooges doing the unwholesome political bidding of Republican carpetbaggers. Responding to the growing sentiments of disdain and contempt for the organization, and over the strenuous objections of Governor Davis, the Texas Legislature on 22 April 1873 repealed the act which three years earlier created the Texas State Police. This left Texas once again without a police organization with statewide jurisdiction, and it was not until 1874 that the Texas Legislature, at the insistence of then Governor Richard Coke, authorized funding for two companies of Texas Rangers. From 1874 until 1935, the Texas Rangers remained the closest thing to a police force with statewide jurisdiction in Texas.

It was not until 1935 that Texas once again had a legislatively authorized and funded state police organization separate and distinct from the Texas Rangers. In the early 1920s Texas experienced a very sharp increase in the amount and kind of motor vehicle traffic on Texas highways. By the 1920s automobiles had replaced horses as the primary and preferred method of transportation within the state. Additionally, the agricultural and natural resources of the state, such as bailed cotton and raw (as well as refined) petroleum products, were being transported by heavy trucks that were unregulated with respect to weight and safety restrictions. Many of these heavy trucks were poorly maintained and often had defective brakes, bad tires, and suspension systems inadequate to handle the weight of their loads. The growing reliance on heavy trucks to move the treasure of the state was seen as a safety threat not only to the motoring public but also to the structural integrity of public roadways and bridges in Texas. To monitor heavy truck traffic and promote the safety of the motoring public the Texas Legislature in 1927 created a group of eighteen regulatory inspectors responsible for licensing and monitoring the weight of heavy trucks. This regulatory unit operated under the auspices of the Texas Highway Department.

In 1929 a significant development occurred which set the stage for the creation once again of a state police organization in Texas. In 1929 the Texas Legislature authorized and provided funding for the expansion of the regulatory weight and licensing unit to 50 men, vested the members of the unit with the statutory authority to enforce all state laws regulating the operation of motor vehicles on public highways, and changed the name of the unit to the Texas State Highway Patrol. In recognition of the growing workload associated with their new statutory responsibilities, the State Highway Patrol was increased by the Texas Legislature to 120 men in 1931.

Between 1929 and 1935 it became increasingly clear to the Texas Legislature that steps needed to be taken to rethink, reorganize, and consolidate the manner in which the state discharged its responsibility for enforcing the law and providing public protection. In late 1934 and early 1935 the Texas Legislature crafted a bill to statutorily create a Texas Department of Public Safety. Two provisions in the bill are of particular importance. First, the legislation stripped the adjutant general of his control and oversight of the Texas Rangers, and second, the legal authority to direct and oversee the State Highway Patrol was taken away from the State Highway Department.

Troopers stand at attention.

(Courtesy of TDPS)

Both the Texas Rangers and State Highway Patrol were merged into a single state police force that included a mandate to enforce the law, provide for the safety of the public, and prevent and detect criminal wrongdoing. Included in the bill was an appropriation of $450,000 to fund the new department, and on 10 August 1935 the legislation creating the Department of Public Safety became effective.

The original organization of the Department of Public Safety consisted of three divisions: the Texas Rangers, the Highway Patrol, and the Headquarters Division. The Headquarters Division consisted of the Bureaus of Identification, Records, and Communications (to operate a new police radio broadcast system), an intelligence unit, and an education unit to operate a training school for Department of Public Safety personnel. To promote the integrity of the new state police organization and to insulate it from political manipulation, the Texas Legislature, as part of the bill creating the Department of Public Safety, also created a three-member Public Safety Commission whose responsibility it was to set policy and oversee the management and operation of the department.

No discussion about the Department of Public Safety would be complete without touching upon the career and contributions of Homer Garrison, Jr. From 1935 until his retirement in 1968, Homer Garrison earned a worldwide reputation for honesty and integrity and for advancing the interests of law enforcement professionalism by incorporating state-of-the-art law enforcement innovations into the operation of the Department of Public Safety. His long and distinguished tenure as director served to shape the destiny of the Texas Department of Public Safety more than any other person in its history. The modern-day Texas Department of Public Safety is unquestionably the legacy of Garrison, and he may rightly be said to be the father of the organization.

Homer Garrison, Jr.
(Courtesy of TDPS)

Homer Garrison was born in Kickapoo, Texas (Anderson County) on 21 July 1901. He began his law enforcement career in 1920, when, at the age of 19, he received an appointment as deputy sheriff in Angelina County. In 1929 he joined the regulatory weight and licensing unit, and in 1930 transferred to the newly reorganized Texas Highway Patrol. During his first few years with the Texas Highway Patrol his law enforcement talents and abilities clearly stood out and he quickly became an obvious choice among his peers where leadership qualities were required. When the Department of Public Safety was created in August 1935, Garrison was appointed by the Public Safety Commission to be its first assistant director. Three years later, in September 1938, Garrison became director of the Department of Public Safety and the Texas Rangers, a position he would hold for 30 years. Garrison took control of an organization that had an annual operating budget of $1.3 million, and by the time of his retirement built the Department of Public Safety into a widely respected state law enforcement agency with over 3,800 employees and an annual operating budget of $28.4 million. He was responsible not only for rehabilitating the tarnished reputation of the Texas Rangers, but was also instrumental in developing a number of programs which served as models for other state law enforcement agencies around the nation, including the first state program of law enforcement training and the department's crime control, traffic supervision, vehicle inspection, safety education, and disaster relief programs.

His reputation as a skilled administrator and law enforcement innovator quickly spread beyond the confines of the state of Texas. At the request of the governor of New Mexico, Garrison organized the New Mexico State Police, and following the end of World War II he was solicited by Gen. Douglas MacArthur to be the principal architect of the postwar national police system for Japan. His many contributions to promoting public safety were recognized in a variety of ways. During his professional career he was the recipient of the Paul Gray Hoffman Award (given annually by the Automotive Safety Foundation for distinguished contributions to enhancing highway safety), and was appointed to numerous state committees, including the directorship of Governor John Connally's Texas Highway Safety Commission. On a regional and national level, Garrison served as a member of the Southern Regional Highway Policy Committee of the Council of State Governments, and in 1967, shortly before his retirement due to health problems, he was appointed to the National Motor Vehicle Safety Advisory Council. Garrison died on 7 May 1968 and is buried in the State Cemetery in Austin.

Today the Department of Public Safety operates under the statutory authority of Chapter 411.002 of the *Texas Government Code*. The mandated mission of the Department of Public Safety is "to maintain public safety in the State of Texas." In discharging its mission, the Department of Public Safety preserves public order by enforcing state laws, providing for the prevention and detection of crime, and promoting and protecting the lives and property of Texans. The motto of the Department of Public Safety is "Courtesy, Service, Protection."

The responsibility for overseeing the general operation of the Department of Public Safety is discharged by a non-salaried, three-member Public Safety Commission that is appointed by the governor with the advice and consent of the Texas Senate. Members of the commission serve six-year terms. The Public Safety Commission appoints the director of the Department of Public Safety and develops plans and policies for the enforcement of criminal and traffic laws in the state, crime prevention, detection and apprehension of law violators, and the education of citizens regarding public safety. Today the Department of Public Safety employs more than 6,600 people, approximately 2,800 of whom are commissioned law enforcement officers, and the Texas Legislature appropriated slightly over $300 million for all of the operations of the Department of Public Safety in 1998.

Over the years since 1935, the scope and diversity of law enforcement and public safety-related functions discharged by the Department of Public Safety have expanded greatly. To effectively and efficiently discharge its current statutory responsibilities, the Department of Public Safety is presently organized into three major divisions that include (1) administration, (2) criminal law enforcement, and (3) traffic law enforcement. It is important to note that today the Texas Rangers are operated as a unit under the auspices of the office of the director of the Texas Department of Public Safety.

The Administrative Division—The Administrative Division is responsible for providing specialized services that support the

ORGANIZATIONAL STRUCTURE ★ TEXAS DEPARTMENT OF PUBLIC SAFETY

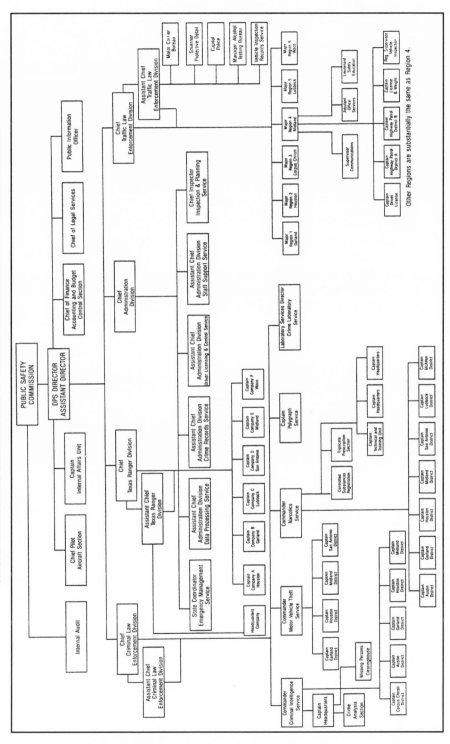

Source: *A Brief Look at the Texas Department of Public Safety.* Texas Department of Public Safety, November, 1995.

mission of the organization. The Administrative Division is organized into three principle units: Staff Support Services, the Crime Records Service, and the Driver Licensing and Control Service.

A. *Staff Support Services*—The Staff Support Services unit includes the Personnel and Training bureaus. The Personnel Bureau is responsible for the recruitment, screening, and employment of highway patrol troopers, which is the entry level position for commissioned law enforcement officers in the Department of Public Safety. Applicants must be at least 21 years of age and have a minimum of 60 semester hours from an accredited college or university. The required number of college credit hours may be waived in lieu of 24 months or more of military or law enforcement experience.

The origin of the Training Bureau dates to 1937, when the Department of Public Safety conducted its first law enforcement training school. Today the Training Bureau conducts, on average, two training schools per year for newly employed troopers. Each training school is 26 weeks long and consists of approximately 1,200 hours of classroom instruction and field practicums. In order to satisfy the legal mandate that all Texas law enforcement officers receive a minimum of 40 hours of advanced in-service training every two years, the Training Bureau conducts extensive and ongoing advanced in-service training programs for not only its experienced troopers, but for county and municipal law enforcement officers from around the state as well. The training programs are designed to keep law enforcement personnel abreast of changes in the law and new developments in crime fighting technologies and tactics.

B. *Crime Records Service*—The Crime Records Service unit includes the Crime Information Bureau and the Fingerprint and Records Bureau. The Crime Information Bureau is responsible for two very important functions: the operation of the Texas Crime Information Center and the Uniform Crime Reporting Section. The Texas Crime Information Center operates the computerized data base that provides information on outstanding criminal warrants, missing persons, and property reported stolen to all Texas law enforcement officers as well as law enforcement officers from other states and the federal government. Any Texas driver who has ever been stopped by a Texas law enforcement officer is indirectly familiar with the work of the Texas Crime Information Center. After the officer has requested to see the driver's license and proof of insurance of the motor vehicle operator, the officer will return to the patrol car and radio his headquarters. What the officer is doing is requesting the dispatcher at headquarters to contact the Texas Crime Information Center and inquire if there are any outstanding warrants for the person listed on the driver's license or if the car he has stopped has been reported stolen. To ensure that accurate and timely information is available to law enforcement officers, the Texas Crime Information Center operates 24 hours a day, 7 days a week, 365 days a year. The operation of the Uniform Crime Reporting Section has been discussed in Chapter 1.

The Fingerprint and Records Bureau is responsible for maintaining the state's fingerprint and criminal records files. The origin of this bureau and its database of fingerprints of known criminals dates to 1935, when the Beaumont Police Department's paper fingerprint files were transferred to Austin, classified, and filed. As the state's central repository for information on known criminals, the Fingerprint and Records Bureau today manages a paper fingerprint file on over five million arrestees, and receives over 600,000 new fingerprint cards a year. In 1991 the Fingerprint and Records Bureau began a project to convert all of its paper fingerprint files to electronic form, using a sophisticated computer technology known as the Automated Fingerprint Identification System (AFIS). The process of converting all of the paper fingerprint files to the AFIS system was completed in May 1993. Today, the AFIS system allows for remarkably rapid searching of the database to ascertain if arrestees have prior criminal records, and aids criminal investigators in using latent fingerprints from a crime scene to identify a possible perpetrator.

Additionally, when the Texas Legislature in 1995 passed

Senate Bill 50, which permitted qualified Texans to lawfully carry a concealed handgun, the Concealed Handgun Unit of the Fingerprint and Records Bureau was created. The unit is responsible for processing concealed handgun permit applications and conducting the necessary criminal background checks to ensure that the applicant has no criminal history.

C. Driver Licensing and Control Service—The Driver Licensing and Control Service is responsible for virtually all of the administrative functions connected with the regulation of motor vehicles and their operators on Texas highways. The Driver Licensing and Control Service provides administrative support to the Driver License Service of the Traffic Law Enforcement Division (discussed on page 122) by verifying an applicant's eligibility to hold a driver's license, and maintaining all driving and accident records.

Criminal Law Enforcement Division—The Criminal Law Enforcement Division is responsible for conducting major criminal investigations that typically involve murder, gambling, narcotics trafficking, and public corruption. The Criminal Law Enforcement Division is organized into five services: Criminal Intelligence, Narcotics, Motor Vehicle Theft, Crime Laboratory, and Polygraph. The Criminal Intelligence Service is principally responsible for identifying and apprehending wanted felons, locating missing persons, and overseeing the operation of the Texas Sexual Offender Registration Program. In 1991 the Texas Legislature passed the Sexual Offender Registration Law, which mandates that criminals convicted of certain sexual offenses after 1 September 1991 must register with the county sheriff or municipal police in the county or city where they intend to reside. The Criminal Intelligence Service was given the responsibility of supplying the necessary sex offender registration forms to county and municipal law enforcement agencies and maintaining the state's database of registered sex offenders. The criminal investigation activities of the Criminal Intelligence Service as well as the Narcotics and Motor Vehicle Theft Services are aided by the Crime

Laboratory and Polygraph Services. Crime laboratories use scientific technologies and methodologies to aid criminal investigators in the identification, apprehension, and prosecution of criminals. The first Department of Public Safety crime laboratory was established in 1937, and in 1944 the DPS established a polygraph unit. Today the Crime Laboratory Services unit consists of a main state crime laboratory headquartered in Austin and 12 field laboratories around the state. The Crime Laboratory Services unit provides state-of-the-art scien-

Polygraph administration.

(Courtesy of TDPS)

tific analysis of a wide range of evidence, including the chemical analysis and identification of controlled substances, ballistics tests for firearms, questioned document analysis for forgeries, toxicological and serological analysis, tool mark comparison, forensic photography, and DNA analysis.

Traffic Law Enforcement Division—The Traffic Law Enforcement Division is responsible for the supervision of motor vehicle traffic on Texas highways. This responsibility is discharged principally through three units: the Driver License Service, the License and Weight Service, and the Highway Patrol Service. The first law requiring that operators of motor vehicles in Texas be licensed took effect on 14 February 1936. The Texas Legislature originally required that each county tax collector be responsible for issuing driver's licenses. Since 1937, however, the Department of Public Safety has been responsible for all aspects regarding the testing and issuance of licenses for motor vehicle operators in Texas. Today the License and Weight Service is responsible for enforcing the laws that regulate and promote motor carrier safety on the public highways in Texas. The License and Weight Service oversees the licensing of commercial truck drivers and ensures that laws and regulations relating to size, weight, cargo, and registration of commercial motor vehicle transports are being enforced.

The Department of Public Safety function that Texans are undoubtedly most familiar with is the Highway Patrol. With an authorized force of more than 1,800 men and women, the Highway Patrol Service is the largest unit today within the Department of Public Safety. The clean and well-maintained black and white patrol units clearly labeled "State Trooper" are a frequent sight on Texas highways. In addition to enforcing laws which promote the safe operation of motor vehicles on Texas highways, the Department of Public Safety Troopers also play a major role in the general enforcement of the criminal law. While patrolling the highways of Texas, Department of Public Safety Troopers make approximately 950,000 arrests each year for violations that range from drunk driving to murder.

*Though vehicles and uniforms may change,
some things remain the same.*

(Courtesy of TDPS)

COUNTY LAW ENFORCEMENT

County Sheriff

HISTORY

The office of sheriff is of English origin, and dates to the time immediately following the Norman Conquest of England in 1066. For purposes of governance and peacekeeping, the Norman kings partitioned England into geographical units called shires, which roughly approximate the modern concept of counties. For each shire, the king appointed a chief conservator of the peace known as a "shire-reeve." It is from this English institution of law enforcement that the modern concept and term "sheriff" evolved. The concept of a county as a governmental unit and the office of sheriff as chief law enforcement officer of a county were both introduced into the North American English colonies by the British in the 1600s.

In Texas the office of county sheriff is the direct descendant of the Spanish and Mexican *alguacil*. The first instance of the use of the term "sheriff" appears in Stephen F. Austin's 1824 document titled *Instructions and Regulations for the Alcaldes*, which authorized the appointment of a sheriff to aid Austin in the execution of civil processes. The office of sheriff first received constitutional status in Article 4, Section 12 of the 1836 Constitution of the Republic of Texas, which provided that "there shall be appointed for each county ... one sheriff ... who shall hold office for two years ... and be elected by qualified voters" (an amendment to the Texas Constitution in 1954 changed the term of office from two years to the present four-year term of service). Article 4, Section 12 also provided that sheriffs, as necessary, could receive their commission directly from the president of the Republic of Texas. David Rusk, a veteran of the Battle of San Jacinto, became Texas' first constitutionally authorized sheriff in 1837. The office of county sheriff has been constitutionally provided for in every subsequent Texas Constitution, and the importance of the office in the overall scheme of law enforcement at the county level in Texas is reflected in the fact that a State Association of Texas Sheriffs has been in existence since 1878. Local law enforcement officers in Texas had no similar organization until 1894, when the City Marshals and Chiefs of Police Union of Texas was founded.

The Modern Texas Sheriff—Since 1836 the sheriff has been the chief law enforcement officer of Texas counties. In this capacity, the sheriff has been vested with the statutory responsible for keeping the peace in the unincorporated and rural areas of Texas counties. The enforcement of law and maintenance of the peace within the geographical limits of cities, towns, and villages has traditionally been left to city police and constables. The specific duties of county sheriffs in Texas have changed very little over the years since 1836. Today the statutory duties and responsibilities of Texas county sheriffs are set forth in two codes. Article 2.17 of the *Texas Code of Criminal Procedure* specifically stipulates the duties and responsibilities of the office of sheriff as a conservator of the peace, while Subchapter B of Chapter 85 of the *Texas Local Government Code* defines additional miscellaneous powers and duties of sheriffs in the discharge of civil law matters. When considered together, the statutory language in these two codes make it clear that the office of county sheriff in Texas is vested with the responsibility of discharging two functions: the county sheriff is both the chief executive and administrative officer for law enforcement in the county and the chief executive officer of the criminal and civil courts of record in the county.

Acting in the capacity of chief executive and administrative officer for law enforcement in the county, a Texas sheriff is responsible for discharging a wide range of functions that extend beyond the traditional role of enforcing the law and maintaining the peace in unincorporated areas of a county. The sheriff of Texas counties is responsible for not only the law enforcement functions associated with the office, but Chapter 351.034 of the *Texas Local Government Code* specifically grants to sheriffs the responsibility to act as the chief jail administrator of the county jail. In this capacity the sheriff is statutorily held accountable for the day-to-day operation of the county jail, including the staffing and management of the jail and the safekeeping and maintenance of pretrial detainees and convicted misdemeanants.

Acting in the capacity of an executive officer of the criminal and civil courts of record in Texas counties, the sheriff is statutorily responsible for the discharge of an even wider range of functions. In this role, the sheriff is responsible for aiding the discharge of business by the criminal and civil courts of record by serving the processes ordered by these courts (i.e., writs, summonses, and subpoenas), summoning veniremen, and executing the judgments of both civil and criminal courts. With respect to the discharge of processes, it is important to note that the sheriff is also statutorily responsible for executing subpoenas and other processes directed and issued to him by the president of the Texas Senate, the Speaker of the Texas House of Representatives, or the chairman of any committee of either house of the Texas Legislature. The responsibilities associated with executing the judgment of a civil court include both the attachment of property pursuant to a court order and presiding over the judicially ordered sale of property.

The sheriff discharges the judgments of criminal courts in three ways. First, the sheriff is responsible for transporting pretrial detainees to their criminal court appearances; second, the sheriff is held responsible for ensuring that a sentence of incarceration for 12 months or less imposed upon a convicted misdemeanant is carried out; and third, the sheriff is responsible for the transportation of convicted felons remanded by the judge to the custody of the Texas prison system.

Additionally, it is interesting to note that in counties with a population of less than 10,000, the sheriff is statutorily authorized to serve in the capacity of tax assessor and tax collector, unless the citizens of the county vote to separate the two offices.

Chapter 85 of the *Texas Local Government Code* also sets forth the requirements necessary to qualify an individual to run for office of sheriff and the authority of county sheriffs to staff their office. To be eligible to run for election to the office of county sheriff in Texas, one must be at least 21 years old, have no record of a felony conviction, and, within two years of their election, pass the state test for peace officer licensing given by the Texas Commission on Law Enforcement Standards and Education. A person elected to the office of county sheriff must, before beginning to perform the statutory duties associated with the position, post a bond made payable to the governor in an amount not less than $5,000 nor more than $30,000. The posting of a bond is for the purpose of insuring that the elected sheriff will faithfully perform the statutory duties of the office, and the amount of the bond is determined by the commissioners court of the county. The appointment of deputy sheriffs is completely at the discretion of the sheriff. The appointment must be made in writing, and all appointed deputies serve at the sheriff's pleasure. The posting of bonds by deputies appointed in writing by the sheriff is not mandated by statute but is left to the discretion of the commissioners court of each county. Today in Texas there are approximately 11,000 deputy sheriffs.

Reserve deputy sheriffs may be appointed by the sheriff only with the approval of the commissioners court of the county. Reserve deputy sheriffs serve at the discretion of the sheriff and may be called into service if the sheriff considers it necessary to have additional officers under his command to preserve the peace and enforce the law. The traditional authority of the county sheriff to appoint reserve deputy sheriffs is founded in the early English common law practice of *posse comitatus*, and is readily recognizable and familiar to many people today as the sheriff's posse that was assembled during the nineteenth century to pursue and capture fleeing felons. In this capacity, reserve deputy sheriffs function in the capacity of peace officers and may legally carry weapons (in the guise of their position) only during the time they are called upon by the sheriff to aid him in the discharge of his statutory duties and responsibilities. Each reserve deputy sheriff is required by statute to file a bond with the sheriff in the amount of $2,000. Additionally, the sheriff of a county that borders the Gulf of Mexico is authorized to organize some of the reserve deputy force to serve as marine reserve deputies and lifeguards for beach and water safety purposes.

Finally, county sheriffs in Texas are statutorily required to employ, with the approval of the county commissioners court, a suitable number of guards to ensure the security of the county jail and the safekeeping of its prisoners.

MUNICIPAL LAW ENFORCEMENT

The law enforcement function at the local or municipal level in Texas today is discharged principally by municipal police departments and constables' offices.

Municipal Police Departments

HISTORICAL DEVELOPMENT AND CONTRIBUTIONS

The Anglo-American tradition of vesting villages, towns, and cities with the responsibility of maintaining order and enforcing law is of English origin and dates to the late period of the Anglo-Saxon kings, about 900 A.D. Following the Norman Conquest in 1066, the frankpledge and tithing systems were established to discharge essential peacekeeping and law enforcement functions at the grassroots community level. Under the frankpledge system every able-bodied male over the age of twelve was required to swear an oath to uphold the king's law and aid in apprehending wrongdoers. Groups of ten frankpledged males formed a tithing, the basic unit of early English community law enforcement. In larger communities, ten tithings were subsequently grouped into a hundred, which was overseen by a town constable. In turn, a varying number of hundreds were grouped together to form a shire (or county), and a reeve was appointed as the chief law enforcement officer and commander of the various constables in his county. This English system of delegated and shared responsibility for the enforcement of law was transplanted to the British colonies of North America, and the general structure was maintained even after the United States declared its independence from England in 1776.

After Texas gained its independence from Mexico in 1836, the term marshal was commonly used to designate the chief law enforcement officer of a village or town. As the population of small villages and towns grew, the title of the chief municipal law enforcement officer changed from town marshal to chief of police. The shift in title was viewed by some community leaders as indicative of their community no longer being a frontier backwater but a thriving metropolis. For example, in 1878 Houston became the first municipality in Texas to shift from a city marshal designation to that of chief of police, and, not to be upstaged, Dallas quickly followed suit in 1881. It is interesting to note that the capital of Texas retained the position of city marshal until 1924, when the city government of Austin changed from the commissioner form to the city manager form, and the title of chief of police was formally adopted.

Typical of both the qualifications for appointment and the job responsibilities of municipal police officers in Texas during the 1880s are those that are described in the *Charter and Revised Civil and Criminal Ordinances of the City of Austin*, adopted in 1886. Under the subheading "Rules and Regulations Governing the Police Force of the City of Austin," no person was to receive an appointment to the city police force unless he was a citizen of the United States and had resided in Texas for at least a year, was able to read and write English, had never been convicted of a crime, was of good health, sound mind, and exhibited good moral character and habits. It is abundantly clear that the primary responsibility of municipal police in Texas, even at this early date, was the prevention of crime by means of high visibility patrol. Patrolmen were expected to be intimately acquainted with the area that comprised their assigned beat. They discharged this responsibility by acquiring a knowledge of all inhabitants residing and routinely working within their assigned beat and watching vigilantly all persons passing their way. The presence of strangers was to be looked into, and known or suspected offenders were to be watched carefully and their presence reported to a sergeant in a timely fashion. In the evening, the patrol officer was required to examine all doors and windows of dwellings and stores to ensure they were properly secured. All of this was done with a view toward insuring an orderly and safe community and preventing the commission of offenses against people and their property. The efficiency with which patrolmen at this time discharged their responsibilities was measured by the absence of crime within their assigned beat. It was assumed that when disturbances of the peace and criminal offenses occurred frequently in an officer's assigned beat there was good reason to suspect either negligence or a lack of ability on the part of the patrolman.

From the 1870s to about 1920 it was common practice for municipal police officers to work twelve-hour shifts. In 1912 Houston was the first city in Texas to go to the now standard three shifts of eight hours each. Dallas made the change from the twelve- to the eight-hour shift in 1917, but as late as 1926 municipal police officers in Austin were still working twelve-hour days.

Municipal police departments in Texas may rightfully be called the bellwether of Texas law enforcement. Those departments have been the major source for initiating change and introducing innovations in police work that have become standard practice across the state. Many of the innovations were only later adopted by state law enforcement agencies and county sheriff departments. Typical of the state's law enforcement innovations first pioneered by Texas municipal police departments were the adoption of standardized uniforms, the creation of training programs, and the utilization of newly emerging technologies.

In 1880 Austin became the first city in Texas to adopt a standard uniform for its police officers. The uniform, which was all wool and indigo-dyed a deep navy blue, consisted of pants with a distinctive white cord on the outer seam, a matching shirt, and a double-breasted frock coat. The coat had a waist that extended to the top of the hips and a flared skirt which fell to about one inch above the bend of the knee. The bulky coat was embellished with two rows of four brass buttons each on the breast. A high crown hat with the word "POLICEMAN" emblazoned on the front in white letters completed the uniform. Despite the reports from Austin of discomfort associated with the heavy, wool uniform, especially during hot Texas summers, both Dallas and Houston adopted wool uniforms of remarkably similar tailoring and coloring in 1881 and 1891, respectively. Accompanying the standardized uniform were common implements of the trade. From the late

1880s until well into the 1920s, municipal police officers in Texas were routinely equipped with a whistle, truncheon, and a revolver, which they commonly referred to as a "smoke wagon." Until the 1950s, most municipal police departments in Texas required their officers to buy their own uniforms and equipment.

Municipal police departments in Texas unquestionably were the pioneers in establishing training for law enforcement officers. In the United States, prior to the beginning of the twentieth century, there existed no formal classes or manuals for training law enforcement personnel in either law or police practices. Learning how to go about enforcing the law was accomplished mainly by apprenticeship experience. New officers were assigned to experienced police veterans, and under their tutelage the process of learning occurred through trial and error. The first formal training classes in the United States for municipal law enforcement officers were begun in 1907 by August Vollmer, police chief of Berkeley, California. Texas quickly followed the lead established by Vollmer.

The credit for establishing the first municipal police training course in Texas belongs to E. C. Noble, the chief of police in Houston. In 1913 Noble organized a cadre of private attorneys knowledgeable in criminal law and criminal procedure, and had them address Houston police officers on the finer points of law. The value of the seminars was quickly recognized, and in 1921, at the urging of the Houston Civil Service Commission, Police Chief Gordon Murphy instituted a 30-day training course. Lectures on criminal law and procedure given by the district attorney's office were supplemented with discussion on city ordinances, police procedure, and departmental policies and regulations. In 1930 Houston was the first city in Texas to establish an advanced in-service training school for detectives.

Following Houston's lead, the Dallas and Fort Worth police departments established in-service training programs in 1925 and 1926, respectively. Dallas police officers were required to attend 40 hours of lecture per year in their off-duty time, and they were not compensated for the time they spent in the classroom. Dallas hired a full-time training instructor in 1933. In 1945 Dallas established a pre-service training academy for police recruits that encompassed all phases of criminal law enforcement and police procedure. When Homer Garrison established the first training program for his Department of Public Safety officers in the late 1930s, he was merely importing to state law enforcement ideas that had already been proven to be of value by municipal law enforcement agencies in Texas.

The credit for the introduction and utilization of new technological innovations, which have since become standard in state and county law enforcement in Texas, clearly belongs to the state's municipal police departments. Municipal police departments in Texas were the first to make use of automobiles, emerging communications technology, and scientific criminal investigation methodologies. The municipal police departments of Dallas and Houston were the first to purchase internal combustion vehicles for their police officers. In 1907 both cities each purchased two Harley-Davidson motorcycles, which were used primarily for traffic enforcement. In 1912 the Dallas Police Department became the first law enforcement agency in Texas to use an automobile for the purpose of routine patrol, and in 1936 the Houston Police Department became the first law enforcement agency in Texas to routinely use an aircraft. The plane was used for traffic enforcement purposes and regularly patrolled the highway between the San Jacinto Battleground and Harrisburg.

Municipal police departments in Texas were first to make use of new communication technologies. In 1878 the first telegraph lines were installed in Texas, and almost immediately city police departments made use of the technology for communicating with one another about crimes and wanted criminals. In 1908 the Dallas Police Department was the first city in Texas to install the Gamewell system of telephone police call boxes. Placed in strategic locations in beats throughout a city, the Gamewell system of police call boxes allowed headquarters to relay information and orders to patrol officers. In 1927 Houston became the first city in the Southwest to install radio receivers in their police patrol cars. Austin quickly followed suit in 1927. The early radio transmitters were of low power, usu-

A state trooper demonstrates the modern marvel of the two-way radio.
(Courtesy of TDPS)

ally ranging from 25 to 100 watts. Patrol officers still had to contact headquarters by telephone because the radios installed in the patrol cars did not have transmitting capabilites. On 11 May 1938 Austin became the first municipal police department in Texas to install two-way radios in patrol cars, and Dallas adopted the technology one year later in 1939.

Finally, the bulk of the credit for introducing innovative criminal investigation techniques into the practice of law enforcement in Texas rests with municipal police departments. The first detective units responsible only for the investigation of crimes reported by patrol officers were created in Austin in 1885 and in Houston in the late 1890s. In 1900 the Houston Police Department created the first organized criminal identification bureau in the state when it purchased Bertillon measurement instruments and photographic equipment to document and identify arrested criminals. In 1913 the nationally renowned criminal identification expert W. R. Ellis reorganized Houston's criminal identification bureau and introduced fingerprinting as a supplement to the Bertillon system, and he developed a sophisticated system of indexing and cross-referencing known criminals with their method of operation, or *modus operandi*. Ellis' reorganization gave the Houston police the reputation of having the most advanced criminal identification bureau of any metropolitan police department in the United States. The first true crime laboratory in Texas was established in Dallas in 1934, when the police department organized a ballistics unit equipped with a comparison microscope. At the time, Dallas and New Orleans were the only two municipal police departments in the South that had the capability of conducting ballistics examinations.

Additionally, it is important to note one final contribution of municipal police departments in Texas: They were the first police organizations in the state to employ minorities and women as law enforcement officers. The first African-American law enforcement officers were employed by municipal police departments in the early 1870s to patrol and enforce the law in black neighborhoods. In 1917 the Houston Police Department hired the first full-time female patrol officer in the state, Eva J. Bracher, and she subsequently went on to become the state's first female detective, when she was promoted to the position in the early 1920s.

CONTEMPORARY MUNICIPAL POLICE DEPARTMENTS

Municipal police, because of their sheer numbers, distinctive uniforms, and readily recognizable patrol vehicles, constitute the most visible component of the Texas criminal justice system. There are today in Texas more than 600 municipal police departments that employ in excess of 31,000 full-time law enforcement officers, the majority of which (about 27,500) are men. Most of the municipal police departments in Texas are small organizations that employ between 25 and 50 police officers. A few cities, such as Austin and San Antonio, have police departments that employ between 1,000 and 2,500 officers.

ORGANIZATION OVERVIEW ★ AUSTIN POLICE DEPARTMENT

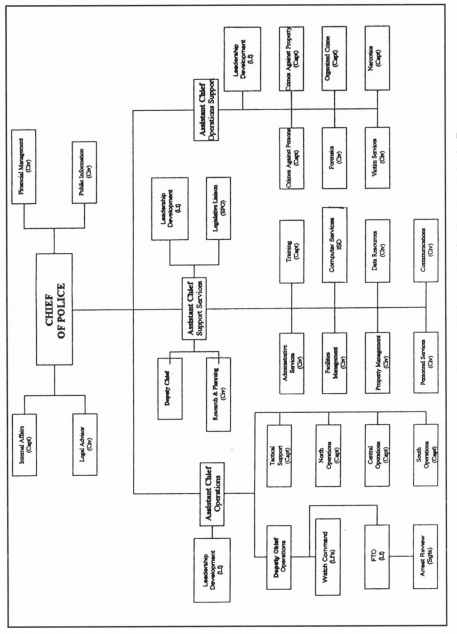

Source: *1996 Program Directory and Resource Guide.* Austin Police Department, Austin, Texas.

The two largest metropolitan police departments in Texas are Houston, which has approximately 7,000 police officers, and Dallas, which has a force of about 3,700 officers. In addition to full-time law enforcement officers, municipal police departments in Texas today employ about 11,000 civilian personnel who support police officers in the discharge of their law enforcement function by providing a wide range of valuable clerical and professional services, such as 911 dispatching, crime scene evidence processing, and data processing. In 1998 Texans spent more than $2 billion to fund and operate municipal police departments. The midrange and larger municipal police departments such as Austin, San Antonio, Dallas, and Houston are funded by annual operating budgets that range from $80 million to greater than $100 million.

To one degree or another, virtually all municipal police departments in Texas perform five basic functions: (1) routine patrol, (2) information gathering (such as conducting criminal investigations), (3) law enforcement (by making arrests for criminal wrongdoing), (4) order maintenance (such as crowd and traffic control), and (5) service-related activities (such as educating the public about crime prevention, establishing neighborhood watch programs, participating in drug abuse resistance education programs, and assisting the injured). How these functions are organized and the degree to which they have been specialized within a municipal police department is directly related to the size of the organization. In the smaller municipal police departments, officers function as generalists and routinely perform all of the five basic functions. In the midrange to large municipal police departments, however, the basic functions are discharged by police officers assigned to very narrow and highly specialized details. The organization and range of specialized law enforcement functions discharged by the Austin Police Department is typical of midrange and larger police municipal police departments in Texas.

The diversity of functional specialization in midrange and larger municipal police departments is most evident in the two areas of patrol and information gathering. The standard patrol function, which has been the backbone of municipal policing in Texas for more than 150 years, continues today to be the law enforcement function where most of a department's economic, personnel, and material resources are invested. In addition to the standard patrol cruiser, many midrange and larger metropolitan police departments today have specialized walking patrols, bicycle patrols, and mounted patrols. The degree of functional specialization is most obvious in the area of information gathering. Midrange and larger municipal police departments typically have highly trained detectives organized into specialized criminal investigation units or bureaus, such as criminal homicide, child abuse, narcotics, robbery, burglary, sex crimes, auto theft, and gang suppression. Additionally, many of these municipal police departments have specialized units to provide tactical support for the law enforcement function, such as canine and special weapons and tactics units, as well as helicopters, aircraft, and armored personnel carriers.

The Office of Constable

HISTORICAL DEVELOPMENT

Like the office of sheriff, the constable also has its origin in England, and makes its first appearance immediately following the Norman invasion in 1066. The modern English term "constable" is derived from the Norman French term *comes stabuli*, meaning head of the stables. While the shire-reeve was responsible to the king for the enforcement of law and the maintenance of public order at the county level, the constable functioned as his counterpart at the local, or village, level. While the office of sheriff no longer exists in the English system of law enforcement, the office of constable has endured, and today in England the function of law enforcement at both the county and local levels is discharged by chief constables and their deputies.

The office of constable was transplanted to the North American colonies by the British in the early 1600s, where they served as the chief law enforcement officers of villages, towns, and cities until the advent of modern police departments in the late nineteenth century. After the rise of large

metropolitan police departments, the law enforcement authority and responsibilities of constables diminished considerably.
Since 1776, 37 states have constitutionally or statutorily authorized the office of constable. Nine states never had the office,
and four states have abolished the position. Today in Texas the
office of constable is inextricably linked with justice of the
peace precincts and their respective courts.

The first mention of the office of constable in Texas is
found in Stephen F. Austin's 1824 document titled
Instructions and Regulations for the Alcaldes. The document
authorized the Anglo-American *alcaldes* to each appoint a
constable to aid them in the execution of their law enforcement as well as their judicial functions. Unlike the sheriff in
Austin's colony, however, the constable's jurisdictional powers were geographically limited to the local, or municipal,
level. During the period prior to the Republic of Texas, the
constable maintained vigilance against disorder in the villages
and towns and served as bailiff and court clerk when the
alcalde's court was in session. After Texas won its independence from Mexico, the Constitution of 1836 formally abolished the *ayuntamiento* system of government, as well as the
alcalde system of law enforcement and the administration of
justice established by Austin, but some of the offices of common law origin created by Austin's *Instructions and
Regulations for the Alcaldes* were retained, including that of
sheriff and constable. The function of the *alcalde* was transformed into a purely judicial function, and following English
common law tradition was renamed "justice of the peace."
The position of constable was maintained, and those holding
that office continued to function in a limited law enforcement
capacity as well as serving as an executive officer of the justice of the peace court.

Every Texas constitution since 1836 has provided for the
office of constable as an adjunct to justice of the peace courts.
Under the Constitutions of 1836, 1845, and 1861 the constable was required to be elected biennially, and candidates for
the office were to be selected from each militia captain's
precinct. Little has changed over the years with respect to the
constitutional mandates for the office of constable. The Con-

stitution of 1876 abolished the requirement that constables be selected from militia precincts, and instead required constables to be elected from each justice of the peace precinct. Article V, Section 18 of the 1954 Texas Constitution was amended to provide for the election of constables to four instead of two-year terms of office.

THE MODERN TEXAS CONSTABLE

Constables in Texas no longer have the broad powers of law enforcement they enjoyed during the period before the Republic of Texas. Subchapter C of Chapter 86 of the *Texas Local Government Code* defines the powers and duties of constables. While constables are authorized peace officers with the power to make arrests both with and without a warrant, their jurisdiction is limited to the geopolitical confines of the justice of the peace precinct to which they were elected, and as such, the law enforcement function of a constable is principally limited to that of a precinct police officer. The more important and fundamental function of the modern Texas constable is discharged through his serving in the capacity of executive officer of the justice of the peace court. A constable is statutorily required to attend each session of the justice of the peace court in the precinct to which he was elected and act as bailiff of the court. In this capacity, he is charged with the responsibility of executing anywhere in the county any civil or criminal process directed to him by the justice of the peace in his precinct or by any judge of a court of record within his county.

The statutory provisions governing the organization and staffing of the office of the constable are found in Chapter 86 of the *Texas Local Government Code*, and are very similar to the requirements attending the organization and staffing of a county sheriff's department. After election and prior to discharge of his official duties, a constable must post a bond with the office of the governor of not less than $500 nor more than $1,500. The posting of the bond is to ensure that the constable will faithfully perform the duties imposed upon him by statute. Like sheriffs, constables have the power to deputize. A constable who desires to appoint a deputy must make application to do so in writing to the commissioners court of the county in which the precinct is located. The written application is basically an argument of justification designed to convince the county commissioners that in order to properly handle the volume of business associated with their law enforcement and justice of the peace functions in the precinct, it is necessary to appoint a deputy constable. If the application has merit and the commissioners court determines that the constable needs the assistance of a deputy, they may approve the appointment of a deputy constable.

Additionally, the commissioners court may also authorize a constable to appoint reserve deputy constables. Reserve deputy constables serve in the capacity of peace officers at the discretion of the constable, and may be called into serve at any time the constable considers it necessary to have additional officers to enforce the law and preserve the peace within the geopolitical boundaries of the justice of the peace precinct. At the time of their appointment, reserve deputy constables must execute a bond with the constable in the amount of $2,000. When called upon to serve in the capacity of reserve deputy constable, they are vested with the same law enforcement authority and power as constables.

It is interesting to note that under current law, if a constable encounters resistance in either enforcing the law or in the discharge of his lawful civil and criminal process functions, he is authorized to place a lawful demand for assistance upon any resident of the county who is present. A person who refuses to obey any such a lawful call for rendering assistance may, on a motion by the constable, be held in contempt of court by the justice of the peace and assessed a fine not to exceed $10.

WORKS CONSULTED AND
SUGGESTIONS FOR FURTHER READING

Adams, Paul. "The Unsolved Murder of Ben Thompson." *Southwestern Historical Quarterly*, vol. 48 (1945), pp. 321-329.

Askins, Charles. "The Texas Ranger and His Guns (Part I)." *American Rifleman*, vol. 130 (November 1982), pp. 44-45, 78-79.

————. "The Texas Ranger and His Guns (Part II)." *American Rifleman*, vol. 130 (December 1982), pp. 28-29, 75.

Barker, Eugene C. "The Government of Austin's Colony, 1821-1831." *Southwestern Historical Quarterly*, vol. 21 (1918), pp. 211-229.

Barkley, Mary Starr. *History of Travis County and Austin: 1839-1899*. Austin, Texas: Austin Printing Company, 1963.

Baenziger, Ann Patton. "The Texas State Police During Reconstruction: A Reexamination." *Southwestern Historical Quarterly*, vol. 72 (1969), pp. 470-491.

Baugh, Virgil E. *A Pair of Texas Rangers: Bill McDonald and John Hughes*. Washington, D.C.: Potomac Corral, 1970.

"Ben Thompson, City Marshall of Austin, Texas." *National Police Gazette*, vol. 37, no. 181 (1881), p. 6.

Burks, Tom. "Texas Ranger Hall of Fame and Museum." *The New Handbook of Texas*. Austin, Texas: Texas State Historical Association, 1996, vol. 6, p. 393.

Cannon, Carl L. *Scout and Ranger: Being the Personal Adventures of James Pike of the Texas Rangers*. New York: Da Capo Press, 1972.

Carter, Bill. "Garrison, Homer, Jr." *The New Handbook of Texas*. Austin, Texas: Texas State Historical Association, 1996, vol. 3, pp. 102.

Charter and Revised Civil and Criminal Ordinances of the City of Austin. Adopted May 17, 1886. Austin, Texas: Warner and Daughon, 1886.

Curtis, James Robert. "The Dallas Police System." M.A. thesis, Southern Methodist University, 1927.

"Dallas Police Department." *The Encyclopedia of Police Science*. William G. Bailey, editor. New York: Garland Publishing, 1989, pp. 128-132.

"Dallas Stoudenmier." *National Police Gazette*, vol. 38, no. 209 (1881), p. 6.

Davis, John L. *The Texas Rangers: Their First 100 Years*. San Antonio, Texas: The University of Texas at San Antonio, Institute of Texan Cultures, 1975.

Day, James M. *Captain Clint Peoples: Texas Ranger*. Waco, Texas: Texian Press, 1980.

Douglas, Claude Leroy. *The Gentlemen in the White Hats: Dramatic Episodes in the History of the Texas Rangers*. Dallas, Texas: Southwest Press, 1934.

Draper, Robert. "The Twilight of the Texas Rangers." *Texas Monthly*, February 1994, pp. 76-82, 107-113, 118.

Durham, George. *Taming the Nueces Strip: The Story of McNelly's Rangers*. Austin, Texas: University of Texas Press, 1962.

Dykstra, Robert R. *The Cattle Towns*. New York: Alfred A. Knopf, 1968.

Engberg, Vernon L. "Municipal Police Training in Texas." M.A. thesis, University of Texas, 1952.

Evans, Dorothy Ellen Saunders. "John Coffee Hays: A Texas Ranger." M.A. thesis, Southwest Texas State University, 1970.

Field, William T. "The Texas State Police." *Texas Military History*, vol. 5 (1965).

Ford, John Salmon. *Rip Ford's Texas*. Stephen B. Oates, editor. Austin, Texas: University of Texas Press, 1963.

Fugitives From Justice: The Notebook of Texas Rangers. Sgt. James B. Gillett. Austin, Texas: State House Press, 1997.

Fuller, Henry C. *A Texas Sheriff: Being a Biography of the Life of A. J. Spradley, Sheriff of Nacogdoches County for Thirty Years*. Nacogdoches, Texas: Nacogdoches Press, 1931.

Gard, Wayne. *Frontier Justice*. Norman, Oklahoma: University of Oklahoma Press, 1949.

Gillett, James B. *Six Years With the Texas Rangers, 1875-1881*. New Haven, Connecticut: Yale University Press, 1925.

Greer, James K. *A Texas Ranger and Frontiersman: The Days of Buck Barry in Texas, 1845-1906*. Phoenix, Arizona: The Southwest Press, 1942.

———. *Col. Jack Hays: Texas Frontier Leader and California Builder*. New York: Dutton, 1952.

"Houston Police Department." *The Encyclopedia of Police Science*. William G. Bailey, editor. New York: Garland Publishing, 1989, pp. 278-282.

Hughes, W. J. *Rebellious Ranger: Rip Ford and the Old Southwest*. Norman, Oklahoma: University of Oklahoma Press, 1964.

Jasinski, Laurie E. "Texas Department of Public Safety." *The New Handbook of Texas*. Austin, Texas: Texas State Historical Association, 1996, vol. 6, p. 322.

Jenkins, John H., and H. Gordon Frost. *I'm Frank Hamer*. Austin, Texas: Pemberton Press, 1968.

"John Chenneville, Austin, Texas Lawman." *National Police Gazette*, vol. 45, no. 4 (1884), p. 5.

Keating, Bern. *An Illustrated History of the Texas Rangers*. New York, New York: Promontory Press, 1980.

Light, Ken, and Suzanne Donovan. *Texas Death Row*. Jackson, Mississippi: University Press of Mississippi, 1997.

Looney, Wesley Hall. "The Texas Rangers in a Turbulent Era." M.A. thesis, Texas Tech University, 1971.

Mahaney, Charles C. "A Review of Police Training and Education in Texas." M.A. thesis, Sam Houston State University, 1970.

Marchiafava, Louis J. "The Houston Police: 1878-1948." *Rice University Studies* (Monograph in History series), vol. 63, no. 2 (Spring 1977).

Martin, Jack. *Border Boss: Captain John R. Hughes, Texas Ranger.* San Antonio, Texas: The Naylor Company, 1942.

Mason, Herbert Molloy. *The Texas Rangers.* New York: Meredith Press, 1967.

Metz, Leon C. *Dallas Stoudenmire.* Norman, Oklahoma: University of Oklahoma Press, 1979.

———. *John Selman.* Norman, Oklahoma: University of Oklahoma Press, 1980.

Monkkonen, Eric H. *Police in Urban America: 1860-1920.* Cambridge, England: Cambridge University Press, 1981.

Nash, Jay Robert. "John Selman." *Encyclopedia of World Crime.* Wilmette, Illinois: Crime Books, Inc., 1990, p. 2727.

Nunn, William Curtis. "A Study of the State Police During the E. J. Davis Administration." M.A. thesis, University of Texas, 1931.

Paine, Albert Bigelow. *Captain Bill McDonald, Texas Ranger: A Story of Frontier Reform.* New York: J. J. Little, 1909.

Prassel, Frank Richard. *The Western Peace Officer: A Legacy of Law and Order.* Norman, Oklahoma: The University of Oklahoma Press, 1972.

Pray, Scott. "Reserve Officer Programs." *Texas Law Enforcement Management and Administrative Statistic Program Bulletin.* Bill Blackwood Law Enforcement Management Institute of Texas, Policy Research Center, Sam Houston State University, Huntsville, Texas, vol. 4, no. 9, December 1997.

Preece, Harold. *Lone Star Man: Ira Aten, Last of the Old Texas Rangers.* New York: Hastings House, 1960.

Procter, Ben H. *Just One Riot: Episodes of Texas Rangers in the 20th Century.* Austin, Texas: Eakin Press, 1991.

———. "Texas Rangers." *The New Handbook of Texas.* Austin, Texas: Texas State Historical Association, 1996, vol. 6, pp. 393-395.

Raymond, Dora Neill. *Captain Lee Hall of Texas.* Norman, Oklahoma: University of Oklahoma Press, 1940.

Rigler, Eric T. "A Descriptive Study of the Texas Ranger: Historical Overtones on Minority Attitudes." M.A. thesis, Sam Houston State University, 1971.

———. "Frontier Justice in the Days Before NCIC." *FBI Law Enforcement Bulletin*, vol. 54 (1985), pp. 16-18, 19, 20-22.

Rigler, Lewis C., and Judyth Wagner Rigler. *In the Line of Duty: Reflections of a Texas Ranger Private*. Houston, Texas: Larksdale Press, 1984.

Samora, Julian, et al. *Gunpowder Justice: A Reassessment of the Texas Rangers*. Notre Dame, Indiana: University of Notre Dame Press, 1979.

Schuster, Stephen William. "The Modernization of the Texas Rangers, 1930-1936." M.A. thesis, Texas Christian University, 1965.

Smith, Dick. "Development of Local Governmental Units in Texas." Ph.D. dissertation, Harvard University, 1939.

Sonnichsen, C. L. "Selman, John." *The Handbook of Texas*. Austin, Texas: Texas State Historical Association, 1952, vol. 2, pp. 591-592.

Spiller, Phillip N. "A Short History of the San Antonio Police Department." M.S. thesis, Trinity University, 1954.

Steen, Ralph W. "Analysis of the Work of the General Council of Texas, 1835-1836." *Southwestern Historical Quarterly*, vol. 41 (1938), pp. 324-348.

Sterling, William W. *Trails and Trials of a Texas Ranger*. Norman, Oklahoma: University of Oklahoma Press, 1969.

Texas Department of Public Safety. *Annual Report*, 1996.

"Texas' First Sheriff." *Sheriffs' Association of Texas Magazine,* vol. 1 (1932), pp. 7-15.

"Texas Rangers." *The Encyclopedia of Police Science*. William G. Bailey, editor. New York: Garland Publishing, 1989, pp. 614-616.

Torres, Donald A. *A Handbook of State Police, Highway Patrols, and State Investigative Agencies*. Westport, Connecticut: Greenwood Press, 1987.

———. "State Law Enforcement Agencies." *The Encyclopedia of Police Science*. William G. Bailey, editor. New York: Garland Publishing, 1989, pp. 578-592.

Vebtal, Stanley. *Bigfoot Wallace: A Biography*. Boston, Massachusetts: Houghton Mifflin, 1942.

Vernon's Texas Codes Annotated, Administrative Code, Sections 211-229.

Vernon's Texas Codes Annotated, Code of Criminal Procedure, Articles 2.12, 2.13, and 2.17.

Vernon's Texas Codes Annotated, Government Code, Chapter 411.002, and 021-023.

Vernon's Texas Codes Annotated, Local Government Code, Chapters 85 and 351.034.

Ward, James Randolph. "The Texas Rangers, 1919-1935: A Study in Law Enforcement." Ph.D. dissertation, Texas Christian University, 1972.

Webb, Walter Prescott. *The Texas Rangers: A Century of Frontier Defense.* Austin, Texas: The University of Texas Press, 2nd edition, 1965.

Weiss, Harold J. "Organized Constabularies: The Texas Rangers and the Early State Police Movement in the American Southwest." *Journal of the West,* vol. 34 (1995), pp. 27-33.

——. "The Texas Rangers Revisited: Old Themes and New Viewpoints." *Southwestern Historical Quarterly,* vol. 97 (1994), pp. 620-640.

——. "Yours to Command: Captain William J. 'Bill' McDonald and the Panhandle Rangers of Texas." Ph.D. dissertation, University of Indiana at Bloomington, 1980.

Whitman, Walt. "Song of Myself," from *The Selected Poems of Walt Whitman.* New York: Walter J. Black, 1942.

Wilkins, Frederick. *The Highly Irregular Irregulars: Texas Rangers in the Mexican War.* Austin, Texas: Eakin Press, 1991.

4.
★ THE TEXAS COURT SYSTEM

PART 1:
CONSTITUTIONAL HISTORY OF THE
TEXAS JUDICIARY

Before the Texas Revolution and the birth of the republic in 1836, justice in the province of Texas was a subject of heated controversy. Stephen F. Austin's appointment of Josiah H. Bell in 1822 as a provisional justice of the peace for the province was displaced by Mexico's implementation of a judiciary which called for the election of three *alcaldes*. Each *alcalde* was responsible for insuring the application of Spanish criminal and civil law upon the citizenry of Austin's Colony. Displeased by this system of justice, unsuccessful attempts at reform were made by the colonists. Ultimately, all reformation efforts were abandoned, as the Texas Revolution ensued.

In 1836 the Constitution of the Republic of Texas created the territory's first independent judiciary. In the Anglo-American legal tradition, the republic's judiciary vested its power in one Supreme Court. The court's jurisdiction, its legal authority, was limited to the review of appeals and to oversight of inferior courts as provided by the legislature.

Since its inception, the legislature has played a significant role in shaping Texas jurisprudence. The legislature not only created the judicial districts of the republic but also selected the chief justice of the Supreme Court, as well as all district court judges. Notably, district court judges also served in the capacity as extra members of the Supreme Court when called upon by the chief justice. Only county judges and justices of the peace were elected by popular vote.

With statehood and the Texas Constitution of 1845, the role of district judges in the Supreme Court was abolished in favor of the appointment of two associate justices. These justices were also nominated by the governor with the recommendation and approval of the senate.

However, the appointment of judges came to an end with the amendment of the state's constitution in 1850, which made all judicial offices elective. With the exception of the period following the Reconstruction Constitution of 1869, Texas has continued to elect its judiciary. As will be discussed later in this chapter, the move to an elected judiciary has at various times been a source of controversy and criticism.

Following the Civil War, Texas benefited from an economic revival. With a growing number of new businesses and citizenry, the Supreme Court found itself unable to manage its growing docket of civil and criminal appeals. The congestion of the appellate process called for a restructuring of the judiciary. To alleviate the burden of the Supreme Court, the Constitution of 1876 created the Court of Appeals to act as a court of last resort in all criminal, probate, and county court cases. The intent of the constitutional restructuring of the judiciary was to allow the Supreme Court to exclusively hear civil appeals from the district courts. The restructuring effort, however, failed as the Supreme Court continued to fall behind in its adjudication of civil appeals.

A second attempt at alleviating the backlog of cases before the Supreme Court was attempted in 1891 as the constitution was amended to establish an intermediate level of appeals for civil cases. The amendment created new courts of civil appeals (not to be confused with the Court of Appeals) which were given jurisdiction over most civil appeals from the county and district courts. The legislative intent of the amendment was to alleviate the burden of the Supreme Court by filtering out most cases through intermediate level courts. The amendment of 1891 proved advantageous. Through the use of discretionary review, the Supreme Court was better able to control the size of its docket. Furthermore, the civil appellate system could be expanded to meet the future needs of the state.

The Court of Appeals was not abolished by the 1891 amendment. Renamed the Texas Court of Criminal Appeals, today it is the court of last resort in all criminal cases originating from district and county courts. It is important to remember that the Texas Supreme Court has no jurisdiction in criminal matters. It serves as the court of last resort only in civil and juvenile cases.

Like the Supreme Court, the Court of Criminal Appeals has suffered its share of growing pains. Paralleling the growth of the state, the caseload of the Court of Criminal Appeals increased at such a rate that many criminal defendants serving short prison sentences completed their term of incarceration before their appeals were decided. Solving the congestion of criminal appeals was hindered by the fact that the Court of Criminal Appeals had no discretion to deny appeals from the county and district court levels. It attempted to alleviate the backlog by adding extra judges through constitutional amendments (3 judges increased to 5 in 1966, increased to 9 in 1978). However, attempts to remedy the courts' congestion by adding more judges proved futile. In 1980 the state constitution was amended so that the Court of Criminal Appeals could better manage its docket. The courts of civil appeals were renamed the courts of appeals and given appellate jurisdiction of non-capital criminal cases. Subject to discretionary review, the decisions of the courts of appeals in non-capital cases can be appealed to the Court of Criminal Appeals.

Though other states have separate intermediate appellate courts for civil and criminal cases, Texas and Oklahoma are unique in that each has separate courts of last resort for both civil and criminal cases. As a consequence of there being two high appellate courts, the Texas Supreme Court and Court of Criminal Appeals must be careful not to violate each other's jurisdiction by issuing conflicting interpretations of the same laws. It is important as you proceed through this chapter that you become familiar with the jurisdictional differences between these two courts. Though our primary focus is Texas criminal justice, the state courts operate in a collective manner which requires one to distinguish as well as understand the interrelationship between criminal and civil justice.

PART 2:
CONTEMPORARY ORGANIZATION
OF TEXAS COURTS

In terms of structure, Texas has three levels of trial courts and two levels of appellate courts. Unlike other states, Texas trial courts do not have uniform jurisdiction (the authority to hear various types of cases without statutorily imposed limitations). Rather, each trial court can only hear cases within the statutory parameters provided to it by the state legislature (subject matter jurisdiction). Ultimately, to be sure of a trial court's jurisdiction, one must be familiar with the statute that created the court in question. A trial court, by definition, is responsible for hearing witnesses, taking testimony, accepting exhibits offered into evidence, and rendering verdicts. Cases may then be appealed to the appellate courts, where the merit of the trial court's verdict is reviewed. The decisions of the appellate courts are based solely on the evidence and exhibits from the trial courts' proceedings. What follows is an overview of the jurisdictional limits and subject matter for each court.

The Inferior Courts: Local Trial Courts of Limited Jurisdiction

Despite being labeled "inferior," justice of the peace and municipal courts play a critical role in providing the essential revenue needed for local governments to exist. If you have ever paid a fine for a criminal misdemeanor (e.g., a speeding ticket), you probably know that the amount of money, depending on the violation, can be quite substantial. Most cases in the inferior courts are traffic offenses. The money collected in such traffic offenses are often the life blood of local governments.

COURT STRUCTURE OF TEXAS
April 1998

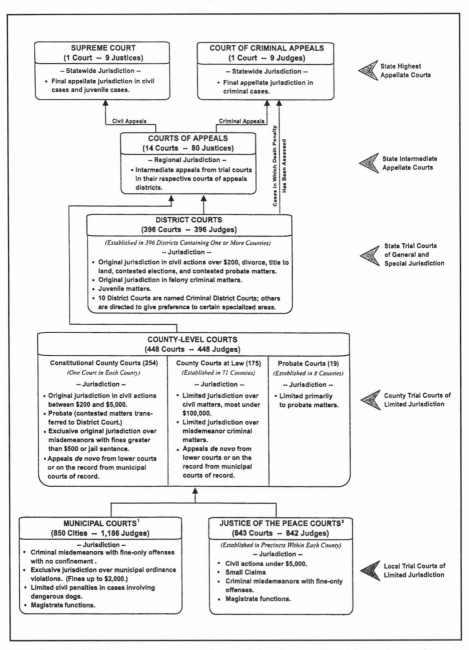

SUPREME COURT
(1 Court -- 9 Justices)

-- Statewide Jurisdiction --
- Final appellate jurisdiction in civil cases and juvenile cases.

COURT OF CRIMINAL APPEALS
(1 Court -- 9 Judges)

-- Statewide Jurisdiction --
- Final appellate jurisdiction in criminal cases.

State Highest Appellate Courts

Civil Appeals

Criminal Appeals

Cases in Which Death Penalty Has Been Assessed

COURTS OF APPEALS
(14 Courts -- 80 Justices)

-- Regional Jurisdiction --
- Intermediate appeals from trial courts in their respective courts of appeals districts.

State Intermediate Appellate Courts

DISTRICT COURTS
(396 Courts -- 396 Judges)

(Established in 396 Districts Containing One or More Counties)
-- Jurisdiction --
- Original jurisdiction in civil actions over $200, divorce, title to land, contested elections, and contested probate matters.
- Original jurisdiction in felony criminal matters.
- Juvenile matters.
- 10 District Courts are named Criminal District Courts; others are directed to give preference to certain specialized areas.

State Trial Courts of General and Special Jurisdiction

COUNTY-LEVEL COURTS
(448 Courts -- 448 Judges)

Constitutional County Courts (254)	County Courts at Law (175)	Probate Courts (19)
(One Court in Each County)	*(Established in 71 Counties)*	*(Established in 8 Counties)*
-- Jurisdiction --	-- Jurisdiction --	-- Jurisdiction --
• Original jurisdiction in civil actions between $200 and $5,000.	• Limited jurisdiction over civil matters, most under $100,000.	• Limited primarily to probate matters.
• Probate (contested matters transferred to District Court.)	• Limited jurisdiction over misdemeanor criminal matters.	
• Exclusive original jurisdiction over misdemeanors with fines greater than $500 or jail sentence.	• Appeals *de novo* from lower courts or on the record from municipal courts of record.	
• Appeals *de novo* from lower courts or on the record from municipal courts of record.		

County Trial Courts of Limited Jurisdiction

MUNICIPAL COURTS[1]
(850 Cities -- 1,186 Judges)

-- Jurisdiction --
- Criminal misdemeanors with fine-only offenses with no confinement .
- Exclusive jurisdiction over municipal ordinance violations. (Fines up to $2,000.)
- Limited civil penalties in cases involving dangerous dogs.
- Magistrate functions.

JUSTICE OF THE PEACE COURTS[2]
(843 Courts -- 842 Judges)

(Established in Precincts Within Each County)
-- Jurisdiction --
- Civil actions under $5,000.
- Small Claims
- Criminal misdemeanors with fine-only offenses.
- Magistrate functions.

Local Trial Courts of Limited Jurisdiction

[1] Some Municipal Courts are courts of record—appeals from those courts are taken on the record to the county-level courts.

[2] All Justice of the Peace Courts and most Municipal Courts are not courts of record. Appeals from these courts are by trial *de novo* in the county-level courts, and in some instances in the district courts.

Justice Courts

Justice of the peace courts, also referred to as justice courts, have jurisdiction within precincts, which are specific geographical areas within a county. Precincts are created based on the population of the county. Each county with a population of 30,000 or more is divided into as many as eight, but not fewer than four precincts. Each precinct has one justice of the peace who serves a term of four years. Currently, more than 60 justice courts share concurrent jurisdiction with county courts. In 1998 there were 843 justice of the peace courts.

The justice courts have original jurisdiction over: (1) civil matters in which exclusive jurisdiction is not in the district or county courts and in which the controversy is not more than $5,000 (exclusive of court costs and interest); (2) cases of forcible entry and detainer (i.e., eviction of tenants from rental property); and (3) foreclosures of mortgages and enforcement of liens on personal property (V.T.C.A. Government Code § 27.031(b)).

Since 1953 justice courts have also served as small claims courts (Govt. Code §§ 28.001-002). Small claims courts provide forums in which common citizens, by filling a petition of basic facts, may represent themselves without hiring a lawyer (Govt. Code § 28.012). Judges in small claims courts have the authority to hear claims no greater than $5000 (exclusive of courts, costs and interests) (Govt. Code § 28.002).

In terms of criminal jurisdiction, justice courts have original jurisdiction in criminal cases: (1) punishable by fine only, and (2) punishable by a fine and/or a sanction (excluding imprisonment) that is rehabilitative or remedial in nature (Tex. Code Crim. Proc. art. 4.01). It is within the original jurisdiction of the justice courts to impose a penalty or sanction which results in the denial, suspension, or revocation of a privilege by another state agency (e.g., denial, suspension or revocation of a driver's license). Justices of the peace regularly preside over Class C misdemeanor violations (punishable by fines not exceeding $500) when such criminal acts are committed in unincorporated portions of counties or on state-owned property. Furthermore, justices of the peace act as magistrates who can issue both arrest and search warrants in felony and misde-meanor cases (Tex. Code Crim. Proc. art. 2.09). Notably, all judges in Texas have the authority to act as a magistrate. Finally, justices of the peace serve as coroners in counties that do not have medical examiners.

Municipal Courts

In 1998 there were 850 municipal courts in Texas. Larger cities often have more than one judge presiding over cases in the municipal courts. Though some municipal judges are elect-ed by the people, most are appointed by the governing body of the city.

Municipal courts have exclusive jurisdiction within the territorial limits of the municipality in all criminal cases that: (1) arise under the ordinances of the municipality, and (2) are punishable by a fine not to exceed $2,000, in all cases per-taining to public safety (e.g., fire safety, public health, sanita-tion) and $500 in all other cases (Govt. Code § 29.003(a)). Municipal courts have concurrent criminal jurisdiction with the justice courts if the municipality is located in the justice courts precinct. Like the justice courts, municipal courts have the authority to impose sanctions and penalties which are either rehabilitative or remedial (e.g., court-mandated coun-seling, community service, license revocation, etc.) (Govt. Code § 29.003(b)). One factor which distinguishes municipal courts from justice courts is that municipal courts have final judgment in setting bail bonds and personal bonds within its criminal jurisdiction (Govt. Code § 29.005(e)).

The judge of a municipal court serves a term of two years unless the municipality provides for a longer term. The laws of Texas do not prevent a justice of the peace from holding, at the same time, the office of part-time municipal judge for a city located with the same precinct (Op. Atty. Gen. JM-422 (1986)).

Appeals

The process of appealing a decision from an inferior court depends on whether the court is a court of record (i.e., courts where its proceedings are transcribed by an official court reporter). The justice courts are not courts of record, thus all appeals from them to the county level courts (or in some instances the district courts) are *de novo* proceedings (i.e., they are completely tried again). Critics have claimed that trials *de novo* encourage appeals, causing huge backlogs of cases. Alleviating backlogs often requires massive dismissals and plea bargains based on expediency rather than the merits of the case. Though most municipal courts are not courts of record, the number of municipal courts of record, created by statute, are growing in number. Appeals from these courts are not *de novo*; rather they are based solely on errors of law shown in the written record of the municipal proceedings (Govt Code §§ 30.11-30.278).

County Level Courts of Limited Jurisdiction

County Courts (Constitutional)

Each of the state's 254 counties has a constitutional county court. In addition to their jurisdiction over appeals from the inferior courts, the constitutional county courts have their own criminal, probate, and civil jurisdiction.

In terms of criminal jurisdiction, the county courts have original jurisdiction of all misdemeanors which are punishable by fines greater than $500 (i.e., Class A and Class B misdemeanors) (Govt Code § 26.045(a)). As you may recall from Chapter 2, a Class A misdemeanor is punishable by: (1) a fine not to exceed $4,000; (2) confinement in jail not to exceed one year; or (3) both a fine and confinement. Examples include public lewdness, nonaggravated assault, criminal nonsupport of a child, theft between $50 and $200, and burglary of a coin-operated vending machine. A Class B misdemeanor is punishable by: (1) a fine not to exceed $2,000; (2) confinement in jail for a term not to exceed 180 days; or (3) both a fine and confinement. Examples include driving while intoxicated and making false reports to police officers. Constitutional county courts also have jurisdiction to enter final judgment in the forfeiture of bonds and recognizance when criminal defendants "jump bail" (Govt. Code § 26.045). It should be noted, however, that if a constitutional county court is located in a county that has a criminal district court, then that constitutional county court has no criminal jurisdiction whatsoever.

Constitutional county courts have jurisdiction to enter final judgment in the forfeiture of bonds and recognizance when criminal defendants "jump bail" (Govt. Code § 26.045). County courts may also have jurisdiction of juvenile matters and may be designated a juvenile court by the legislature (Govt. Code §§ 23.001 & 26.042).

County Courts at Law (Statutory)

In 1998 there were 175 county courts at law in Texas. Unlike the constitutional county courts, which are created by the state constitution and cannot be eliminated by the legislature, statutory county courts are created by the legislature under constitutional authority (Govt. Code § 21.008). Statutory county courts are created primarily to reduce the caseload of constitutional county courts in heavily populated counties. In at least 74 counties the constitutional county court's judicial duties have, in whole or part, been given to statutory county courts. A statutory court exercising concurrent civil jurisdiction with a constitutional county court may hear disputes where the amount in controversy is between $200 and $100,000 (exclusive of interest, damages, and court costs) (Govt. Code § 25.0003). The criminal, civil, probate and family-law jurisdiction of these courts varies from county to county. Some exercise jurisdiction typically reserved for the district courts, while others have jurisdiction concurrent with the justice courts. Each statutory county court at law has one judge who is elected to a four-year term.

Appeals

County courts have appellate jurisdiction over criminal and civil appeals from judgments rendered in justice and municipal courts (Govt. Code §§ 26.043, 26.046). While criminal convictions of Class C misdemeanors rendered in the inferior courts may be appealed to the county court for trial *de novo*, subsequent convictions at the county level cannot be appealed unless: (1) the fine is in excess of $100 (exclusive of court costs) or (2) the sole issue on appeal is the constitutionality of the statute or ordinance on which the conviction is based (Tex. Code of Crim. Proc. art. 4.03). Civil appeals from a judgment in a county court may be appealed to the Court of Appeals when the amount in controversy exceeds $100 (exclusive of costs and interest) (Govt. Code § 22.220(a)).

State Trial Courts of General and Special Jurisdiction

The jurisdiction of the constitutional district courts is provided by Article V, § 8, of the Texas Constitution (Govt. Code § 24.007). As the trial courts of general jurisdiction in law and equity, district courts serve as the primary trial venue for the most serious criminal and civil cases. A constitutional district court's jurisdiction cannot be reduced by the legislature. However, just as it may create statutory county courts, the legislature has the authority to establish specialized district courts (Tex. Const. Art. V, § 1).

Constitutional District Courts

Constitutional district courts generally exercise jurisdiction over criminal, civil, and family-law cases, except in metropolitan areas where cases are sorted by their subject matter.

In terms of criminal jurisdiction, constitutional district courts have original jurisdiction in all criminal cases of the grade of felony (i.e., punishable by fine, imprisonment, or death). The various degrees of felonies are detailed in Chapter 2. In addition to felonies, district courts have jurisdiction over all misdemeanors involving "official misconduct" (i.e., any intentional violation of law committed by a public servant while acting in an official capacity) (Tex. Code Crim. Proc., Art 3.04 & 4.05).

In civil matters in which the controverted amount exceeds $500 (not including court costs and interests), district courts

Nationally, Texas is known for the grand architecture of some of its older courthouses. The Denton County Courthouse (pictured above) was built for $179,000 in 1897.

(Courtesy of Stephanie Becan)

In 1998 Denton County opened a new courthouse for $18 million.

(Courtesy of Stephanie Becan)

have exclusive original jurisdiction in: (1) all suits on behalf of the state to recover a penalty or forfeiture from a citizen, (2) cases of divorce, (3) suits for slander or defamation of character (i.e., spoken or written words which injure one's public reputation), (4) disputed land titles and liens, and (5) cases where election results are contested (Govt. Code § 24.007). In relation to the other trial courts, district courts exercise concurrent jurisdiction with constitutional county courts (controversies $200-$5,000) and statutory county courts (controversies $200-$100,000). There is no statutory maximum on the dollar amount which may be sought at the district court level.

Specialized District Courts

Similar to statutory county courts, specialized district courts exist in densely populated urban areas and exercise limited jurisdiction over specific subject matter. In 1998 there were 10 district courts which exclusively dealt with criminal matters. Other specialized district courts deal with family and juvenile matters. In 1977 all existing domestic relations courts and juvenile courts were renamed family district courts. Family district courts have primary responsibility for hearing cases which include, but are not limited to, birth and adoption records, divorce and marriage annulments, child welfare and custody, child support, parent-child relations, and husband-wife relations (Govt. Code § 24.601). In areas that do not have specialized family courts (less populated areas), family law cases are heard by constitutional district courts (Govt. Code § 24.601(c)).

Judicial Districts

The Texas Constitution divides the state into geographic regions known as judicial districts (Tex. Const. Art. V, § 7). Each judicial district contains at least one district court whose jurisdiction is limited to that territory. There is no constitutional requirement, as in the case of county courts, that there be a district court for each county. Accordingly, judicial districts which are sparsely populated may entail more than one county. In such cases, the district judge travels from county seat to county seat. This practice has come to be known as "riding the circuit." In contrast, highly populated counties such as Dallas and Harris have in excess of 30 district courts. Despite such disparity, the geographic area of the average judicial district is one county. Each court has one judge, who serves a four-year term.

State Intermediate Appellate Courts

Texas has only one level of intermediate appellate courts, the Texas Courts of Appeals. Each court of appeals has intermediate appellate jurisdiction in both civil and criminal cases appealed from the district or county court level. (The only exception being appeals in death penalty cases, which go directly to the Texas Court of Criminal Appeals.) There are 14 courts of appeals located throughout the state. With the exception of Houston, which has two separate courts of appeals, the remaining twelve are located in Fort Worth, Austin, San Antonio, Dallas, Texarkana, Amarillo, El Paso, Beaumont, Waco, Eastland, Tyler, and Corpus Christi (Govt. Code §§ 22.202-22.215). Each court is presided over by a chief justice and at least two associate justices. The specific number of justices on a particular court of appeals ranges from three to thirteen and is determined by statute. Presently there are 80 justices serving the courts of appeals. Most appeals are heard by a panel of three justices, unless an *en banc* hearing is ordered, in which instance all justices of that particular court of appeals consider the case (Govt. Code §§ 22.222-22.223). Cases are heard *en banc* when the issues involved are unusually novel and the outcome of the case is anticipated to have significant impact on the law or citizenry of the state.

Writ Power

The appellate courts have authority to issue writs of mandamus and writs of habeas corpus as necessary to enforce their jurisdiction (Govt. Code § 22.221(a)). A writ of mandamus is a court order which requires a public official or corporation to act in a specific manner to ensure compliance with the law. Each court of appeals may issue writs of mandamus against a district or county judge within its district to ensure compliance with state law (Govt. Code § 22.221). A writ of habeas corpus challenges the legality of an individual's detention. While the concept of detention may evoke images of criminal proceedings, one should remember that individuals can also be detained in civil proceedings for committing criminal acts such as perjury and/or contempt (Govt. Code § 22.002). Concurrent with the Court of Criminal Appeals and the Supreme Court, all courts of appeals have the authority to issue writs of habeas corpus when lower courts improperly detain a citizen for violating an order, judgment, or decree. Such detention can occur in divorce, child support, and child custody cases. Pending an application for habeas corpus, the courts of appeals may order lower courts to grant bail to criminal defendants who were either denied bail or received bail set at an excessive amount (Govt. Code § 22.221).

Civil Cases

Appeals may be heard in civil cases in which the amount in controversy exceeds $100 (Govt. Code § 22.220). The courts of appeals have final judgment in resolving municipal and county election contests, appeals from most interlocutory orders, and appeals from temporary injunctions (Govt. Code § 22.225).

Scope of Review

While in limited instances the courts of appeals may examine disputed factual contentions (i.e., questions of fact), the scope of appellate review is generally limited to disputed legal contentions (i.e., questions of law). To appeal any issue it must be raised at the trial level and "preserved on the record" (officially noted by the judge or court reporter). While questions of law may be further appealed, to the highest appellate courts (i.e., Texas Supreme Court and Texas Court of Criminal Appeals), the intermediate appellate courts have final determination of most questions of fact (Govt. Code § 22.225).

Courts of Last Resort: The High Courts

Members of the Court of Criminal Appeals and Supreme Court are each elected in statewide elections for overlapping six-year terms. The Court of Criminal Appeals is composed of one presiding judge and eight judges. The Supreme Court is composed of one chief justice and eight justices. Notice that while the number of members on each court is the same, their judicial titles are different (i.e., the Supreme Court has "justices" presiding, while the Court of Criminal Appeals has "judges"). When vacancies occur in either court, the governor appoints court members with the advice and consent of the senate.

Ultimately, on appeal, it is the goal of the petitioner/ appellant (the party seeking a reversal or modification of the trial court's decision) to obtain a writ of error. A writ of error is issued from a court of appellate jurisdiction ordering the lower court to remedy an error which was incorporated into its final judgment. A writ of error may order that the lower court's judgment be reversed, corrected, or affirmed. The party opposing the petitioner is referred to as the respondent/appellee.

Texas Court of Criminal Appeals

Decisions of the courts of appeals in criminal cases may be appealed to the Court of Criminal Appeals by petition for discretionary review (PDR) filed by the defendant, state, or both. Review may be denied without explanation. The court may also review decisions on its own motion. As the highest criminal court in the state, it holds final appellate jurisdiction in most criminal cases (the exception being those appealed from an inferior court to a county court at law with an imposed fine which does not exceed $100, in which the only appeal is the United States Supreme Court).

Determinations of cases by the Court of Criminal Appeals are final unless they involve a question of federal constitutional law. In such instance, the case enters the federal court system. There are no appeals from the Texas Court of Criminal Appeals to the Texas Supreme Court.

Besides reviewing appeals from the intermediate courts, the Court of Criminal Appeals has three primary additional duties. First, it is responsible for hearing direct appeals of death penalty convictions and denials of bail from the trial court level. In such cases, the court has the power to issue writs of habeas corpus and mandamus to ensure that the law is properly carried out by the lower courts. Second, along with the Supreme Court, the Court of Criminal Appeals has jurisdiction to answer questions of state law certified from a federal appellate court issued when the federal courts seek guidance in interpreting Texas law. And third, the legislature has authorized the Court of Criminal Appeals to create rules of evidence and criminal procedure. Such rules govern the proceedings of the lower criminal courts.

Supreme Court of Texas

As the highest civil court in the state, the Supreme Court of Texas has final appellate jurisdiction in most civil and juvenile cases. (Juvenile justice is discussed in Chapter 9.) The Supreme Court has discretionary appellate jurisdiction in five instances: (1) if a dissenting opinion is filed in the court of appeals; (2) where the courts of appeals issue conflicting opinions; (3) where the construction or constitutional validity of a statute is involved; (4) where state revenue is involved; and (5) where the Railroad Commission is a party. The Supreme Court has discretionary appellate jurisdiction in civil cases in which: (1) an error of law has been committed by the court of appeals; (2) the error is of such importance to the jurisprudence of the state that in the opinion of the Supreme Court it requires correction; and (3) the decision of the court of appeals is not made final by statute (Govt. Code § 22.001).

To ensure the effective administration of justice in Texas, the legislature has assigned five primary administrative duties to the Supreme Court. First, the court is responsible for creating all rules of evidence and procedure in civil proceedings. Second, the court is responsible for creating rules of judicial conduct which regulate the conduct and performance of all members of the Texas judiciary. Such rules are enforced by the Commission on Judicial Conduct (Govt. Code § 33.001). Third, the court has statutory authority to supervise the State Bar of Texas, a quasi-public agency which governs all licensed attorneys. The court assists the State Bar in promulgating rules for admission, discipline, and disbarment of attorneys, as well as standards for accrediting law schools in the state. Fourth, the court creates the rules of operation for the Court Reporters Certification Board. Court reporters are sworn public officers who record and transcribe court proceedings and depositions. Finally, the court is responsible for assessing the need for adding, consolidating, eliminating, or reallocating existing appellate courts and recommending such changes to the legislature.

Built in 1951, the Supreme Court Building located on the northwest grounds of the State Capitol is home not only to the state's highest civil court, but also to the court of last resort in criminal matters—the Texas Court of Criminal Appeals.

(Courtesy of authors)

PART 3:
THE TEXAS JUDICIARY

The early days of Lone Star justice have come to be a great source of nostalgia. Men like Judge Roy Bean have come to immortalize the rugged individualism that many Americans associate with Texas. Undoubtedly, the actions of Judge Roy Bean, the only "Law West of the Pecos," are worthy of the mythology and Texas folklore. Reportedly, Bean once found a dead man with $40 in gold and a pistol in the corpse's pockets. He fined the corpse $40 for carrying a concealed weapon and pocketed the money. Before announcing

Judge Roy Bean
(From Rose Collection,
University of Oklahoma Library)

Judge Roy Bean, Law West of the Pecos, mounted on horse in front of the Lily Langtry Courthouse and Saloon.
(Courtesy of Western History Collections,
University of Oklahoma)

that court was in session, Bean would "suggest" that everyone buy "a good snort" to liven up the proceedings. While Bean may have been a proponent of gun laws and a persuasive proprietor of whiskey, matrimony was another matter entirely. His wedding ceremonies were somber affairs in which after rushing through the rites he would stare at the groom and announce: "May God have mercy on your soul," a comment traditionally reserved for those sentenced to death (*Handbook of Texas* at 288-289).

As the population of the state has shifted from rural to urban communities, the law has supposedly overshadowed the men who administer it (Interpretative Commentary to Tex. Const. Art. V, § 19). Perhaps this is true to a degree. There are certainly no judges in Texas whose antics measure up to those of Judge Roy Bean. However, to say that the "law" has overshadowed the people who operate the Texas judicial system is debatable in light of the fact that the law of Texas prescribes, for the most part, an elected judiciary. Endowed with human flaws, and with their jobs on the line in any given election year, judges' decisions are inherently based on their personal and institutional biases as well as political considerations. As a group, Texas judges may be more impartial and less political than legislators and governors, but for better or worse they are political beings. As acknowledged by one Texas judge, "This job is more politics than law, there's no two ways about it. Hell, you can have all kinds of dandy ideas, but if you don't get yourself elected, you can sell your ideas on a corner somewhere. Politics is not a dirty word in my mouth" (Kraemer & Newell at 301).

For most of the state's history the Democratic Party has dominated the Texas judiciary. It was not until the 1980s that the Republican Party in Texas emerged as a contending political force to be reckoned with. Straight ticket voting has in recent years swept incumbent Democratic judges from their benches. Benefiting from the immense popularity of Governor George W. Bush, the Republican Party swept all statewide elections in 1998. As of 1999, Republican judges exclusively make up the Texas Supreme Court and the Texas Court of Criminal Appeals.

While most judicial races do not entail as much media attention or fundraising as other state elected offices, one would be mistaken to think that the Texas judiciary has not been tainted by its share of political scandals. Most notably, in 1976 Donald B. Yarbrough, a Houston attorney with no political experience, ran for associate justice of the Texas Supreme Court, and handily defeated respected jurist Charles Barrow. Thousands of Texans voted for Yarbrough, thinking

By Ben Sargent
(copyright 1976; used by permission)

that he was either former Senator Ralph Yarborough or Don Yarbrough, a Democrat who ran for governor in 1962. Imagine the surprise when it was discovered that Yarbrough was a defendant in 16 civil suits on charges of fraud, negligence, and failure to repay debts. Yarbrough resigned during impeachment proceedings, was convicted for aggravated perjury, and sentenced to prison. In 1981, while his case was on appeal and he was free on bail, Yarbrough fled the United States to the Caribbean island of Grenada and enrolled in medical school. He was eventually extradited and returned to Texas, where he received an additional seven years in the penitentiary.

The Yarbrough scandal has been used by critics of the Texas elected judiciary to illustrate that popularity does not necessarily correlate with qualifications. Despite proposals to "reform" the judiciary (via selection by a non-partisan process), all measures have been quashed, including a proposed 1974 amendment to the constitution which was rejected by Texas voters.

Qualifications

The qualifications required of candidates for the state's judiciary increases with the level of the court. Although justices of the peace are required to take a course on legal fundamentals, there are no specific statutory or constitutional requirements for being elected to office. In fact, in 1994, only 5% of the state's 885 justices of the peace were lawyers. In the past, practices such as basing a portion of the justices' salary on a percentage of fines levied have tarnished the court's image. Additionally, legal scholars have criticized the practice of having judges untrained in the law presiding over potentially complex legal problems. Other commentators, however, believe that judicial reform, such as mandatory training and increasing the scope of the justice court's small claims function, have attracted more qualified lawyers to seek this office.

The qualifications of municipal judges vary, except that all statutorily created municipal courts of record require that judges be licensed to practice law in Texas. Also, many municipalities have passed ordinances that require candidates for municipal judge to have two to five years' experience practicing law or serving in the judiciary. In recent years, municipal courts have been criticized for the informality of their proceedings (e.g., judges seldom wear robes, patrons do not have to rise when the judge enters the courtroom, bailiffs often participate in taking pleas). Critics claim that though such informal court proceedings may expedite the processing of cases, important constitutional rights are potentially hampered by the confusion concerning general courtroom procedure.

Judges of the constitutional county courts are constitutionally required to be "well informed in the law of the state" (Tex. Const. Art. V, § 15). This does not mean, however, that candidates must have a license to practice law or have attended law school. In fact, about 85% of constitutional county judges are not lawyers. In contrast, statutory county judges must be licensed to practice law in Texas, have at least four years' experience as a lawyer, and be at least 25 years old.

Candidates for district court judge must be at least 25 years of age, a practicing attorney or judge of a Texas court for

Justices Ward, Henenberg, and Brazzil in the all-woman Texas Supreme Court, 1925.

at least four years, and a resident of the district in which he or she is elected for at least two years prior to election (Tex. Const. Art. V, § 7; Govt. Code § 24.001).

All judges and justices in the appellate courts must be at least 25 years old and have been a practicing lawyer or a judge for a court of record for at least 10 years (Tex. Const. Art. V, §§ 2, 6; Govt. Code § 22.228). Currently, both the Texas Court of Criminal Appeals and the Texas Supreme Court are composed of six men and three women.

While high courts across the United States have historically been dominated by men, it is a little known fact that in one instance in 1925 the Texas Supreme Court was composed entirely of women. The incident occurred when all sitting justices found themselves legally disqualified to hear a case before them on appeal from El Paso County. After certifying their disqualifications to Governor Pat Neff, the governor appointed Hortense Ward of Houston as special chief justice and Hattie L. Henenberg of Dallas and Ruth Brazzil of Galveston as special associate justices to hear and determine the case of *W. T. Johnson et al. v. J. M. Darr, et al.* The three special justices were sworn in 8 January 1925. The case was decided on 23 May 1925, affirming the judgment of the intermediate court of appeals.

Oversight and Regulation
of the Texas Judiciary

In 1965 the constitution was amended to mandate the retirement of all members of the judiciary at age 75. Though it has yet to exercise its authority, the legislature has the discretion to lower the mandatory retirement age to 70. The Commission on Judicial Conduct (composed of five judges from all levels, two lawyers, and four citizens) has the legal authority to discipline and/or remove members of the judiciary for incompetence, willful violation of the Code of Judicial Conduct, or for conduct which clearly suggests impropriety and discredits the judiciary or the administration of justice. A judge may be removed or involuntarily retired for permanent disabilities that interfere with the performance of his or her duties (Govt. Code § 33.001).

WORKS CONSULTED AND SUGGESTIONS
FOR FURTHER READING

(Note: Unless otherwise stated, all statutory citations noted (Govt. Code) in this chapter are from the Texas Government Code.)

Jones, Eugene, et al. *Practicing Texas Politics*. 3rd ed. Geneva, New York: Houghton Mifflin, 1977.

Kane, Joseph. *Famous First Facts*. 3rd. ed. New York: H. W. Wilson, 1964.

Kramer, Richard, and Charldean Newell. *Texas Politics*. 4th ed. St. Paul, Minnesota: West, 1990.

Lucko, Paul. "Texas Court of Criminal Appeals." *The New Handbook of Texas*, vol. 6. Austin, Texas: Texas State Historical Association, 1996, pp. 312-313.

Schulze, Enika, P. Michael Jung, and Rebecca Adams. *Texas Courts*. 4th ed. Dallas, Texas: Pearson, 1996.

Sonnichsen, C. L. *The Handbook of Texas*, vol. 1. Austin, Texas: Texas State Historical Association, 1952, pp. 129-130.

Womack, Paul. "Judiciary." *The New Handbook of Texas*, vol. 3. Austin, Texas: Texas State Historical Association, 1996, pp. 1012-1014.

5.
TEXAS CRIMINAL PROCEDURE: FROM ARREST TO APPEAL

OVERVIEW

In contrast to the Texas Penal Code, which defines crimes and prescribes punishments, the Texas Code of Criminal Procedure provides the rules which regulate how the government goes about enforcing the criminal law. In countries such as the United States, which put a premium on individual rights (e.g., the right to privacy), enforcing the law is no simple task. The United States Constitution's Bill of Rights, the Texas Constitution, and laws passed by the Texas Legislature impose strict limitations on the government that are designed to protect the individual rights of all citizens (detailed in Chapter 2). As a consequence of the concern for such rights, the task of actors in the criminal justice system (police officers, prosecutors, defense attorneys, judges, juries, and correctional officers) is often complicated because they are duty-bound to enforce the law, but without violating the law protecting individual rights. While the scope of this text precludes addressing the entire array of issues pertaining to Texas criminal procedure, this chapter will provide a detailed foundation of the subject matter.

Our discussion begins with an analysis of arrest. Though arrest is the formal beginning point at which criminal procedure comes into play, it is worth noting that arrest is actually the second step in the criminal process. Usually, detection and investigation occur before arrests are made. With the assistance of citizens, law enforcement agencies control the detection and investigative stage of the criminal process. A pre-arrest investigation may be general in that it does not focus on a specific suspect. However, when an investigation shifts its focus on to a specific suspect(s), the process enters the accusatory stage. It is at this point that an arrest may occur and individual rights may impose greater limits on the actions of the police.

PART 1:
PROCEDURE PRIOR TO TRIAL

Arrest

Would you know if you were "arrested"? Despite the common notion of the average citizen, there has been great controversy over just what constitutes an arrest. In Texas, courts examine the nature of the detention (*Amores v. State*, 816 S.W.2d 407 (Tex. Crim. App. 1991)). If a peace officer has a reasonable, articulable suspicion that you are connected with criminal activity, you may be detained for a reasonable period of time so that an inquiry may be made. Such investigatory "stops" do not necessarily constitute an arrest; rather, they are merely for the gathering of potential information. However, if subsequent to the stop the officer through reasonable deduction believes he has probable cause (sufficient evidence to believe that you have committed or are committing a criminal act) you may be placed under arrest. Probable cause is the quantum of proof required by the Fourth Amendment for arrest.

In Texas, courts review the officer's determination of probable cause to arrest or search without a warrant by applying the "totality of the circumstances" test. Under the test, the burden is on the State to establish that:

- facts and circumstances within the officer's knowledge
- of which the officer has reasonably trustworthy information
- are sufficient in themselves to warrant a person of reasonable caution
- in the belief that a particular person has committed or is committing an offense.

Determination of probable cause by the police officer, however, does not mark the precise moment that an individual is under arrest. A person is arrested when "actually placed under restraint" (CCP art. 15.22). As you can imagine, the actual point in time that an arrest has occurred can be a source of controversy. The circumstances of the case are almost always determinative. Thus, courts have construed an arrest to have occurred:

- when a person is handcuffed (*Johnson v. State*, 722 S.W.2d 417, 419 (Tex. Crim. App. 1986)).
- when a person is taken into custody legally or physically under the control of law enforcement (*McCrory v. State*, 643 S.W.2d 725, 726 n.3 (Tex. Crim. App. 1982)).
- when a person's liberty or movement is substantially or significantly restricted or restrained (*Amores v. State*, supra)
- when a person is not physically detained, but reasonably believes that he or she is not free to leave (*United States v. Mendenhall*, 446 U.S. 544, 554 (1980)).

Arrest with a Warrant

Generally, an arrest in Texas without a warrant is considered to be unreasonable unless a statutory exception to the general warrant requirement is applicable. Consequently, failure to obtain an arrest warrant when no statutory exception exists invalidates the arrest and precludes prosecution (regardless of the fact that blatant probable cause may have existed).

An arrest warrant is a written order from a magistrate to a peace officer ordering that a specific person accused of an offense be taken into custody and dealt with as prescribed by law (CCP art. 15.01). A warrant is issued by a magistrate after being provided sufficient information in the form of an affidavit (also known as a complaint). In order to be sufficient an affidavit must:

- state the name of the accused, if known, and if not, it must give some reasonably definite description of the accused
- show that the accused has committed some offense against the laws of the State and that the affiant (the individual swearing to the affidavit) has direct knowledge or a good reason to believe that the accused has committed the offense

PROCESS OF A FELONY OFFENSE IN TEXAS

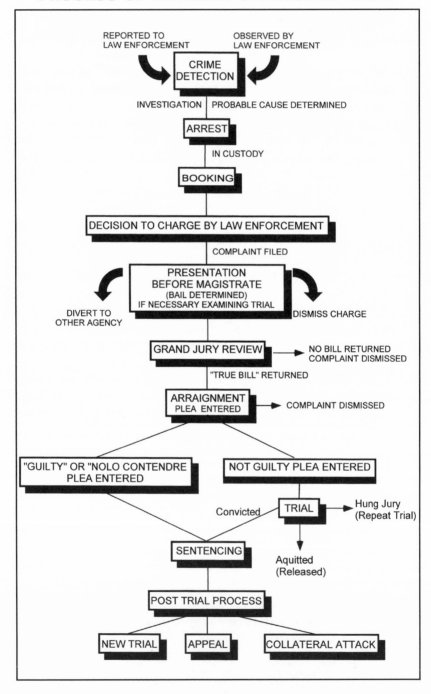

- state as definitely as possible the time and place of the commission of the offense
- contain the signature, name, or mark of the affiant (the person attesting to the truth of the information) (CCP art. 15.05).

For an arrest warrant to be valid it is critical that the basis for probable cause be stated within the four corners of the affidavit (the "four corners" rule). This means that the State cannot justify an arrest made under a warrant containing insufficient information by claiming that the police orally gave the magistrate additional information that amounted to probable cause. Failure to comply with the "four corners" rule can result in the invalidation of an arrest (*Jones v. State*, 568 S.W.2d 847, 855 (Tex. Crim. App [en banc] 1978)).

Execution of Arrest

Generally, Texas courts are reluctant to suppress evidence based on technical failures to comply with the warrant and arrest requirements (e.g., typos in the warrant, the failure of a police officer to knock on the door before entering the accused's premises). However, the manner in which the arrest is executed, with or without an arrest warrant, can result in the evidence not being admissible at trial. Under the "fruit of the poisonous tree doctrine," all evidence derived from illegally obtained evidence is deemed tainted, and thus inadmissible at trial. Though no statute specifically addresses the execution of arrest, the Texas Court of Criminal Appeals has invalidated arrests when based on warrants which failed to adequately describe "unknown" individuals (e.g., general descriptions such as two black females will not suffice) (*Visor v. State*, 660 S.W.2d 816 (Tex. Crim. App. 1983)).

To remedy situations where facial defects in a warrant (such as inadequate descriptions of suspects) have invalidated arrests and resulted in the exclusion of evidence, the legislature in 1987 adopted the "good faith" rule which allows "evidence obtained in good faith reliance upon a warrant issued by a neutral magistrate based on probable cause" to be used at trial against the accused in a criminal case (CCP art. 38.23).

With weapons drawn and the suspect surrounded, there is little doubt that the passengers in this airplane knew they were under arrest.

(Courtesy of TDPS)

Arrests Without a Warrant

Despite the State's preference that warrants be procured before an arrest is executed, warrantless arrests are commonplace in Texas. In contrast to the federal constitution which allows warrantless arrests to be made in public places (regardless of how easily a warrant could have been obtained), a warrantless arrest in Texas must fall within narrower statutory exceptions (*United States v. Watson,* 423 U.S. 411 (1976); *Dejarnette v. State*, 732 S.W.2d 346, 349 (Tex. Crim. App. 1987)).

OFFENSES WITHIN VIEW—When an offense, regardless of its penal classification, is committed "in the presence" or "within the view" of a peace officer an arrest may be made without a warrant (CCP art. 14.01(b)). The "within view" rule also applies to bonded peace officers even when they are outside of their jurisdiction, as long as the offense is either a felony or an act of disorderly conduct (CCP art. 14.03(d)). Similarly, ordinary citizens may make arrests upon witnessing a felony or disorderly conduct (CCP art 14.01(a)). Additionally, all persons have the right to make a citizen's arrest to prevent the theft of personal property (CCP art. 18.16).

PEACE OFFICER AUTHORITY—In order to protect and serve the public, peace officers, subject to probable cause, have statutory authority to make warrantless arrests when persons whom they did not see commit a crime are:

- found in "suspicious places" and are reasonably believed to have committed a felony or to have engaged in disorderly conduct
- believed to have committed assault and thought to pose a continuing threat to the victim
- believed to have violated a court protective order
- believed to have committed an act of domestic violence (CCP art. 14.03).

Additionally, when a felony has been committed a peace officer may pursue and arrest a person if:

- the person who reports the crime to the police officer is deemed to be credible
- the offense is a felony
- the offender is about to escape, and
- there is no time to procure a warrant (CCP art. 14.04).

Search and Seizure

With a Warrant

Like the requirement for an arrest warrant, a search warrant may not be issued unless an affidavit sets forth facts to establish probable cause:

- that a specific offense has been committed
- that specifically described items constitute evidence that a particular person committed an offense, and
- that the property or items which constitute evidence are located at a particular person, place, or thing to be searched (CCP art. 18.01).

Basically, search warrants may be issued to retrieve:

- *contraband*—legally prohibited items

- *fruits and instrumentalities of a crime*—tools used to effectuate a particular crime and the proceeds of the crime ("loot")
- *mere evidence*—proof that the suspect committed a particular crime, and
- *particular persons* (CCP art. 18.02; Reamey & Steele at 46).

A search warrant must be based upon an affidavit which shows probable cause to believe that one of the above items will be found at the specified location. As with an arrest warrant the sufficiency of the affidavit is critical. The information contained in the affidavit may be challenged in a pre-trial hearing known as a "Franks" hearing. In such a hearing the veracity of the affiant and the existence of probable cause are generally at issue (*Dancy v. State*, 728 S.W.2d 772 (Tex. Crim. App. 1987)). Just as the courts look to the four corners of an affidavit to determine if the issuance of an arrest warrant is proper, they similarly may examine the underlying merits of a search warrant.

Absent a showing of prejudice, Texas courts have been reluctant to use administrative errors to exclude evidence seized in otherwise proper searches. Accordingly, typos and administrative errors in the search warrant do not necessarily invalidate a search (*Pecina v. State*, 516 S.W.2d 401, 404 (Tex. Crim. App. 1974)). However, a warrant is invalid (*functus officio*) if not executed within three days from issuance (excluding day of issuance and day of execution unless the police can show good cause for not executing the search within three days of issuance) (CCP art. 18.06; *Gonzales v. State*, 768 S.W.2d. 436, 437 (Tex. App.-Houston [1st Dist.] 1989, no pet.)).

Without a Warrant

Just as there are statutory exceptions to the general arrest warrant requirement, there are also statutory exceptions to the general search warrant requirement. Many, if not most, searches are done without a warrant. A search without a warrant is permitted in the following three situations.

INCIDENT TO LAWFUL ARREST—If an officer properly arrests a suspect, the officer may search the area within the suspect's immediate control (i.e., all the areas within the suspect's immediate reach, commonly referred to as "wing span") (*Linnet v. State*, 647 S.W.2d 672 (Tex. Crim. App. 1983)). Before taking the suspect into custody for booking, such searches are conducted for the limited purposes of:

(1) protecting officers whom suspects may injure or kill, and
(2) preserving evidence the suspect may destroy (Samaha at 284).

VEHICLE INVENTORY—When a vehicle is either discovered abandoned or the owner is taken into custody, an inventory of the vehicle's contents (also known as an administrative search) may be conducted to protect the owner's property rights. Due to the administrative nature of such searches, vehicle inventories are not protected by the Fourth Amendment. However, to prevent abuse of such inventories, they must be necessary for the protection of the owner's property. If an inventory is not necessary to protect the owner's property, any incriminating discoveries may be held unlawful (*Benavides v. State*, 600 S.W.2d 809 (Tex. Crim. App. 1980)).

PLAIN VIEW SEARCHES—While protecting individual privacy often requires excluding evidence which is not *specifically* described in the search warrant, one narrow exception exists. Specifically, peace officers executing a proper search warrant may seize property within the "plain view" of the officer. Such "plain view" discoveries commonly occur when:

(1) law enforcement inadvertently discovers additional evidence of the crime contemplated in the warrant, and
(2) when law enforcement discovers mere evidence of other crimes not contemplated in issuance of the warrant.

While it is generally accepted that evidence which is contraband, fruits or instrumentalities of a crime, or mere evidence of the crime contemplated in the warrant may be lawfully seized, it is less clear as to whether items of mere evidence of a different crime not contemplated in the warrant may be taken. In interpreting the U.S. Supreme Court's discussion of the plain view exception, the Texas Court of Criminal Appeals set forth two conditions that must be met before the warrantless seizure is valid:

- the initial intrusion must be proper so that the police have the right to where they are, and
- it must be immediately apparent to the police that they have evidence of a crime before them (*White v. State*, 729 S.W.2d 737 (Tex. Crim. App. 1987)).

Seizure and Forfeiture of Contraband

In 1989 the Texas Legislature implemented provisions permitting the seizure and forfeiture of property related to various criminal offenses (CCP art. 59.02). Items that may be seized include property used, or intended to be used, in the

Every year law enforcement seizes millions of dollars in weapons and other valuable assets.   (Courtesy of TDPS)

commission of (1) major criminal offenses, and (2) drug offenses defined in the Controlled Substance Act. Consequently, in civil proceedings, separate from criminal proceeding, any property deemed to be the "proceeds," or "acquired" with proceeds from the stated classes of crimes, may be subject to seizure and forfeiture. Items obtained in forfeiture proceedings are generally used to supplement the resources of Texas criminal justice and law enforcement agencies.

Statements by the Suspect

Texas law has historically provided more restrictions regarding the admissibility of statements by the accused than the United States Constitution. While the Fifth Amendment and federal case law treat oral and written confessions similarly, Texas law has only in recent decades begun to admit oral statements. For most of the state's history, only written confessions have been admissible. Though a preference for written statements remains, legislative modifications in the Code of Criminal Procedure make it much easier for oral statements to be used against the accused in court.

Texas law distinguishes statements made by suspects who are not detained for custodial interrogation from those who are officially in custody. Oral statements made by individuals who are not in custody may be used if made "freely and without compulsion or persuasion" (CCP art. 38.21). In contrast, statements made by suspects who are in custody generally must be in writing. Miranda-like warnings must appear on the same page as the confession, the statement must be the exact statement of the accused, and the statement must be signed by the accused.

The Miranda warnings which must appear on the face of the statement are the warnings that peace officers are required to provide to a person they choose to question while in custody. Such Miranda warnings, which are named after the landmark United States Supreme Court decision of *Miranda v. Arizona* (384 U.S. 436 (1966)), are a no-frills crash course in constitutional law for the average citizen. One's Miranda rights are based on the Fifth Amendment right against self-incrimination. By the time most children reach adolescence they are likely to be familiar with Miranda. Consider how many times in television programs or films you have overheard the following:

- You have the right to remain silent and not make any statement at all;
- Any statement you make may be used against you as evidence at trial;
- You have the right to a lawyer present to advise you during any questioning;
- If you are unable to employ a lawyer, you have the right to have a lawyer, appointed to you prior, to and during any questioning;
- You have the right to terminate an interview at any time (CCP art. 38.22).

Under Texas law, regardless of whether a confession is an oral or written statement, to be admissible the statement cannot be induced by promises of benefit (e.g., "If you admit to the crime, I'll make sure the prosecutor goes easy on you") (*Hardesty v. State*, 667 S.W.2d 130 (Tex. Crim. App. 1984)). The voluntariness of the statement is of critical importance. Texas courts have gone so far as to rule that informing a suspect that any statement made can be used "for or against him" is inadmissible because it is a promise of a benefit, which as a matter of law makes the statement involuntary (*Dunn v. State*, 721 S.W.2d 325 (Tex. Crim. App. 1986)).

Though Texas law may appear to totally prohibit oral statements from being used against a suspect, it is important to recognize that the prohibition of oral statements is only *general*. Texas law contains what has been described by legal scholars as a "series of disorganized and somewhat confusing exceptions to the general rule." While the scope of this chapter prevents describing these exceptions in detail, the general categories of admissible oral statements include:

- audio or video taped confessions
- assertions by the accused which establish guilt and are proven to be true by other evidence

- statements which are not the product of a custodial interrogation
- *"res gestae"* statements (utterances made immediately and spontaneously upon arrest or during the commission of the crime)
- statements made at trial, before a grand jury or at an examining trial
- statements used to impeach the credibility of the defendant after he testifies at trial (CCP art. 38.22).

Booking

Booking is the clerical process by which the police make an administrative record of the suspect's arrest. A suspect is "booked" upon arriving at the police station, jail, or other detention facility. Ordinarily, the suspect's name, time of arrival and suspected offense are entered into an official record (commonly referred to as a "blotter" or "log"). Additionally, the suspect's fingerprints and photograph are taken. Afterward, the charges against the suspect are explained and the suspect is allowed to make a phone call.

When suspects are arrested for minor offenses, they may be able to secure their release on what is known as "station house bail" (either a small cash security payment or a promise to appear before a magistrate at a designated time). If they are arrested for a serious crime or are unable to post adequate security, they will be incarcerated until their initial appearance before a magistrate.

Before being placed in the "holding" cell the suspect is searched more thoroughly (this may entail being strip-searched). Though the suspect was searched upon arrest, the purpose of a second search is to make a personal inventory of the suspect's belongings, to prevent contraband from entering the holding cell unit, and to discover any evidence which may have eluded the arresting officer.

The Decision to Charge

Following booking, the police decide whether to send the case to the prosecutors for formal charging and possible trial. In making their decision the police may consider whether:

- proper procedures were followed in executing the arrest and/or search
- evidence was collected in a valid manner and properly preserved
- whether the police believe they have enough evidence to convict
- the suspect may be utilized as an informant (in exchange for reduced charges or foregoing charges entirely).

If it is decided that formal proceedings should be instigated, the responsibility to carry the criminal process forward is shifted from the police to prosecutors. Depending on the facts of the case the prosecutors will decide to:

- dismiss the case
- divert the case into some non-criminal justice agency, or
- charge the suspect with a specific crime.

If the prosecutor decides to charge the suspect, a complaint (or formal charging document) is filed with the magistrate. Upon filing, the arrested individual is no longer a mere suspect but a defendant, who though presumed innocent is formally charged with crimes. In misdemeanor cases the complaint (i.e., the ticket or citation) serves as the formal charging document to be used in all subsequent proceedings. In felony cases the complaint is merely the first charging document. As discussed later, upon being processed by a grand jury or a judge, the complaint will be replaced by an indictment or information.

Presentation Before the Magistrate

All arrested persons must be brought before a magistrate "without unnecessary delay" (CCP art. 14.06). Generally, the arrestee is brought before a magistrate in a matter of hours. However, when persons are arrested during a weekend or after the court's working hours, they may be detained without violating the statutory requirement of an appearance (*Hokr v.*

State 545 S.W.2d 463 (Tex. Crim. App. 1977)). Courts have been reluctant to use the "unnecessary delay" requirement to automatically invalidate otherwise proper confessions (*Boyd v. State*, 811 S.W.2d 105, 124-125 (Tex. Crim. App. 1991)).

Upon presentation to the magistrate, the accused is told specifically what law he is accused of violating. His Miranda rights are repeated to him for a second time. Additionally, if charged with a felony, the suspect is informed of his right to an examining trial. Examining trials must be held before the accused is indicted by a grand jury and are conducted by a magistrate. The purpose of the examining trial is to:

- determine if sufficient evidence of guilt justifies further criminal proceedings
- determine if bail should be allowed and if so, at what amount
- obtain the testimony of witnesses (*Harris v. State*, 457 S.W.2d 903 (Tex. Crim. App. 1970)).

Bail

Bail is the security given by the accused to assure the court that he will appear at the proper time and answer the charges which have been brought against him (CCP art. 17.01).

Determining the Amount

The amount of bail is generally determined when the suspect is initially brought before the magistrate. In setting bail the law requires that the courts:

- set bail at an amount that assures that the accused will appear before the court
- not set bail at an amount is so high that bail acts as an "instrument of oppression"
- consider the accused's financial resources in setting the amount of bail
- consider the accused's ties to the community (length of residence, length of employment, location of family, etc.) (CCP art. 17.15).

Securing a Bail Bond

In order to be released from detention, the accused must secure a bail bond. There are three forms of bonds (CCP arts. 17.01-17.08). A surety bond is the most common bail bond. If the accused can pay a non-refundable fee (generally 10%-20% of the amount of bail), a surety (or bondsperson) will write a bond that obligates them to pay the entire amount of bail if the accused fails to appear before the court. A personal bond is a bail bond which is obtained without a surety; in fact, no money is required. Rather, subject to the discretion of the court, the accused may be released on his own recognizance by signing a personal pledge to appear before the court as ordered. A cash bond is a bail bond involving money but involving no surety. Rather, the accused pays a percentage of the bail directly to the court. Upon the conclusion of the case, and if the accused makes all of his scheduled appearances before the court, the accused receives a full refund.

Conditions of Release

While at a minimum the accused's release is conditioned on his promise to appear before court at a designated time, courts have discretionary authority to impose other conditions. For example, if the accused is charged with a sexual offense against a minor younger than 12 years of age, bail may be conditioned on the accused having no contact with the particular child (or other children) (CCP art. 17.41). Additionally, courts may release the accused on personal bond upon the condition that he agree to submit to a home curfew and electronic monitoring (CCP art. 17.43).

Preventive Detention

In setting the amount of bail, courts are allowed to consider the future safety of the victim, the victim's family, and the safety of the community (CCP arts. 17.15 & 56.02). Texas is one of 32 states that statutorily allows preventive detention. Despite the fact that the U.S. Supreme Court has ruled that bail may not be used as a means of protecting public safety, it has not ruled whether such statutes are constitutionally impermissible. In Texas, even after bond is posted, the accused can be detained for 24 hours. Furthermore, upon the order of a court, custody can be extended an additional 20 hours.

Denial of Bail

Bail is not available to suspects of all crimes. Article 1, Section 11 of the Texas Constitution states that "all prisoners shall be bailable by sufficient sureties, unless for a capital offense, when the proof is evident." Additionally, Article 1, Section 11a provides district judges with discretion to deny bail to persons charged with non-capital offenses:

- if the suspect has previously been convicted twice of committing a felony and is seeking bail after being charged with a third felony offense
- while on bail for one felony, the accused seeks bail for another felony
- the accused has a prior felony conviction and is now seeking bail for a crime involving the use of a deadly weapon.

Grand Jury Review

While in some states formal felony charges are drafted and filed by state prosecuting attorneys, Texas formalizes felony charges through grand jury review. Historically, grand juries were organized at the local level to consider law enforcement allegations that specified individuals had committed particular crimes. To protect the grand jurors from undue criticism and harassment, meetings were conducted in secret. At the conclusion of the private meetings, the grand jurors would determine if sufficient grounds for prosecution existed. If it was determined that the state should proceed with a criminal prosecution, a "true bill" was issued. If it was determined that there were inadequate grounds for prosecution a "no-bill" was returned. Though some states have abandoned the process of grand jury review, it is required under the Constitution of the State of Texas. This is not to say that all felony prosecutions are the result of a grand jury indictment. Since 1971, Texas law has allowed felony defendants to waive their right to grand jury indictment for all felonious acts with the exception of capital offenses (CCP art. 1.141).

Waiver of Grand Jury

Defendants who opt out of their right to a grand jury hearing may be prosecuted by information, a written statement filed and presented in behalf of the State by the district or county attorney, charging the defendant with an offense (CCP art. 21.20). As the functional equivalent of a grand jury indictment, an information is the process by which the State prosecutes misdemeanors and is used by criminal defendants who wish to avoid the drawn out process of grand jury indictment. Accordingly, an information allows criminals who wish to plea bargain to accelerate the procedural process.

Composition of the Grand Jury

Grand juries are composed of 12 citizens who reside in the jurisdiction where the offense was committed. The grand jury may be selected by local commissioners who are appointed by local district judges or they may be chosen by random lottery (the latter being the less common of the selection methods). Regardless of what selection process is utilized, as a matter of law a grand juror must:

- be a citizen of the state and county
- be eligible to vote
- be of sound mind and good moral character
- be able to read and write
- not have been convicted of any felony
- not be under indictment or accused of theft or any other felony (CCP art. 19.23).

The only people who can be excused from grand jury service are persons over the age of 65, a person responsible for child care, a person attending an institution of higher learning, and any other person deemed by the court to have a "reasonable excuse" (CCP art. 19.25).

Assembly of the Grand Jury

Depending on the size of the county, the grand jury may meet once or several times a week, for a period of four to six months. Nine members of the grand jury must be present to conduct business. Regardless of the number of grand jurors present, a "true bill" requires nine affirmative votes. In proving sufficient evidence for prosecution, the prosecutor may call witnesses, and read both witnesses' statements and crime reports (CCP art. 20.21).

Unlike procedure at a trial, the accused may be compelled to testify by subpoena. The accused does not have the right to counsel during the hearing. He may, however, consult his attorney outside the grand jury room before answering any questions. Furthermore, he has the right to refuse to answer any question which may incriminate him. All testimony given before the grand jury is under oath and can be used against the accused in subsequent proceedings (CCP art. 20.17).

Dismissal or Indictment

After the prosecutor presents evidence, the grand jury deliberates outside the presence of prosecuting lawyers. If the grand jury returns a "no bill" the accused must, if no other charges are pending, be released from custody. If, on the other hand, a "true bill" is returned, the prosecutor prepares an indictment (a statement by the grand jury accusing a person of an act or omission which is a legal offense). Everything should be stated in the indictment which must be proven at trial (e.g., elements of the offense) (CCP art. 21.03). The indictment is then signed by the foreman of the grand jury, filed with the court clerk, and a copy is delivered to the accused which notifies him of his court date. If the defendant is not already in custody, the judge may issue a warrant for his or her arrest.

Arraignment

After indictment in all felony cases, and all misdemeanor cases punishable by imprisonment, there must be arraignment (CCP art. 26.01). If at the arraignment it is determined by the court that the defendant is indigent and in need of an attorney, the court appoints defense counsel (CCP art. 26.04). In 1995 attorneys were appointed to represent indigent defendants in 98,804 felony cases. While larger counties have public defender programs which provide counsel to indigent defendants, smaller counties appoint local lawyers who have general experience in criminal law. Court-appointed lawyer fees vary but are generally substantially less than the lawyer would normally charge.

Generally, after being provided counsel, the defendant is informed once more of the specific charges against him and asked how he wishes to plead to the indictment or information: either not guilty, nolo contendere, or guilty.

Not Guilty—A plea of not guilty contests the charges and challenges the State to prove them beyond a reasonable doubt. In capital punishment cases, a not guilty plea is mandatory (CCP art. 26.13).

Nolo Contendere—A plea of *nolo contendere* (no contest) allows the defendant to avoid contesting the State's charges. It has the same legal implications as a guilty plea (CCP art. 27.13).

Guilty—A plea of guilty is an admission by the defendant that the charges brought by the state are true. Approximately 97% of all felony convictions in Texas are the result of a guilty plea. By pleading guilty the defendant waives the right to have the State prove the charges against him. While there is no trial, the defendant may still opt to have a jury set punishment (CCP art. 26.14). Due to the significant consequences of waiving the right to trial, a judge must be convinced that a plea of guilty is made both "voluntarily and knowingly" before accepting a guilty plea (CCP art. 26.13).

Even though a guilty plea my expedite judicial proceedings, the State still has various obligations following the defendant's plea. For instance, the State must still present evidence which proves the defendant's guilt. This is often accomplished by means of a written confession that sets out the elements of the offense the State would have been obligated to prove at trial.

Additionally, the State must provide to the court a victim impact statement, describing how the defendant's actions have affected the life of the victim. The judge or jury in turn considers such information in sentencing the defendant.

Plea Bargaining—Often defendants plead guilty either because they have negotiated a plea with the State in return for reducing charges or lesser sentences, or because the case against them is so strong that they believe it is futile to contest it. Though plea bargains are often reached at arraignment, they can occur at an earlier or later stage of the criminal process. Plea bargains take various forms (any of which can be merged with one another):

- *Agreement not to file additional charges*: In cases involving multiple charges, the State may agree that in exchange for pleading guilty to more serious charges it will not prosecute less serious offenses.
- *Parole eligibility bargaining*—In cases involving multiple charges, the defendant agrees to plead guilty only to charges which would entitle them to earlier eligibility for parole.
- *Sentence Bargain*—The defendant pleads guilty in exchange for a specific sentence.

In accepting a guilty plea, the court may inquire if it is the result of a plea bargain. If it is, the court may refuse to accept the plea (in such instances, the court must allow the defendant the opportunity to withdraw his plea of guilty).

Pre-Trial Motions

A pre-trial motion is an order of the court that governs the conduct of the trial. Generally, pre-trial motions are requested by either the defense or prosecution to fix the scope of the trial (e.g., what evidence is admissible, what particular witnesses can testify about, what issues can be raised, what issues cannot be raised). Consequently, pre-trial motions often have great influence on the outcome of the trial. Pre-trial motions are used by the defense to request either a jury trial (case is decided by members of the defendant's community) or a bench trial (case is decided by a judge) (CCP arts. 1.13-1.15). Additionally, pre-trial motions are often made to:

- request additional time to prepare court documents and the case for trial (through a continuance) (CCP art. 28.01); additionally, in cases where the mental state of the defendant is in question, either the defense counsel, prosecutor, or judge may request that a mental health expert be appointed to determine if the defendant is competent for trial (CCP art. 46.02);
- suppress evidence from being used by the prosecution, the legal merits of which are debated in what has come to be known as a "Jackson v. Denno hearing" (named after the U.S. Supreme Court case which required the merits of questionable evidence to be appraised by the court) (CCP art. 28.01);
- change the venue of the trial due to the defendant's inability to receive a fair trial (such a motion is often used when a case receives so much negative press that finding an impartial jury is believed to be unreasonably difficult) (CCP arts. 29.04-29.13.);
- discover evidence possessed by the prosecution. By making what is commonly referred to as a "Brady motion" (named after the U.S. Supreme Court case of *Brady v. Maryland*), the prosecution is legally obligated to turn over all evidence which might prove the defendant's innocence (*Juarez v. State*, 439 S.W.2d 346 (Tex. Crim. App. 1963). In contrast, the defense is not required to turn over any evidence to the prosecutor. While civil cases generally entail extensive discovery from both sides, criminal cases usually entail significantly less. For this reason criminal trials in Texas can be described as "trial by ambush."

PART 2:
TRIAL

Legal Principles at Trial

Depictions of trial procedure in television and film often emphasize the dramatic aspects of what can occur at trial. As a result, the average consumer of pop culture often is not as well versed on the underlying legal principles which form the foundation for the trial proceeding.

Constitutional Rights

The federal and state constitutional protections (detailed in Chapter 2) are of central importance at trial. The promise of fundamental fairness extended to all criminal defendants is often apparent at trial through two procedural rights, which follow.

THE RIGHT TO CALL AND CONFRONT WITNESSES—The defense counsel on behalf of his client has the right to call witnesses who may vindicate him of criminal wrongdoing. Similarly, the defense counsel has the right to cross examination in order to discredit any witness called by the prosecutor.

THE RIGHT AGAINST SELF-INCRIMINATION—The defendant cannot be called by the prosecution for questioning. If, however, the defendant chooses to take the stand and testify on his own behalf, he cannot refuse to answer questions.

Burden of Proof

Trial would be futile without some standards by which to measure the evidence and to decide whether the accused has been proven guilty. In criminal cases the "burden of proof" refers to the amount of evidence which must be brought forward by the prosecutor in order to establish the defendant's guilt. Remember, all criminal charges are filed in the name of the State and must be proven by the State's attorney (the prosecutor). While in civil cases the party bringing the lawsuit must prove the case against the defendant by a preponderance of the evidence (a 51% probability), criminal cases involve a higher standard. Criminal charges must be proven beyond a reasonable doubt (doubt based on reason and common sense after a careful and impartial consideration of all the evidence in the case). It is this kind of doubt that would make a reasonable person hesitate to act in the most important of his or her own affairs (*Geesa v. State*, 820 S.W.2d 154 (Tex. Crim. App. 1991)).

Rules of Evidence

Now that you know how much proof is necessary to find a defendant guilty under Texas law, it is important to know that a complex series of rules drafted by the Texas Court of Criminal Appeals governs the admission of evidence at trial. The Texas Rules of Criminal Evidence, based on comparable federal rules, are divided into 11 articles and set forth the rules regulating what evidence can be introduced at trial. While the admissibility of evidence often depends on the facts and circumstances of a particular case (as well as how those facts and circumstances are portrayed by the prosecutor and defense lawyer), there are certain concepts that are fundamental at trial: relevance, hearsay, and privileges.

RELEVANCE—Whether or not a particular piece of evidence makes an important issue at trial more or less likely to be true. Evidence must be relevant to be admissible.

HEARSAY—Testimony given by a witness who relates not what he knows personally but what has been said by others. Since the truthfulness of such statements can only be tested on individuals not present in court, it is per se inadmissible as evidence. However, there are in Texas 24 exceptions to the general rule prohibiting hearsay. For example, "excited utterances" may be admitted into evidence (i.e., statements made by persons immediately after a startling event).

PRIVILEGES—The right of certain individuals not to testify about certain matters. While Texas does not recognize a physician-patient privilege, it does recognize:

- the attorney-client privilege, protecting communications between lawyers and clients
- communications with clergy, protecting communications between defendants and their ministers, priests, preachers or rabbis when occurring in the clergy's professional capacity
- interspousal privilege, allowing married people not to testify against each other (inapplicable when the victim of the crime is the spouse, a minor child, or a member of either spouse's household).

The Rule of Witnesses

Commonly referred to as simply "the Rule," Texas law allows either the prosecutor or defense lawyer to exclude all witnesses from the courtroom except when they are testifying. "The Rule" does not apply to the defendant, whose constitutional protections allow him to remain present to hear all witnesses (unless his conduct is disruptive). The purpose of "the Rule" is to prevent witnesses from changing their testimony after hearing the testimony of other witnesses. It is ultimately, however, within the discretion of the court as to whether a witness may remain in the courtroom while other witnesses testify. Additionally, judges have the discretion to ban the testimony of any witness who fails to comply with "the Rule" (CCP art. 36.05).

Court Personnel

While the process of trial is often associated with the work of lawyers and judges, the administration of justice involves various individuals who are fundamental to the operation of the judicial process. To understand trial procedure is to appreciate collectively the responsibilities of the court personnel:

- The *court administrator* is responsible for coordinating and scheduling matters before the court.
- The *court clerk* maintains the files on all cases which come before the court and often administers the oath to witnesses.
- The *bailiff* leads the jury in and out of the courtroom, escorts witnesses to the stand, announces when the court is in session, and maintains order in the court during proceedings.
- The *court reporter* keeps a written record of all words spoken before the court and oversees the inventory, collection, and preservation of all evidentiary exhibits (photographs, diagrams, murder weapons, etc.).
- The *judge* determines how much time will be allotted for trial, manages all proceedings, and decides all legal matters raised during the course of the trial.
- The *prosecutor* represents the State of Texas and has the burden of proving each element of the crime alleged against the defendant.

- The *defense lawyer* represents the defendant often by showing inconsistencies in the State's case, highlighting insufficient proof of essential elements of the crime, and raising doubt as to the guilt of his client.

Jury Selection

A jury trial may be requested by either the defendant or the State. If the request is granted by the court, registered voters and holders of Texas driver's licenses are randomly selected and summoned by mail to appear before the court at a designated time. If a person summoned fails to appear, an "attachment" may be issued ordering the individual to be brought before the court, and a maximum fine of $50 may be imposed (CCP art. 35.01).

Upon gathering, the *venire* (a Latin term referring to all citizens who have been called to appear before the court) are each assigned an identification number, placed on a list, and generally assigned a seat corresponding to their identification number. After being seated, each attorney is given the opportunity to visually examine the composition of the panel. If either attorney believes that the panel was selected through a process which is legally corrupt or motivated by racism they may "challenge the array" (CCP art. 35.07). A successful challenge to the array results in the dismissal of the current panel and the selection of a new panel of prospective jurors (this rarely occurs and is often difficult to prove). Furthermore, upon examining the order in which members of the panel are listed, either attorney may request that the order of the list be randomly reorganized (shuffled). The right to a "shuffle" is guaranteed by law (CCP art. 35.11). Shuffling results in a new listing of the prospective jurors. While the order of the list may seem trivial, you shall soon appreciate the importance of the order in which prospective jurors ultimately appear on the list.

General Qualifications

Qualifications for jury service are quite similar to those for service on the grand jury (as are the exemptions, previously discussed). Once sworn to truthfulness, the court determines if the prospective jurors are generally qualified. Veniremen (the individual members of the prospective panel) are legally required to:

- be eligible to vote in the state and county of the proceeding
- not have been convicted of any felony
- not be under indictment or accused of theft or any other felony
- be of sound mind
- be free from any sensory impediment that would legally preclude jury service (i.e., being legally deaf or blind)
- not have had any previous involvement in the case either as a grand juror or witness
- be free from bias or prejudice for or against the defendant (CCP art. 35.16).

The Size of the Jury

The number of jurors and alternate jurors depends on the type of charges brought by the State. If the State alleges a felony, 12 jurors and 4 alternate jurors are empaneled. If the State alleges a misdemeanor, 6 jurors and up to 2 alternate jurors are empaneled (CCP art. 33.01).

The only situation in which the size of the jury is not determined by the type of charges alleged is in the event of waiver by the defendant. In December 1997 the Court of Criminal Appeals ruled in a controversial 5-4 ruling that a jury trial in a felony case, other than capital murder, can be decided by fewer than 12 jurors if the defendant and prosecutor both agree to waive the requisite number of jurors. In its ruling, the majority held that constitutionally the right to a jury trial cannot be "violated"; however, it can be "regulated" by the legislature. It went on to construe a 1985 law passed by the legislature to allow such waiver. Dissenting judges claimed the 1985 law was intended to apply to civil, not criminal, cases (*Hatch v. State*, 958 S.W.2d 813).

Voir Dire

Upon establishing the basic qualifications of the potential jurors, attorneys for the defense and prosecution are allowed to question the jurors in a process known as *voir dire* (French, meaning to "speak the truth") (CCP art. 35.17). *Voir dire* provides attorneys an opportunity to discover the individual biases and attitudes of jurors which may be legal grounds for dismissal. When it is determined during questioning that legal grounds exist which justify excluding ("striking") a venireman from the jury, the attorney makes a challenge for cause. Challenges for cause may be made due to the fact that the venire is:

- prejudiced against the defendant, the victim, or the State
- unwilling to enforce the law as explained by the court
- ineligible due to failure to comply with any of the general qualifications required by law (as previously discussed) (CCP art. 35.16).

Peremptory Challenges

After *voir dire* is complete, and the challenges for cause are resolved by the court, each attorney exercises his or her peremptory challenges (challenges made without explanation) by striking out the number assigned to the prospective juror on his or her copy of the court's listing of prospective jurors. The only limitation on the use of peremptory challenges is that they may not be based on sex or race (CCP art. 35.261). In most misdemeanor cases, both the defense and prosecution have three peremptory challenges. In felony cases not punishable by death, both sides have 10 peremptory challenges. In death penalty cases both sides have 15 peremptory challenges (CCP art. 35.15).

Assembling the Jury

Though it is not inappropriate to refer to the process of assembling a jury as "jury selection," the term is fairly deceptive. Juries are not "selected" by attorneys or by judges. Rather, through a process of elimination and chance, juries are assembled. After determining which jurors to "strike," the prosecution and defense return their lists to the court clerk. Upon recording how each side exercised their peremptory strikes, the judge dismisses the jurors "struck" from the list. There-after, the clerk seats the first remaining 12 (or six) potential jurors who were not eliminated for cause or by peremptory challenge (CCP art. 35.26). These individuals are empaneled and sworn as jurors. Thus, as previously alluded to, while the order of the list may seem trivial at the outset of jury selec-tion, in the end the order in which prospective jurors ulti-mately appear on the list determines who ends up on the jury.

A Special Note on Capital Cases

The procedures in selecting a jury in capital cases differ from those used in non-capital cases. In non-capital cases, *voir dire* examination is conducted in the presence of the entire panel of prospective jurors. In capital cases, questions pertaining to principles applicable to the case (e.g., reasonable doubt, burden of proof, grand jury indictment, presumption of innocence, and opinion) may be asked before the entire panel. However, both the state and the defendant have the right to examine each juror individually and apart from the entire panel.

Due to the extremely controversial nature of the death penalty and the emotions it often evokes, Texas law gives spe-cial attention to the qualification of jurors in capital cases. Regardless of personal beliefs, to be qualified for jury service a venireman must be able to impose the penalty if it is pre-scribed by law. Upon being deemed qualified by the court, the State is given the right to question jurors and make any chal-lenge (for cause or peremptory) prior to examination by the defendant.

Juror Compensation

While proposals now before the Texas Supreme Court would raise jury pay to $40 a day in all cases lasting more than one day (potentially the highest pay in the country), Texas jurors cur-rently receive a meager $6 a day (the lowest pay in the coun-try). Critics have commented that $6 particularly does not go far in cities like Dallas, where jurors pay $3 a day to park their cars and must buy their own lunches.

Trial Before the Jury

Criminal trials in Texas are bifurcated. In other words, the jury trial is separated into two distinctive phases: a guilt phase and a punishment phase.

Phase One: Determination of Guilt

After the jury is empaneled, trial begins to determine if the defendant is guilty of the charges alleged by the State. There are seven stages in the "guilt phase" of the trial (CCP art. 36.01).

1. FORMAL PRESENTATION OF THE INDICTMENT OR INFORMATION

The trial begins with the prosecutor reading to the jury the indictment or information. Afterward, the defense counsel, on behalf of the defendant, responds to the allegations by entering a plea of guilty or not guilty.

2. OPENING STATEMENTS

On behalf of the State, the prosecution has the first opportunity to address the jury. In its opening statement, the prosecutor informs the jury of the nature of the offense in which the defendant is charged, the facts it expects to establish during trial, and specifically how it plans to prove the elements of the alleged offense. At the conclusion of the State's opening, the defense may either deliver its opening statement or postpone its remarks until the prosecution finishes presenting its case.

3. PRESENTATION OF CASES

Following opening statements, the prosecutor begins the State's case by calling witnesses to the witness stand. All witnesses called to the stand must first pledge before the court to be truthful in all testimony. On direct examination the prosecutor questions the witness in order to establish particular aspects of its case against the defendant. During direct examination, neither the State nor the defense is allowed to ask leading questions (questions which imply an answer, such as,

The Texas Bill of Rights assures criminal defendants the right of trial by jury. Every day across the state, empaneled citizens participate in the criminal justice process.

(Photo provided by authors)

"You saw the defendant kill the victim, didn't you?") After finishing direct examination, the witness is "passed." "Passing the witness" signifies the defense's opportunity to cross-examine the State's witness. As previously discussed, cross-examination is the right to question and discredit any witness called by the opposing side of the case. Regardless of whether it is the prosecutor or the defense, the party conducting cross-examination may pose leading questions to the witness.

In presenting their cases both the State and defendant may want to introduce particular items proving or negating the commission of the crime (physical evidence, mere evidence, fruits of the crime) and visual aids to assist witnesses in their testimony (demonstrative evidence). Before either type of evidence can be brought before the witness and jury, it must be identified usually with a sticker as either "State's Exhibit #" or "Defendant's Exhibit #." After the evidence is labeled, usually by the court reporter, the attorney who wants the evidence to be considered by the jury must establish a "proper predicate" for its admission. This requires the attorney to factually verify (through sworn affidavit or testimony) that the evidence is accurate, genuine, and (in cases involving scientific proof) uncontaminated. The opposing lawyer may object to the item's admissibility on the basis that the evidence was illegally obtained or that an inadequate foundation has been established. The judge then rules on the admissibility of the evidence.

Upon calling all of its witness, the State rests its case. If not already delivered, the defendant's case begins with the defense lawyer's opening statement. Then witnesses and exhibits are offered in the same manner as presented by the prosecution. Since the prosecution bears the burden of proof, the defense is not obligated to present any witnesses or evidence whatsoever. At the conclusion of its case, assuming that it presents one, the defense also rests.

4. REBUTTAL

Once the defense concludes its case, the prosecution has the opportunity to present witnesses in an effort to discredit the defendant's case and reinforce its own. After the State's rebuttal, the defense may call additional witnesses (often called "sur-rebuttal") to counteract the State's rebuttal witnesses. Generally, few additional witnesses are called to testify in rebuttal. Upon the conclusion of rebuttal, both sides close their case.

5. JURY CHARGE

Once each side has presented its case and rebuttal has concluded, the judge will read aloud the jury's instructions for reaching a verdict. Generally, both the prosecution and the defense cooperate with the court in drafting such instructions before the trial begins. Such instructions make up the "jury charge" (CCP art. 36.14). Without commenting on how much weight the jury should give particular evidence and testimony, the jury charge:

- sets forth the applicable law in the case
- explains the issues the jury must determine

- provides guidelines for deliberating a verdict
- contains forms for recording the jury's verdict.

Generally, the jury charge asks the jury to determine if the defendant is guilty or not guilty of one or more of the charges alleged by the State. Additionally, upon request of either the prosecution or defense, the court may incorporate specific questions of fact into the jury charge. Such "special charges" may be used to ascertain particular facts, such as whether the defendant was or was not mentally competent at the time the crime was committed (CCP art. 36.15).

6. FINAL ARGUMENTS

Final arguments provide the last opportunity for the attorneys to convince the jury of the merits of their case. Generally, the prosecution summarizes the case against the defendant by correlating the evidence directly to the legal elements of the crime charged. In contrast, the defense may emphasize the weaknesses in a particular aspect of the prosecution's case and/or argue that the State has failed to meet its burden of proving the charges against the defendant beyond a reasonable doubt. Since the State has the burden of proof, final arguments are made in the following order: prosecution, defendant, prosecution rebuttal.

7. DELIBERATION AND VERDICT

Under the supervision of the bailiff, jurors are adjourned to a jury room where they are left alone to deliberate a verdict. No person shall be allowed without the permission of the court to interact with the jury while it is deliberating. Any communication whatsoever must occur in the presence of the court (CCP art. 36.22). Anyone, including a juror, who violates the prohibition of out of court communications may be held in contempt and punished by a fine not to exceed $100 and three days in jail (CCP art. 36.23). The jury may request that exhibits admitted into evidence be delivered to the jury room (CCP art. 36.25). All communications between the jury and the court must be in writing. The substance of the message and any issue arising from the message must be brought to the attention of the prosecuting and defense attorneys. Any additional instructions given to the jury by the court must be delivered verbally in open court and in the presence of the defendant (CCP art. 36.27). During deliberation the jury may have witnesses reexamined or particular testimony read back to them by the court reporter (CCP art. 36.28).

Unlike civil cases, which only require a majority vote to reach a verdict, criminal cases require a unanimous verdict. If the jury is not able to reach a unanimous verdict (i.e., "hung jury"), the court must declare a mistrial and a new jury is selected. In essence, the trial process starts all over again.

If the defendant is found not guilty, the trial is over and the defendant is released from custody. Under the federal and state constitution, the principal of "double jeopardy" prohibits the defendant from ever standing trial again for the same charges once he or she has been "acquitted" (found not guilty by the jury).

If the defendant is found guilty, either the judge or jury will set punishment. (The decision as to who imposes punishment is the defendant's and is generally made before trial.) If it has been predetermined that the judge shall set punishment, the jury is dismissed. The judge may decide to hear evidence and impose a sentence immediately or delay sentencing to a later time. If the jury is to impose punishment, the judge will generally begin the sentencing phase immediately.

Phase Two: The Imposition of Punishment

The punishment phase of the trial closely parallels the guilt phase with one major exception. Not until the punishment phase may evidence of the defendant's prior criminal history (other crimes or bad acts) be admitted as evidence. Prior convictions of the defendant are generally incorporated into the "penalty paragraphs" of the indictment. In front of the jury the defendant is asked to plea whether the information contained in the penalty paragraph is "true" or "not true." Prior offenses, ultimately established in the penalty paragraph, increase the possibility of more severe punishment (enhancements).

GENERAL ORDER OF PROCEEDINGS

The following is an overview of the order of proceedings in the punishment phase of trial:

1. *Opening Statements*: Both sides inform the jury what they believe the evidence and testimony will prove is the appropriate punishment for the defendant.

2. *Prosecution's Case*: In addition to any prior offenses that may exist, the prosecutor presents evidence and testimony (in the same manner as the guilt phase) which suggests a course of punishment from the State's perspective.

3. *Defense's Case*: The defense will offer evidence and testimony to mitigate or lessen punishment. It is not uncommon for family, friends, and work colleagues to be called to testify about defendant's upbringing, character, and disposition. Additionally, mental health professionals (psychologists, psychiatrists, and psychotherapists) may be called to testify on what punishment they believe is appropriate in light of the defendant's current mental state.

4. *Jury Charge*: After each side "rests its case" (all witnesses and evidence are presented) and each side "closes its case" (all rebuttal witnesses are called) the jury is read another jury charge. This jury charge, which pertains specifically to factors for consideration in imposing a sentence, is compiled by the court with the cooperation of the prosecuting and defense attorneys.

5. *Final Arguments*: While specific to sentencing, the goals of final arguments in the punishment phase are the same as previously described in the guilt phase.

6. *Deliberation and Verdict*: After deliberating, the jury is returned to the courtroom so that the verdict may be read. The verdict states the length of prison or jail time the defendant must serve, as well as the dollar amount of any fine. If the

imprisonment term is less than 10 years, and the defendant is deemed eligible by the court, the jury can suspend the sentence and place the defendant on probation. The judge will set the terms and length of probation (further discussed in Chapter 8).

SPECIAL NOTE: THE PUNISHMENT PHASE IN CAPITAL CASES

While there is no difference in the order of proceedings in the punishment phase of a capital murder case, only two punishments are possible: life in prison or death by lethal injection. In contrast to the penalty phase of criminal trials, described above, the jury does not actually "choose" the punishment. Rather, the court submits as part of the jury charge two issues for the jury to determine:

1. the probability that the defendant will commit further violent criminal acts which make that person a continuing threat to society;
2. whether the defendant actually caused, intended, or anticipated that a human life would be taken (CCP art. 37.071).

On the basis of the jury's responses to these two issues, the judge sentences the defendant to either life in prison or death by lethal injection. (The enforcement of these sentences is detailed in Chapter 7.)

In October 1997 four U.S. Supreme Court justices questioned Texas death sentencing law. In an appellate opinion rejecting a death penalty appeal, Justice John Paul Stevens criticized the above stated "two issue" jury charge. "Although juries are required to assess a capital defendant's 'future dangerousness,' [the defendant] is prohibited from presenting truthful information to the jury about when he would be eligible for parole if sentenced. . . . The Texas rule unquestionably tips the scales in favor of the death sentence that a fully informed jury might not impose" (*Brown v. Texas*, 118 U.S. 355 1997). In contrast, juries considering punishment in noncapital cases must be told when a defendant would be eligible for parole. Commentators believe that Stevens' opinion should serve as a notice to all Texas courts: The U.S. Supreme Court is carefully watching how the State lets juries choose between death or life in prison for convicted murderers. Since 1976, almost a third of all executions in the United States have occurred in Texas. More than half of all U.S. executions in 1997 occurred in Texas (of the 59 executions carried out nationwide, 31 occurred in Texas).

PART 3:
POST-TRIAL PROCESSES

Three principal mechanisms exist to review proceedings after sentencing: (1) new trials, (2) appeals, (3) collateral attacks.

New Trials

A "new trial" is the rehearing of a criminal case after a finding or verdict of guilty has been set aside by the trial court. Upon defendant's motion for new trial, a new trial shall be granted for the following reasons (Texas Rules of Appellate Procedure 21.3):

1. *Absence of Defendant/Counsel*: The case was tried in the absence of the defendant or the defendant was not provided counsel (inapplicable in misdemeanor cases in which the maximum punishment is a fine).

2. *Material Error of Law by the Court*: The court has misdirected the jury as to the law or has committed some other material legal error which injured the rights of the defendant.

3. *Improper Deliberation*: The verdict was reached by the jury in an improper manner (flipping a coin, drawing straws, etc.).

4. *Jury Tampering*: A juror has received a bribe to convict the defendant or is guilty of other corrupt conduct.

5. *Witness Intimidation/Concealment of Evidence*: Through force, threat or fraud, a material witness for the defendant was

prevented from attending court or evidence tending to show the defendant's innocence was intentionally destroyed or withheld from use at trial.

6. *Exculpatory Evidence*: New evidence favorable to the accused has been discovered since trial.

7. *Jury Misconduct:*

- While deliberating, a juror discussed the case with individuals prohibited by the court.
- A juror rendered his or her verdict while intoxicated.
- The conduct of the jury prohibited the defendant from receiving a "fair and impartial" trial.

8. *Legally Insufficient Verdict*: The verdict is contrary to the law and evidence.

Appeals

The appellate courts do not reconsider facts in a case; rather, they examine the legal rulings of the trial court. For legal errors committed at trial to be reviewable on appeal, they must be prejudicial in nature (i.e., not harmless) and they must be "properly preserved" at trial. Defense counsel properly preserves error by objecting verbally or in writing to the court (via a "bill of exception"). Additionally, the evidence excluded by the court should also be preserved verbally or in writing (as an "offer of proof") so that the court of appeals may examine it. To properly preserve error for appellate review all objections, motions, and requests must be timely, specific, and have been ruled upon the court during trial. Since the trial transcript becomes part of the record on appeal all attempts to preserve error should appear in the trial transcript. Errors not properly preserved are legally presumed waived and are not reviewable on appeal. Accordingly, a criminal defendant's chances for a successful appeal often rely on how well the defense counsel detected and preserved error at trial.

The appeals process serves as a safety mechanism to ensure the correctness of the defendant's conviction. However, contrary to popular belief, most defendants who win on appeal are not set free. Rather, upon reversing the conviction, the case is usually remanded for retrial in the trial court following instructions of the appellate court to assure that the initial mistakes are avoided at retrial. Appellate decisions, which are written and published, often affect how laws are interpreted and applied in future cases.

The process of appeal in Texas depends to a certain degree on the sentence imposed at trial. If the defendant is sentenced to imprisonment, the process is the same regardless of the offense. However, if the defendant is sentenced to death, his or her appeal automatically bypasses the court of appeals and goes directly to the Court of Criminal Appeals. (The structure of the appellate process in criminal cases is detailed in Chapter 4.)

The state prosecuting attorney represents the state in all proceedings before the Court of Criminal Appeals. Additionally, upon request from local prosecutors or where State interests require, the state prosecuting attorney may assist district or county attorneys before a court of appeals (intermediate level of appeals for non-capital offenses). The state prosecuting attorney deals only with appellate criminal cases.

Many assume that convicted defendants remain incarcerated during their appeals. The truth of the matter may be surprising. Criminals can avoid prison for years during appeals. Many end up being rearrested. The issuance of appeal bonds has increasingly become one of the most controversial aspects of Texas criminal appellate procedure. An appeal bond is a written instrument of debt which allows a criminal defendant to remain free after conviction while his or her case is being appealed. An appeal bond may be procured by depositing cash with the county or paying a fee, generally 10 percent of the total amount set by the judge, to have a surety guarantee the defendant will appear before the judge and surrender to authorities if so ordered by the court. While the manner for setting appeal bond may vary from county to county (and even among judges), in some counties appeal bonds are set at $1,000 per year of prison sentence. Thus, a 10-year sentence may result in a $10,000 appeal bond. With the secured guarantee of a surety, a convict could stay out of jail (in some instances for as long as five years) for only $100.

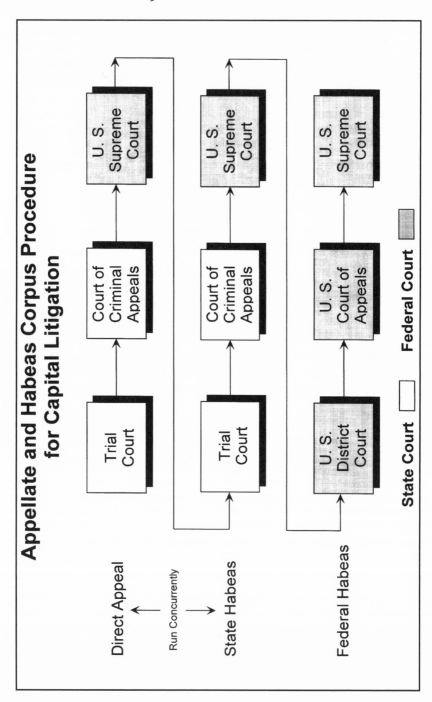

Appellate and Habeas Corpus Procedure for Capital Litigation

Under Texas law, appeal bonds are available to defendants convicted of any offense, as long as their sentence is 15 years or less. Other states deny appeal bonds for certain violent and sexual offenses. Attempts to modify criteria for appeal bonds in Texas have, as of date, been unsuccessful. While appeal bonds can be revoked if a person commits a subsequent offense, one of Texas' larger counties reports that over 25% of its appeal bond holders have been rearrested while free on bond, without having their appeal bond canceled. Prosecutors claim that they lack the resources to track offenders who breach the terms of their bond. While criminal defense lawyers may be justified in protesting the abolition of appeal bonds, victims' rights advocates persuasively argue that appeal bonds in Texas currently serve as "bail for the guilty," which allows some offenders to commit additional crimes.

Collateral Attacks

After all appeals are exhausted and the offender is imprisoned, his conviction may still be challenged on a limited basis by what is known as a "collateral attack." In contrast to a "direct" appeal, which immediately follows the defendant's conviction and sentence, a collateral attack is a separate and new lawsuit which attempts to defeat the judgment of the trial courts on new grounds not raised in the direct appeal. In the context of criminal cases the most common means of collateral attack is through a writ of habeas corpus. As you recall from Chapter 4, habeas corpus challenges the constitutionality of the offender's imprisonment. In this form of collateral attack, inmates rely on their state and federal constitutional rights.

Partially due to the increased number of executions in Texas, the availability of unlimited use of habeas corpus in death penalty cases has been a subject of controversy. In 1995 Texas enacted legislation which generally limits condemned inmates to one habeas corpus review at the state level (CCP art. 11.071). Opponents of capital punishment claim that most of Texas' death row inmates receive inadequate legal representation before and after trial. Consequently, they contend that streamlining habeas corpus review only adds to the injustice of the death penalty in Texas. Proponents of streamlining habeas corpus review at the state level claim that the law provides a full, complete, and meaningful review of applications filed by condemned inmates. In 1996 the Court of Criminal Appeals upheld the constitutionality of the 1995 legislation (*Ex Parte Davis*, 947 S.W.2d 216 (Tex. Crim. App. 1996)).

WORKS CONSULTED AND SUGGESTIONS FOR FURTHER READING

(Note: Unless otherwise stated, all statutory citations noted (CCP) in this chapter are from the Texas Code of Criminal Procedure.)

Anderson, Ken. *Crime in Texas*. Austin, Texas: University of Texas, 1997.

Curriden, Mark. "State Panel Seeks Pay Raise for Juries." *Dallas Morning News*, 15 September 1997: A1.

Dawson, Robert, and George Dix. *Texas Criminal Procedure*. New York: Matthew Bender, 1984.

Fikac, Peggy. "Appeals Court Ends 12-Juror Mandate." *Austin American-Statesman*, 11 December 1997: B1.

Guide to Texas State Agencies. Austin, Texas: State of Texas, 1996.

Inciardi, James. *Criminal Justice*. 3rd ed. San Diego, California: Harcourt Brace Jovanovich, 1990.

Reamey, Gerald, and Walter Steele, Jr. *Texas Criminal Procedure*. 3rd ed. Dallas, Texas: Academia, 1993.

Samaha, Joel. *Criminal Procedure*. St. Paul, Minnesota: West, 1990.

Slover, Pete, and Ed Housewright. "Criminals Avoid Prison For Years During Appeals." *The Dallas Morning News*, 13 December 1997: 1A.

"Texas Death Sentencing Questioned." *Austin American-Statesman*, 22 October 1997: B1.

6.
HISTORY OF THE TEXAS
PRISON SYSTEM

PART 1:
MEXICAN COLONIAL ADMINISTRATION

The first development of a prison system in what is now the state of Texas can be traced to 1829, when the Congress of the Mexican state of Coahuila and Texas adopted a resolution authorizing the colonial administration to arrange for the private construction and operation of the first buildings for penal incarceration in Texas. Decree 93 of the *Congreso del Estado de Coahuila y Tejas* resulted in five log cabin prisons of one and two rooms being built before Texas won its independence in 1836. The five Mexican colonial prisons (called *carcels*) were financed and built by private venture capitalists. Private individuals contracted with the Mexican colonial government to finance and erect the prisons. Upon completion of the prison, the labor of the prisoners was used to manufacture products within the prison, such as ceramic pottery and woven textiles, the proceeds of which, when sold on the open market, were used by the private contractors to recoup their initial investment and turn a profit.

While Decree 93 might appear at first glance to be a form of institutionalized slave labor, it was far from that. Private contractors who operated the five prisons were held responsible for teaching the prisoners a marketable trade which they could later use to earn an honest living. Upon completion of sentence, the discharged prisoner was sent to the town of his

211

choosing. The contractor was required to give the discharged prisoner the equivalent of $30 and supply him with the rudimentary tools of the trade he practiced while incarcerated. To ensure that the prison operators were carrying out their contractual obligations, all discharged prisoners were required to report directly to colonial authorities of the town where they wished to relocate. Upon arrival, the colonial authorities would then inspect the belongings of the discharged prisoner to insure he had the means necessary to sustain himself by honest labor.

PART 2:
THE REPUBLIC OF TEXAS

Texas declared its independence from Mexico on 2 March 1836. During the period of the Republic of Texas, which lasted until 1846, no provision was ever made for the establishment of a penitentiary system. Francis Moore, Jr., M.D., a member of the Texas Senate from Harris, Liberty, and Galveston counties in the 4th, 5th, and 6th congresses, led the movement to establish a prison system in the Republic of Texas. In 1839 Dr. Moore introduced a penitentiary bill in the 5th Congress, but owing to the pressing economic problems facing the fledgling republic, the bill was not passed. Rather, the government of the Republic of Texas authorized county sheriffs to rent or buy structures to use for incarcerating prisoners.

PART 3:
THE STATE OF TEXAS

The Congress of the United States of America authorized the admission of Texas into the Union on 29 December 1845, but it was not until 16 February 1846 that the state government of Texas was organized and the Republic of Texas passed into history. After Texas formally joined the Union in early 1846, the impetus of the Texas Legislature to establish a state penitentiary was initially slow.

On 13 March 1848 the 2nd Texas Legislature finally passed a bill which provided for the erection of the Texas State

Penitentiary. The bill appropriated $10,000 for the construction of a prison, and gave to Governor Wood the authority to appoint a board of three commissioners to investigate a site for its location and oversee its construction. While the search was under way to locate a site for the state's first prison, one of the commissioners appointed by Governor Wood was asked to pay a visit to the Mississippi State Penitentiary with a view to acquiring ideas about how to design and manage the convict population in the planned Texas State Penitentiary.

Erected near the capital at Jackson in the early 1840s, the cell houses of the Mississippi State Penitentiary were enclosed by a massive wall, and convicts were managed under the philosophy of the Auburn system of prison discipline. In the late 1840s there were two philosophies of prison discipline and convict management operating in the United States: the Pennsylvania system and the Auburn (or New York) system. In the Pennsylvania system convicts were lodged in separate cells, where they were required to work alone at such jobs as shoemaking, weaving, and wool spinning. During the entire time of their confinement they were never permitted to see or communicate with one another. The Auburn system, on the other hand, confined and isolated convicts in separate cells only during the night. During daylight hours the convict population labored together in prison workshops. The Texas commissioner was favorably impressed with Mississippi State Penitentiary's walled style of construction and its congregate system of prison labor, and returned to Texas with the recommendation that Texas adopt both its architecture and method of prison discipline.

The East Texas town of Huntsville, located in Walker County, was selected by the commissioners as the location for the Texas State Penitentiary, and subsequently 98.8 acres were purchased for $493. Construction began on 5 August 1848 under the supervision of Abner Hugh Cook. Almost all of the bricklaying, blacksmithing, and carpentry was performed by convicts who were brought to Huntsville by the sheriffs of counties where they were incarcerated. A crude log cabin structure was built on the site of the prison to house the convict laborers. The prison at Huntsville, which quickly came to be referred to as "The Walls," was laid out in a square, enclosed by a massive wall of locally manufactured coarse red brick. The walls were 100 yards long, three feet thick, and 15 feet high. Within the 10,000-square-yard enclosure were an administration building, a kitchen, a workshop for prisoners, and three cell houses containing a total of 266 regular cells and two dark cells for the punishment of recalcitrant and incorrigible convicts. The smallest of the three cell houses contained 36 cells reserved exclusively for female convicts. The 230 cells intended for male convicts were five feet by seven feet in size, while the 36 cells set aside for female convicts were six feet by seven feet in size. The two dark cells for punishment were seven by ten feet in size.

The first prisoner, a farmer convicted of cattle theft in Fayette County named William G. Sansom, was received by the Texas State Penitentiary on 1 October 1849. Prisoner number two, Stephen Perry, convicted of murder at Jefferson,

"The Walls" of Huntsville Prison, circa 1895.

Texas, arrived in early November, followed a few days later by prisoner number three, Thomas Short, a horse thief convicted in Washington County and sentenced to two years' incarceration. The first female prisoner, a 23-year-old house servant named Elizabeth Hoffman, was convicted of infanticide in San Antonio, and was remanded into the custody of the penitentiary at Huntsville on 8 April 1854 to begin a one-year sentence. Abner Hugh Cook, the contractor responsible for overseeing the construction of the prison, served until 1850 as the first superintendent of the Texas State Penitentiary.

After the opening of the Texas State Penitentiary at Huntsville in 1849, the Texas prison system went through a number of distinct and rather well-defined historical periods: the State Account Period, from 1849 to 1871; the Prison Lease Period, from 1871 to 1882; the Convict Lease Period, from 1883 to 1912; the Post-Convict Lease Period, from 1912 to 1948; the Ellis and Beto Era, from 1948 to 1972; and the Post-Beto Era, from 1972 to the present.

The State Account Period (1849 to 1871)

The single most outstanding influence on the history and development of the Texas prison system, from its very inception in 1849 to the present day, has been the Texas Legislature's enduring economic philosophy of prison operation and management. The state legislature has always stressed the importance of, and sought ways to use, convict labor as a source of revenue to defray the operating costs associated with running the Texas prison system and to make it as economically self-supporting as possible.

The first indications of this philosophy were evidenced when convict labor was employed to erect the Texas State Penitentiary at Huntsville and workshops were built with a view to using convict labor for the purpose of manufacturing whatever products were deemed most profitable and useful to the state. Under this system convicts were made to labor inside the walls of the Texas State Penitentiary at Huntsville at various jobs, including shoemaking, blacksmithing, carpentry, tailoring, wagon making, harness and saddle manufacturing, the fabrication of basic agricultural implements, and cooking. It is important to emphasize that under the public account system of prison operation and management, the state government of Texas retained total responsibility for the care, control, custody, and labor of the convicts.

A significant development in the State Account Period of the Texas prison system occurred when the 5th Legislature on 11 February 1854 passed legislation authorizing the State to spend $35,000 for the construction of a cotton and wool textile mill to be worked by convicts within the walls of the penitentiary. Convict labor was used to construct the mill building, and after its completion, convicts were immediately put to work producing Osnaburg textile, cotton jeans, kersey, and other cotton and wool products. By 1859 forty looms were in operation that yielded a profit of $14,849 for the state treasury. During the Civil War additional looms were installed that produced gross revenues in excess of $1.5 million. The production of cotton and woolen textiles remains today the oldest continuous convict labor enterprise in the Texas prison system.

A period of general civil unrest and lawlessness in Texas occurred immediately after the conclusion of the Civil War and during the early years of reconstruction in the 1870s. The convict population swelled beyond manageable limits, and the ability of the Texas State Penitentiary to keep convicts employed was seriously threatened. To relieve the overcrowding at the Texas State Penitentiary and maintain the economic self-sufficiency upon which the prison system was predicated, the Texas Legislature, faced with inadequate facilities to house the growing number of convicted felons and stymied by a depressed post-war economy, took an ominous step that would greatly influence the operation of the Texas prison system for almost the next half century. On 12 November 1866 the 11th Texas Legislature passed a bill establishing a five-member Board of Public Labor to operate the Texas State Penitentiary at Huntsville and to oversee the profitable employment of convict labor in the private sector. In February 1867 the board contracted for the lease of convict labor to private, civilian contractors. Civilian contractors paid approximately $3 per month per convict for the right to use their labor in a variety of ways, including on farms, on railroad construction projects, and in quarrying stone. While the contracting of convict labor to private parties succeeded in initially reducing the over-crowded conditions at the Texas State Penitentiary, the reve-nues it generated during its first few years were insufficient to cover the escalating costs of operating the prison system. Something had to be done.

The Prison Lease Period (1871 to 1882)

At the close of the State Account Period in 1871 the Texas prison system held 520 convicts. Strapped for cash and re-luctant to allocate limited state economic resources for the operation of a prison system that was supposed to be self-sustaining, the Texas Legislature passed a bill in 1871 which required the governor to lease the entire prison system to the highest bidding private contractor. This was not an entirely new idea, however. The legislature was merely resorting to a pattern and precedent first established in 1825, when Kentucky became the first state to lease its entire prison sys-tem to a private contractor. Under the prison lease system, the State of Texas leased to a private party all of its land holdings, prison buildings, and prisoners for an agreed upon annual dollar amount. Under terms of the lease, the private operator took complete control of the Texas State Penitentiary and fur-nished everything needed to operate the prison, including feeding, clothing, and providing for the medical needs of the convicts, paying the salaries of the prison officials and guards, and maintaining the upkeep of the physical facilities. The con-victs were employed by the lessee (or, as was the case in some instances, sublet by the leaseholder to other parties) either at the site of the prison or at work camps in the eastern part of Texas.

During the Prison Lease Period, the Texas prison system was leased to two major contractors. The first lease took effect on 5 July 1871 when the entire Texas State Penitentiary was leased to Ward, Dewey, and Company of Galveston for a period of 15 years. The lease stipulated that they were to pay the State of Texas $5,000 annually for the first five years, $10,000 per year during the second five-year period, and $20,000 per year during the last quinquennium. Ward, Dewey, and Company subsequently subleased the labor of the convicts under its charge to farmers, timber harvesters, tanners, bricklayers, stone quarries, and railroad construction firms. Reports of mismanagement and abuse of prisoners, coupled with cash flow problems and political differences between Ward, Dewey and Company and Governor Richard B. Hubbard, resulted in the cancellation of their lease in 1877. The second lessee was the firm of Cunningham and Ellis. Edward H. Cunningham and L. A. Ellis had extensive agricultural holdings south and west of Houston, where they used convict labor to work their fields of sugar cane, feed grains, and cotton. Cunningham and Ellis also sublet Texas convicts to private farmers, industrial concerns, and railroad construction contractors.

A combination of circumstances led to the demise of the Prison Lease Period in Texas. First, the venture proved so profitable that many in the state legislature adopted the view that the profits from convict labor which had been reaped by Cunningham and Ellis should be going to the state. Second, because the private contractor incurred the responsibility for convict management, care, and discipline, wholesale abuses were rampant. Convicts suffered from overwork, physical abuse, meager diets, and received little or no medical care. Reports of death and injury, and the increasing number of escapes by convicts, shocked the senses of the general public. Subsequently, the 15th Texas Legislature in 1883 abandoned the practice of leasing the entire prison system to private contractors and replaced the practice with contracting only the labor of the prisoner while retaining the responsibility for the discipline, care, and control of the convicts. On 15 May 1883 control of the prison system reverted to the State.

The most significant development which occurred during the Prison Lease Period was the construction of Texas' second enclosed penitentiary, which more than doubled the state's capacity to incarcerate convicted felons. As early as 1859 the governing board of the Texas State Penitentiary wisely foresaw

A leased prison inmate plows
while a guard called a "high rider" looks on.
(Courtesy of TDCJ)

Leased prison inmates quarrying for granite and limestone for the
State Capitol building break for a rare photo opportunity.
(Courtesy of TDCJ)

the future necessity of more cell space to accommodate convicts, and proposed that the legislature give serious consideration to the building of a second penitentiary. The proposal was quickly dismissed by the 9th Texas Legislature because the urgent necessity of preparing for the inevitable onset of the Civil War consumed most of the legislature's attention and fiscal allocations. No longer able to avoid the overcrowding crisis at Huntsville which was occasioned by the general unrest following the conclusion of the Civil War, the 14th Texas Legislature in 1875 passed legislation authorizing the construction of the state's second walled penitentiary. A committee of three commissioners appointed by Governor Coke chose the East Texas town of Rusk, in Cherokee County, as the site for the new prison, which was formally designated the East Texas State Penitentiary, but which later was simply known as Rusk Penitentiary. Rusk was chosen as the site to build a new prison chiefly because it was the intent of the state to use leased convict labor to exploit the iron-ore resources and to manufacture pig iron and cast iron in East Texas.

The Rusk Penitentiary was built in two stages by the Cunningham and Ellis lease between 1877 and 1883. On 14 January 1879 Governor Hubbard reported to the legislature that the buildings for the new prison at Rusk had been completed at a total cost of $160,000. Governor Hubbard pointed out, however, that the new prison could not be used to incarcerate convicts until a wall was built, and that it was estimated the wall would cost almost as much as the buildings. When the Rusk Penitentiary opened in 1883, it contained 528 doubled-bunked cells that could accommodate 1,056 convicts. A brick wall 20 feet high and one and one-half feet thick enclosed a seven-acre site within which were contained a large, two-story cell house and ancillary buildings.

Two iron smelters with a capacity of producing 30,000 tons annually were also constructed at this time. The first iron furnace completed, nicknamed "Old Alcalde," was fired up for the first time on 27 February 1884. In the mid to late 1880s convicts from Rusk Penitentiary were responsible for manufacturing much of the new State Capitol building's interior decorative and functional cast-iron work which can still be seen today, including its iron dome, columns, stairs, and balusters. Convicts from the Rusk Penitentiary were also responsible for quarrying much of the granite and limestone used in the construction of the new State Capitol in Austin.

The iron ore as well as the wood used to fuel the smelter at Rusk Penitentiary were supplied by the Texas State Railroad. The ten-mile railway line of narrow gauge track that ran between the prison and the ore field was owned by the State, constructed between 1896 and 1903 using convict labor, and operated by the Texas prison system. (In 1972 the 61st Texas Legislature turned the railroad over to the Texas Parks and Wildlife Department, and once again convict labor was used to rehabilitate the line. The Texas State Railroad Historical Park was opened for public recreation in 1977, and continues today to operate a steam train that provides visitors an opportunity to ride the old route traveled so frequently by convicts in the late nineteenth and early twentieth centuries. The 517-acre park is only 50 to 200 feet wide in most places, making it the longest and narrowest state park in the United States.)

The iron furnaces and cast iron industry at the Rusk Penitentiary eventually proved to be an economic failure, and its smelting and fabrication operations were closed down in 1910, after a quarter century of operation. The penitentiary closed in 1917, leaving Huntsville as the only remaining walled prison in the state. In 1919 the land and buildings became the Rusk State Hospital for the insane. The land and its buildings came full circle in 1988, when the Texas Department of Corrections once again took control of them to use as a prison for the incarceration of mentally ill convicts, and it was renamed the Skyview Unit. At the close of the Prison Lease Period in 1882 the Texas prison system held 2,301 convicts. As a final note of interest, in 1888 Rusk Penitentiary became the first prison in Texas to be equipped with electric lighting. The penitentiary at Huntsville did not receive electricity until 1890.

The dominant figure associated with this period in the history of the Texas prison system was Thomas Jewett Goree, an ex-Confederate army officer and Huntsville attorney. In 1877 Governor Hubbard appointed Goree superintendent of the Texas State Penitentiary, a position that he held until his retirement in 1891. His 14-year tenure as superintendent spanned the great majority of years that constitute the entire Prison Lease Period, and eight years of the Convict Lease Period. As such, he was the principal governmental agent responsible for administering the prison lease system, overseeing the construction of the Rusk Penitentiary, and transitioning Texas from the prison lease system to the convict lease system. Despite the troubling times during which he served as superintendent, he was honored in 1900 by having a small prison farm located outside of Huntsville named in his honor. Thomas Goree died in 1905.

The Convict Lease Period (1883 to 1912)

Under this system, only the labor of convicts was leased to private contractors by the State on a monthly basis. In 1883 a rate of $6 per convict per month was obtained by the State under the convict lease system. The lessee was required to furnish all the tools and equipment necessary for the successful employment of the convicts, as well as feeding, clothing, and housing the convicts at the work site. The prison system retained full responsibility for the management and control of the convicts. Convicts were leased to cotton and rice growers on the Texas Gulf Coast, East Texas timber harvesting companies, and railroad construction firms. By 1898, the State was charging $35 per month per convict, but had taken over all other interests affecting its prisoners, including their feeding, clothing, and medical care.

The most outstanding development of the prison system during the Convict Lease Period was the purchase and development of large state prison farms in the eastern and southeastern parts of the state, a legacy that is still one of the hallmarks of the Texas prison system today. Agriculture was seen as a cost effective way to offset the funding of the prison system. In 1885 the first prison farm, the 2,500-acre Harlem Farm (now the Jester Units I and II), in Fort Bend County, was purchased for $25,000. By 1909 there were seven prison farms in operation: Harlem, Clemens, Ramsey (now Ramsey I and II),

Imperial, Goree, Wynne, and Central. Due to complaints of unfair labor competition from private sector labor interests, sales boycotts of prison agricultural products, and poor farm management practices and internal corruption, the prison's agricultural system was not successful in offsetting the State's outlay of financial resources for the operation of the prison system.

The end of the Convict Lease Period in Texas began with a series of articles written by George Waverly Briggs and published in the *San Antonio Daily Express* between 5 December 1909 and 11 January 1910. The series of articles exposed the mismanagement, corruption, and physical abuse associated with the leasing of convict labor and the management of the prison system. The articles got the attention of the legislature, which appointed a special committee to investigate the allegations published by Briggs. Following the publication of the investigating committee's report, a special session of the Texas Legislature was called by Governor Thomas M. Campbell in the summer of 1910. On 17 September 1910 Governor Campbell signed a bill that resulted in the most sweeping changes in the prison system since its inception in 1849.

Governor Campbell's bill provided that the governance of the prison system was to be overseen by a Prison Commission consisting of three members appointed by the governor who were to serve two-year terms. Furthermore, the bill provided for a major restructuring of the Texas prison system, including notification to private contractors that there would be no renewal of existing convict lease contracts. Additionally, the bill required that punishments would be humane, and that the use of the stocks as a means of disciplining convicts would stop. Under the new law convicts would be classified, and only the third, or worst, class would wear the traditional striped suit. The lash was to be restricted for use on only the third class of prisoners, and even then the lashing was to be carefully supervised. A small per diem was to be paid to convicts in return for their labor. The Prison Commission was to supply an adequate amount of reading material to convicts, and convicts were to be provided with access to doctors, preachers, and teachers.

All leases were terminated by the end of 1912, and the Convict Lease Period formally ended. At the close of the Convict Lease Period in 1912 the Texas prison system held 3,691 convicts.

The Post-Convict Lease Period (1912 to 1948)

The first thirty-six years following the close of the Convict Lease Period were troubled times for the Texas prison system. In an attempt to defray the cost of running the system by continuing to rely on the financial proceeds realized from the convict prison farms, the State purchased in 1918 the 6,747-acre Darrington Farm, and the 7,428-acre Retrieve Plantation on Oyster Creek, near Lake Jackson, in Brazoria County. By 1921 the state prison farms had a combined acreage of slightly more than 80,000 acres, but operated in the red.

Investigating committees in 1913, 1915, 1923, 1925, and 1928 all concluded that there were serious problems with the management and administration of the Texas prison system. The most influential of these investigations was carried out by Robert Homes Baker, a politically influential Texas businessman who was president of a private prison reform organization called the Texas Committee on Prisons and Prison Labor. The 38th Texas Legislature authorized the Texas Committee on Prisons and Prison Labor to conduct an independent survey of the Texas prison system. The report, completed in 1924, revealed a litany of abuse and mismanagement plaguing the Texas prison system, including lax and fraudulent bookkeeping and accounting practices, unqualified and unfit prison system personnel, inhumane and unsanitary living conditions, and political corruption. Typical of the graft, fraud, and inefficient management which the Texas Committee on Prisons and Prison Labor exposed was the prison system's beef cattle operation. The prison system branded their cattle with a five-pointed star. The committee discovered that landowners near and adjacent to the prison farms were using the star brand with the addition of a letter or numeral to, in effect, rustle cattle. This practice, which helped explain the failure of the prison herds to increase, was carried out with the knowledge and collusion of prison officials.

   The first real attempt to reform the system during the Post-Convict Lease Period occurred when Governor Daniel Moody appointed Marshall Lee Simmons as general manager of the Texas prison system in April 1930. At the time of his appointment as general manager, Simmons, a member of the Prison Board, had a reputation for being a charismatic individual who was very good at public relations. Simmons was given the job of general manager with the understanding that he was to reform the system and promote a positive public image of the prison system. His five-year tenure as general manager, however, resulted in no meaningful, long lasting, or substantive changes that served to address the shortcomings of the troubled system and usher in the beginning of a new era for Texas prisons. Rather, Simmons is best remembered today for the creation of the Texas Prison Rodeo, which was open to the public and held in October from 1931 until 1986. Billed as the "Fastest and Wildest Rodeo in Texas," the prison rodeo

Inmates compete before a captive audience in what became known as the "Fastest and Wildest Rodeo in Texas."   (Courtesy of TDCJ)

in Huntsville proved to be a very successful public relations tool that captured the attention of the general public and cast the prison system in a favorable light. The rodeo received national attention, and attendance at the October event in the late 1960s topped 100,000 and continued to draw large crowds through the 1970s.

Ardent advocates for prison reform, however, continued to monitor the progress of the prison system, and argued that Simmons' attempt to effect meaningful change amounted only to window dressing. Disillusioned with those critical of his ability to reform the system, Simmons resigned as general manager in November 1935. After resigning, Simmons was hired in 1936 as clerk of the United States Court for the Eastern District of Texas, a post he held until 1941, when he resumed ranching. In the late 1950s Simmons began work on a book he titled *Assignment Huntsville: Memoirs of a Texas Prison Official*. The book, published in 1957, is a very frank account of his experiences as general manager of the Texas prison system. Marshall Simmons died in Austin on 12 October 1957 while on a trip to check on the galley proofs of his book.

After the resignation of Simmons, the Texas prison system drifted along aimlessly from 1935 to 1948, with no strong leadership, no vision, and not one single reform of any lasting significance. Texas Prison Board member Dave Nelson succeeded Simmons as general manager in November 1935, but died after only two weeks in office. Nelson was succeeded by O.J.S. Ellingson. Ellingson's tenure as general manager was lackluster. Continuing reports of prison mismanagement and brutality resulted in his firing in October 1941. Douglas W. Stakes replaced Ellingson in November 1941. His leadership, and subsequent legacy, fared no better than that of his predecessor. Public criticism and indignation about the state of the prison system continued during Stakes' administration. Stakes was forced to resign under pressure from the Texas Prison Board, after a report (which was commissioned by the board) by internationally renowned prison reformer Austin MacCormick concluded that the Texas prison system was in no better shape in 1947 than it had been in 1930.

At the conclusion of the Post-Convict Lease Period in December 1947, the Texas prison system held 5,675 convicts in eleven prison farms and the main walled prison at Huntsville, all of which were located predominantly in the southeastern part of Texas. Total income from agricultural and industrial operations was slightly more than $4 million, and the average per diem cost of maintaining a convict in the Texas prison system was 84 cents.

The Ellis and Beto Era (1948 to 1972)

What is unquestionably the golden era in the history of the Texas prison system began in 1948, when Oscar Byron Ellis assumed the position of general manager, and ended with the retirement of Dr. George Beto as director of the Texas Department of Corrections in 1972, almost a quarter of a century later.

Following the disgrace and resignation of General Manager Douglas Stakes in the wake of the Austin MacCormick investigation, the Texas Prison Board began to look for a truly progressive and enlightened individual who could bring leadership and vision to the general manager's position, and effect meaningful reform of the troubled Texas prison system.

Oscar Byron Ellis (1902-1961) came to the attention of the Texas Prison Board because of the national reputation he earned as commissioner of the Shelby County Penal Farm, located on the outskirts of Memphis, Tennessee. Following his

Oscar Byron Ellis—
Pioneer of Texas prison reform.
(Courtesy of TDCJ)

election to the position in 1937, Ellis transformed the penal farm into a model correctional facility by his humane methods of prison discipline and his efficient management of the penal farm's agricultural operations, which subsequently became a model for efficient agricultural practices for farmers in the region. His pioneering agricultural initiatives at the Shelby County Penal Farm and the agricultural character of the troubled Texas prison system made Ellis the obvious choice to bring about much needed reform. He assumed the position of general manager of the Texas prison system on 1 January 1948, and thus began the single greatest period of reform in the history of the Texas prison system.

Ellis took charge of a prison system that had major problems. The prison system was in debt, and its operations were outdated. The agricultural program was in a state of virtual collapse. Of the almost 81,000 acres of land owned by the Texas prison system, only 20,000 were in cultivation. Fields were worked with Georgia stock plows pulled by mules. Despite owning some of the best agricultural and grazing land in the Gulf Plains, the prison system spent more than a half million dollars a year purchasing beef and vegetables on the open market. Prison employees were untrained, underpaid, and morale was low. Additionally, due to years of negligence, the physical plant and infrastructure of the prison system was in a state of disrepair and disintegration.

Ellis' vision of reforming the Texas prison system was embodied in five basic initiatives which have collectively come to be known as the Ellis Plan. The Ellis Plan of reforming the Texas prison system included (1) professional management, modernization, and diversification of agricultural operations, (2) upgraded physical facilities and improvement of living conditions for convicts, (3) upgraded standards of recruitment, pay, and training of prison guards, (4) the expansion of convict rehabilitation programs, and (5) reorganization and management of the prison system's industries. During his 13-year tenure as head of the Texas prison system, Ellis worked in harmony with Governors Beauford H. Jester, Allan Shivers, and Price Daniel, Sr., as well as the Texas Legislature, which from 1948 to 1961 appropriated more than $19 million for the Ellis Plan.

The reforms instituted by Oscar Ellis forever changed the Texas prison system. The Texas prison farms were consolidated into one managerial unit, and a professional agricultural specialist was hired to manage all farming operations. Tractors were purchased to replace the inefficient use of mules to work the land. Thousands of low lying acres on the Texas Gulf Coast which were unusable due to flooding were brought into productive operation by the adoption of modern drainage techniques. The prison system's beef and dairy herds were upgraded, with the result that, by 1961, Texas convicts were producing most of the beef and dairy products they consumed. New cell blocks were constructed to accommodate the growing convict population, which grew rapidly after the end of World War II, and the prison system's infrastructure was improved by the use of convict labor to build new industrial workshops, guard towers, fences, and other facilities. The diet and medical care of convicts was upgraded, and Ellis introduced television sets into the cell blocks, and on weekends convicts were entertained with Hollywood films, with the result that convict morale was greatly improved. He summarily fired brutal and corrupt convict guards and prison wardens, and to insure that qualified and competent personnel were hired to carry out his reforms, in 1958 he started the first pre-service training program for Texas prison guards. Between 1948 and 1961 the annual starting salaries of guards almost tripled, and competent prison guards were rewarded by subsidized housing and other amenities such as barber and laundry services.

Convict rehabilitation programs were a priority for Ellis. Between 1950 and 1955 vocational training programs were begun with the goal of enabling convicts to acquire meaningful skills by which they could earn an honest living after their discharge from prison. Programs of vocational instruction in the construction arts, television repair, metal welding, auto mechanics, and carpentry were created and made available to convicts. In 1956 Ellis began the General Education Development Program, which provided convicts the opportunity to earn a high school diploma. In 1956 the first religious chapel was completed at Huntsville. Alcoholics Anonymous programs were started to help convicts with alcohol problems. In order to maximize the effect of rehabilitation programs, Ellis reorganized the convict classification system to group convicts according to factors such as age, offense, prior record, and potential for rehabilitation.

Ellis was a hands-on general manager. His management philosophy (which, incidentally, was not lost on his successor, Dr. George Beto) was that a prison system could not be run from behind a desk. Ellis made frequent inspection visits to all the prison system units (often traveling by car over 4,500 miles each month) to ensure that his reforms were being implemented and the prison system was being run according to his vision. His successful program of reforming the Texas prison system further contributed to his national reputation as a penologist, and in 1958 he was elected president of the American Correctional Association. By the time Ellis died suddenly of a heart attack in 1961, he had succeeded in transforming what Austin MacCormick and others had considered the worst state prison system in the United States into one of the best. In recognition of his contributions, two Texas prison facilities have been named after him. The Ellis I Unit opened in 1963, and the Ellis II Unit opened in 1983. At the time of Ellis' death the Texas prison system held 12,011 convicts.

Within hours after the sudden and unexpected death of Ellis, Texas Prison Board Chairman H. H. Coffield was on the telephone with Dr. George John Beto (1916-1991), president of Concordia Theological Seminary, in Springfield, Illinois. Beto was Coffield's first and obvious choice to be director of the Texas Department of Corrections. While the choice of a theological seminary president to run the Texas prison system may at first seem odd, Beto was no stranger to either the field of penology in general or to the Texas prison system specifically.

Beto was born in Hysham, Montana, in 1916, the son of a Lutheran minister. He took his undergraduate degree at Indiana's Valparaiso University and completed theological studies in 1939 at Concordia Seminary in St. Louis, Missouri. From 1939 to 1949 he taught history at Concordia Lutheran College in Austin, Texas, and served as its president from 1949 to 1959. While at Concordia Lutheran College he was ordained a minister in the Lutheran Church (1944) and matriculated at the University of Texas at Austin, where he earned a master of arts degree in history in 1944, and a Ph.D. in educational administration in 1955.

His first official exposure to and involvement with the Texas prison system occurred in 1953, when Governor Allan Shivers appointed him to the Texas Prison Board. During his six years of service on the board, Beto was a staunch supporter of Ellis' reform efforts, and he was instrumental not only in crafting the language of the bills deemed vital to promoting the success of the Ellis

Dr. George J. Beto—Theologian and penologist. He revolutionized the state's implementation of industrial prison operations.
(Courtesy of the Beto family)

Plan but also lobbied for their passage in the Texas Legislature. His administrative abilities, energy, and progressive penological vision impressed all who came into contact with him. When Beto resigned from the Texas Prison Board in 1959 to become president of Concordia Theological Seminary, in Springfield, Illinois, his presence was greatly missed by Ellis, the board, and all Texans interested in the continued success of the Ellis Plan.

During his tenure as president of Concordia Theological Seminary, Beto continued his involvement in prison issues. He became a very close friend of Joseph E. Ragen, the superintendent of Illinois' famous Stateville Penitentiary. Beto's philosophy about how a prison should best be managed was greatly influenced by Ragen's no-nonsense approach to convict control and his emphasis on attention to detail, efficiency, and routine. On the strength of his previous Texas reputation and with the support of Ragen, Beto was appointed by Illinois Governor Otto Kerner to the Illinois Board of Pardons and Paroles, and during this period he also served as the chairman of the governor's committee that evaluated the Illinois Youth Commission, the state agency charged with the care, custody, and control of delinquent youth. During this time Beto also began to acquire an international penological perspective. In 1960 he visited and evaluated a number of European prison systems, including those of England, France, Germany, Denmark, and Holland.

It is therefore not surprising that this Lutheran minister and seminary president with a proven track record in prison affairs and a growing international reputation in the field of penology was Coffield's first choice to continue the legacy of reform so ably begun by Ellis. Beto accepted Coffield's offer to become director of the Texas Department of Corrections (and chief of chaplains) on 1 March 1962. Thus began the second phase of the greatest era in the history of the Texas prison system.

Beto left his mark on the prison system in two ways: through his philosophy of prison management, and by his reform accomplishments. His influence on the management and administration of the Texas prison system was immediately felt, and the lessons he learned from Ragen were apparent. There was never any question about who was in charge. He quickly gained the reputation as a stern disciplinarian who would tolerate neither convict misbehavior nor brutal or inhumane prison guards. One observer euphemistically characterized him as "a preacher with a baseball bat in one hand and a Bible in the other." Beto demanded that the Texas prison system be a safe, humane, and productive environment that was conducive to the rehabilitation of convicts. To insure that the prison system was being run according to his vision, Beto frequently showed up unannounced at the various prison units, where he talked with convicts, visited with staff, ate the food that was given to convicts, and inspected the working and living conditions of the convicts. Given his reputation for this type of direct oversight, both convicts and prison employees

soon came to refer to him by the nickname "Walking George."
His philosophy of order, discipline, and convict control has
subsequently come to be referred to in the literature of penology as the control model of prison management, and resulted
in what many considered the safest and most humane prison
system in the United States during the 1960s.

Beto's reform accomplishments, which were the natural
and complementary extensions of what Ellis had begun in
1948, fall into three broad categories: educational opportunities, rehabilitation, and the economic base of the prison system. In the area of convict education, Beto will best be remembered as the father of the Windham School District, the first
school district created in the United States with no geographical boundaries, designed solely to serve the primary, sec-
ondary, and vocational education needs of convicts in the
Texas prison system. He was also responsible for creating programs of higher education within the prison system that
allowed convicts the opportunity to earn college credit and
university degrees. A staunch supporter of rehabilitation, Beto
was the driving force behind the first pre-release program in
the state of Texas, which was an eight-week program of counseling to help soon-to-be-discharged convicts make a successful transition from prison life to life in the free world. He was
also responsible for establishing the Texas prison system's first
work furlough program, which allowed qualified convicts (those
with less than a year remaining on their sentence) to be released from the confines of the prison during the day for private employers. After the conclusion of the work day, the fur-
loughed convicts returned to the prison, where they remained
confined during nights and on weekends. And not surprisingly,
he significantly upgraded the prison system's chaplaincy program. Finally, in strengthening the economic base of the prison
system, he continued to improve its fiscal self-sufficiency by
creating new ways to productively make use of convict labor.
Beto was instrumental in expanding the industrial base of the
prison system by creating school bus repair shops, a tire recap-
ping plant, garment manufacturing facilities, a dental laboratory, a license plate factory, and a number of computer data
entry offices for conversion of state records to computer format,

all of which were worked by convicts. Additionally, in 1963 he convinced the Texas Legislature to enact a bill allowing the prison system to sell its agricultural and industrial products to other state agencies and non-profit private organizations. Agricultural operations on approximately 100,000 acres of land combined with prison industries and construction projects utilizing convict labor were a major source of income and saving to taxpayers that gave Texas one of the lowest per-capita convict costs to taxpayers in the United States, with a daily cost per convict of $3.61. It is worth noting that Beto was responsible for hiring the first African-American correctional officers in the Texas prison system. In 1969 Beto was elected president of the American Correctional Association.

When Beto retired as director of the Texas Department of Corrections on 31 August 1972, the golden era of the Texas prison system came to a close. The reforms achieved during the Ellis and Beto Era represented a sea change in not only the Texas prison system but also in the public's perception of the system. In 1968 Austin MacCormick summed up the progress he had seen occur since his landmark 1947 report which ushered in the Ellis and Beto Era. In a communication to the Texas Prison Board, MacCormick remarked, "I saw the Texas Prison System come up from close to the bottom of the rating list to its present position in the top half-dozen. Under Dr. Beto, it is going steadily forward. Nothing in my entire career of fifty years in the correctional field has given me such satisfaction as the remarkable transformation that has taken place."

After retiring, Beto was the driving force behind the creation of Sam Houston State University's Institute of Contemporary Corrections and the Behavioral Sciences, in Huntsville, Texas. Under his professorship, the institute quickly grew into one of the premier centers of criminal justice higher education and research in the world. In 1990 the institute was renamed the George J. Beto Criminal Justice Center. Beto died suddenly and unexpectedly of a heart attack at his Austin home on 4 December 1991. He is buried in the State Cemetery at Austin.

The Post-Beto Era
(1972 to Present)

George Beto was succeeded in 1972 by Ward James Estelle. During Estelle's eleven-year tenure as director of the Texas prison system, he continued to build upon the legacy begun by Ellis and Beto. Under Estelle's stewardship, the Texas prison system experienced growth in additional prison unit construction, prison industrial programs continued to expand in number and variety, and opportunities for convict rehabilitation continued to increase with the growth of educational and vocational training programs.

The most significant development during Estelle's tenure as director of the Texas prison system was what has come to be known as the *Ruiz* case. A federal lawsuit was filed in June 1972 by Texas prison convict David Ruiz (*Ruiz v. Estelle*, 503 F. Supp. 1265 (1980)). The lawsuit alleged that the living and working conditions in Texas prisons violated the Eighth Amendment protection against cruel and unusual punishment and the due process and equal protection clauses of the 14th Amendment to the United States Constitution. On 12 April 1974 eight other similar lawsuits were consolidated with the *Ruiz* case and converted into a class action suit. The trial began on 2 October 1978 and ended 159 days later on 20 September 1979. It remains today the longest running prison class action

Ward J. Estelle—He and his successors have been marred by issues ranging from prison overcrowding to financial mismanagement and impropriety. (Courtesy of TDCJ)

Cruel and unusual punishment? The subject of prison overcrowding continues to be a controversial issue in which human rights and ideal notions of punishment are often at odds.   (Courtesy of TDCJ)

suit in American history. During the trial, testimony was taken from 349 witnesses and 1,565 exhibits were received into evidence. At the conclusion of the trial U.S. Federal District Court Judge William Wayne Justice ruled that the State of Texas operated a prison system that was overcrowded, and violated the Eighth Amendment protections of Texas convicts against cruel and unusual punishment.

Following the ruling, Texas entered into a consent decree with the federal government. The consent decree gave the federal government powers to oversee the operation of the Texas prison system and to insure that the sweeping changes Judge Justice mandated to rectify Eighth Amendment violations were being met. Minimum standards were set by Judge Justice in the areas of convict management practices, prison guard hiring and training programs, health care, feeding, clothing, recreational opportunities, and improved prison physical facilities to alleviate the overcrowding problem. To ensure that over-crowding would not again occur, the decree required Texas to leave five percent of its prison housing capacity (at that time approximately 2,000 beds) vacant every night.

The *Ruiz* lawsuit spurred Texas into the largest prison con-struction program in its history, with the result that today Texas has the third largest prison system in the world. In 1992 the lawsuit was finally ended with a final judgment that released Texas from the consent decree and returned control of the Texas prison system to the State.

The controversy surrounding the *Ruiz* case, along with alle-gations of financial mismanagement in the early 1980s, took its toll on Estelle, who resigned on 7 October 1983. Following the resignation of Estelle, the Texas prison system never fully recov-ered from the leadership vacuum created after the resignation of Beto and the problems exposed by the *Ruiz* case. Daniel V. "Red" McKaskle acted as director of the prison system for six months in 1983 and 1984 following the resignation of Estelle. Raymand T. Procunier served as director from March 1984 until June 1985. Procunier was replaced by O. Lane McCotter, a retired army colonel who served as director from June 1985 until late 1986, when he was asked to resign by Governor William Clements. In early 1987 James A. Lynaugh, an accoun-tant by training with 19 years' experience in state government, replaced McCotter. In 1989 the Texas Department of Correc-tions was merged with both the Board of Pardons and Paroles and the Texas Adult Probation Commission to form the Texas Department of Criminal Justice, and the Texas Department of Corrections became the Institutional Division of the Texas De-partment of Criminal Justice. Lynaugh became the first executive director of the newly formed Texas Department of Criminal Justice, and James A. Collins was named director of the Institu-tional Division. A few years later Collins succeeded Lynaugh as executive director of the Texas Department of Criminal Justice.

The tenure of Collins as both the Texas prison chief (in the capacity of director of the Institutional Division), and later as the executive director of the Texas Department of Criminal Justice, was marred by scandal. Collins retired from his $120,000-a-year job in January 1996 amid growing allegations of an illegal $33.7 million prison purchase of a soy-based meat substitute called VitaPro. The contract was awarded without competitive bids by Collins, who, it was alleged, had directed prison officials to buy VitaPro through a method called direct purchasing, which allowed him to bypass the formal competitive bidding procedures. Evidence has suggested that in 1994 Collins pressured subordinates to purchase millions of dollars worth of VitaPro, and personally directed food service officials to serve the soy product food extender to prisoners at least once a day. The initial investigation into the illegal purchasing agreements resulted in the firing or forced resignation of the purchasing director and the chief of the prison industries program that oversaw the VitaPro purchases, both of whom were top ranking administrators in the prison system. A month before his retirement in January 1996 Collins was paid a $20,000 "commission" by VitaPro. After leaving the Texas Department of Criminal Justice, Collins subsequently became an occasional $1,000-a-day consultant for the Montreal-based VitaPro firm. Both federal and state investigations into the scandal continue to this day.

WORKS CONSULTED AND
SUGGESTIONS FOR FURTHER READING

Allen, Sandra Fuller. "The Iron Men: An Historical Review of the East Texas Penitentiary." M.A. thesis, Stephen F. Austin State University, 1982.

Anderson, Marcus. "Rehabilitation Activities of the Texas Prison System." M. A. thesis, East Texas State Teachers College, 1941.

Ayers, Edward L. "Prisons." *Encyclopedia of Southern Culture*. Edited by Charles Reagan Wilson and William Ferris. Chapel Hill, North Carolina: The University of North Carolina Press, 1989, pp. 1494-1496.

Bancroft, Hubert Howe. *The Works of Hubert Howe Bancroft. Volume XVI: History of the North Mexican States and Texas, 1801-1899.* San Francisco: The History Company, 1889.

Birmingham, Billy Martin. "An Historical Account of the East Texas Prison at Rusk." M.A. thesis, Sam Houston State University, 1979.

Briggs, George Waverly. "The Texas Penitentiary: A Study of the Texas Convict System and Suggestions for its Betterment." *San Antonio Express*, 5 December 1909-11 January 1910. (Reprint of a series of articles from the *San Antonio Daily Express*.)

Brinkerhoff, I. R. "The Convict Contract Labor System." *Proceedings of the National Conference of Charities and Correction*, 1887, p. 107.

Cable, George Washington. "The Convict Lease System in the Southern States." *Century Magazine*, vol. 27 (1884), pp. 593-595.

———. "Lease of Convicts in the South." *Proceedings of the National Conference of Charities and Correction*, 1883, p. 265.

Carleton, Mark T. "Convict Lease System." *The Encyclopedia of Southern History*. Edited by David C. Roller and Robert W. Twyman. Baton Rouge, Louisiana: Louisiana State University Press, 1979, p. 294.

———. "Convict Leasing." *Encyclopedia of Southern Culture*. Edited by Charles Reagan Wilson and William Ferris. Chapel Hill, North Carolina: The University of North Carolina Press, 1989, p. 1502.

———. "Penal Systems." *The Encyclopedia of Southern History*. Edited by David C. Roller and Robert W. Twyman. Baton Rouge, Louisiana: Louisiana State University Press, 1979, pp. 962-963.

Carroll, H. Bailey. "Texas Collection." *The Southwestern Historical Quarterly*, vol. 58 (1954), p. 292.

Carter, Dan T. "Convict Lease." M.A. thesis, University of Wisconsin, 1964.

Copeland, Ronald Craig. "The Evolution of the Texas Department of Corrections." M.A. thesis, Sam Houston State University, 1980.

Costilow, Donna. "Prison Cemetery." *Texas Historian*, vol. 43 (1983) pp. 15-17.

Crouch, Ben M., and James W. Marquart. *An Appeal to Justice: Litigated Reform of Texas Prisons*. Austin, Texas: University of Texas Press, 1989.

Crow, Herman Lee. "A Political History of the Texas Penal System, 1829-1951." Ph.D. dissertation, University of Texas, 1964.

DeHay, James Harvey, Jr. "Recreation in the Texas Prison System." M.A. thesis, University of Texas, 1952.

Dollar, Ray Gordon. "A Study of the Organizational Structure of the Administration Unit of the Texas Prison System." M.A. thesis, University of Texas, 1954.

Duncan, J. S. "Richard Bennett Hubbard and State Resumption of the Penitentiary, 1876-1878." *Texana*, vol. 12 (1974), pp. 47-55.

Estill, Harry F. "The Old Town of Huntsville." *The Quarterly of the Texas State Historical Association*, vol. 3 (1900), pp. 265-271.

Felton, Charles E. "Prison Labor." *Proceedings of the Annual Congress of the National Prison Association of the United States*, 1886, p. 216.

Flinty, Tom. "The Texas Prison Investigation." *The Survey*, vol. 23 (1909), pp. 387-391.

Goree, James Langston, and Deborah Bloys Hardin. "Goree, Thomas Jewett." *The New Handbook of Texas*. Austin, Texas: Texas State Historical Association, 1996, vol. 3, p. 252.

Hafertepe, Kenneth. "Cook, Abner Hugh." *The New Handbook of Texas*. Austin, Texas: Texas State Historical Association, 1996, vol. 2, pp. 301-302.

Hardin, Stephen L. "Jester State Prison Farm." *The New Handbook of Texas*. Austin, Texas: Texas State Historical Association, 1996, vol. 3, p. 396.

Hart, Brian. "Simmons, Marshall Lee." *The New Handbook of Texas*. Austin, Texas: Texas State Historical Association, 1996, vol. 5, pp. 1052-1053.

Henderson, John N. "The Lease System in Texas." *Report of the National Prison Association*, 1897, p. 298.

Hutson, Marvin. "Mississippi's State Penal System." M.A. thesis, University of Mississippi, 1939.

Jeffords, Charles, and Jan Lindsey. "George J. Beto." *Encyclopedia of American Prisons*. Edited by Marilyn D. McShane and Frank P. Williams III. New York: Garland Publishing, 1996, pp. 58-61.

Kennedy, Riley. *Facts, Features, and Fotos: Prison in Texas*. Tyler, Texas: Riley Kennedy, 1972.

Lucko, Paul M. "A Missed Opportunity: Texas Prison Reform During the Dan Moody Administration, 1927-1931." *Southwestern Historical Quarterly*, vol. 96 (1992), pp. 27-52.

————. "The Next Big Job: Women Prison Reformers in Texas, 1918-1930." *Women and Texas History: Selected Essays*. Downs, Fan and Nancy Baker Jones, editors. Austin, Texas: Texas State Historical Association, 1993.

————. "Beto, George John." *The New Handbook of Texas*. Austin, Texas: Texas State Historical Association, 1996, vol. 1, pp. 511-522.

————. "Ellis, Oscar Byron." *The New Handbook of Texas*. Austin, Texas: Texas State Historical Association, 1996, vol. 2, pp. 831-832.

————. "Retrieve Plantation." *The New Handbook of Texas*. Austin, Texas: Texas State Historical Association, 1996, vol. 5, pp. 551-552.

————. "Rusk Penitentiary." *The New Handbook of Texas*. Austin, Texas: Texas State Historical Association, 1996, vol. 5, pp. 726-727.

————. "Texas Committee on Prisons and Prison Labor." *The New Handbook of Texas*. Austin, Texas: Texas State Historical Association, 1996, vol. 6, pp. 306-307.

Martin, Steve J., and Sheldon Ekland-Olson. *Texas Prisons: The Walls Came Tumbling Down*. Austin, Texas: Texas Monthly Press, 1987.

McAdams, Kelly E. "A Social Study of the Women's Penitentiary of Texas." M. A. thesis, Texas Agricultural and Mechanical College, 1932.

McAlister, J. P. "The Toughest, Roughest Rodeo Behind Bars." *Texas Historian*, vol. 43 (1983) pp. 22-24.

McFarlane, W. D. *The Penitentiary System of Texas*. Austin, Texas: Von Boeckmann Jones Company, 1930. A speech of W. D. FcFarlane in the Senate of the state of Texas, 26 February 1930.

McKelvey, Blake. *American Prisons: A History of Good Intentions*. Montclair, New Jersey: Patterson Smith, 1977.

Morris, Joe Dale. *The Texas State Railroad*. Austin, Texas: Branch Line Graphics, 1979.

Nowlin, James Robertson. "A Political History of the Texas Prison System, 1849-1957." M. A. thesis, Trinity University, 1962.

"Our Penal System and its Purpose." A series of articles published in the *Galveston News* and the *Dallas Morning News* during the summer of 1909.

Paddock, W. A. "Texas Prison System." *The State of Texas Book: One Hundred Years of Progress*. Published for the Bureau of Research and Publicity in Austin, Texas, by Capital Printing Company, 1937.

Potts, C. S. "The Convict Labor System in Texas." *Annals of American Academy of Political and Social Sciences*, vol. 30 (1903).

Ragen, Joseph E. *Inside the World's Toughest Prison*. Springfield, Illinois: Thomas Publishing Company, 1962.

Rambo, Ernest Steele. "A Study of Education in the Texas Prison System." M.A. thesis, Texas Agricultural and Mechanical College, 1932.

Reynolds, James Robert. "The Administration of the Texas Prison System." M.A. thesis, University of Texas, 1925.

Richards, Amy. "Texas State Railroad." *The New Handbook of Texas*. Austin, Texas: Texas State Historical Association, 1996, vol. 6, p. 432.

Rives, William T. "Rogues' Rodeo." *Colliers*, vol. 120, no. 16, 22 November 1947.

Rosenquist, C. M. "Prison System." *The Handbook of Texas*. Austin, Texas: Texas State Historical Association, 1952, vol. 2, pp. 411-414.

Ruiz v. Estelle, 503 F. Supp. 1265 (1980).

Simmons, Lee. "Observations on Horses Across Seventy-five Years." *The Southwestern Historical Quarterly,* vol. 58 (1954), p. 217.

———. *Assignment Huntsville: Memoirs of a Texas Prison Official.* Austin, Texas: University of Texas Press, 1957.

"State Penitentiary Statistics." *The Texas Almanac for 1857.* Galveston, Texas: Richardson and Company, 1856.

"Statistics of Convict Labor in the United States." *Public Opinion*, vol. 21 (1896), p. 305.

Stone, William E. *A Brief History of the Texas Department of Corrections.* Huntsville, Texas: Texas Department of Corrections, 1974.

Tatum, Bowen C. "The Penitentiary Movement in Texas, 1847-1849." M.A. thesis, Sam Houston State University, 1970.

"Texas Penitentiary." *Journal of Prison Discipline and Philanthropy,* vol. 15 (1860), pp. 7-17.

Texas Prison Board: Annual Reports, 1928-1932, 1934-1946.

Walker, Donald R. *Penology for Profit: A History of the Texas Prison System, 1867-1912.* College Station, Texas: Texas A&M University Press, 1988.

———. "Convict Lease System." *The New Handbook of Texas.* Austin, Texas: Texas State Historical Association, 1996, vol. 2, pp. 298-299.

———. "Texas State Penitentiary at Huntsville." *The New Handbook of Texas.* Austin, Texas: Texas State Historical Association, 1996, vol. 6, pp. 430-432.

Welch, June Rayfield. *People and Places in the Texas Past.* Dallas, Texas: G. L. A. Press, 1974, pp. 68-71.

Whitman, Sylvia. "Texas Prison Rodeo." *The New Handbook of Texas.* Austin, Texas: Texas State Historical Association, 1996, vol. 6, pp. 390-391.

Zimmerman, Hilda Jane. "Penal Systems and Penal Reform in the South Since the Civil War." Ph.D. dissertation, University of North Carolina at Chapel Hill, 1947.

7.
THE TEXAS PRISON SYSTEM TODAY

OVERVIEW

The Texas prison system is today the third largest prison system in the world. Only the People's Republic of China and the state of California have more penal facilities and incarcerate more prisoners than the state of Texas. By the end of 1998, the state of Texas had 111 penal facilities scattered across the state for the incarceration of convicted felons. Eighty-four of these facilities are classified as prisons and twenty-seven are state jails. Of the 84 prisons, seven are dedicated to exclusively housing female convicts. The prison system also operates its own hospital at Galveston and a health delivery system employing more than 200 physicians, 1,300 nurses, 100 dentists, and 20 pharmacists.

Texas currently incarcerates almost 150,000 convicts, approximately 135,000 of whom are locked up in state prison facilities and about 10,000 are confined in the state jail system. This represents about 12% of the entire prison convict population in the United States, and is second only to California, which has a prison convict population of almost 140,000. This gives Texas a prison incarceration rate of 659 convicts per 100,000 population, the highest recorded rate of any state in the United States since the federal government began keeping uniform prison statistics in 1925. This figure is a little less than double the national prison rate of incarceration, which is 388 per 100,000 population. Additionally, Texas has the highest per capita rate of felon incarceration of any Western democracy. By way of comparison, England, France, Germany, Spain, and Italy have incarceration rates of between 80 and 90 convicts per 100,000 population.

In the past ten years, the growth of the Texas prison system, both in numbers of prison units and the size of the convict population, has been phenomenal. In 1990 the convict population in Texas was approximately 48,000. Today it is almost 150,000. This represents a 180% increase in seven years in the size of the convict population, and is the largest reported increase in the felon convict population of any state prison system in the United States. Texas receives approximately 900 new prisoners every month, and the projected number of convicts incarcerated in Texas prisons in the year 2000 is expected to be 206,000. This will result in a prison incarceration rate of 1,029 per 100,000 population, and will be slightly more than double the projected national rate of 501 prison convicts per 100,000 population. If this projection holds true, Texas prisons in the year 2000 will hold approximately one-fifth of all the convicted felons in the United States.

The growth in the Texas prison system's capacity to incarcerate convicts represents the largest prison expansion program undertaken in the United States during the twentieth century. The growth in the number of prison units is a direct result of the *Ruiz v. Estelle* lawsuit (see Chapter 6) and the State's meeting the conditions mandated in the consent decree. The building boom began in 1987 with legislative appropriations that provided for the construction of prison facilities to hold 15,000 new convicts. This was followed in 1989 with a $400 million legislative appropriation to finance the construction of facilities to hold 11,100 more convicts. Since 1990, the State of Texas has spent an additional $2 billion on prison expansion. The Texas prison system today has the capacity to incarcerate in excess of 145,000 convicts, and more prison construction is planned for the future. The growth in the size of the convict population in Texas has been attributed to the fact that the number of convicts being granted parole has dropped significantly, and the number of parole revocations has increased. Additionally, it has been argued that given the increased capacity to incarcerate convicted felons, Texas district court judges are today sentencing more violent felons to prison.

PART 1:
MANAGEMENT STRUCTURE AND OVERSIGHT: THE TEXAS DEPARTMENT OF CRIMINAL JUSTICE

The management structure of the Texas prison system has undergone considerable change since the first prison was opened at Huntsville in 1849. Originally, the prison system was managed by a superintendent appointed by the governor. In 1881 management and oversight of the prison system became the responsibility of the Board of Prison Commissioners, a three-member board appointed by the governor. The Board of Prison Commissioners was responsible for hiring a superintendent. Texas voters in 1926 adopted a constitutional amendment which allowed the legislature to abolish the Board of Prison Commissions and replace it with the Texas Prison Board.

The new Texas Prison Board consisted of nine members appointed by the governor for six-year terms. The members of the Texas Prison Board served without benefit of compensation, except for a small per diem when they were actually engaged in prison system business. The Texas Prison Board was required to employ a general manager who was directly responsible for managing the day-to-day affairs of running the prison system and for implementing and administering the plans and policies of the Texas Prison Board. The Texas Prison Board functioned in much the same capacity as the board of directors of a large corporation. Except for minor name changes, this structure of managerial oversight and governance remained in place until 1990.

In 1957 the Texas Legislature passed legislation that resulted in three name changes associated with the prison system: the Texas prison system was renamed the Texas Department of Corrections, the Texas Prison Board became the Texas

Board of Corrections, and the position of general manager was changed to director.

The greatest managerial restructuring in the history of the Texas prison system occurred on 1 January 1990, when House Bill 2335 (passed by the 70th Legislature) went into effect. House Bill 2335 created the Texas Department of Criminal Justice, and today it operates under the legal authority of Chapter 412 of the *Texas Government Code*. This new state agency was created to provide centralized and integrated managerial oversight over three functions of criminal justice administration in Texas that were previously managed by three separate agencies of state government: the Texas Department of Corrections, the Texas Board of Pardons and Paroles, and the Texas Adult Probation Commission. Sometimes referred to as the Omnibus Criminal Justice Bill, the 1990 legislation created three divisions within the Texas Department of Criminal Justice: the Institutional Division (previously the Texas Department of Corrections), the Pardons and Paroles Division (to supervise parolees), and the Community Justice Assistance Division (previously known as the Texas Adult Probation Commission). (The work of the Pardons and Paroles Division and the Community Justice Assistance Division is discussed in Chapter 8.) Additionally, in 1993 the Texas Legislature created the State Jail Division of the Texas Department of Criminal Justice to oversee the management and operation of the state jail system. The mandated mission of the Texas Department of Criminal Justice is to provide public safety, promote positive change in the behavior of criminal offenders, and to successfully reintegrate them into mainstream society.

The Texas Department of Criminal Justice is today the largest single agency in Texas state government, and its annual budget is the fifth largest of any state agency. Only the Departments of Education, Health, Human Services, and Transportation receive larger annual legislative appropriations than does the Texas Department of Criminal Justice. The Texas Department of Criminal Justice has more than 42,000 employees, and in 1998 the cost to the citizens of Texas of operating the deparatment was in excess of $2.5 billion.

The Texas Department of Criminal Justice is governed by

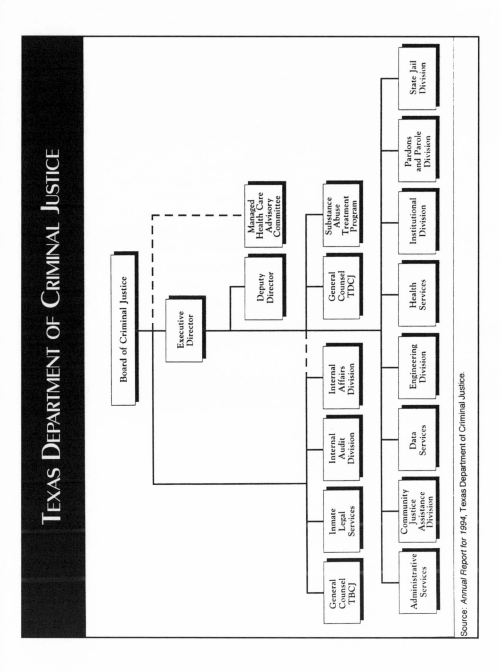

TEXAS DEPARTMENT OF CRIMINAL JUSTICE

Board of Criminal Justice

Executive Director

Deputy Director

Managed Health Care Advisory Committee

General Counsel TBCJ

Inmate Legal Services

Internal Audit Division

Internal Affairs Division

General Counsel TDCJ

Substance Abuse Treatment Program

Administrative Services

Community Justice Assistance Division

Data Services

Engineering Division

Health Services

Institutional Division

Pardons and Parole Division

State Jail Division

Source: *Annual Report for 1994*, Texas Department of Criminal Justice.

the Texas Board of Criminal Justice, which is composed of nine non-salaried members appointed by the governor with the advice and consent of the senate for six-year terms. The governor appoints one member of the board to serve as chairman, and the board employs an executive director who is responsible for both implementing the policy of the board and for the day-to-day management and operation of the Texas Department of Criminal Justice. The board meets at least once every three months to formulate managerial, administrative, and operational policy initiatives for Texas Department of Criminal Justice to follow, and to provide oversight and review of the Texas Department of Criminal Justice's implementation of its policies.

Two advisory boards provide guidance to the Texas Board of Criminal Justice in its formulation of policy initiatives. A ten-member Legislative Criminal Justice Board provides the Texas Board of Criminal Justice with information about legislative intent of recently passed bills that deal with the prison system, parole, and probation. A twelve-member Judicial Advisory Council, appointed jointly by the chief justice of the Texas Supreme Court and the presiding judge of the Texas Court of Criminal Appeals, provides advice to the Texas Board of Criminal Justice on policy matters of interest to the Texas judiciary.

The Institutional Division

The Institutional Division of the Texas Department of Criminal Justice is headed by a director who is responsible for the overall management and operation of the prison system and the secure and humane confinement of convicted felons. The practical aspects of the day-to-day management and operation of the Texas prison system is broken down into two broad, functional divisions of labor—operations and support services—each of which is overseen by a deputy director.

Operations

The deputy director of operations is responsible for the management oversight and operation of all the prison units, in-

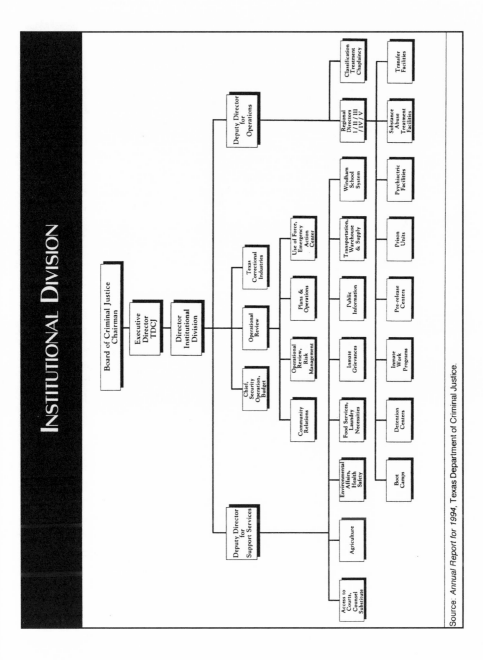

INSTITUTIONAL DIVISION

Source: *Annual Report for 1994*, Texas Department of Criminal Justice.

cluding the classification and processing of new convicts, convict work programs, and the State's privately operated prison facilities. The Bureau of Classification evaluates all new convicts remanded to the custody of the Institutional Division with respect to their age, offense, and prior criminal record, and then screens them psychologically with respect to mental health, as well as educational and vocational skill levels. These diagnostic procedures aid prison operations personnel in making decisions about the appropriate assignment of newly arrived convicts to a prison unit based upon the convict's security risk, rehabilitation and medical needs, and work assignments that are complementary to both the specific labor needs of the prison unit and the job skills and vocational training requirements of the convict.

CUSTODY ASSIGNMENTS AND GOOD TIME ELIGIBILITY

For purposes of supervision and control, the Texas prison system classifies convicts into one of two major custody levels: Trusty convicts and Line Class convicts. Each of these two major custody classifications is further broken down into grades.

The Trusty grades I through IV are used to designate convicts who are minimum custody and minimum security risks. All newly arriving convicts, except those sentenced to death or those with prior prison records that include violence and attempted flight, are assigned a Trusty IV designation. Trusty levels IV and III are allowed to work outside the confines of the prison but only under the direct supervision of an armed correctional officer, and they may work inside the prison under a correctional officer's periodic supervision. A convict with a Trusty II designation is allowed to work outside the prison with only periodic supervision by an unarmed correctional officer, and is permitted to work inside the prison with no direct supervision. A convict with a Trusty I designation (the lowest custody assignment level) may work either outside or inside the prison with no direct supervision by correctional officers.

Line Class grades I, II, and III are assigned to convicts who are classified as medium or maximum custody and security risks. A level III classification within this grade identifies a convict as the highest security risk requiring maximum custodial supervision. While working outside the confines of the prison, Line Class convicts require constant supervision by armed correctional officers, and their movements while inside the prison are strictly controlled by escort at all times. A convict's assigned custody level and grade determines to a very large degree which prison unit in the system the convict will be assigned to serve his sentence. As a general rule, the Texas prison system attempts not to commingle Trusty level and Line Class level convicts within the same prison unit. Hence, each of the 84 prison units that comprise the Texas prison system are typically designated as a minimum, medium, or maximum security facility.

Whether a convict moves to a reduced or enhanced custody level and grade is dependent on his behavior and attitude while in prison. A convict's assigned custody grade and level is important not only for the purposes of determining what prison unit he will be assigned to and the amount of freedom he will subsequently be allowed, but it also determines the amount of good time credit a convict may earn while incarcerated.

The good time allowance (or good time credit) is the amount of time that may be earned by a convict and applied toward fulfilling his sentence. When accumulated good time credits are added to his calendar time (the amount of time he has actually served in prison), the overall time a convict must remain in prison to satisfy the calendar time requirement of the sentence may be reduced significantly. A convict may earn good time for both good behavior and for participating in work programs and educational, vocational, and rehabilitation programs.

The formulas for awarding of good time credit are determined by the Texas Legislature, and are set forth in the *Texas Government Code*. The maximum amount of good time credit a convict can earn is presently a function of both his custody classification and grade and the date the offense for which he was convicted was committed. Convicts who are classified in the Trusty level at either grades I, II, or III and who committed their felony offense before 1 September 1987 may earn good time credit at the maximum rate of 45 days for each 30 calendar days served. In the past few years, the Texas Legislature

Interior and exterior views of the Estelle Maximum Security Unit.
(Courtesy TDCJ)

has reduced by one-third the good time earning potential of Trusty level I, II, and III convicts whose criminal offense was committed on or after 1 September 1987. Today, convicts with Trusty level status who were convicted of felonies committed on or after 1 September 1987 are eligible to earn good time credits at a maximum rate of only 30 days for each 30 calendar days served. All Trusty level I, II, and III convicts, regardless of the date their offense was committed, are also eligible to earn an additional 15 days of good time credit per month by their satisfactory participation in educational, vocational, and rehabilitation programs. Trusty IV convicts must earn the privilege of receiving good time credits by exhibiting positive behavior that makes them eligible for reclassification as a Trusty III.

Line Class I and II convicts are eligible to earn 10 days of good time credit for each 30 calendar days served. Line Class III convicts are not eligible for earning good time credits, and are expected to serve their sentences on a day-for-day calendar basis.

THE CONVICT POPULATION

The convicts who comprise the bulk of the prison population in Texas may generally be described as overwhelmingly young, non-white, borderline functionally illiterate males with prior prison records. With regards to gender, 93% of the convicts incarcerated in the Texas prison system are male. About 9,000 females are incarcerated in seven prisons reserved exclusively for women. With respect to race and age, 46% of the convict population is African-American, 27% is white, 26% is Hispanic, and 1% is classified as other, which would include Native Americans, Asians, and Pacific Islanders. Fully 73% (or almost three-quarters) of the convict population of the Texas prison system has minority status with respect to either race or ethnicity. The average age of a convict incarcerated in the Texas prison system is 33.5 years. With respect to education, 64% of the convicts incarcerated in the Texas prison system never completed high school. The typical convict has an educational achievement score equivalent to a seventh-grade education. The average IQ is 92. With respect to the crimes for which they are incarcerated, 41% of the convict population committed violent offenses, 28% committed property offenses, and about 25% are incarcerated for having committed drug-related offenses. The remaining 6% are incarcerated for other miscellaneous felony offenses. The average sentence length is 20 years, and 50% of the convicts incarcerated in the Texas prison system have been in prison before.

A popular misconception about convict life in Texas prisons is that they lounge about watching color television all day. Today about 88 percent of all Texas convicts have a job assignment. Unless excused for reasons of physical health, psychiatric imbalance, or educational remediation reasons, every convict in the Texas prison system has an assigned job and is expected to work a full eight-hour shift. Inmates work in a variety of capacities in the Texas prison system, including agriculture, industrial production, and support service areas such as food service preparation, laundry, and facilities maintenance. No convict is paid for working. Convicts do have access to color televisions, but television viewing is considered to be a privilege reserved for those who complete their work shifts and who do not violate prison rules and regulations that govern inmate behavior. Televisions are located in day rooms that accommodate 50 to 100 inmates, and only basic channels are available. Convicts do not have access to cable or premium channels. Additionally, the televisions are not paid for with tax dollars, but are purchased with the proceeds of commissary sales to convicts.

The Institutional Division maintains very high standards for the general appearance of the convicts under its care, control, and custody. All convicts incarcerated in the Texas prison system wear white cotton uniforms made by the prison system's textile industries. Additionally, all convicts are required to keep their hair closely cropped and their faces clean-shaven. No other prison system in the United States either requires or enforces these type of appearance standards.

CORRECTIONAL PERSONNEL

The convict population in Texas is managed and supervised

by approximately 32,000 correctional officers whose entry level salary is approximately $17,000, well below the national average of $20,252. Texas currently ranks 35th among the 50 states for the entry level salary paid to prison guards. New Jersey is the highest at $31,805 and Arkansas is the lowest at $12,616. Currently, the Institutional Division requires that applicants for the position of correctional officer be 21 years of age, have a high school diploma or general educational development (GED) degree, and no criminal record. All newly hired correctional officers are required to successfully complete a pre-service training course that consists of approximately 400 hours of training.

PRIVATE PRISONS

Managerial oversight of the various privately operated prisons in the state is also a responsibility of the operations unit of the Institutional Division. In 1987 the Texas Legislature first authorized the Texas Department of Corrections to contract with commercial confinement companies for the financing, construction, operation, maintenance, and management of privately operated prisons. Currently, seven of the 84 prison facilities that comprise the Institutional Division of the Texas Department of Criminal Justice are operated by private corporations. Three prisons are operated by the Corrections Corporations of America, three are operated by the Wackenhut Corrections Corporation (both of which have stock that is publicly traded on the New York Stock Exchange), and one prison is privately operated by United States Corrections Corporation.

The seven privately operated prisons incarcerated about 5,000 convicts at an average per diem cost of $33.61 per convict. The private corporations which contract with the State of Texas to build and operate prison facilities are required to comply with all federal constitutional standards applicable to the operation and management of prisons, and receive and retain accreditation from the American Correctional Association. Additionally, to insure compliance with all laws and standards associated with the operation and management of prisons, contracts for the operation of private prisons provide for the on-site monitoring of the facilities by the Texas Department of Criminal Justice.

Despite the demonstrated per-diem cost savings associated with the operation of Texas' seven priviate prisons, there is currently an ongoing value-laden controversy with respect to whether or not prison operations should be privatized in Texas. Proponents of prison privatization in Texas advance several arguments. From an economic perspective, proponents argue that private sector commercial confinement companies can build prisons faster and cheaper than the state government. Additionally, capital budget restraints may be avoided through the use of creative lease or lease-purchase arrangements. From a management perspective, proponents argue that contracting for the private operation of a prison will enhance public and convict safety through increased staff training and professionalism, and that privatization increases public accountability because the market mechanisms of control are added to those of the political oversight process. In short, commercial confinement companies can build and operate prisons more cheaply and more efficiently than can state governments.

On the other hand, opponents of prison privatization argue that the protection of society incarcerating convicted felons is the business of the government, and that commercial confinement companies are motivated not by public interest in safety, but by profit. Additionally, opponents argue that contracting for the private operation of prisons may contribute to an increase in the rate of incarceration by making cheaper confinement more readily available. Furthermore, contracting on a per diem inmate rate gives the commercial confinement company an incentive to keep convicts incarcerated for as long as possible.

The question of whether or not Texas should contract for the operation of private penal facilities is one that is not likely to be resolved any time soon. Indeed, with the increasing reliance of not only Texas but other states as well on the services of commercial confinement companies for the construction and operation of a wide range of penal institutions, including prisons, state jails, substance abuse facilities, and halfway houses, the public dialogue surrounding the question of prison privatization is likely to intensify in coming years.

Support Services

The deputy director of support services is responsible for providing programs and services that support both the day-to-day operation of the prison units and the educational, vocational, and correctional needs of convicts. Included within this responsibility is the managerial oversight of the operation of the Texas prison system's agricultural and industrial programs and the Windham School District.

AGRICULTURAL PROGRAMS

Agricultural work by convicts and the production of crops and livestock for consumption by the convict population has been a major feature of the Texas prison system for more than 100 years. The managerial and operational reform of the prison system's farming and ranching practices instituted by Oscar Ellis in the early 1950s represents the most enduring legacy of his administration.

Today the Texas prison system efficiently operates the largest prison agricultural program in the United States, with farming and ranching operations on more than 138,000 acres (about 210 square miles) on 45 prison units in 37 Texas counties. Additionally, the prison system has one of the largest cattle and horse herds in the state, with more than 10,000 head of beef cattle and approximately 1,500 horses. More than 300 full-time agricultural professionals, including agronomists, animal husbandry specialists, and agricultural economists, are employed by the prison system to utilize in the most efficient manner possible the prison system's farming and ranching resources.

Approximately 6,000 convicts work in the Texas prison system's farming and ranching programs. Crops planted and harvested by the prison agricultural crop program for consumption by convicts include a variety of fruits and vegetables,

The commercial sale of poultry and livestock is a multimillion-dollar industry and is used to offset the cost of the Texas prison system.

(Courtesy TDCJ)

ABOVE: *The agricultural programs of the prison system help provide for its sustenance.*
BELOW: *Inmates at the Huntsville Unit produce 3.5 million yards of cloth annually.*
(Courtesy TDCJ)

corn, rice, and pecans. The harvested comestible crops provide convicts with a fresh supply of vegetables and fruits, and a vegetable canning plant insures a year-round supply of seasonal fruits and vegetables. Alfalfa, grain sorghum, hay, and silage are also grown and used for feeding the prison system's beef cattle, chickens, and hogs. The prison system operates its own meat processing plant to prepare the livestock it raises for consumption by the convict population. Cotton is also grown by the prison system. The harvested cotton is processed by the prison system's cotton gins before being shipped to the prison's textile and garment factories, where it is processed into the cotton cloth from which the uniforms for all prison convicts and prison guards are made.

The agricultural programs produce in excess of $34 million worth of comestible crops and livestock per year for the prison system, resulting in significant savings to the taxpayers of the state of Texas.

INDUSTRIAL OPERATIONS

The industrial operations of the Texas prison system are also immense, and they remain today one of the two great legacies of Beto's administration. From modest beginnings in 1963, the prison system today operates more than 46 industrial factories and plants on 36 prison units. The industrial operations program produces a wide variety of products and services relating to automotive fabrication and repair, metal and wood products, printing, soap and janitorial products, and cardboard and concrete products, and both raw and finished textile products. For example, in 1996 the prison system's textile mills produced 3.5 million pounds of finished yarn that was subsequently woven into 32 million yards of cloth. While most people know that the Texas prison system is the source of all Texas motor vehicle license plates (over seven million were stamped out in 1996), few people realize that Texas convicts are also responsible for making license plate validation stickers, motor vehicle inspection stickers, and all of the highway signs that direct speed limits and indicate travel routes. In 1996 convicts manufactured more than 205,000 signs for the State Highway Department, and produced more than 19 million license plate validation stickers and motor vehicle inspection stickers. Additionally, the prison system's industrial factories and plants manufacture all of the steel bunks, mattresses, and stainless steel sinks and commodes that each cell is equipped with, and all of the janitorial supplies used by the prison system, including laundry, bath, and dishwashing soap, general purpose cleansers, brooms, mops, and mop handles.

More than 8,000 convicts work in the industrial factories and plants, and produce in excess of $100 million worth of goods and services yearly for the prison system, state agencies, cities, counties, and school districts in the state of Texas. The overall economic savings to Texas taxpayers of the combined industrial and agricultural operations is significant. Texas ranks 35th among the states in the United States for per diem cost of keeping a convict in prison. The average per diem cost of keeping a convict in the Texas prison system is $39.51, and is below the national average per diem cost of $53.85. By way of comparison, Alaska ranks first with a per diem cost of $106.63, while Alabama has the lowest average per diem cost of $25.10 per convict.

THE WINDHAM SCHOOL DISTRICT

The growth and success of the Windham School District and the important role it serves in aiding the rehabilitation of convicts and preparing them for reintegration into the community as law-abiding and contributing members of society is attributable to the vision of Dr. George Beto, and represents the second great legacy of his administration. Since its founding by Beto in 1968, the goal of the Windham School District (named after longtime Texas Prison Board member James A. Windham) has been to reduce convict recidivism by providing them with an opportunity to acquire the academic, vocational, and social and civic skills necessary for an adult to earn a living and make a life for himself in mainstream society. To accomplish this goal, the Texas prison system's Windham School District offers a wide variety of accredited academic and vocational programs, including remedial education programs for the functionally illiterate, instruction in English as a second language for non-English speaking convicts, high school equivalency programs, and vocational instruction and apprenticeship training programs.

Participation in the Windham School District's academic programs is mandatory for convicts who cannot read at the 6th grade level. Participation in academic programs is voluntary for convicts who are literate but have less than a high school diploma. Enrollment in vocational training programs, while strongly encouraged for convicts who are unskilled, is voluntary. Today approximately 50,000 convicts are enrolled in the Windham School District's academic and vocational programs, and approximately 5,000 high school general education development (GED) certificates are earned every year, along with 10,000 vocational certificates of completion. Additionally, baccalaureate and graduate degrees may be earned by convicts through the prison system's cooperative programs in higher education. Today, approximately 300 associate of arts degrees, 50 baccalaureate degrees, and 20 master's degrees are earned every year by convicts during their incarceration.

The State Jail Division

In 1993 the 73rd Texas Legislature passed a bill altering the *Texas Penal Code* by creating a new degree of felony punishable by a potential term of incarceration ranging from 180 days to two years. This new felony degree is called a "state jail felony." (See Chapter 2 for a discussion of the various offenses that constitute a state jail felony in Texas.) To provide for the incarceration of offenders convicted of state jail felonies, the Texas Legislature created the State Jail Division of the Texas Department of Criminal Justice to oversee the management and operation of the state jail system. The state jail system in Texas was developed to provide a lower cost alternative to expensive prison incarceration for non-violent felons convicted of property and drug offenses. Two distinct benefits are associated with the state jail system: first, the state jail system

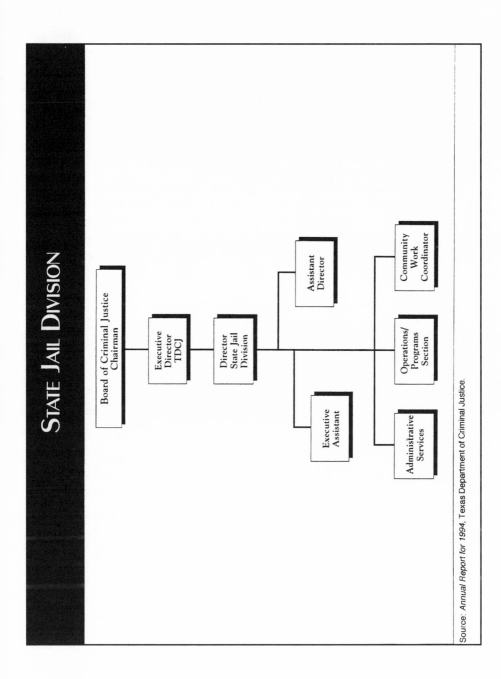

STATE JAIL DIVISION

Board of Criminal Justice Chairman

Executive Director TDCJ

Director State Jail Division

Executive Assistant

Assistant Director

Administrative Services

Operations/ Programs Section

Community Work Coordinator

Source: *Annual Report for 1994*, Texas Department of Criminal Justice.

frees up valuable and limited prison space for the incarceration of criminals convicted of violent crimes; and second, the state jail system provides a means of delivering community-based rehabilitation services.

Today there are approximately 10,000 convicts serving sentences in 27 state jails throughout Texas. Two of the state jails are reserved exclusively for housing female convicts. Six of the state jails are operated by private companies with which the State of Texas has contracted. Corrections Corporation of America operates two state jail facilities: Wackenhut Corrections Corporation operates two state jails, and Management and Training Corporation operates one. It is estimated that by the year 2000 the state jail population in Texas will almost double. The per diem cost of maintaining a convict in a state jail is approximately $28, about $11 cheaper per day than incarceration in a state prison facility.

PART 2:
CAPITAL PUNISHMENT IN TEXAS

There currently are in excess of 455 convicts under sentence of death in Texas. This represents a little more than 10% of the approximately 4,000 convicts who are today under sentence of death in the United States. Approximately two to three convicts are sentenced to death each month in Texas. Convicts sentenced to death in Texas are incarcerated pending their execution at the Ellis I Unit about 20 miles northeast of Huntsville. Convicts awaiting execution are segregated from the rest of the Ellis I convict population in six special wings of the prison known as death row. Each death row cell is five feet by nine feet, and contains a bunk and a steel sink and toilet. Death row convicts are identified for custody and security purposes by a three-digit number preceded by 999.

At the end of 1998 there were nine women under sentence of death in Texas. The death row facility for condemned women in Texas is located at the Mountain View women's prison unit, which is located about four miles north of Gatesville, in Coryell County. Texas has always been very reticent

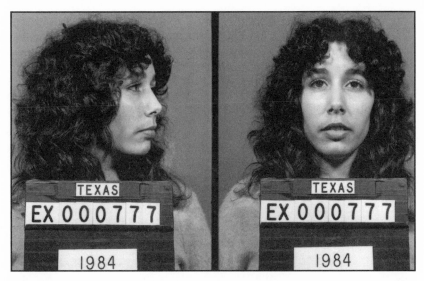

Should a pick-axe murderer who finds spiritual redemption on death row have her sentence commuted to life in prison? Did the State of Texas in its ready use of capital punishment inadvertently create an effective spokesperson against the death penalty in the case of Karla Faye Tucker? The execution of Tucker generated many interesting questions which are likely to linger in the collective conscience of the American people.   (Courtesy TDCJ)

about putting condemned female murderers to death. Prior to 1998, the last time Texas executed a woman was in 1863, when Chipita Rodriguez was hanged in San Patricio County for the murder of a horse trader. Between 1863 and 1976, when the death penalty was reinstated in Texas, only five women have been sentenced to death. All of them, however, subsequently had their death sentences commuted to life in prison. This legacy of reticence changed on Tuesday, 4 February 1998, when 38-year-old Karla Faye Tucker became the first woman executed in Texas since the Civil War. Despite a plea from Pope John Paul II to spare Tucker's life, the Texas Board of Pardons and Paroles rejected her plea for clemency, and Tucker was subsequently executed by lethal injection for the bloody, brutal, and wanton hacking to death of two people with a pick axe in a Houston apartment in June 1983.

Today Texas is the most execution-active state in the United States. Seventy-four convicts were executed in the United States in 1997, and 37 of them were executed in Texas. With the execution of 37 convicted murderes in 1997, Texas broke its previous year high record of 20 executions, which occurred in 1935. Since 1930 Texas has carried out more than 400 executions, and more than 125 of these have taken place since 1982. In years past, the average length of time spent on death row in Texas awaiting execution was in approximately nine to twelve years. The pace of executions in Texas in 1997, however, significantly and dramatically altered this. It has been only recently that the average time spent on death row in Texas between imposition of sentence and execution has fallen to approximately seven and a half years.

The dramatic reduction in the average number of years spent on death row awaiting execution and the recent record pace at which executions are taking place in Texas both result from two factors: long-term convicts on death row exhausting their appeals, and a 1995 law limiting the use of post-conviction habeas corpus appeals. A lull in executions in 1996 was caused by an unsuccessful challenge to this Texas statute limiting the appeals process. When the statute was ruled constitutional, the appeals process was subsequently shortened, and the way was cleared for executing more convicts whose appeals were now exhausted.

Hanging

Since the time of the Republic of Texas, three methods of execution have been employed: hanging, electrocution, and currently, lethal injection. Prior to 1924 hanging was the method employed in Texas to execute condemned convicts. Executions by hanging were carried out in public by the sheriff of the county in which the convict was tried and condemned to death. A well-oiled length of pliable five-strand manila hemp rope approximately 3/4 to 7/8 of an inch in diameter was employed to produce almost instantaneous death by means of what is sometimes called the hangman's fracture. The knot of the hangman's noose was placed high up under the left jaw, where it would produce a violent snapping back of the chin when the condemned fell through the trap door of the gallows upon which he stood. The violent snapping back of the chin, caused by the knot quickly and forcefully pressing against the side of the head, resulted in a ruptured spinal cord, cutting off of oxygen to the brain, and immediate paralysis in the rest of the body.

The first legal hanging carried out by Anglo government in Texas is believed to have occurred during Stephen F. Austin's administration of the colony at San Felipe de Austin on 15 March 1835. Joseph Clayton was convicted and condemned to death by a judicial tribunal presided over by Austin for the stabbing death of Abner Kuykendall. The last legal execution by hanging occurred on 31 August 1923 at Angleton, in Brazoria County, when a condemned murderer named Nathan Lee was hanged.

Electrocution

Public hangings in Texas, as elsewhere, often degenerated into carnival-like public spectacles. J. W. Thomas, from Rogers, Texas, was so appalled by a public hanging he witnessed in 1922 that he ran for election to the Texas Senate on a platform advocating changing the manner in which execution of condemned convicts was carried out. After his election to the state senate, Thomas was successful in introducing and passing legislation that resulted in the most sweeping changes in Texas history regarding the way capital punishment is discharged. Thomas' bill, which was passed by the 38th Texas Legislature in 1923, resulted in three major changes: first, the method of execution was changed from hanging to electrocution; second, it put an end to public executions; and third, his bill required the State, rather than counties, to be responsible for executing death warrants.

The electric chair is of very simplistic design and operation. Made of stout oak, the chair has four legs and extra wide arms that are fitted with strong leather straps to pinion the arms of the condemned. Other leather straps are provided to go around the condemned's chest, abdomen, and legs. The wiring around the chair is protected by heavy rubber insulation. Copper electrodes are attached to the calf of one leg, and

Bonnie and Clyde criminal associate Raymond Hamilton awaits electrocution in the infamous electric chair "Old Sparky."
(Courtesy Mary Carey)

a felt helmet containing another copper electrode is fixed to the top of the condemned's shaved head. The felt helmet is soaked in brine to increase its conductivity. The process of electrocution begins when the executioner throws a switch completing an electrical circuit, which sends a surge of alternating current of approximately 2,000 volts through the body of the condemned criminal. This initial surge initiates a current of eight to ten amperes through the body, which results in almost instantaneous unconsciousness by paralyzing the brain, causing cardiac arrest, and inducing a failure of the respiratory system. After three to four seconds the voltage output is reduced to between 1,000 and 500 volts, producing between three to four amperes, where it is held steady for about one minute. The surge reduction is necessary in order to prevent the body from bursting into flame and to hold the paralysis of the body's normal life sustaining functions. When the switch is thrown, every muscle in the condemned's body violently and rigidly contracts, causing him to strain enormously against his bindings. As the current continues to flow through the condemned's body, the skin begins to slowly take on the reddish hue of a beet. Sometimes a thin gray wisp of smoke is emitted from the helmet, and a faint odor of burning flesh may be evident. Immediately after the current is halted, it is not uncommon for the temperature of the body to be approximately 140 degrees Fahrenheit, and the temperature of the internal brain often approaches the boiling point of water. After the body has been allowed to cool down for approximately seven to ten minutes, the prison physician examines the condemned and pronounces him dead.

The electric chair, nicknamed "Old Sparky," was used for the first time in Texas on 8 February 1924, when Charles Reynolds, a convicted murderer from Red River County, was electrocuted. Four other condemned men followed Reynolds that same day. Between 1924 and 1964, 361 condemned convicts were executed by electrocution in Texas. Joseph Johnson, a condemned murderer from Harris County, was the last person electrocuted in Texas. He was executed on 30 July 1964. Today "Old Sparky" is on public display behind a glass partition at the Texas Prison Museum in Huntsville.

Lethal Injection

In 1982 the Texas Legislature did away with electrocution as the preferred method of execution, substituting in its place lethal injection. The current law governing execution by lethal injection in Texas is set forth in Articles 43.14 to 43.26 of the *Texas Code of Criminal Procedure*, and includes procedures for the drawing and delivery of the death warrant, scheduling of the execution date, conveyance of the condemned from the Ellis I Unit to the death chamber at the Huntsville Unit, the designation of an executioner, the listing of persons permitted to be present at the execution, and instructions on what to do with the corpse of the executed convict.

The procedure for initiating death by means of lethal injection requires the intravenous introduction of a chemical solution directly into the bloodstream of the condemned convict. The lethal chemical solution is composed of an admixture of sodium thiopental (a rapidly acting anesthetic which renders the condemned unconscious), pancuronium bromide (or pavulon, which paralyzes the respiratory system), and potassium chloride (which arrests the heart).

The Texas death chamber at the old prison in Huntsville consists of a small, windowless room, twelve by sixteen feet, painted pastel blue, which contains a hospital gurney. One wall of the death chamber contains a small square hole which opens into a closet-sized room that holds the lethal injection apparatus operated by the executioner. The apparatus is very similar to the equipment used in a hospital to intravenously feed or deliver medication to patients. In the death chamber, the condemned convict is strapped to the hospital gurney, and two catheters attached to a tube connected to the chemical solution held by the intravenous apparatus are passed through the small hole in the wall to the death chamber. The needles are inserted into a vein in both arms of the condemned. After being asked if the condemned has any final statement to make, the unidentified executioner presses a button and the lethal chemicals begin to flow into the bloodstream of the condemned prisoner. First the sodium thiopental is administered, followed immediately by approximately 50 cubic centimeters of pancuronium bromide, followed immediately thereafter by another approximately 50 cubic centimeters of potassium chloride. Death occurs very rapidly, and usually within seven minutes after the lethal chemicals begin flowing, the condemned is officially pronounced dead.

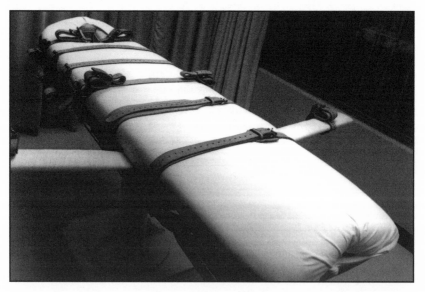

The execution gurney in the death chamber at Huntsville Prison.
(Courtesy TDCJ)

Because the process is essentially a medical procedure, ethical questions have arisen within the medical profession about active physician participation in the lethal injection process. While the entire process is supervised by a prison system physician, the actual preparation of the chemicals, insertion of the needle, and opening of the petcocks are all performed by personnel who are not licensed physicians.

On 7 December 1982, Charlie Brooks, Jr., became the first person executed by lethal injection in Texas. Texas leads the nation in carrying out capital punishment, and accounts for more than one-third of all executions in the United States since the U.S. Supreme Court in 1976 allowed the states to resume carrying out executions.

SOME HIGHLIGHTS OF CAPITAL PUNISHMENT IN TEXAS

NUMBER OF YEARLY EXECUTIONS

1982	1	1990	4
1983	0	1991	5
1984	3	1992	12
1985	6	1993	17
1986	10	1994	14
1987	6	1995	19
1988	3	1996	4
1989	4	1997	37

Average time on death row: **9 years**
Longest time on death row: **21 years**
Shortest time on death row: **8 months and 18 days (252 days)**
Second shortest time on death row: **1 year and 5 months**
Age of current oldest death row convict: **61 years of age**
Age of youngest person arriving on death row: **24 years of age**
Average age of executed convict: **37 years**
Age of oldest executed convict: **59 years**
Age of youngest executed convict: **24 years**
Fastest growing population on death row: **Teenagers**

Today, 27 states and the federal government have adopted lethal injection as the preferred method of execution. Following several legal challenges, the U.S. Supreme Court in *Heckler v. Chaney* upheld the constitutional validity of lethal injection in 1984.

WORKS CONSULTED AND SUGGESTIONS FOR FURTHER READING

Anderson, Ken. *Crime in Texas*. Austin, Texas: The University of Texas Press, 1997.

Barr, James. "The Mechanics of Hanging." *Popular Science Monthly*, vol. 27 (1885), pp. 503-508.

Brister, Richard C. "Changing of the Guard: A Case for Privatization of Texas Prisons." *Prison Journal,* vol. 76 (1996).

Brownlee, Shannon, et al. "The Place for Vengeance." *U.S. News and World Report* (June 16, 1997), pp. 25-29, 31-32.

Chronology of Texas Prison Reform, 1972 to 1994. Austin, Texas: Senate Research Center, 1994.

Corrections Corporation of America: 1995 Annual Report. Nashville, Tennessee, 1996.

Corrections Yearbook 1996. South Salem, New York: Criminal Justice Institute, 1996.

Crime State Rankings 1997. Lawrence, Kansas: Morgan Quinto Press, 1997.

Curtis, Gregory. "Seven Women." *Texas Monthly* (October 1997), pp. 7, 10, 12.

Directory of Juvenile and Adult Correctional Departments, Institutions, Agencies, and Paroling Authorities. Lanham, Maryland: American Correctional Association, 1996.

Fabelo, Tony. "Prisons After the Building Boom: Where Do We Go From Here?" *Prison Journal*, vol. 76 (1996).

Feeley, Malcomb M. "The Privatization of Prisons in Historical Perspective." *Criminal Justice Research Bulletin* (Huntsville, Texas: Criminal Justice Center, Sam Houston State University), vol. 6, no. 2, (1991).

Gilliard, Darrell K., and Allen J. Beck. *Prison and Jail Inmates at Midyear 1996*. Bureau of Justice Statistics Bulletin, U.S. Department of Justice, January 1997.

Holley, Joe. "Guarded: What do Private-Prison Officials Have Against the Public's Right to Know?" *Texas Monthly* (February 1997), p. 22.

"How They Kill Them at Huntsville's Death Row." *The Texas Observer*, 15 April 1961, p. 1.

Johnson, Robert. *Death Work: A Study of the Modern Execution Process*. Pacific Grove, California: Brooks/Cole, 1990.

———. "Prison System." *The New Handbook of Texas*. Austin, Texas: Texas State Historical Association, 1996, vol. 5, pp. 341-344.

Marquart, James W., et al. *The Rope, the Chair, and the Needle: Capital Punishment in Texas, 1923-1990*. Austin, Texas: University of Texas Press, 1990.

Mumola, Christopher, and Allen J. Beck. *Prisoners in 1996*. Bureau of Justice Statistics Bulletin, U. S. Department of Justice, June 1997.

Nellis, Ashley. "Doing Well v. Doing Good: Private Prisons and Corporate America." Unpublished St. Edward's University Honors Program Senior Thesis, 1997.

Robinson, Rita. "The Great Texas Prison Caper." *Civil Engineering*, vol. 65 (1995), p. 67.

Seaholm, Megan. "Texas Department of Criminal Justice Hospital." *The New Handbook of Texas*. Austin, Texas: Texas State Historical Association, 1996, vol. 6, p. 318.

Sharp, John. *Texas Crime, Texas Justice: A Report From the Texas Performance Review*. Austin, Texas: Texas Comptroller of Public Accounts, 1992.

Shichor, David. "Private Prisons." *Encyclopedia of American Prisons*. Marilyn D. McShane, and Frank P. Williams III, editors. New York: Garland Publishing, 1996, pp. 364-372.

———. *Punishment for Profit*. Thousand Oaks, California: Sage, 1995.

Texas Department of Criminal Justice: Annual Report for 1995.

"Texas Department of Criminal Justice." *Guide to Texas State Agencies*. Austin, Texas: Bureau of Governmental Research, Lyndon B. Johnson School of Public Affairs, University of Texas at Austin, 1996, pp. 74-79.

Wackenhut Corrections Corporation: Corporate Overview. Palm Beach Gardens, Florida, 1997.

8.
PAROLE AND PROBATION IN TEXAS

PART 1:
PAROLE

In Texas today there are approximately 700,000 people under supervision of one kind or another for having committed criminal offenses. Stated differently, one out of every 25 Texas residents is under the care, control, and custody of the Texas criminal justice system. This includes about 150,000 convicts incarcerated in Texas prisons and state jails, about 75,000 pre-trial detainees and convicted misdemeanants held in county jails, approximately 80,000 on parole and mandatory release, and 410,000 on probation.

The Historical Development of Parole in Texas

The term "parole" comes from the French word *parole*, meaning "word." In French, the word *parole* is used in the context of a promise, or giving one's word of honor. With respect to its use in a criminal justice sense, parole has come to mean a convict's pledge or promise to conduct himself in a law-abiding manner in exchange for an early release from prison. In other words, parole is the discretionary, conditional, and supervised release from prison of a convict who has served less than the amount of time to which he was sentenced. Two distinct purposes are said to be served by parole. First, the primary objective of parole is to help convicts readjust to life in the free world by providing them with the necessary counseling and social service support mechanisms they need. Second, parole is designed to protect society by closely monitoring the behavior and activity of convicts released early from prison and imposing sanctions on them for inappropriate behavior. It is important to note that a convict on parole legally remains under the care, control, and custody of the state.

Convicted felons are released early from prison to serve the remainder of their sentence under the supervision and control of a parole officer by means of a parole contract. The parole contract is a written, legally enforceable document which clearly spells out the behavioral expectations that the paroling authority has of a convict who is being released from prison prior to the expiration of his sentence. Today parole is the most frequently employed method of releasing a convict from incarceration in a Texas prison.

Zebulon Reed Brockway, the founder of the American reformatory movement, created the first supervised parole program in the United States in 1876, at the Elmira Reformatory in Elmira, New York. Following Brockway's lead, the practice of supervised parole spread rapidly in the United States. By 1900, legislatures in 20 states had passed parole statutes, and by 1922, 44 states had adult parole laws which allowed for the early release from prison of convicts who had yet to complete their sentences. Texas was very slow to embrace the practice of parole, and did not statutorily provide for supervised parole until 1957.

Prior to 1936, convicts serving sentences in Texas prisons were released prior to completing their sentence by two distinct forms of gubernatorial (or executive) clemency. This was accomplished by means of a pardon or by means of conditional release (which has sometimes been referred to as executive parole). A pardon was a gubernatorial act that released a convict from the remainder of his sentence, and restored back to him the rights and privileges forfeited by him after his conviction. From 1845 to 1936 the broad and virtually unchecked power to pardon was exclusively vested in the office of the governor by the Constitutions of 1845, 1861, and 1866. The

Texas courts during this period steadfastly struck down all challenges to the governor's constitutional pardoning power.

As the number of requests for pardons grew over the years in Texas, governors found themselves unable to personally attend to all the requests for early release. In 1893 the Texas Legislature provided the governor's office with some relief in the pardoning area by passing a bill authorizing the creation of a two-member Board of Pardons Advisors. Membership on this statutorily created board was by gubernatorial appointment. The governor delegated to the Board of Pardons Advisors the responsibility of reviewing and screening all requests for pardons and recommending to him which requests ought to be granted or denied. As the number of requests for pardons grew, so did the number of pardons granted by the governor. For example, Governor James E. Ferguson granted 1,774 pardons between 1915 and 1917, and his predecessor, Governor William P. Hobby, granted 1,319 pardons between 1917 and 1921. The number of gubernatorial pardons granted during this period are especially significant in light of the fact that the total number of convicts incarcerated in the Texas prison system ranged from 3,699 in 1915 to 3,146 in 1921. The public's perception that the pardoning power was being corrupted by influence peddling led to an attempt by the Texas Legislature to remedy the problem. In 1929 the legislature amended its 1893 statute by abolishing the Board of Pardons Advisors, and creating a three-member Board of Pardons and Paroles. The three members of the new Board of Pardons and Paroles were still appointed by the governor, but now the gubernatorial nominees had to be approved by the Texas Senate, and they served six-year staggered terms.

The new 1929 law resulted in the use of a second practice associated with early release of convicts in Texas. This was executive parole, or conditional release, whereby a convict's remaining sentence was discharged by the governor, and the convict was released from prison without supervision, and allowed to serve the balance of his sentence in the community provided he did not commit any new criminal offenses. Unlike a gubernatorial pardon, however, the criminal record of a convict conditionally released from prison early was not erased, and he was not relieved from the civil disabilities that accompanied a felony conviction. This early form of parole in Texas differed from both the concept of parole employed by Brockway and the modern practice of parole in that the convict was released from prison early without any supervision in the community. Despite the 1929 legislative attempt to reform the practice of pardoning and paroling of Texas convicts, allegations of misuse, corruption, and influence peddling persisted. The use of parole or conditional release continued, however, and the public's confidence in the gubernatorial use of both of these early release mechanisms remained low.

The practice of pardoning and paroling convicts underwent significant change in 1936, when the Texas Constitution was amended to create a three-member Board of Pardons and Paroles that was totally independent of the governor's office. For the first time since 1845, the executive clemency powers associated with the officer of the governor of Texas were significantly limited in two ways. First, of the three members that comprised the board, one was appointed by the governor, the second by the chief justice of the Texas Supreme Court, and the third by the presiding judge of the Texas Court of Criminal Appeals. All three appointments were subject to the consent and approval of the Texas Senate. Second, the amendment to the Texas Constitution provided that in all cases except treason and impeachment, the governor would have the power to grant pardons and conditional paroles only pursuant to the written recommendation of the Board of Pardons and Paroles. The constitutional amendment was further strengthened in 1947 when the Texas Legislature passed the Adult Parole Law. This statute allowed the Board of Pardons and Paroles, with the approval of the governor, to conditionally release on parole any convict confined in the Texas prison system with the exception of those convicts under sentence of death.

It is interesting to note that until 1958 the Texas Legislature never appropriated funds to be used for the supervision of convicts released on parole. Supervision of paroled convicts was provided for entirely by volunteers on a county-by-county basis. The State of Texas did not officially take responsibility for professionally supervising convicts released on parole until 1957, when the Texas Legislature, at the urging of Oscar Ellis, the general manager of the Texas prison system, passed a bill establishing and funding an enforcement arm of the Board of Pardons and Paroles called the Division of Parole Supervision. Vincent O'Leary, the director of the parole supervision authority in Washington state, was hired to reorganize and supervise the Division of Parole Supervision in Texas. Texas was one of the last three states in the United States to adopt a state-funded parole supervision agency.

Before proceeding, it is important to understand that the traditional parole process in Texas today has been augmented with another early release mechanism called "mandatory release." Under the Texas mandatory release law, some convicts must, by law, be released from prison after having served a specific amount of their sentence. While the eligibility requirements for release on parole differ from the requirements for mandatory release, both parole and mandatory release are similar in that convicts released early from prison remain under the care, control, and custody of the state.

Parole in Texas Today: The Bifurcated Early Release Function

The practice of parole and mandatory release of convicts in Texas today is split into two distinct components: the release function and the supervision function. This bifurcation of early release responsibilities is carried out by two separate and distinct governmental entities: the Board of Pardons and Paroles makes the decision to grant early release, and the Pardons and Paroles Division of the Texas Department of Criminal Justice assembles all the necessary documentation for the board to consider, and supervises all convicts granted early release from prison by the board.

The Texas Board of Pardons and Paroles

The Texas Board of Pardons and Paroles is an agency of the

executive branch of government in Texas, and derives its statutory mandate and authority from Article 42.18 of the *Texas Code of Criminal Procedure*. Unlike the early three-member board, the Board of Pardons and Paroles today consists of 18 members appointed by the governor with the advice and consent of the Texas Senate, and is exclusively vested with the authority to release convicted felons prior to the full completion of their sentence and revoke their release if they violate the conditions of their early release.

Members of the Board of Pardons and Paroles are full-time, salaried, governmental appointees who work five days per week, and who serve six-year staggered terms. The chairman of the board is designated by the governor. The granting, denial, and revocation of early release are decided by panels of three board members, with decisions being made by majority vote. In the past few years the board's approval rate for granting early releases has decreased dramatically, from about 80% of all applications in 1991 to about 20% today. Currently in Texas there are approximately 60,000 convicted felons on parole and about 20,000 on mandatory release. This represents a rate of 774 early releasees per 100,000 population in Texas. With an overall national early release rate of 330 per 100,000 population in the United States, the Texas early release rate is exceeded only by Pennsylvania and New Jersey. Today the State of Texas spent in excess of $110 million on the parole and mandatory release function.

PAROLE HEARINGS

Several months before a convict becomes eligible for parole he or she will be interviewed by a transitional case manager. The case manager prepares a parole summary which includes information of the facts and circumstances of the convict's crime, the convict's personal history, his or her disciplinary record while in prison, and an overview of any positive or negative factors that would impact on the decision to release the convict early. This information is used to prepare a release plan which addresses where the convict will live if and when released on parole, prospective employment opportunities, and any special treatment and counseling programs that may be undertaken upon early discharge from prison.

Decisions to grant early release to eligible convicts are made by panels consisting of three members of the Board of Pardons and Paroles. The panel reviews all pertinent information relating to the prisoner that has been assembled by the Review and Release Processing Section of the Pardons and Paroles Division of the Texas Department of Criminal Justice. This information generally includes, but is not limited to, the history and criminal record of the convict, a record of the convict's behavior and attitude while in prison, and any written information or comments which may aid the panel in deciding whether or not the early release of a convict from prison is in the best interest of promoting both community safety and the rehabilitation needs of the convict. In making this decision the members of the parole panel will take into consideration a number of factors, including the circumstances and seriousness of the offense for which the convict was sentenced to prison and whether or not a deadly weapon was used, the convict's prior criminal record (including a propensity for alcohol and drug abuse, violent or assaultive behavior, and deviant sexual behavior), the convict's behavior and attitude while in prison, his or her emotional stability, and relevant input from victims, family members, and trial officials. Additionally, the parole panel also considers the convict's release plan, which details where the releasee intends to live and work.

A convict denied parole on first review with the panel is given either a "Serve-All" or a "Next Review" date (sometimes referred to as a "Set-Off"). A Next Review means that the Board of Pardons and Paroles has decided that the convict is not ready for release back into the community, and that a subsequent review should be conducted within the next one to three years. A Serve-All means the convict is not considered fit for parole and that no future parole reviews will be scheduled, and the convict will be released from prison only upon having served the entire sentence. A Serve-All may only be given to convicts who have less than three years until their discharge or scheduled release to mandatory supervision.

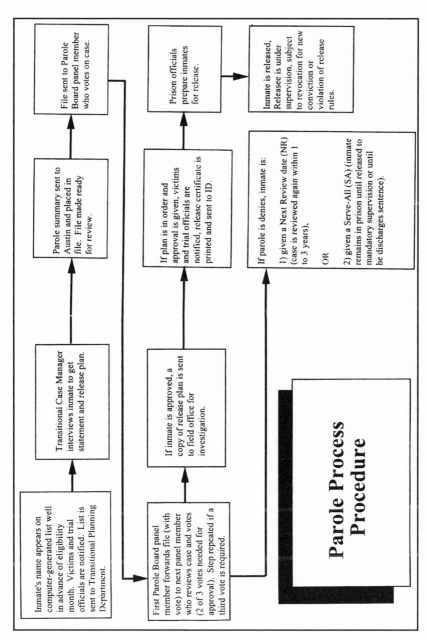

Parole Process Procedure

Inmate's name appears on computer-generated list well in advance of eligibility month. Victims and trial officials are notified. List is sent to Transitional Planning Department.

Transitional Case Manager interviews inmate to get statement and release plan.

Parole summary sent to Austin and placed in file. File made ready for review.

File sent to Parole Board panel member who votes on case.

First Parole Board panel member forwards file (with vote) to next panel member who reviews case and votes (2 of 3 votes needed for approval). Step repeated if a third vote is required.

If inmate is approved, a copy of release plan is sent to field office for investigation.

If plan is in order and approval is given, victims and trial officials are notified, release certificate is printed and sent to ID.

Prison officials prepare inmates for release.

Inmate is released, Releasee is under supervision, subject to revocation for new conviction or violation of release rules.

If parole is denies, inmate is:

1) given a Next Review date (NR) (case is reviewed again within 1 to 3 years),

OR

2) given a Serve-All (SA) (inmate remains in prison until released to mandatory supervision or until he discharges sentence).

Source: *Parole in Texas*, Texas Department of Criminal Justice, 1995.

EARLY RELEASE ELIGIBILITY

The power of the Board of Pardons and Paroles to release incarcerated felons before the full expiration of their sentence is limited by mandates set by the Texas Legislature. In limiting the power of the Board of Pardons and Paroles to grant early releases to convicts, the Texas Legislature has been guided by the general principle that offenders convicted of perpetrating crimes of violence must serve a greater percentage of the calendar time of their sentence before being eligible for early release. Conversely, offenders convicted of nonviolent felonies are eligible for early release after having served a smaller percentage of the calendar time of their sentence.

Given the general principle that ties early release eligibility with the nature of the convicted offender's crime, the eligibility of convicts for early release from prison by the Texas Board of Pardons and Paroles is dependent upon which of three offense categories the offender's conviction falls into. These three categories are: (1) the parole release eligibility of 7(g) offenders convicted of certain felony offenses that have enhanced parole requirements; (2) the parole release eligibility of 3(g) offenders; and (3) the non-discretionary mandatory release of non 7(g) and 3(g) offenders (all to be discussed below). Additionally, the date the crime was committed must be considered. The result of this general rule is that, depending on the nature of the crime for which the offender was convicted and incarcerated, most of the convicts in the Texas prison system today are eligible for either parole or mandatory release after having completed a statutorily fixed percentage of their sentence (i.e., calendar time served plus good time). Convicts who are sentenced to death are never eligible for either parole or mandatory release.

The Parole Release of 7(g) Offenders—Section 7(g) of Article 42.18 of the *Texas Code of Criminal Procedure* (which the Texas Legislature has now moved to Chapter 508.046 of the *Texas Government Code*) all but exempts certain convicted offenders from the possibility of early release from prison on parole. Offenders convicted of indecency with a child, aggravated sexual assault, or any criminal offense that carries a mandatory minimum 40-year calendar sentence, will, for all intents and purposes, never be released on parole. An offender convicted for one of the above statutorily enumerated offenses may be released on parole only after serving one-half of the calendar time of his or her sentence and has received a two-thirds vote of all 18 members of the Board of Pardons and Paroles. To date, this has never occurred in Texas. Therefore, offenders who have been convicted of indecency with a child, aggravated sexual assault, or any criminal offense that carries a mandatory minimum calendar sentence of 40 years or more may reasonably expect to serve 100% of the calendar time of the sentence before being released from prison. After completing 100% of the calendar time of the sentence, the offender will be released back into society without parole supervision.

The Parole Release of 3(g) Offenders—Offenders whose convictions were for a special class of violent crimes are referred to for parole eligibility purposes as "3(g)" convicts. The parole eligibility designation "3(g)" is derived from Section 3(g) of Article 42.12 of the *Texas Code of Criminal Procedure*. Those 3(g) convicts whose crimes of violence were committed after 31 August 1993 are not eligible for early release from prison on parole until after they have served a minimum one-half of the calendar time of their sentence, or 30 years, whichever is less. The crimes of violence specified in Section 3(g) which govern when a convict can become eligible for parole include murder, aggravated robbery, sexual assault, aggravated kidnaping, and any felony conviction where the record demonstrates that the criminal brandished or actually used a deadly weapon in the commission of the felony. A deadly weapon can be any instrument likely to or calculated to produce death or serious bodily injury. Examples of possible deadly weapons (depending on how they are used) include a wooden two-by-four, a broken beer bottle, or a brick. It is becoming increasingly difficult for 3(g) convicts to gain parole in Texas, so much so that from a practical standpoint, parole for 3(g) convicts has virtually been abolished. At the present time, the philosophy of the Board of Pardons and Paroles governing the release on parole of 3(g) convicts is that they are expected to serve up to 90% of the calendar time on their sentence before parole will be seriously considered.

For example, under this limitation, an offender convicted of aggravated robbery (which is a first-degree felony punishable by a term of incarceration of not less than five nor more than 99 years and a fine not to exceed $10,000 and an enumerated 3(g) offense) is sentenced by the judge to 50 years of incarceration. The convict has been in prison for 10 actual, or calendar years, during which time he has accumulated 12 years of good time credit. The convict is neither eligible for mandatory release, nor is he eligible to come before a parole panel for release on parole. He will be eligible for release from prison only after he has served either 100 percent of his 50-year sentence, or he will be eligible for release on parole by the parole panel only after he has served a minimum of 25 calendar years (one-half of his actual sentence) and has received two out of three votes from the parole panel.

Before the panel considers parole for an eligible convict who is serving a sentence for a crime against a person, a reasonable effort must be made to notify the victim that the offender is being considered for early release on parole. The parole panel is required by law to allow the notified victim to provide a written victim impact statement to the parole panel. The parole panel must consider the statements and the information contained in the victim impact statement in determining whether or not to recommend parole. If granted, the parole panel must notify the victim of the pending early release of the convict on parole. When considering whether to grant or deny parole to a parole eligible convict, the parole panel may, at its discretion, require the convict to personally appear before it to answer questions. This, however, is hardly ever done.

Mandatory Supervision Release—The Board of Pardons and Paroles must, by statute, mandatorily release some convicts on parole prior to the completion of their sentence. The program was instituted in 1977 as a relief valve on a prison system so overcrowded that it had to release some convicts in order to make room for new ones entering the prison system. This is referred to as "mandatory release" or "mandatory supervision." Offenders convicted and sentenced to prison for felony offenses that do not fall within the 7(g) and 3(g) categories and who are not subject to certain limitations imposed on the Board of Pardons and Paroles by the Texas Legislature are eligible for mandatory release on parole.

Two basic concepts are important to understanding mandatory release eligibility in Texas: calendar time and good time. Calendar time is the amount of actual time a convict has served in prison on his sentence. Good time is the amount of time credited toward a convict's sentence for good behavior (see Chapter 7 for a discussion about good time). The awarding of good time has the effect of reducing the actual time a convict must spend in prison to satisfy the calendar time requirement of the sentence imposed upon him, but the good time allowance does not reduce the sentence itself. Calendar time plus good time equals the length of the sentence itself, and dictates the eligibility for mandatory release. For example, consider a convict sentenced to five years' incarceration after conviction for a non 7(g) or 3(g) offense, and who has already been imprisoned for two years in the Texas prison system. Suppose that during this time he has accumulated good time credits equal to three years. The two years he has actually served (calendar time) plus the three years accumulated good time equals five years—the length of the sentence imposed upon him following conviction. In this example, the convict is eligibile for mandatory release, and will be under the care, control, and custody of a parole officer for three years (the time equal to his earned good time).

Eligibility for mandatory release is calculated by counting the actual calendar time served plus accumulated good time. When that total is equal to the length of the judicially imposed sentence, the Board of Pardons and Paroles must release the convict from prison. Mandatory releasees are required to complete the remaining portion of their sentences under the supervision of the Pardons and Parole Division of the Texas Department of Criminal Justice. For example, suppose an offender is convicted of selling or purchasing a child (a third-degree felony punishable by a term of incarceration of not less than two nor more than 10 years and a fine not to exceed $10,000) and receives a sentence of five years. The convict has been in prison for two actual, or calendar years, during which time he has accumulated three years of good time. In this example the Board of Pardons and Paroles must mandatorily release him. Offenders convicted for non 7(g) or non 3(g) offenses committed after 31 August 1987 are not eligible to come before a parole panel until they have served a minimum of one-quarter of their sentence, or 15 years, whichever is less. The time served on the sentence is calculated by adding calendar time served to the accumulated amount of good time they have earned.

It is very important to note, however, that the Texas Legislature has imposed stringent limitations on the power of the Board of Pardons and Paroles to mandatorily release convicts from prison. The Board of Pardons and Paroles is not empowered to mandatory release offenders who were convicted and are serving a prison sentence for first- or second-degree aggravated assault, first-degree injury to a child, the elderly, or the disabled, first-degree arson, second-degree robbery, first-degree burglary, or violation of the drug-free zone statute in Section 481.134 of the *Texas Health and Safety Code*. Offenders sentenced to prison after having been convicted of any one of the above mentioned statutorily enumerated felony offenses are not eligible for mandatory release, and can obtain their freedom only by serving either 100 percent of the calendar time of their sentence, or by receiving a majority vote of two out of the three members that constitute a parole panel. To be eligible for consideration before the parole panel an offender convicted of one of the above enumerated offenses, the convict must have served at least one-half of the calendar time of his sentence.

There is now an additional exception to the eligibility of convicts for mandatory release. Section 8(c-1) of Chapter 42.18 of the *Texas Code of Criminal Procedure* (now located in Chapter 508.046 of the *Texas Government Code*), which became effective on 1 September 1996, allows a parole panel to veto mandatory release of an eligible convict if a majority of the panel feel that the calendar time served by the offender

Parole and Mandatory Supervision Eligibility Chart
(Revised 10/11/95)

Offense Date	Legislature	Offense	Parole Eligibility
Prior to 1-1-66	55th	All Offenses*	Calendar Time = 1/3, including any bonus & blood donations* Maximum = 15 yrs. * (Art. 42.12 was amended on 1-1-66 to allow good time and 1/4 time for all persons confined in TDC.)
1-1-66 thru 8-28-67	59th	All Offenses*	Calendar Time + Good Time = 1/4, including any bonus & blood donations Maximum = 15 yrs.
8-29-67 thru 8-28-77	60th	All Offenses* *TDCJ Data Services calculates eligibility dates on all offenses prior to 8-28-77 utilizing calendar time + good time = 1/3, regardless of the law in effect when the offense was committed. This apparently due to court rulings during that time period.	Calendar Time + Good Time = 1/3, including any bonus & blood donations Maximum = 20 yrs. No Mandatory Supervision: Inmate discharges sentence when calendar time + good time = total sentence. Sentence is effectively reduced by the amount of good time earned.
8-29-77 thru 8-31-87	65th 69th	Capital Murder, Agg. Kidnapping, Agg. Rape, Agg. Sexual Abuse (8-31-85; Agg. Rape and Agg. Sexual Abuse combined into Aggravated Sexual Assault) Agg. Robbery, Any Offense with Affirmative Finding of Deadly Weapon	Art. 42.12 Sec. 3f(8-29-77 thru 8-31-83) Art. 42.12 Sec. 3g (9-1-83 thru 8-31-87) Calendar Time = 1/3 Minimum of 2 yrs. Maximum of 20 yrs.
		All other offenses	Calendar Time + Good Time = 1/3, including A, B, or C credits and bonus Maximum of 20 yrs. All cases eligible for Mandatory Supervision
9-1-87 thru 8-31-89	70th	3g Offenses: Capital Murder Agg. Kidnapping Agg. Sexual Assault Agg. Robbery Any Offense with Affirmative Finding of Deadly Weapon	Calendar Time = 1/4 Minimum of 2 yrs. Maximum of 15 yrs.
		All other offenses	Calendar Time + Good Time = 1/4, including work credits and bonus Maximum of 15 yrs. All Offenses Eligible for Mandatory Supervision except: All 3g Offenses Murder, 1st Degree Sexual Assault, 2nd Degree Aggravated Assault, 2nd & 3rd Degree Deadly Assault on Law or Corrections Officer; Court Participant; Probation Personnel; Member or Employees of the BPP; Employees of TYC Injury to Child or Elderly, 1st Degree Arson, 1st Degree Robbery, 2nd Degree Burglary Punishable under Subsection d(2) or d(3)
9-1-89 thru 8-31-93	71st-72nd	3g Offense: Capital Murder (Capital Felony) - Life Sentence 1) Murders a peace officer or fireman on official duty, 2) Murders while committing a kidnapping, burglary, robbery, aggravated sexual assault, or arson, 3) Murders for remuneration, 4) Murders while escaping from a penal institution, 5) Murders an employee of a penal institution, or 6) Murders more than one person during the same criminal transaction, or during different criminal transactions but the murders are committed pursuant to the same scheme.	Calendar Time = 1/4 Minimum of 2 yrs. Maximum of 15 yrs. Calendar Time = 35 yrs. effective 9-1-91.

Source: *Parole in Texas*, Texas Department of Criminal Justice, 1995.

Offense Date	Offense	Legislature	Parole Eligibility
9-1-93 to 8-31-94	**3g Offense:** Capital Murder (Capital Felony) - Life Sentence	73rd	Calendar Time = 40 yrs.
	1) Murder of a peace officer or fireman on official duty, 2) Murders a person in the course of committing a kidnapping, burglary, robbery, aggravated sexual assault, arson, obstruction, or retaliation, 3) Murders while escaping or attempting to escape from a penal institution, 4) Murders for remuneration, 5) Murders an employee of a penal institution, 6) Murders with intent to establish or participate in an alliance of individuals, 7) A person convicted of murder who murders while incarcerated, 8) Murders while serving a sentence of Life or 99 years for Aggravated Kidnapping, Aggravated Sexual Assault, or Aggravated Robbery, 9) Murders more than one person during the same criminal transaction, or during different criminal transactions but the murders are committed pursuant to the same scheme, 10) Murders an individual under six years of age.		
	3g Offenses: Agg. Kidnapping, Agg. Sexual Assault, Agg. Robbery, Any Offense with Affirmative Finding of Deadly Weapon		Calendar Time = ½ Minimum of 2 yrs. Maximum of 30 yrs.
	Murder, Indecency With a Child		
	Special Needs Parole Elderly, Physically Handicapped, Terminally Ill		3g cases are excluded. At a date earlier than normally calculated (No longer a threat to society; appropriate supervision plan)
	Mentally Retarded, Mentally Ill		Above criteria + approval by Texas Council on Offenders with Mental Impairments

Offense Date	Offense	Legislature	Parole Eligibility
Continued 9-1-89 thru 8-31-93	**3g Offenses:** Agg. Kidnapping, Agg. Sexual Assault, Agg. Robbery, Any Offense with Affirmative Finding of Deadly Weapon		Calendar Time = 1/4 Minimum of 2 yrs. Maximum of 15 yrs.
	Special Needs Parole (Effective 12-1-91) Elderly, Physically Handicapped, Terminally Ill		3g cases are excluded. At a date earlier than normally calculated (No longer a threat to society; appropriate supervision plan)
	Mentally Retarded, Mentally Ill		Above criteria + approval by Texas Council on Offenders with Mental Impairments
	All other offenses		Calendar Time + Good Time = 1/4, including work credits and bonus Maximum of 15 yrs.
			Must earn time credit on all sentences, one after another, until eligibility is reached on the last sentence
			All Offenses Eligible for Mandatory Supervision except: All 3g Offenses, Murder, 1st Degree, Sexual Assault, 2nd Degree, Aggravated Assault, 2nd & 3rd Degree, Deadly Assault on Law or Corrections Officer; Court Participant; Probation Personnel; Member or Employees of the BPP; Employees of TYC, Injury to Child or Elderly, 1st Degree, Arson, 1st Degree, Robbery, 2nd Degree, Burglary Punishable under Subsection d(2) or d(3)

Offense Date	Offense	Legislature	Parole Eligibility
Continued 9-1-93 to 8-31-94	All other offenses		Calendar Time + Good Time =1/4, including work credits and bonus Maximum of 15 yrs.
			Must earn time credit on all sentences, one after another, until eligibility is reached on the last sentence.
	Drug-Free Zones: Institution of higher learning or a playground (1000 ft.), youth center, public swimming pool or video arcade (300 ft.)		Calendar Time = 5 yrs. or maximum term, whichever is less
			All Offenses Eligible for Mandatory Supervision except: All 3g Offenses: Murder 1st Degree; Sexual Assault, 2nd Degree; Aggravated Assault, 1st & 2nd Degree; Injury to Child or Elderly, 1st Degree; Arson, 1st Degree; Robbery, 2nd Degree: Burglary punishable under Subsection d(2) or d(3); A Felony increased under Health & Safety Code (Drug-Free Zones)
9-1-94 to 8-31-95	3g Offense: Capital Murder (Capital Felony) - Life Sentence 1) Murder of a peace officer or fireman on official duty, 2) Murders a person in the course of committing a kidnapping, burglary, robbery, aggravated sexual assault, arson, obstruction, or retaliation, 3) Murders while escaping or attempting to escape from a penal institution, 5) Murders an employee of a penal institution, 6) Murders with intent to establish or participate in an alliance of individuals, 7) A person convicted of murder who murders while incarcerated, 8) Murders while serving a sentence of Life or 99 years for Aggravated Kidnapping, Aggravated Sexual Assault, or Aggravated Robbery, 9) Murders more than one person during the same criminal transaction, or during different criminal transactions but the murders are committed pursuant to the same scheme, 10) Murders an individual under six years of age.	73rd	Calendar Time = 40 yrs. (Full Board vote)
Continued 9-1-94 to 8-31-95	3g Offenses: Agg Kidnapping Agg Sexual Assault Agg Robbery Any Offense with Affirmative Finding of Deadly Weapon Murder Indecency With a Child		Calendar Time = ½ Minimum of 2 yrs. Maximum of 30 yrs.
	Special Needs Parole Elderly Physically Handicapped Terminally Ill		At a date earlier than normally calculated (No longer a threat to society; appropriate supervision plan) Above criteria + approval by Texas Council on Offenders with Mental Impairments
	Mentally Retarded Mentally Ill		Calendar Time + Good Time = 1/4, including work credits and bonus Maximum of 15 yrs.
	All other 1st, 2nd, and 3rd degree felony offenses (a court may reduce the punishment of a 3rd degree felony by imposing the confinement of a Class A Misdemeanor)		Must earn time credit on all sentences, one after another, until eligibility is reached on the last sentence.
	Drug-Free Zones: Institution of higher learning or a playground (1000 ft.), youth center, public swimming pool or video arcade (300 ft.)		Calendar Time = 5 yrs. or maximum term, whichever is less
	State Jail Felonies		Parole eligibility is not applicable (confinement is to a state jail for any term of not more than two years or less than 180 days.
			All Offenses Eligible for Mandatory Supervision except: All 3g Offenses: Murder 1st Degree; Sexual Assault, 2nd Degree; Aggravated Assault, 1st & 2nd Degree; Injury to Child or Elderly, 1st Degree; Arson, 1st Degree; Robbery, 2nd Degree; Burglary punishable under Subsection d(2) or d(3); A Felony increased under Health & Safety Code (Drug-Free Zones)

Offense Date	Offense	Legislature	Parole Eligibility
9-1-95 to 8-31-96	3g Offense: Capital Murder (Capital Felony) - Life Sentence 1) Murder of a peace officer or fireman on official duty. 2) Murders a person in the course of committing a kidnapping, burglary, robbery, aggravated sexual assault, arson, obstruction, or retaliation. 3) Murders for remuneration. 4) Murders while escaping or attempting to escape from a penal institution. 5) Murders an employee of a penal institution. 6) Murders with intent to establish or participate in an alliance of individuals. 7) A person convicted of murder who murders while incarcerated. 8) Murders while serving a sentence of Life or 99 years for Aggravated Kidnapping, Aggravated Sexual Assault, or Aggravated Robbery. 9) Murders more than one person during the same criminal transaction, or during different criminal transactions but the murders are committed pursuant to the same scheme. 10) Murders an individual under six years of age.	74th	Calendar Time = 40 yrs. (Full Board vote + written report from Texas Department of Criminal Justice)
....	Agg. Sexual Assault Agg. Kidnapping (with intent to violate or abuse victim sexually)* Indecency with a Child (sexual contact) Burglary of a Habitation with intent to commit a felony other than Felony Theft, or committed or attempted to commit a felony other than Felony Theft or Sexual Assault or Indecency with a Child.* * Two prior felonies, one of which was a sex related offense.		Calendar Time = 35 yrs. (Full Board vote + written report from Texas Department of Criminal Justice)

Offense Date	Offense	Legislature	Parole Eligibility
Continued 9-1-95 to 8-31-96	3g Offenses: Agg. Kidnapping Agg. Robbery Any Offense with Affirmative Finding of Deadly Weapon Murder Indecency With a Child Sexual Assault ((a)(2) with a Child)		Calendar Time = ½ Minimum of 2 yrs. Maximum of 30 yrs. *Aggravated Sexual Assault remains a 3g Offense, but eligibility is Calendar Time = 35 yrs.*
....	Special Needs Parole Elderly Physically Handicapped Terminally Ill		At a date earlier than normally calculated (No longer a threat to society; appropriate supervision plan)
	Mentally Retarded Mentally Ill		Above criteria + approval by Texas Council on Offenders with Mental Impairments
....	All other 1st, 2nd, and 3rd degree felony offenses (a court may reduce the punishment of a 3rd degree felony by imposing the confinement of a Class A Misdemeanor)		Calendar Time + Good Time = 1/4, Including work credits and bonus Maximum of 15 yrs.
	The length of a sentence can be affected by the enhancement law (Sec. 12.42 of the Penal Code, Habitual & Repeat Offenders)		Must earn time credit on all sentences, one after another until eligibility is reached on the last sentence.
....	Drug-Free Zones: Institution of higher learning or a playground (1000 ft.), youth center, public swimming pool or video arcade (300 ft.)		Calendar Time = 5 yrs. or maximum term, whichever is less
....	State Jail Felonies* * A state jail felony can be enhanced to a 2nd or 3rd degree felony.		Parole eligibility is not applicable. *Confinement is to a state jail for any term of/not more than two years or less than 180 days.* *Effective 1-1-96: Confinement to a state jail is not more than two years or less than 90 days.*

Offense Date	Offense	Legislature	Parole Eligibility
Continued 9-1-95 to 8-31-96			**All Offense Eligible for Mandatory Supervision except:** **All 3g Offenses:** Murder 1st Degree Sexual Assault, 2nd Degree Aggravated Assault, 1st & 2nd Degree Injury to Child or Elderly, 1st Degree Arson, 1st Degree Robbery, 2nd Degree Burglary, 1st Degree A Felony increased under Health & Safety Code (Drug-Free Zones) *Effective 9-1-96:* *Injury to Disabled Individual* *Previous Conviction for 3g Offense* *Previous Conviction for Offense with an Affirmative Finding of a Deadly Weapon* *A case may be denied Mandatory Supervision by a Parole Panel.*

does not adequately reflect the amount of time necessary to meet his or her rehabilitation and correctional needs, and that the convict poses a continuing risk to society.

CONDITIONS OF PAROLE AND MANDATORY RELEASE

The Board of Pardons and Paroles may release convicted felons back into the community before they have completed their entire sentence of imprisonment only when the convicts agree to abide by certain conditions. Parole and mandatory release conditions, set by the Board of Pardons and Paroles, are of two basic types: standard (or general) and special (or individual). The standard conditions for parole and mandatory release which the Board may require of all convicts eligible for early release are set forth in Article 42.12, Section 11, of the *Texas Code of Criminal Procedure*, and relate principally to reasonable behavioral expectations associated with promoting community safety and the efficient supervision and management of parolees by parole officers. Typical of the standard conditions of parole and mandatory release imposed upon the convict are requirements that no federal or state laws or municipal ordinances be violated. The convict also should refrain from the use of intoxicants and not frequent any place where intoxicants are sold for consumption on premises; avoid injurious or vicious habits; not associate with disreputable characters, including known criminals, nor be in possession of a firearm; work regularly at a lawful occupation; maintain reasonable hours; support legal dependents; not leave the community to which he has been released without the permission of his parole officer; notify his parole officer immediately if there is a change in the place of his residence; report punctually as directed by his parole officer and follow all of the parole officer's advice and instructions; and permit the parole officer to visit at any time his home, place of employment, or anywhere else he may be.

Special conditions of early release may also be imposed on the convict eligible for parole or mandatory release at the discretion of the Board of Pardons and Paroles. Special parole conditions particularly address any unique and reasonable community safety needs or treatment and rehabilitative needs of the convict, such as mandating his residence in a halfway house, or his compulsory participation in a sex offender therapy program or a substance abuse program. The general and special conditions under which the board is willing to release a convict eligible for parole or mandatory release are clearly and succinctly stated in a legally binding contract which both the convict and the board sign off on prior to the release of the convict from prison.

The Board of Pardons and Paroles will release a convict only after it has determined that (1) an eligible convict is suitable for early release; (2) the convict's early release from prison will not increase the likelihood of harm to the public; (3) arrangements have been made for the convict's employment or for his or her maintenance and care while free in the community; and (4) the convict is willing and able to abide by all of the general and specific conditions of an early release.

Every convict released early from prison is remanded to the legal custody of the Pardons and Paroles Division of the

Texas Department of Criminal Justice. The period of time the released convict spends on parole or mandatory release before being fully discharged from the care, control, and legal custody of the Pardons and Paroles Division is equivalent to the maximum term for which the convict was sentenced less the calendar time actually served in prison plus the amount of accumulated good time.

RELEASEE REVOCATION

Failure to abide by either the general or special conditions of parole or mandatory release can result in the issuance of a warrant for the arrest of the releasee. A violation of the conditions of the release contract will not necessarily result in a revocation of parole or mandatory release and the return of the convict to prison. A parole or mandatory release violation that does not endanger the public or does not constitute a crime is often referred to as a "technical violation," and usually does not result in the convict being returned to prison. Examples of technical violations include getting fired from a job, going to a bar, or missing a scheduled meeting with a parole officer. On the other hand, consistent and repeated failure to abide by the conditions of the release contract, or the commission of a new crime while on parole or mandatory supervision, will result in a revocation proceeding.

The procedure used by the Texas Board of Pardons and Paroles for parole and mandatory release revocation is a two-step process, and follows the procedural requirements set forth by the 1972 U.S. Supreme Court case *Morrissey v. Brewer* (408 U. S. 471). The first step is an initial hearing (often referred to as a "Morrissey Hearing") which focuses on whether there is probable cause to believe the violation of a condition of early release alleged by the parole officer did in fact occur. If probable cause is established at the initial hearing, the second step is to convene a revocation hearing to determine whether the violation did in fact occur and whether the violation justifies the revocation of early release agreement. If early release is revoked, the convict is remanded back to the custody of the prison system. If the revocation is based upon commission of a new crime, the releasee may be subject to further prosecution, conviction, and incarceration for the new crime. Both hearings are handled by a hearings officer, whose findings are then forwarded to a panel composed of three members of the Board of Pardons and Paroles for a vote based on the officer's findings. The decision of the panel to revoke early release is decided by majority vote. The panel does not see or hear from the convict directly. After a convict's parole or mandatory release has been revoked, any previously earned good time days are forfeited, and future parole or mandatory release eligibility must then be calculated on the number of good time days newly acquired.

GUBERNATORIAL EXECUTIVE CLEMENCY

The pardoning power of the governor of Texas has been greatly reduced from what it was in the past. The old pardoning power of the governor is today referred to as "executive clemency," and is clearly specified in Article 48.01 of the *Texas Code of Criminal Procedure*. In all criminal cases arising from violations of state law, except those involving treason or impeachment, the governor of Texas has the authority to (1) grant a full or conditional pardon, (2) grant a full pardon based on innocence, (3) commute the sentence of the convicted offender by changing or reducing the sentence imposed by the court after conviction, (4) grant remission of a fine or forfeiture resulting from a criminal conviction, (5) grant an emergency medical reprieve, or (6) grant a thirty-day reprieve of execution. With the exception of a thirty-day reprieve of execution, the Texas Constitution forbids the governor from granting executive clemency without the recommendation and approval of the Board of Pardons and Paroles.

A full executive pardon has the effect of restoring to an offender certain citizenship rights forfeited as a consequence of a criminal conviction. Typical of the rights forfeited by law upon conviction for a felony are the right to vote, the right to serve on a jury, and the right to hold public office. It is important to mention that under the current *Texas Election Code*, the right to vote is restored to Texas residents two years after the discharge of a felony sentence. Additionally, a full pardon removes the restrictions which attach to some, but not all, forms of professional licensing and employment. For example, a full pardon will not restore an individual's eligibility to be licensed as a peace officer in Texas. Additionally, a full pardon does not result in either the expungement of the criminal record nor does it legally exonerate an individual. The only exception to this is if the pardon is granted on the grounds that the person was wrongfully convicted and is actually innocent of the crime. Innocence pardons are extremely rare.

The statutory power of the governor to reprieve, commute punishment, and pardon is used very sparingly today. For example, from September 1995 to August 1997 approximately 400 convicts applied to the Board of Pardons and Paroles for full pardons. Of the 400 applications, the Board of Pardons and Paroles recommended to Governor George W. Bush that 71 receive full pardons. Of those recommended by the board for full pardon, Governor Bush granted pardons to only 15.

The Pardons and Paroles Division of the Texas Department of Criminal Justice

The Pardons and Paroles Division of the Texas Department of Criminal Justice represents the second half of the parole and mandatory release process in Texas. The Pardons and Paroles Division is responsible for two principal functions. First, it is responsible for keeping track of and calculating parole and mandatory release eligibility dates for all convicts in the Texas prison system. Other responsibilities include preparing and assembling all the necessary data and documentation that the board's parole panels will consider when making decisions to grant or deny early release, and in making recommendations to the board's parole panel to grant or deny early release on a case-by-case basis. Second, the Pardons and Paroles Division is responsible for the supervision and management of all parolees and mandatory releasees. Because the Pardons and Paroles Division operates in concert with the Board of Pardons and Paroles and serves it as a managerial arm, the statutory authority for the division emanates from Section 42.18 of the

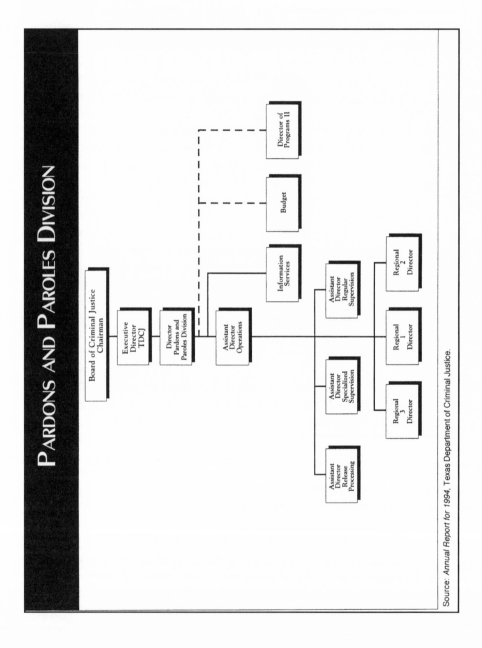

PARDONS AND PAROLES DIVISION

Source: *Annual Report for 1994*, Texas Department of Criminal Justice.

Texas Code of Criminal Procedure—the same statutory source from whence the power of the Board of Pardons and Paroles is derived. The director of the Pardons and Paroles Division is appointed by the executive director of the Texas Department of Criminal Justice.

PAROLE OFFICERS IN TEXAS

The actual supervision of parolees and mandatory releasees is conducted by parole officers working out of district offices in three regional field headquarters located in Austin, Dallas, and Houston. Texas parole officers are appointed by the director of the Pardons and Paroles Division. The legal duties and responsibilities of parole officers in Texas are set forth in Article 42.18, Section 2(3) of the *Texas Code of Criminal Procedure*, and include a variety of functions, including the assessment of parolee risks and needs, investigation, case management, the supervision and monitoring of the activities of parolees to insure their compliance with the conditions of their release, and assisting parolees with their continuing rehabilitation needs, and providing support and referral services to help parolees with their successful reintegration into society. Article 42.18, Section 19 of the *Texas Code of Criminal Procedure* requires that all Texas parole officers have a four-year college degree and two years of full-time and paid experience in either adult or juvenile corrections. Typically, Texas parole officers have an undergraduate degree in one of the behavioral and social sciences, usually criminal justice, psychology, or social work. State law forbids any Texas peace officer or prosecuting attorney from acting in the capacity of a parole officer.

The approximately 60,000 parolees and 20,000 mandatory releasees in Texas are supervised and managed by more than 1,200 parole officers in 70 district field offices located around the state. At the beginning of 1997, there were in excess of 19,000 3(g) parolees, and more than 13,000 paroled felons were at large with outstanding warrants for their arrest. Of these fugitive Texas parolees, 2,011 were considered armed and dangerous. While parole officers in approximately half of the states in the United States are allowed to carry firearms, parole officers in Texas are not. This has been a continuing source of concern and dissatisfaction among Texas parole officers, and despite attempts to introduce legislation allowing them to carry firearms, the Texas Legislature has not yet passed a bill allowing them to do so.

PAROLE SUPERVISION PROGRAMS AND SERVICES

There is currently a very wide range of diverse and specialized parole supervision programs and services available in Texas to ensure that paroled convicts are afforded every opportunity to receive the help they require in order to reintegrate into mainstream society and not lapse back into criminal behavior. These parole programs and services fall into four basic categories: regular parole supervision, intensive parole supervision, residential parole, and specialized parole.

Regular parole supervision is the most frequent type of parole program used in Texas, and it is the type of parole program the average person most readily associates with the practice of parole. Upon release from prison the parolee lives and works in the community, and reports periodically with his parole officer. The parole officer monitors the parolee's compliance with the general and special conditions of the parole agreement, and provides the parolee with referrals to programs and services in the community to help facilitate a successful transition from prison to the free world. The average Texas parolee on regular supervision remains on parole for a little more than two years, after which time he or she is discharged from monitoring and supervision by the state. The per diem cost of regular parole supervision for one parolee is about $2.25, and parole officers assigned to regular parole supervision typically have a caseload of approximately 75 parolees.

A second type of parole supervision used in Texas is called ISP, or intensive supervision parole. ISP is a type of parole program that the Texas Legislature specifically requires the Pardons and Paroles Division to operate. The ISP program is intended for parolees who pose a potentially high risk to community safety or are at a greater than average risk of not being able to successfully meet the general or specific conditions of their parole. Parolees under intensive supervision parole are monitored more closely than parolees on regular parole supervision, and have more frequent contacts with their parole officer than do non-ISP parolees. Electronic monitoring is frequently used with ISP parolees, and also with those parolees who are not responding well to regular parole supervision and are considered by their parole officer to be at a potentially high risk of violating one or more conditions of their parole. Where this is the case, a non-removable electronic device which either continuously or intermittently transmits signals over a telephone line is attached to the parolee's ankle or wrist. The device allows a parole officer to monitor and verify a parolee's compliance with one or more conditions of his release which state that he be in a certain place at a specified time. Texas was the first state to use electronic monitoring for paroled felons. The per diem cost of intensive supervision parole for one parolee is about $6.25, and parole officers assigned to intensive supervision parole typically have a caseload of approximately 30 parolees.

A third type of parole supervision used in Texas is community residential parole. Article 42.18, Section 25 of the *Texas Code of Criminal Procedure* requires that the Pardons and Paroles Division establish and operate community residential parole facilities for parolees who are required, as a special condition of their early release from prison, to live in a controlled and structured environment. This type of parole program is thought by the Texas Legislature to be the most conducive to providing a wide range of specialized, community-based services to parolees who have special needs. There are three principal forms of community residential parole used in Texas: the Halfway House Program, the Pre-parole Transfer Placement Program, and the Intermediate Sanction Facility Program.

- The *Halfway House Program* provides paroled convicts who do not have a permanent place to live, do not have a job, or lack the essential social skills to live on their own, with a place to live and a wide variety of counseling services to help them readjust to life outside of prison. Halfway houses provide parolees with a reliable, stable, and safe living environment where they receive counseling and training in commonplace skills that most of us take for granted, such as how to manage and budget money and balance a checkbook, how to shop for groceries, and how to prepare your own meals. Additionally, parolees in halfway houses receive job-readiness and employment placement counseling that helps them locate employment opportunities and teaches them job interview skills.

- The *Pre-parole Transfer Placement Program* is similar to the halfway house program in the wide variety of counseling services provided, but differs in two fundamental respects: first, the convicts residing in these residential facilities have not yet technically been released on parole (but are prime candidates), and second, the physical security arrangements associated with the operation of the facility are much greater than halfway houses. Unlike halfway houses, pre-parole transfer placement facilities are required by Texas law to have complete perimeter fencing and external lighting as well as controlled ingress and egress. These facilities help prepare the prospective parolee with an opportunity to gradually adjust to life outside prison by providing a structured and closely monitored and supervised living environment that helps the convict gradually adjust to life outside of prison. While in the pre-parole transfer placement facility, the convict receives a wide range of assistance, including help in locating a suitable place to live on his own after he has been paroled, help in finding a job, and help in establishing contacts with social service programs deemed essential to meeting all conditions of release.
- The *Intermediate Sanction Facility Program*, or ISF, combines elements from both the intensive supervision parole and residential parole programs. The intermediate sanction facility program represents a last chance alternative for parolees who have had their parole revoked for violating a general or specific condition of their parole, but who are believed to deserve one last chance before being returned to prison.

Specialized parole programs represent the fourth type of

parole supervision used in Texas. The Texas Legislature has mandated that the Pardons and Paroles Division provide highly specialized services and supervision, counseling, and support systems to parolees who have special problems that are directly related to the criminal behavior for which they were convicted and sentenced to prison, and, which left unaddressed, could pose a significant threat to the safety of the general public, or place the parolee in a high risk category for having their parole revoked. Article 42.18, Section 23 of the *Texas Code of Criminal Procedure* requires special parole programs for parolees who have a history of substance abuse offenses, sex offenses, or whose criminal behavior is attributable to mental impairment or mental retardation. Special parole programs created by the Pardons and Paroles Division to meet the mandate established by the Texas Legislature include:

- *Substance abuse programs*. These are specialized programs designed to aid parolees who have prior records of alcohol or drug abuse that may interfere with their successful reintegration into society and place them at high risk of having their parole revoked. Parolees in substance abuse programs are closely scrutinized and monitored, undergo frequent drug and alcohol testing, and receive special psychological counseling and medical treatment fortheir substance abuse problems.
- *Sex offender programs* represent another form of specialized parole. The goal of this program is twofold. First, the program promotes public safety interests by intensively monitoring and supervising parolees who were convicted for crimes of a sexual nature that involved either children, adults, or animals. Second, the program mandatorily requires that paroled sex offenders participate in psychological counseling aimed at preventing the parolee from relapsing into further sexually predatory behavior. Research tends to suggest that sex offenders are apt to be repeat offenders, and therefore merit intense supervision and monitoring in conjunction with special therapeutic counseling.
- The *Mentally Retarded Offender Program* was created in 1984 to upgrade the level of monitoring and supervision

of convicted criminals released from prison on parole who are mentally retarded or borderline mentally retarded. The program is designed to reduce the mentally retarded parolee's potential for having parole revoked because of a violation of a general or special condition by providing him with the necessary educational, vocational, and job readiness skills he needs in order to successfully live outside of a penal or mental institution.

- The *Mentally Impaired Offender Program* is a specialized form of parole service for parolees who have a history of in-or-out patient care and treatment for debilitating psychiatric disorders such as chronic depression, manic depression, psychosis, or schizophrenia. The goal of the program is to reduce the potential for parole revocation and recidivism among parolees with psychiatric problems by ensuring they receive the specialized medical services and psychiatric treatment they need.

- *Project RIO* (Reintegration of Offenders) is an innovative and nationally recognized Texas program created with a view to reducing parole revocations and recidivism by providing parolees with special assistance in finding employment suitable to their educational and vocational skills level. Project RIO, a joint governmental endeavor combining personnel and resources from the Pardons and Paroles Division of the Texas Department of Criminal Justice and the Texas Employment Commission, has been recognized as a unique model program by the United States Department of Labor, the National Governor's Association, and Harvard University's John F. Kennedy School of Government.

Parole will undoubtedly continue in the immediate future as the most frequently employed means of releasing convicted felons from prison in Texas. It is expected, however, that the Texas Legislature in the future will continue to pass statutes that make it increasingly difficult to meet minimal eligibility requirements for parole. Additionally, it is expected that the Texas Legislature will continue the process of expanding the number of crimes that are not parole eligible, and increasing the minimum calendar time that offenders must serve before they become parole eligible. Furthermore, if the current trend of the Texas Board of Pardons and Paroles is any indication of what the future holds, it is highly likely that the board will continue to defer the granting of parole to convicts when they first become parole eligible, and, as new prison facilities open, the board will no doubt revoke more paroles for failure to strictly abide by the letter and spirit of the conditions of the parole contract.

PART 2:
PROBATION

The Historical Development
of Probation in Texas

Community supervision (the new term for probation in Texas) is a sentencing option available today to both judges and juries in Texas that is an alternative to incarcerating a convicted misdemeanant or felon. When a convicted criminal is sentenced to a term of probation, he is allowed to remain in the community under the supervision of a probation officer instead of going to prison. Probation differs from parole in that parole is a status determined by an agency of the executive branch of government, and follows a period of confinement in the Texas prison system. Probation, on the other hand, is a disposition vested with the judicial branch of government. The principal goal of probation is to maximize the convict's effective reintegration into society by not having his ties with the community and mainstream society severed by incarcerating him in a jail or prison. Probation is seen as a valuable sentencing option for first-time nonviolent offenders whose chances for rehabilitation and reintegration into mainstream society as law-abiding citizens are maximized by remaining in the community instead of going to prison.

The contemporary practice of probation in Texas is synonymous with the term "community supervision," and is defined by Article 42.12, section 2(2) of the *Texas Code of Criminal Procedure* as "the placement of a defendant by a court under a continuum of programs and sanctions, with conditions imposed by the court for a specified period during which imposition of sentence is suspended."

The first adult probation laws in the United States were passed by the Massachusetts Legislature in 1878. The practice of probation was introduced into the federal courts in 1925. By the middle of the 1930s the use of probation was statutorily authorized in 36 states. Texas was one of the last states in the United States to formally adopt the practice. Probation was first legislatively authorized in Texas in 1947. By 1956 every state in the United States had provided statutorily for the use of probation as an alternative to incarceration after a finding of criminal liability.

The historical development of the use of probation in Texas is characterized by the Texas Legislature's uncertainty with respect to the appropriate use of probation, its failure to authorize funding to support probation supervision, and its confusion with respect to creating the best mechanism to administer and manage probation services in the state. The origin of the use of probation in Texas as a sentencing alternative to incarceration in prison is founded in the 1913 Texas Suspended Sentence Act. Under traditional common law practice, a suspended sentence was a type of judicial disposition that followed a conviction for either a misdemeanor or felony offense. When a judge suspended sentence he sentenced the convicted offender to a term of incarceration in jail or prison, but unconditionally released the convicted criminal offender into the community with the understanding that the judge would not actually impose the sentence of incarceration as long as the convicted offender committed no further crimes and exhibited good behavior. Under the provisions of the 1913 Texas Suspended Sentence Act, a suspended sentence could be imposed by a judge only pursuant to the jury's recommendation. A judge did, however, have sole authority and discretion to impose a suspended sentence only in bench trials. Additionally, the 1913 Suspended Sentence Act mandated that the use of a suspended sentence be exclusively reserved for first-time felony offenders, and that revocation of the suspended sentence could occur only for the commission of another felony offense.

Between 1913 and 1941 the Suspended Sentence Act was amended by the Texas Legislature on three occasions. In 1931 the legislature authorized judges presiding over jury trials to suspend sentences independent of a jury recommendation. In 1935 the legislature again amended the Suspended Sentence Act, this time taking away from juries the authority and discretion to recommend a suspended sentence in lieu of incarceration, and vesting the power to suspend sentences only with judges presiding in Texas courts having original jurisdiction. In 1941 the Texas Legislature expanded the power of Texas judges to revoke a suspended sentence. The 1941 amendment to the 1913 Suspended Sentence Act authorized judges to revoke a suspended sentence and impose incarceration where the convicted criminal was found to have committed a misdemeanor offense.

The Texas Legislature's patchwork approach to crafting a workable probation law from 1913 to 1941 resulted in two serious shortcomings. First, the lack of any meaningful standards and guidelines for the use of suspended sentences by judges resulted in allegations of judicial corruption and favoritism associated with its granting and revocation. Second, no provision was ever made by the Texas Legislature for the supervision of convicts released back into the community under the Suspended Sentence Act. Similar to the early supervision practices associated with parolees in Texas, the supervision of convicts released on suspended sentence was carried out by interested community volunteers on a county-by-county basis.

The Texas Legislature in 1947 attempted to reform the two principal shortcomings associated with the practice of suspended sentencing by passing the Adult Probation Law. First, the 1947 Adult Probation Law attempted to set minimal guidelines for the use of probation by restricting the authority of judges to grant probation in felony cases only to certain enumerated felonies whose maximum potential punishment did not exceed ten years of incarceration. Second, the issue of supervising convicted first-time felony offenders released on probation was addressed by awkwardly divorcing the authority to hire probation officers from the authority to manage and supervise probation functions. The authority to appoint probation officers was vested with Texas district court judges, while the overall responsibility for managing and supervising probation officers and probation practices was given to the Texas Board of Pardons and Paroles. The major problem associated with this attempt by the Texas Legislature to provide for the management of probation practices and the supervision of probationers by full-time, professional, probation officers was its failure to appropriate funding for these endeavors!

An attempt was made in 1957 to address these problems by amending the 1947 Texas Adult Probation Law. The reform effort by the Texas Legislature in 1957 resulted in removal of the state probation oversight function from the Board of Pardons and Paroles and giving county governments the authority to create county probation departments. Additionally, the legislature set statewide standards for the employment of probation officers, and gave to county commissioners' courts the authority to both employ probation officers and fund and set their salaries. In late 1957 the first full-time, professional probation officers appeared on the criminal justice scene in Texas.

The most sweeping changes in probation law and practice occurred in 1965, when the Texas Legislature revised the *Texas Code of Criminal Procedure.* Five major revisions to the *Code of Criminal Procedure* contributed greatly to shaping and defining the practice of probation in Texas today. First, the Texas Legislature repealed the 1913 Suspended Sentence Law. Second, the legislature authorized the use of probation for misdemeanor as well as felony convictions. Third, the revised *Code of Criminal Procedure* authorized the use of probation for all felonies whose maximum potential sentence did not exceed 10 years. Fourth, juries were once again given the authority to recommend probation. The authority of a jury to recommend probation extended to all misdemeanor convictions, but in felony cases it was limited only to first-time felony offenders. And lastly, the Texas Legislature gave to district court judges the authority to both hire probation officers and administer probation programs, but the responsibility for funding the programs remained with the county commissioners' court. Despite these sweeping changes, problems associated with the use of probation in Texas persisted. Lack of uniform probation services and facilities on a county-by-county basis, a lack of interest by some judges in using probation as an alternative to incarceration, and a lack of equity in the disbursement of funds on a county-by-county basis to operate probation services resulted in an almost complete absence of uniformity in the use of probation and the management and supervision of probationers in Texas. It is interesting to note that even as recently as 1971, only 210 of the 254 counties in Texas routinely provided for professional probation services.

In 1977 the 65th Texas Legislature was finally successful in passing legislation that standardized on a statewide basis the management of adult probation practices and services, and provided for the first time a state source of funding for probation in Texas.

This was accomplished through the creation of a state agency known as the Texas Adult Probation Commission. The statutory responsibility of the Texas Adult Probation Commission was threefold. First, the commission was mandated to establish uniform and minimum standards for the operation and management of probation programs, services, and facilities. Second, the commission was responsible for coordinating the equitable distribution of state funds for the operation of probation programs statewide. And finally, the Adult Probation Commission was statutorily charged with the task of providing training and technical assistance to the newly designated community supervision and corrections departments (entities previously known as county probation departments).

In 1989 the Texas Adult Probation Commission was absorbed into the Texas Department of Criminal Justice and renamed the Community Justice Assistance Division. Today the responsibility for the administration and delivery of probation services remains bifurcated, with the state oversight responsibility being given to the Community Justice Assistance Division, and the responsibility for actually supervising probationers being vested with community supervision and corrections departments that operate at the community level under the auspices of judicial district court judges.

The Community Justice Assistance Division of the Texas Department of Criminal Justice

Today the Community Justice Assistance Division is charged with the overall responsibility for managing and operating the state's system of probation. The director of the Community Justice Division is guided in implementing probation policies, programs, and practices by a twelve-member Judicial Advisory Council. Appointments to the Judicial Advisory Council are made jointly by the chief justice of the Texas Supreme Court and the presiding judge of the Texas Court of Criminal Appeals. There are currently in excess of 410,000 people on probation in Texas, and the Texas Legislature allocated more than $230 million in 1997 for discharging the probation function.

To ensure uniformity and high professional standards in the administration of probation programs and services across the state of Texas, the Texas Legislature, through Article 42.13 of the *Texas Code of Criminal Procedure*, mandated that the Community Justice Division discharge a number of specific responsibilities. The Community Justice Division is statutorily charged with the responsibility for establishing, certifying, and enforcing minimum, statewide standards for the efficient and economic operation of probation programs, services, and community correctional facilities by community supervision and corrections departments, and for the equitable disbursement of state funds for the operation of the departments. The division is also responsible for overseeing, inspecting, auditing, and evaluating the performance of community supervision and corrections departments, and for insuring minimal standards of professional proficiency in probation officers by operating training and certification programs for Texas probation officers.

The Probation Function in Texas Today

Today in Texas the language of the law technically refers to probation as community supervision. Judges of courts of record having original criminal jurisdiction are wholly vested by statute with the responsibility for (1) determining when the imposition of sentence in criminal cases should be suspended

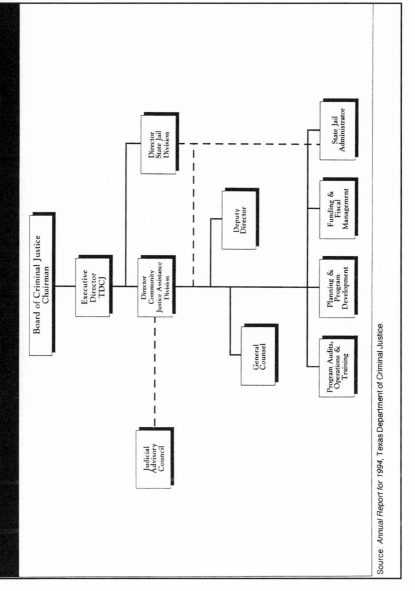

COMMUNITY JUSTICE ASSISTANCE DIVISION

Board of Criminal Justice
Chairman

Executive
Director
TDCJ

Director
Community
Justice Assistance
Division

Director
State Jail
Division

Judicial
Advisory
Council

Deputy
Director

General
Counsel

State Jail
Administrator

Funding &
Fiscal
Management

Planning &
Program
Development

Program Audits,
Operations &
Training

Source: *Annual Report for 1994*, Texas Department of Criminal Justice.

and probation granted, (2) the conditions of probation, and (3) the supervision of convicts placed on probation. Only the court in which the defendant was convicted may grant probation, impose conditions, revoke probation, or discharge the convict from probation.

Probation is the sentence most frequently imposed upon convicted misdemeanants and felons. Today the more than 410,000 convicted criminals on probation in Texas represents the largest population of probationers of any state in the United States. Additionally, there were 3,119 convicted criminals on probation for every 100,000 people in Texas, the highest rate of any state in the United States (the overall national rate of adults on probation was 1,573 per 100,000 population). Probation in Texas today is used as an alternative to incarceration with such frequency and regularity for three principal reasons. First, the supervision and management of probationers and the delivery of probation programs and services is a much cheaper post-conviction alternative than is incarceration. For example, in 1997 the average per diem cost of supervising a probationer was $1.77. Second, probation is used primarily with offenders who have been convicted of nonviolent misdemeanors and nonviolent felonies. Allowing these nonviolent offenders to remain free in the community under the supervision of a probation officer frees up limited prison space for the incarceration of violent criminals. And third, the burden on Texas taxpayers to support governmental crime control programs is lessened because probationers are required to pay probation fees to help defray the cost of their supervision, pay for court costs associated with their case, make financial restitution to their victims, and pay all fines that were assessed along with the probation sentence.

Probation Eligibility—After conviction or a plea of guilty or *nolo contendere*, a judge may suspend imposition of sentence and place the convicted criminal offender on probation. Any offender convicted of a crime whose sentence does not exceed 10 years' incarceration and who has not previously been convicted of a felony is eligible for probation at the discretion of the jury. A judge may grant probation to a probation-eligible offender regardless of the offender's number of prior offenses. Probation is not a sentencing option available to judges for criminals convicted for any of the violent crimes that constitute 3(g) status for parolees, but probation in such cases may be allowed on recommendation of the jury. In other words, the crimes of violence for which convicts are ineligible for probation are capital murder, murder, aggravated robbery, aggravated sexual assault, sexual assault of a child, indecency with a child, aggravated kidnaping, and conviction of any crime where the record demonstrates that the criminal brandished or actually used a deadly weapon in the commission of the crime. A recommendation made by a jury for probation must be honored by the presiding judge. The authority for setting the conditions of probation, however, are the sole, statutory responsibility of the judge.

Conditions of Probation—Probation is granted to an eligible convicted offender only upon his agreeing to abide by certain conditions. The conditions of probation as set by the judge are virtually identical to those conditions imposed upon parolees and mandatory releasees by the Board of Pardons and Paroles, and are derived from the same statutory source (Article 42.12, Section 11 of the *Texas Code of Criminal Procedure*). Like the conditions for parole, those for probation reflect minimal behavior requirements that are considered to be in the best interests of promoting the correctional and rehabilitative needs of the convict and insuring public safety.

Probation conditions are of two types: standard (or general) and special (or individual). Standard conditions apply to all convicts on probation and relate principally to minimal behavioral expectations associated with the supervision and management of the probationer. The standard conditions of probation imposed upon the convict are the same as those listed for parole on page 292. In addition, the probationer must pay all fines and make good on all victim restitution orders of the court, and pay a monthly fee to help offset the costs associated with probation supervision. A judge granting probation may fix a fee of not less than $25 nor more than $40 per month to be paid to the court during the term of probation. The judge may waive the fee as a condition of probation if the judge determines that payment of the fee would cause the probationer significant financial hardship.

Similar to parole, the judge may impose any reasonable condition on a probationer that is designed to protect the community, protect the victim, or serves the best interests of punishing, rehabilitating, or reforming the convict. Examples of special probation conditions include mandating the probationer's participation in drug or alcohol treatment programs or requiring attendance at special counseling or educational programs. The judge of the court having jurisdiction of the case may, at any time during the period of probation, alter or modify the conditions.

In felony cases the minimum period the probationer spends under community supervision is the same as the minimum potential term of incarceration applicable to the offense for which he has been convicted, or a maximum period not to exceed ten years. The maximum period of probation for misdemeanor convictions is two years. The period of probation may be reduced or terminated by the judge granting probation any time after the probationer has satisfactorily completed one-third of the original period of community supervision or two years, whichever is less.

Probation Revocation—Probation may be revoked from any probationer who fails to abide by any of the standard or special conditions of probation. Any time during the period of probation the judge may issue a warrant for violation of any of the conditions of probation and cause the defendant to be arrested and brought before the judge for a hearing. The revoked probationer can be incarcerated without conviction for a new offense where evidence during a probation revocation proceeding demonstrates that the probationer violated one or more conditions of probation. Where this is the case, no part of the time the convict was on probation is considered as fulfilling any portion of the time that the revoked probationer is sentenced to by the judge. If a new criminal offense is the basis for the probation revocation, the revoked probationer will be liable for prosecution for the new offense.

Community Supervision and Corrections Departments

In Texas the responsibility for actually supervising probationers and delivering services to them is discharged entirely at the community level. Community Supervision and Corrections Departments are organized to serve one judicial district. The local judicial district judge employs a director for the judicial district's Community Supervision and Corrections Department, and the director is delegated the authority to hire probation officers to supervise convicts placed on probation by that judicial district.

Article 42.131, Section 3 of the *Texas Code of Criminal Procedure* requires that a Community Justice Council be established in each judicial district that has a Community Supervision and Corrections Department. The council serves in an advisory capacity to the district judge and the director of the local Community Supervision and Corrections Department, and helps provide guidance in developing probation programs, services, and facilities that best fit the needs of the local probationer population. The council is required by law to be diverse in its composition, and as such, it is calculated to embrace as wide a range of community viewpoints as feasibly possible on how the probation function is being locally discharged. Included on Community Justice Councils are the county sheriff, a county commissioner, a city council member of the most populous municipality in the county served by the department, no more than two state legislators elected from the county served by the department, a county attorney with criminal jurisdiction, a criminal district attorney from the judicial district served by the department, and an elected member of the board of trustees of an independent school district in the county served by the department. Additional community input usually comes in the form of an appointed community justice task force which provides staff support for the council and the development of comprehensive community justice plans.

PROBATION OFFICERS

Probation departments in Texas are officially known as Community Supervision and Corrections Departments, of which there are approximately 120 in Texas. While the management and supervision of probationers in Texas is carried out at the local judicial district level, the state's Community Justice Assistance Division of the Texas Department of Criminal Justice sets the standards for probation programs and services and provides the funding to local community supervision and corrections departments.

There are currently about 3,500 probation officers employed by the various community supervision and corrections departments around the state. To be employed as an adult probation officer in Texas, one must have a bachelor's degree from an accredited college or university in corrections, counseling, criminology, law, social work, sociology, psychology, or a discipline that has been approved by the Community Justice Assistance Division. If an applicant's bachelor's degree is in a discipline other than the ones specified, the applicant must have either one year of full-time experience in client counseling and casework or one year of graduate study in one of the required disciplines.

Probation officers in Texas discharge three principal responsibilities. First, they assist judges in matters relating to the eligibility and suitability of a convict for probation. This is done by conducting investigations that furnish a judge with information about the convicted offender's criminal and social history, rehabilitative needs, and any other pertinent information that will aid the judge in assessing the convict's suitability for probation. This information is packaged and presented to the judge in what is called a pre-sentence investigation report, or PSI. Second, probation officers promote the interests of public safety by monitoring and supervising the behavior and activities of convicts on probation. Third, probation officers assist convicts in their rehabilitation by ensuring that they receive whatever services are necessary to promote their successful transition and reintegration into society as productive and law-abiding citizens.

PROBATION SUPERVISION PROGRAMS AND SERVICES

The range of options that today constitute probation services in Texas run the gamut, from programs that afford probationers a great measure of freedom to those programs that severely restrict their freedom and movements. This wide array of probation programs and services includes:

- *Pretrial Intervention Probation* (or Deferred Prosecution). This form of probation is usually employed prior to the filing of formal criminal charges, and is always used prior to a finding of guilt by a court of law. In lieu of going to trial, the criminal defendant agrees to be placed on probation and abide by any and all general and specific conditions of his or her probation. If the defendant successfully completes the term of probation, no further legal actions are pursued and the probationer will have no record of conviction.

- *Deferred Adjudication.* This type of probation resembles pretrial intervention, but requires that the defendant formally respond to the criminal charge for which he or she was arrested by entering a plea of guilty or no contest. Upon doing so, the court halts or defers final judicial settlement of the defendant's charge (adjudication) and does not formally pass sentence but instead places the defendant on probation. Like pretrial intervention probation, if the defendant successfully completes his term of probation, the charges against the defendant will be dropped and the individual will have no record of conviction.

- *Regular Probation.* This is the type of probation with which the general public is most familiar. Following conviction, a defendant is sentenced to a term of incarceration, but the actual imposition of sentence of imprisonment is suspended in lieu of an agreement to abide by the general and/or specific conditions of probation. If the convict successfully completes term of probation he or she will be discharged from management and supervision by a probation officer, but will have a record of conviction.

- *Intensive Supervision Probation.* This type is similar to regular probation but is used to divert borderline high-risk, nonviolent, first-time felony convicts from prison while at the same time providing a much greater level of supervision. Unlike those on regular probation, convicts on intensive supervision probation are subject to daily contacts with their probation officers; rigidly enforced nightly curfews; weekly criminal record checks with law enforcement officials; and weekly drug and alcohol testing.

- *Surveillance Probation*. This type is very similar to intensive supervision probation but is used primarily to intensively monitor convicts who are at a very high risk of having their probation revoked because they are failing to abide by the general and/or specific conditions of their probation.
- *Specialized Supervision Probation*. This type of probation is used for convicts who have very specific and highly specialized service needs associated with their rehabilitation. Typical of such probationers are individuals whose criminal convictions are directly related to alcohol or drug abuse. The special conditions of their probation require them to be diverted into intensive and special therapy programs designed to address the substance abuse problems that are seen as being the principal causes of their criminal behavior.
- *Shock Probation*. This type of probation, which has been in use in Texas since 1977, is actually a type of split sentence involving a very brief term of incarceration followed by regular probation. It is used almost exclusively with young, first-time criminals convicted of petty and nonviolent offenses. The convict is required to serve a very brief period of incarceration to expose them to the harsh realities of imprisonment. The term of incarceration may be up to a maximum of 180 days. It is hoped that this brief exposure will "shock" young, first-time offenders into reevaluating their behavior and that they will desist from further involvement in crime.
- *DWI Probation*. This type of probation is very similar to shock probation because it requires a very brief period of incarceration but is used exclusively for first-time offenders with no previous record of incarceration who have been convicted for driving while intoxicated.
- *Residential Services Probation*. This is the most restrictive of all the types of probation programs currently offered in Texas, and is used principally for convicts who do not have a permanent home or convicts who may require specialized assistance and monitoring in a highly structured

and controlled environment to helping them successfully reintegrate into mainstream society. In this type of probation convicts are not allowed to live and operate out of their home, as all the other types of probation allow. Instead, convicts on residential services probation are required to live on the premises of a closely monitored and supervised residential facility, and are free to leave the confines of the facility only to go to work or to receive specialized medical, rehabilitative, or educational services that are not available on the premises. A variety of specific residential service facilities are in operation throughout the state, including residential programs for mentally retarded and developmentally disabled probationers and substance abuse treatment centers.

- *Boot Camp*. This is a relatively new and unique type of probation that is principally designed for young, nonviolent, first-time offenders between the ages of 17 and 25 who have failed at regular probation or are recidivist nonviolent offenders. First authorized by the Texas Legislature in 1987 (in Article 42.12, Section 18 of the *Texas Code of Criminal Procedure*), convicts are sentenced to a short term of incarceration (usually 90 to 120 days) in a highly structured and specialized program that stresses a military style of discipline employing uniformed drill instructors, a platoon structure of organization, and military customs and courtesies. The goal of boot camp programs is to foster a sense of self-esteem and acceptance of personal responsibility for one's behavior through rigorous physical and mental training.

Probation will continue to be the most popular and frequently employed sentencing alternative used in Texas, and its use will certainly increase well into the twenty-first century. Its attractiveness stems in great part not only from the cost savings as compared to incarceration in a Texas prison unit, but also from the flexibility it affords in specifically tailoring treatment and rehabilitation programs and services to fit the needs of individual criminal offenders.

WORKS CONSULTED AND
SUGGESTIONS FOR FURTHER READING

Anderson, Ken. *Crime in Texas*. Austin, Texas: The University of Texas Press, 1997.

Crime State Rankings 1997. Lawrence, Kansas: Morgan Quitno Press, 1997.

del Carmen, Rolando V., et al. *Probation Law and Practice in Texas*. Huntsville, Texas: Criminal Justice Center, Sam Houston State University, 1989.

Directory of Juvenile and Adult Correctional Departments, Institutions, Agencies, and Paroling Authorities. Lanham, Maryland: American Correctional Association, 1996.

Lucko, Paul M. "Board of Pardons and Paroles." *The New Handbook of Texas*. Austin, Texas: Texas State Historical Association, 1996, vol.1, pp. 614-617.

MacCorkle, Stuart A. "Pardoning Power in Texas." *Southwestern Social Science Quarterly,* vol. 15 (1934), pp. 113-127.

Morrissey v. Brewer (408 U. S. 471).

Rhine, Edward. "Parole Boards." *Encyclopedia of American Prisons*. New York: Garland Publishing Company, 1996, pp. 342-347.

Sharp, John. *Texas Crime, Texas Justice: A Report From the Texas Performance Review*. Austin, Texas: Texas Comptroller of Public Accounts, 1992.

Vernon's Texas Codes Annotated, Code of Criminal Procedure, Articles 42.12 and 42.18, and Chapter 48.

Vernon's Texas Codes Annotated, Government Code, Chapter 508.046.

Vernon's Texas Codes Annotated, Health and Safety Code, Section 481.134.

"Texas Department of Criminal Justice." *Guide to Texas State Agencies*. Austin, Texas: Bureau of Governmental Research, Lyndon B. Johnson School of Public Affairs, University of Texas at Austin, 1996, pp. 74-79.

9.
THE ADMINISTRATION OF TEXAS JUVENILE JUSTICE

INTRODUCTION:
A STATE OF EMERGENCY

Juvenile crime in the last decade has become a problem of epidemic proportions. In 1996, 85% of Texans polled considered juvenile crime a major problem. Crime statistics support society's concern. The number of violent offenders entering the juvenile justice system has increased 141% since 1991. Far surpassing the national average, arrests of Texas juveniles for violent crimes increased 71% since 1990.

In the last decade violence in Texas schools has become increasingly evident. While gang violence is usually associated with metropolitan areas, dramatic increases in the number of youths carrying guns in rural Texas schools suggest that violent juvenile crime is more than a "big city" problem. In 1991 a 17-year-old boy was shot to death before classmates while sitting in the local high school cafeteria. While such incidents may be associated with inner-city crime, this tragedy happened in Crosby, a quiet town with a population of under 2,000.

Most Texas schools are not prepared to handle the new breed of violent juveniles. Taxpayers are bearing the burden of repairing vandalism instead of educational programs. Frightened youth are less likely to learn and more likely to drop out. Concerned citizens are likely to flee, resulting in declining tax bases. In turn, smaller tax bases and increased

319

school violence make it increasingly difficult for schools to hire and retain quality teachers.

Permanently expelling violent students may seem essential to restoring and ensuring order in Texas' classrooms. However, children expelled are likely to roam the streets in search of the status and acceptance that they cannot find at home or at school. Experts agree that herein lies the source of Texas' emerging gang problem.

A 1992 survey conducted by the Office of the Attorney General revealed that in 12 major Texas cities there were an estimated 13,000 gang members. Statewide, 38 cities have reported the formation of gangs and violent gang activity. Reportedly, delinquent youth gangs account for 30% of all gangs and gang membership.

In response, the Governor's Office and the Texas Legislature have implemented policies intended to help all juvenile justice agencies "crack down" on juvenile crime. But how much can legislation alone remedy the problem? A substantial number of juvenile justice professionals and data collected by the federal government suggest that juvenile crime is a result of inadequate adult care and supervision. If so, can any legislative remedy that stops short of policing parents and guardians make any difference? As we proceed through the history of juvenile justice in Texas and the structure of the modern system you may ponder and deduce your own answer.

PART 1:
HISTORICAL OVERVIEW
TO THE PRESENT

Juvenile justice in Texas is historically rooted in English common law and the concept of *parens patriae* (which allows the government to act in the authoritative capacity as a parent for minor children). By contemporary standards, early treatment of juveniles was often extremely harsh. Nearly all offenses were felonies punishable by death, and children over the age of seven were executed just the same as adults.

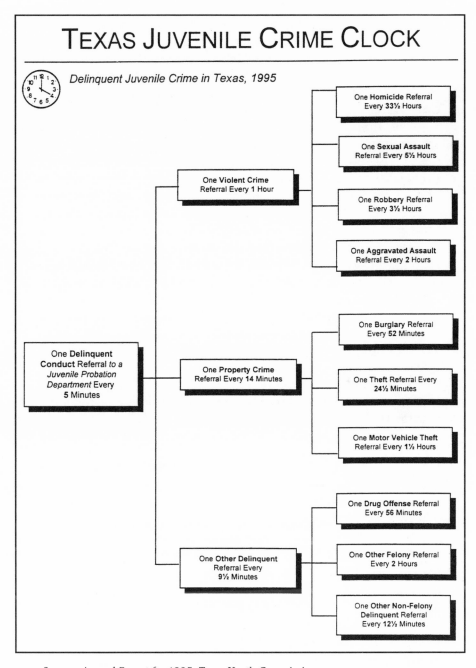

TEXAS JUVENILE CRIME CLOCK

Delinquent Juvenile Crime in Texas, 1995

One Homicide Referral
Every 33½ Hours

One **Sexual Assault**
Referral Every 5½ Hours

One **Violent Crime**
Referral Every 1 Hour

One **Robbery** Referral
Every 3½ Hours

One **Aggravated Assault**
Referral Every 2 Hours

One **Burglary** Referral
Every 52 Minutes

One **Delinquent
Conduct** Referral *to a
Juvenile Probation
Department* Every
5 Minutes

One **Property Crime**
Referral Every 14 Minutes

One **Theft** Referral Every
24½ Minutes

One **Motor Vehicle Theft**
Referral Every 1½ Hours

One **Drug Offense** Referral
Every 56 Minutes

One **Other Felony** Referral
Every 2 Hours

One **Other Delinquent**
Referral Every
9½ Minutes

One **Other Non-Felony**
Delinquent Referral
Every 12½ Minutes

Source: *Annual Report for 1995,* Texas Youth Commission.

In 1856 the legislature raised the age of criminal responsibility to nine years and prohibited youth under the age of 13 from being convicted if they failed to appreciate the consequences of their criminal conduct. Additionally, the same year the legislature revised its death penalty policy to prohibit children under 17 years of age from being executed.

The first year that the legislature acknowledged the need for separate correctional facilities for juveniles and adults was 1859. However, it was not until 1887 that funds were appropriated to build the state's first reformatory, the Gainesville State School for Boys. During this time the state also experienced a growth of independent institutions for delinquent boys and girls.

In 1907 a Juvenile Court Act was passed which provided funding for juvenile probation officers and established juvenile delinquency courts. However, few delinquency courts were created and children still faced the same criminal laws as adults. Consequently, in 1918 all criminal courts were required by the legislature to transfer all children's cases (aged 7 to 17 for boys and 7 to 18 for girls) to a juvenile delinquency court.

It was not until 1943 that the concept of *parens patriae* was extended to all children under the jurisdiction of the state courts. Under such arrangement, the State was able to act in the capacity of a legal guardian for minor children. With the adoption of the Gilmer-Aiken act in 1949, the State established the Texas Youth Development Council. Renamed the Texas Youth Council (TYC) in 1957, this agency was created to provide administrative oversight for the state's juvenile institutional corrections system. In 1961, TYC implemented a parole system for institutionalized delinquents.

In the 1971 case of *Morales v. Turman* (383 F. Supp. 53, 69 (1974)), Judge William W. Justice ruled that TYC's administration of the state's juvenile detention facilities violated the constitutional due process rights of its detainees. *Morales* today is considered a landmark case because it secured the following rights for juveniles:

(1) right to notice of hearing and notice of charges;

(2) the Miranda warning must be given before a confession, guilty plea or judgment is made;
(3) right to a hearing in open court;
(4) opportunity to confront and cross-examine witnesses;
(5) opportunity to present evidence;
(6) right to trial by jury;
(7) right to a transcript of the proceedings;
(8) right to an explanation of the possible consequences of the hearing; and,
(9) an explanation of the right to appeal.

Additionally, the court ruled that detainees have a constitutional right to particular "treatment" while institutionalized. The opinion addressed eight key aspects of TYC supervision and treatment:

(1) physical brutality and abuse;
(2) disciplinary procedures;
(3) assessment and placement;
(4) academic education;
(5) vocational education;
(6) institutional life;
(7) medical and psychiatric care; and
(8) casework and child care (del Carmen, et al., at 115-116).

In 1973 the legislature enacted Title 3 of the Family Code. To date, Title 3 remains the primary statutory source of juvenile law in Texas. When Title 3 was enacted, youthful offenders were presumed salvageable human beings (a presumption which has recently been questioned). For most of the state's history, juvenile justice has not been about punishment, but about rehabilitation. The goal of juvenile justice agencies has been to protect children and to work in their best interest while protecting the public.

Under Texas law, a "child" is defined as a person who is:

(1) 10 years of age or older and under 17 years of age; or
(2) 17 years of age or older and under 18 years of age who is alleged or found to have engaged in *delinquent conduct or conduct indicating a need for supervision* as a result of acts committed before becoming 17 years of age (FC § 51.02).

Texas law holds that children under the age of 10 who engage in prohibited conduct are not of the age of reason (i.e., because of age they lack the requisite mental culpability for criminal responsibility discussed in Chapter 2). In contrast, Texas law states that a person who is 17 years old and who has no history of delinquency or has never been deemed as exhibiting conduct indicating a need for supervision (CINS) can be prosecuted as an adult. Title 3 provides that juvenile probation departments have jurisdiction over 17-year-olds who have committed punishable offenses before their seventeenth birthdays, while Texas juvenile courts have jurisdiction over juveniles who have either engaged in "delinquent conduct" or "conduct in need of supervision."

Delinquent conduct is conduct other than a traffic offense which violates the penal code of the state and is punishable by imprisonment or by confinement in jail. Delinquent conduct can also be a violation of a reasonable and lawful order which was entered by a juvenile court. In general, juvenile delinquency results from either a violation of the Texas Penal Code or one's conditions of probation (FC § 51.03).

In contrast, conduct indicating a need for supervision (CINS) covers certain "status offenses" (non-criminal or less serious law violations) including: (1) three or more fineable misdemeanor offenses or ordinance violations; (2) truancy; (3) runaway; (4) the second or first DWI; and (5) violation of any city ordinance or state law prohibiting inhalant abuse. The principal difference between juvenile delinquency and CINS under Title 3 is that while a child who has been adjudicated a juvenile delinquent can be committed to TYC, a child adjudicated CINS (i.e., a status offender) can only be placed on probation.

In 1974 TYC began residential contract programs for community placement of youth. The following year the state increased its focus on community care programs. Community care includes the use of halfway houses, primary treatment programs, and independent living facilities.

In 1980 the federal government passed the Juvenile Justice and Delinquency Act which required all state governments to remove all juveniles from adult detention facilities.

Texas law requires county juvenile boards to designate separate facilities for delinquent youth.

In 1981 the Texas Juvenile Probation Commission was created to establish standards for local juvenile probation departments and to oversee the distribution of state funds. This function had previously been held by TYC. Two years later, the Texas Youth Council was renamed the Texas Youth Commission.

In the last decade the state legislature has created and modified the law in order to curtail juvenile crime and ensure the efficient operation of juvenile justice in Texas. In 1987 the legislature passed into law the Determinate Sentencing Act (DSA), which established that juveniles between the ages of 10 and 16, adjudicated for a certain violent offense, could receive a sentence of 30 years. In 1991 the legislature raised the maximum sentence to 40 years for commission of capital murder or aggravated possession of a controlled substance. In 1995 the DSA was renamed the Violent or Habitual Offender Sentencing Act (VHSA) and the scope of punishment was expanded to cover second-degree felonies, punishable by a maximum 20-year sentence, and third-degree felonies, punishable by a maximum sentence of 10 years. Violent offenses have been expanded to include:

- capital murder
- murder
- aggravated kidnapping
- aggravated sexual assault
- aggravated robbery
- habitual felony conduct
- felonious deadly conduct involving the discharge of a firearm
- certain offenses involving controlled substances
- injury to a child, elderly individual, or disabled individual
- aggravated assault
- criminal solicitation
- indecency with a child
- criminal solicitation of a minor, and
- attempted murder and capital murder

Under the new act, youths serve their terms at TYC until the age of 18. Prior to his or her eighteenth birthday each youth receives a hearing in which he or she may be retained in the juvenile system or transferred to adult prison (FC § 53.045). In 1995, 43% of youths who turned 18 were transferred to the Texas Department of Criminal Justice. If retained by TYC, the youth must be discharged at age 21.

Legislative changes in 1995, such as the VHSA, have made the juvenile justice system "more judicial, more adversarial, more criminal and less confidential than before" (*State Bar Report: Juvenile Law* at 3). Title 3 of the Family Code was renamed the Juvenile Justice Code and the concept of "punishment" was adopted as part of the state's juvenile justice reform initiative. With legal consequences becoming more retributive in nature and less rehabilitative, it appears that the legislature has effectively banished delinquency from the realm of "family" law and exiled it into the realm of "criminal" law.

PART 2:
OVERVIEW OF
ADMINISTRATIVE AGENCIES

In Texas there are three agencies responsible for the administration of juvenile justice: local organizations, the Texas Juvenile Probation Commission, and the Texas Youth Commission. While each of the agencies work together, they operate structurally independent from one another.

Local Level

Each county has a juvenile board and separate juvenile services. A juvenile board is generally composed of the district, county, and statutory judges of the locality. The board's duties include:

- selection and employment of county's chief probation officer;

- approval of the chief's appointments for probation department personnel;
- approval of expenditures;
- approximating the amount of county funds necessary to operate its juvenile court system;
- making recommendations and reports to the commissioner's court regarding the management and oversight of local juvenile justice operations; and
- inspecting the quality of local detention facilities.

Juvenile services are generally provided by local juvenile probation departments. Each probation department is responsible for intake, detention, and field services. In some counties, probation departments may also supervise TYC parolees. Some probation departments may service more than one county. Accordingly, they may vary in structure and organization.

Texas Juvenile Probation Commission

Prior to the TJPC's establishment in 1981, many Texas counties had no juvenile probation services or detention facilities. Texas lacked uniform standards for the administration of juvenile justice. Furthermore, the state lacked a central source of information on juvenile crime as well as a system for ensuring fiscal accountability for local use of state funds. TJPC was created to remedy these problems as well as to remove barriers to interagency collaboration.

Today TJPC works in partnership with 160 local probation departments in all of Texas' 254 counties by providing training, technical assistance, and monitoring, and by dispersing state funds to the county level. TJPC helps provide the resources and guidelines in an effort to help juvenile probation succeed at the local level. Keeping youths in their communities improves chances for success and is less costly than institutionalization. Intensive probation supervision costs less than $7 per day as compared with more than $100 per day for institutional care.

Texas Youth Commission

TYC is the sole juvenile correction agency for the state of Texas and is responsible for serving violent and seriously delinquent youth, ages 10 through 16, who are committed to state's custody. Through a combination of state and privately operated institutional and community-based programs, TYC's four primary goals are prescribed by law (attempted implementation of these goals is covered later in this chapter):

Protection—"To protect the public and control the commission of unlawful acts by youth committed to the agency by confining them under conditions that emphasize their positive development, accountability for their conduct, and discipline training."

Productivity—"To habilitate youth committed to the agency to become productive and responsible citizens through education and productive work."

Rehabilitation—"To rehabilitate and re-establish in society youth committed to the agency through a competency-based program of resocialization."

Prevention—"To study problems of juvenile delinquency, focus public attention on special solutions for problems and assist in developing, strengthening and coordinating programs aimed at preventing delinquency."

PART 3:
MOVEMENT OF JUVENILES THROUGH THE SYSTEM

Youths enter the juvenile justice system through referrals from police agencies, parents, schools, victims, and probation officers. Pursuant to probable cause, a youth may be arrested and taken into custody (FC § 52.01). After being arrested, police have the discretion to either release or transfer the juvenile to the county's probation department (FC §§ 52.02-52.03). A referral may involve the juvenile being detained until his or her case goes to juvenile court or released to the care of a parent or guardian until the court date (Sharp ~ᵗ 31). In 1995

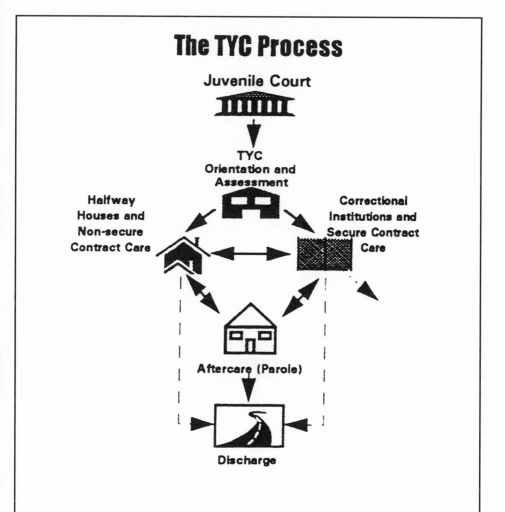

The TYC Process

Juvenile Court

TYC Orientation and Assessment

Halfway Houses and Non-secure Contract Care

Correctional Institutions and Secure Contract Care

Aftercare (Parole)

Discharge

Source: *Annual Report for 1995*, Texas Youth Commission.

Texas police arrested 180,546 children and made 120,101 referrals. Additionally, 13,765 referrals were made by social agencies, parents, and schools. A total of 133,866 cases were referred to juvenile probation departments, a notable increase from 80,560 in 1989.

Juvenile Probation System

Once a referral is made, youths are taken into the authority of the county probation department. All youths go through an "intake" procedure in which the juvenile courts screen cases. After reviewing the case to determine if sufficient probable cause exists, the county intake officer decides whether to place the child on informal probation, file a formal petition with the court, or dispose of the referral (FC §§ 53.01-53.03). Deferred prosecution (also called deferred adjudication or informal probation) is a voluntary agreement in which the youth agrees to temporary court-ordered supervision (FC § 53.03). Informal probation generally involves offenses which are serious but not serious enough to warrant court involvement. When cases are disposed of it is generally because the juvenile is either a first-time offender, has adequate supervision at home, or is capable and willing to make restitution to the victim. Other informal services and measures are used at the intake stage to divert court involvement (e.g., counseling and release, voluntary or court placement outside the home). In 1995, 48% of juveniles referred into the system were counseled, released, diverted, or dismissed by local juvenile probation services. Another 16% received deferred prosecution.

During "intake," the intake officer also determines if the child should be kept in detention. The following factors are considered:

- whether the child is likely to flee the jurisdiction
- whether the child, if released, would have sufficient supervision

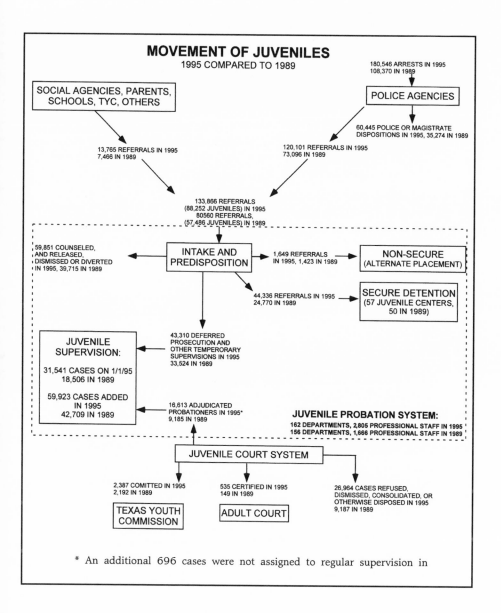

MOVEMENT OF JUVENILES
1995 COMPARED TO 1989

180,546 ARRESTS IN 1995
108,370 IN 1989

SOCIAL AGENCIES, PARENTS, SCHOOLS, TYC, OTHERS

POLICE AGENCIES

60,445 POLICE OR MAGISTRATE DISPOSITIONS IN 1995, 35,274 IN 1989

13,765 REFERRALS IN 1995
7,466 IN 1989

120,101 REFERRALS IN 1995
73,096 IN 1989

133,866 REFERRALS
(88,252 JUVENILES) IN 1995
80560 REFERRALS,
(57,486 JUVENILES) IN 1989

59,851 COUNSELED, AND RELEASED, DISMISSED OR DIVERTED IN 1995, 39,715 IN 1989

INTAKE AND PREDISPOSITION

1,649 REFERRALS IN 1995, 1,423 IN 1989

NON-SECURE
(ALTERNATE PLACEMENT)

44,336 REFERRALS IN 1995
24,770 IN 1989

SECURE DETENTION
(57 JUVENILE CENTERS, 50 IN 1989)

JUVENILE SUPERVISION:

31,541 CASES ON 1/1/95
18,506 IN 1989

59,923 CASES ADDED IN 1995
42,709 IN 1989

43,310 DEFERRED PROSECUTION AND OTHER TEMPERORARY SUPERVISIONS IN 1995
33,524 IN 1989

16,613 ADJUDICATED PROBATIONERS IN 1995*
9,185 IN 1989

JUVENILE PROBATION SYSTEM:
162 DEPARTMENTS, 2,805 PROFESSIONAL STAFF IN 1995
156 DEPARTMENTS, 1,666 PROFESSIONAL STAFF IN 1989

JUVENILE COURT SYSTEM

2,387 COMITTED IN 1995
2,192 IN 1989

535 CERTIFIED IN 1995
149 IN 1989

26,964 CASES REFUSED, DISMISSED, CONSOLIDATED, OR OTHERWISE DISPOSED IN 1995
9,187 IN 1989

TEXAS YOUTH COMMISSION

ADULT COURT

* An additional 696 cases were not assigned to regular supervision in

- if no parent is available, is there an adult to ensure his or her return to court
- is the child a threat to the safety of the public
- does the child have a history of prior jailable offenses and disposition which suggest recidivism (FC § 53.02(b)).

There are no provisions in Texas juvenile law which provide bail for juvenile detainees. Consequently, youths may be detained for up to six months prior to their court hearing. Detention, however, is not intended for punishment purposes. Rather it is legally defined as "the temporary secure custody of a child pending court disposition or transfer to another jurisdiction or agency" (Texas Administrative Code, Title 37 § 343.1). Secure and non-secure juvenile detention centers provide a structured agenda for detainees, including educational and rehabilitation programs. In this sense, juvenile detention provides a stable, therapeutic environment that troubled youth often cannot find elsewhere.

Certifying Juveniles to Adult Courts

If certain conditions exist, juvenile courts have the discretion to waive their exclusive jurisdiction and transfer youths to a criminal court for prosecution as adults. Such transfers are made only after the youth has received a certification hearing. Before the hearing, the juvenile courts are required, by law, to order a complete investigation of the circumstances surrounding the alleged offense, as well as a complete diagnostic and social evaluation of the child. In determining whether to transfer the case to adult courts, the juvenile courts consider the result of their investigation as well as the following:

- whether the alleged offense was against person or property (with greater weight in favor of transfer given to offenses against the person)
- the sophistication and maturity of the child
- the record and previous history of the child, and
- the prospects of adequate protection for the public and the likelihood of the rehabilitation of the child by use of

procedures, services, and facilities currently available to the juvenile (FC § 54.02).

In 1995 the certification age was lowered from 15 to 14, but only in cases involving capital and first-degree felonies (15 remains the age for all other felonies). While some believe that lowering the age of transfer in the most serious cases is a justifiable measure in combating juvenile crime, others believe it does nothing more than contribute to the already sharp increase of juveniles certified to adult courts. In 1996, 508 juveniles younger than 17 were certified to stand trial as adults. Nearly 110 of all certifications were in homicide cases.

Mental Health Hearing

The underlying philosophy of Texas law dictates that a child who is alleged to have engaged in juvenile crime but appears to be mentally ill or retarded should not enter the juvenile justice system. Rather, after being diagnosed, such children should be transferred into the care of the state's mental health or retardation system. If mental illness is suspected, the juvenile courts may initiate proceeding for temporary hospitalization, observation, and treatment. If found mentally ill, youths can be committed for up to 90 days to the Texas Department of Mental Health and Mental Retardation (TDMHMR) so that proper placement may be arranged.

Adjudication Hearing

Similar to the trial of an adult, an adjudication hearing is held to determine whether the juvenile engaged in delinquent conduct. As in trial proceedings against an adult, the district or county attorney represents the State. Many of the constitutional protections extended to adults accused of criminal activity have been extended to children and incorporated into Texas law:

- the right to be notified of the pending charges

- the right to counsel
- the right to confront and cross-examine hostile witnesses
- the privilege against self-incrimination (FC § 54.03(b)).

Additionally, in some instances Texas law provides more rights to accused juveniles than are assured by federal law. For instance, while the U.S. Supreme Court held that due process does not require the right to a jury trial in juvenile adjudication hearings, Texas law provides that a child has a right to a trial by jury and that the jury verdict must be unanimous (comparing *McKeiver v. Pennsylvania,* 403 U.S. 528 (1971) to FC §§ 54.03(b)(6),(c)). (In practice, however, adjudication hearings rarely feature a jury.)

An adjudication hearing is similar to criminal trials of adults. The State must prove the allegations against the juvenile beyond a reasonable doubt. The testimony of accused accomplices must be corroborated by other sources of proof. Evidence illegally seized or unlawfully obtained is inadmissible (FC § 54.03 (e)-(f)). The juvenile court in which the adjudication hearing is held has jurisdiction over the child only if the child is a resident of the county in which the court is located, or if the child committed the offense while in that county (FC § 51.06).

Disposition Hearing

If at the adjudication hearing the child is found delinquent or CINS (conduct indicating a need for supervision), a disposition hearing is held, separate and distinct from the adjudication hearing. Except in a determinate sentence case (previously discussed) there is no right to a jury at a disposition hearing. The purpose of the hearing is to determine where to place the child. In making this decision the court and/or jury determines both the best interests of the child and of the community. No action may be taken by the court unless it is determined that the child is in need of rehabilitation or the public is in need of protection from the child (FC § 54.04).

In determining disposition, the juvenile court may consider case-history reports prepared by the probation department, as well as the testimony of witnesses. It is not uncommon for the juvenile's probation officer to testify as to the child's background, behavior, and educational status. Such information, including the child's prior history of detention, may be considered by the judge or jury in deciding whether the child should be placed on CINS probation or committed to TYC. Juvenile courts also have the authority to dismiss the case, suspend the juvenile's driver's license, order parents to act in the best interest of the child, order community service be performed, and provide restitution to victims.

PART 4:
POST-ADJUDICATION

In 1995, 13% of all disposition hearings ended in court-ordered probation. Nearly 2% resulted in commitment to TYC. Approximately 21% of cases before the court were dismissed or otherwise disposed by the court. (As detailed previously, 64% of all juvenile offenders are dealt with by the juvenile probation system.)

Children placed on CINS probation may be placed in their own homes or in the custody of a relative or other suitable guardian (including foster homes, public and private residential facilities). However, the child may not be placed outside his or her home unless the court concludes that the quality of care and level of supervision is inadequate (FC § 54.04). If no suitable home or residential facility is available, a court may have no other option but to commit the child to TYC.

If the child is placed in foster care, guardianship, or a residential facility, the juvenile courts retain control of the child and may modify the child's placement. A probation modification hearing may be necessary to change the disposition of the child's case. However, if the child is committed, TYC assumes full jurisdiction and determines how long the child shall remain in custody (the only exception being determinate sentencing cases in which detention is determined by statute).

PART 5:
COMMITMENT TO
TEXAS YOUTH COMMISSION

TYC receives the state's most hardened juvenile delinquents (three-quarters were committed for felony offenses). Juveniles committed to TYC are overwhelmingly male (93%) and mostly minority (42% Hispanic, 39% African-American). After being committed to TYC, youth must serve a minimum period (a minimum length of stay, or MLOS) before they can be discharged or eligible for parole supervision. The MLOS for offenders who receive a determinate sentence is based on the felony level of the offense and is set by the court. The MLOS for other criminal acts is determined by the most serious of the relevant offenses documented in the youth's record (i.e., classifying offense):

- Type A Violent—capital murder, murder, attempted capital murder or attempted murder—minimum 24 months.
- Type B Violent—all other violent crimes including aggravated assault, robbery, and sexual assault—minimum 12 months.
- Chronic Serious Offender—committed for felony offenses on three previous and separate occasions—minimum 12 months.
- Controlled Substance Dealer—minimum 12 months.
- Firearm Offender (use of a firearm during the offense)—minimum 12 months.
- General Offender—meets none of the above criteria—minimum 9 months.

Orientation and Assessment

Youth committed to TYC are sent to the Orientation and Assessment (O&A) unit at Marlin, Texas, where they undergo medical, educational, and psychological testing. Test findings, as well as information such as age, nature of offense, and length and degree of criminal activity are used in compiling a need and risk assessment for each youth. Psychiatric evaluations are conducted for all serious offenders and for other youth referred by assessment staff for such testing. After testing and social summaries are completed by TYC, initial recommendations for placement are made by the staff.

Community-Based Programs

Due to the seriousness of their offenses, most youth are initially placed in a TYC institution or correctional facility. Some, however, are placed in community-based programs such as halfway houses. The underlying theory of such placements is that children in halfway houses may be rehabilitated by remaining involved in their communities through school, training, and employment. TYC operates nine halfway houses which are located in Austin, Corpus Christi, Dallas, El Paso, Fort Worth, Harlingen, McAllen, Roanoake, and San Antonio. Each of these facilities provides specialized services which ultimately prepare teens to live independently. Additionally, some facilities provide substance abuse treatment.

Another community-based program, referred to as contract care, allows TYC to contract with the private sector providers for residential programs, including group homes, vocational training programs, residential treatment centers, foster care, and non-residential day treatment services. The progress of the youth, as well as the services of the contract providers, are monitored by TYC for program compliance and service delivery. Since only 7% of the TYC population is female, contract care allows female offenders needing secure placement to be placed in privately operated secure residential facilities. Additionally, many youths are transferred to such community-based residential programs before being discharged from TYC.

Institutional Program

TYC's institutional program is generally reserved for violent juvenile offenders who have a chronic history of delinquency and who have previously run away from a residential facility. In addition to the Marlin O&A facility, TYC operates 13 correctional institutions. State training schools exist in Beaumont, Brownwood, Crockett, Gainesville, Giddings, Pyote, and San Saba. The Corsicana Residential Treatment Camp provides special services for emotionally disturbed and learning-disabled delinquent youth. Additionally, TYC operates Evins Regional Juvenile Center in Edinburg, a boot camp in Sheffield, and a sanction unit in Brownwood. The average daily population of TYC correctional facilities in 1996 was 2,213 (a 27% increase from 1995). Consequently, in 1997 TYC increased its capacity by opening Victory Field Correctional Academy in Vernon and the J.W. Hamilton Jr. State School in Bryan.

Basic Correctional Treatment: Resocialization

All TYC treatment programs are centered around a comprehensive rehabilitation program called "Resocialization." The four cornerstones of such correctional therapy are:

1. correctional therapy;
2. education;
3. work;
4. discipline training.

By creating a therapeutic environment which consists of 16-hour days that engage youth in constructive activities, youths have fewer opportunities to get into trouble. Ideally, the program is designed to enhance accountability of delinquent youth by removing justification for continued delinquency. By reinforcing skills which enable youths to make prosocial choices, TYC hopes that all detainees obtain the tools to detail their lives and identify thinking errors. For this to occur, youths must learn to understand the choices that led them to commit criminal acts and to develop victim empathy and a prosocial value system.

By placing youths in a multi-phase program which rewards constructive, positive behavior, "Resocialization" allows youths to gradually move from high-restrictive confinement to post-institutional supervision. Transition from restrictive confine-

Percent of Youth in Each Treatment Category Who Received Specialized Treatment Prior to Release—Fiscal Year 1996	
Capital Offenders	28%
Sex Offenders	65%
Chemically Dependent Youth	27%
Emotionally Disturbed Youth	35%

Source: Texas Youth Commission, 1996.

ment is conditioned on successful completion of the MLOS (minimum length of stay, discussed previously) and the mastery of predetermined objectives. Resocialization consists of five phases:

1. assessment—evaluating mental processing and behavioral;
2. providing a therapeutic environment;
3. intervention—stopping negative antisocial behavior;
4. rehabilitation—promoting positive prosocial behavior;
5. reintegration—helping youths successfully return to their community.

TYC has devised a checklist of objectives that each youth must achieve in order to advance to the next phase. Basic correctional treatment requires youths to distinguish between rights and privileges. Only through compliance with program rules (which emphasize personal responsibility, self-control, academics, vocational skills, and social skills) and completion of the Resocialization phases may youths earn rewards and privileges. Privileges may include listening to music or choosing their own hairstyle (military-style haircuts are generally mandatory).

Specialized Correctional Treatment

Of course, many youths committed to TYC require specialized treatment in addition to Resocialization. For example, TYC's Capital Offender Program (COP) located at Giddings requires youth to reenact their crimes while role-playing both the perpetrator and the victim. Statistics in fiscal year 1996 show that one year rearrest rates for capital offenders receiving specialized treatment is 26.7%, compared with 35.4% for capital offenders receiving basic treatment.

Specialized treatment for sex offenders is provided by TYC and contract providers. The sex offender treatment program (SOTP) is based on a cognitive-behavioral and relapse prevention model which not only focuses on correcting the offending behavior but also on the cognitive distortions ("thinking errors") that motivate criminal behavior. Statistics for 1996 suggested that one year after their release, sex offenders receiving specialized treatment were rearrested at a rate of 35.7% compared to 52.9% for sex offenders receiving basic treatment.

Aftercare

To ensure that progress made while in a TYC program is maintained after a youth is released, TYC operates an aftercare program. Aftercare, a parole system operated by TYC, provides intensive supervision for all youths upon release. TYC employs parole officers and contracts with various juvenile justice agencies to ensure that youths comply with all terms of their parole. Parole officers often help juveniles reintegrate into the community by providing emotional and psychological support. Often this entails assisting in school enrollment and monitoring the youth's attendance. Additionally, parole officers often refer families to social services, provide crisis intervention, and give guidance in the youth's rehabilitation efforts. Failure to abide by the terms of parole may result in revocation. In such instances, youths may be returned to the Brownwood Sanction Unit or another residential program for further detention and rehabilitation.

Interstate Compact on Juveniles

The Interstate Compact on Juveniles (ICJ) provides a national network which allows states to communicate with each other in the instance that a parolee or probationer moves from one state to another. TYC administers the ICJ for the state of Texas in an attempt to provide nationwide cooperative supervision of juvenile delinquents.

PART 6:
THE FUTURE OF
JUVENILE JUSTICE IN TEXAS

While much of this chapter has been dedicated to detailing the various levels and stages of the juvenile justice system, minds are likely to differ as to whether the system ultimately works. The fact remains that the alarming rate of juvenile crime in the last decade has left law enforcement, the legal system, and the legislature with more questions than answers. While funding for more TYC institutions has been approved, and "tougher" laws have been passed, some policymakers believe that rather than addressing the problems, the State's response has merely addressed the "symptoms" and not the actual problem of juvenile crime. Most scholars agree that further social science research is needed so that Texas may better tailor a solution to the problem.

Accordingly, the legislature in 1997 approved funding for the first academic institution in the state to focus solely on minors who commit crimes. Located at Prairie View A&M near Houston, the center will bring together scholars in education, sociology, psychology, and criminal justice to study juvenile crime. By examining ways to break the cycle of juvenile crime before it starts, Texas hopes to make a positive difference in the lives of its children as they enter a new millennium.

WORKS CONSULTED AND
SUGGESTIONS FOR FURTHER READING

*(Note: Unless otherwise stated, all statutory citations noted (FC)
are from the Texas Family Code.)*

Back to Basics: Annual Report. Austin, Texas: Texas Youth
    Commission, 1996.

del Carmen, Rolando, et al. *Texas Juvenile Law and Practice*.
    Huntsville, Texas: Sam Houston State University, 1991.

Jones, Ronald. Telephone interview, 9 July 1997.

Sharp, John. *Texas Crime, Texas Justice*. Austin, Texas: Office of
    State Comptroller, 1992.

State Bar Report: Juvenile Law, vol. 9, no. 3, August 1995.

Strategic Plan for the 1997-2007 Period. Austin, Texas: Texas Youth
    Commission, 1996.

Texas Juvenile Probation Commission. *12th Annual Report*. Austin,
    Texas: Texas Juvenile Probation Commission, 1995.

Texas Juvenile Probation Commission (agency literature).

Texas Youth Commission (web site and agency literature).

"Trial Monday for 14-Year-Old in Teacher's Slaying." *Austin
    American-Statesman*, 28 September 1997.

APPENDICES

APPENDIX A
THE TEXAS BILL OF RIGHTS

Article 1: Bill of Rights

That the general, great and essential principles of liberty and free government may be recognized and established, we declare:

Sec. 1. FREEDOM AND SOVEREIGNTY OF STATE. Texas is a free and independent State, subject only to the Constitution of the United States, and the maintenance of our free institutions and the perpetuity of the Union depend upon the preservation of the right of local self-government, unimpaired to all the States.

Sec. 2. INHERENT POLITICAL POWER; REPUBLICAN FORM OF GOVERNMENT. All political power is inherent in the people, and all free governments are founded on their authority, and instituted for their benefit. The faith of the people of Texas stands pledged to the preservation of a republican form of government, and, subject to this limitation only, they have at all times the inalienable right to alter, reform or abolish their government in such manner as they may think expedient.

Sec. 3. EQUAL RIGHTS. All free men, when they form a social compact, have equal rights, and no man, or set of men, is entitled to exclusive separate public emoluments, or privileges, but in consideration of public services.

Sec. 3a. EQUALITY UNDER THE LAW. Equality under the law shall not be denied or abridged because of sex, race, color, creed, or

343

national origin. This amendment is self-operative. (Added Nov. 7, 1972.)

Sec. 4. RELIGIOUS TESTS. No religious test shall ever be required as a qualification to any office, or public trust, in this State; nor shall any one be excluded from holding office on account of his religious sentiments, provided he acknowledge the existence of a Supreme Being.

Sec. 5. WITNESSES NOT DISQUALIFIED BY RELIGIOUS BELIEFS; OATHS AND AFFIRMATIONS. No person shall be disqualified to give evidence in any of the Courts of this State on account of his religious opinions, or for the want of any religious belief, but all oaths or affirmations shall be administered in the mode most binding upon the conscience, and shall be taken subject to the pains and penalties of perjury.

Sec. 6. FREEDOM OF WORSHIP. All men have a natural and indefeasible right to worship Almighty God according to the dictates of their own consciences. No man shall be compelled to attend, erect or support any place of worship, or to maintain any ministry against his consent. No human authority ought, in any case whatever, to control or interfere with the rights of conscience in matters of religion, and no preference shall ever be given by law to any religious society or mode of worship. But it shall be the duty of the Legislature to pass such laws as may be necessary to protect equally every religious denomination in the peaceable enjoyment of its own mode of public worship.

Sec. 7. APPROPRIATIONS FOR SECTARIAN PURPOSES. No money shall be appropriated, or drawn from the Treasury for the benefit of any sect, or religious society, theological or religious seminary; nor shall property belonging to the State be appropriated for any such purposes.

Sec. 8. FREEDOM OF SPEECH AND PRESS; LIBEL. Every person shall be at liberty to speak, write or publish his opinions on any subject, being responsible for the abuse of that privilege; and no law shall ever be passed curtailing the liberty of speech or of the press. In prosecutions for the publication of papers, investigating the conduct of officers, or men in public capacity, or when the matter published is proper for public information, the truth thereof may be given in evidence. And in all indictments for libels, the jury shall have the right to determine the law and the facts, under the direction of the court, as in other cases.

Sec. 9. SEARCH AND SEIZURES. The people shall be secure in their persons, houses, papers and possessions, from all unreasonable seizures or searches, and no warrant to search any place, or to seize any person or thing, shall issue without describing them as near as may be, nor without probable cause, supported by oath or affirmation.

Sec. 10. RIGHTS OF ACCUSED IN CRIMINAL PROSECUTIONS. In all criminal prosecutions the accused shall have a speedy public trial by an impartial jury. He shall have the right to demand the nature and cause of the accusation against him, and to have a copy thereof. He shall not be compelled to give evidence against himself, and shall have the right of being heard by himself or counsel, or both, shall be confronted by the witnesses in his favor, except that when the witness resides out of the State and the offense charged is a violation of any of the anti-trust laws of this State, the defendant and the State shall have the right to produce and have the evidence admitted by deposition, under such rules and laws as the Legislature may hereafter provide; and no person shall be held to answer for a cirminal offense, unless on an indictment of a grand jury, except in cases in which the punishment is by fine or imprisonment, otherwise than in the penitentiary, in cases of impeachment, and in cases arising in the army or navy, or in the militia, when in actual service in time of war or public danger. (Amended Nov. 5, 1918.)

Sec. 11. BAIL. All prisoners shall be bailable by sufficient sureties, unless for capital offenses, when the proof is evident; but this provision shall not be so construed as to prevent bail after indictment found upon examination of the evidence, in such manner as may be prescribed by law.

Sec. 11a. MULTIPLE CONVICTIONS; DENIAL OF BAIL. (a) Any person (1) accused of a felony less than capital in this State, who has been theretofore twice convicted of a felony, the second conviction being subsequent to the first, both in point of time of commission of the offense and conviction therefor, (2) accused of a felony less than capital in this State, committed while on bail for a prior felony for which he has been indicted, (3) accused of a felony less than capital in this State involving the use of a deadly weapon after being convicted of a prior felony, or (4) accused of a violent or sexual offense committed while under the supervision of a criminal justice agency of the State or a political subdivision of the State for a prior felony, after a hearing, and upon evidence substantially showing the guilt of the accused of the offense in (1) or (3) above, of the offense committed while on bail in (2) above, or of the offense in (4) above committed while under the supervision of a criminal justice agency of the State or a political subdivision of the State for a prior felony, may be denied bail pending trial, by a district judge in this State, if said order denying bail pending trial is issued within seven calendar days subsequent to the time of incarceration of the accused; provided, however, that if the accused is not accorded a trial upon the accusation under (1) or (3) above, the accusation and indictment used under (2) above, or the accusation or indictment used under (4) above within sixty (60) days from the time of his incarceration upon the accusation, the order denying bail shall be automatically set aside, unless a continuance is obtained upon the motion or request of the accused; provided, further, that the right of appeal to the Court of Criminal Appeals of this State is expressly accorded the accused for a review of any judgment or order made hereunder, and said appeal shall be given preference by the Court of Criminal Appeals.

(b) In this section:

(1) "Violent offense" means:

(A) murder;

(B) aggravated assault, if the accused used or exhibited a deadly weapon during the commission of the assault;

(C) aggravated kidnapping; or

(D) aggravated robbery.

(2) "Sexual offense" means:

(A) aggravated sexual assault;

(B) sexual assault; or

(C) indecency with a child. (Added Nov. 6, 1956; amended Nov. 8, 1977; Subsec. (a) amended and (b) added Nov. 2, 1993.)

Sec. 12. HABEAS CORPUS. The writ of habeas corpus is a writ of right, and shall never be suspended. The Legislature shall enact laws to render the remedy speedy and effectual.

Sec. 13. EXCESSIVE BAIL OR FINES; CRUEL AND UNUSUAL PUNISHMENT; REMEDY BY DUE COURSE OF LAW. Excessive bail shall not be required, nor excessive fines imposed, nor cruel or unusual punishment inflicted. All courts shall be open, and every person for an injury done him, in his lands, goods, person or reputation, shall have remedy by due course of law.

Sec. 14. DOUBLE JEOPARDY. No person, for the same offense, shall be twice put in jeopardy of life or liberty, nor shall a person be again put upon trial for the same offense, after a verdict of not guilty in a court of competent jurisdiction.

Sec. 15. RIGHT OF TRIAL BY JURY. The right of trial by jury

shall remain inviolate. The Legislature shall pass such laws as may be needed to regulate the same, and to maintain its purity and efficiency. Provided, that the Legislature may provide for the temporary commitment, for observation and/or treatment, of mentally ill persons not charged with a criminal offense, for a period of time not to exceed ninety (90) days, by order of the County Court without the necessity of a trial by jury. (Amended Aug. 24, 1935.)

Sec. 15-a. COMMITMENT OF PERSONS OF UNSOUND MIND. No person shall be committed as a person of unsound mind except on competent medical or psychiatric testimony. The Legislature may enact all laws necessary to provide for the trial, adjudication of insanity and commitment of persons of unsound mind and to provide for a method of appeal from judgments rendered in such cases. Such laws may provide for a waiver of trial by jury, in cases where the person under inquiry has not been charged with the commission of a criminal offense, by the concurrence of the person under inquiry, or his next of kin, and an attorney ad litem appointed by a judge of either the County or Probate Court of the county where the trial is being held, and shall provide for a method of service of notice of such trial upon the person under inquiry and of his right to demand a trial by jury. (Added Nov. 6, 1956.)

Sec. 16. BILLS OF ATTAINDER; EX POST FACTO OR RETROACTIVE LAWS; IMPAIRING OBLIGATION OF CONTRACTS. No bill of attainder, ex post facto law, retroactive law, or any law impairing the obligation of contracts, shall be made.

Sec. 17. TAKING, DAMAGING, OR DESTROYING PROPERTY FOR PUBLIC USE; SPECIAL PRIVILEGES AND IMMUNITIES; CONTROL OF PRIVILEGES AND FRANCHISES. No person's property shall be taken, damaged or destroyed for or applied to public use without adequate compensation being made, unless by the consent of such person; and, when taken, except for the use of the State, such compensation shall be first made, or secured by a deposit of money; and no irrevocable or uncontrollable grant of special privileges or immunities, shall be made; but all privileges and franchises granted by the Legislature, or created under it authority shall be subject to the control thereof.

Sec. 18. IMPRISONMENT FOR DEBT. No person shall ever be imprisoned for debt.

Sec. 19. DEPRIVATION OF LIFE, LIBERTY, ETC.; DUE COURSE OF LAW. No citizen of this State shall be deprived of life, liberty, property, privileges or immunities, or in any manner disenfranchised, except by the due course of the law of the land.

Sec. 20. OUTLAWRY OR TRANSPORTATION FOR OFFENSE. No citizen shall be outlawed. No person shall be transported out of the State for any offense committed within the same. This section does not prohibit an agreement with another state providing for the confinement of inmates of this State in the penal or correctional facilities of that state. (Amended Nov. 5, 1985.)

Sec. 21. CORRUPTION OF BLOOD; FORFEITURE; SUICIDES. No conviction shall work corruption of blood, or forfeiture of estate, and the estates of those who destroy their own lives shall descend or vest as in case of natural death.

Sec. 22. TREASON. Treason against the State shall consist only in levying war against it, or adhering to its enemies, giving them aid and comfort; and no person shall be convicted of treason except on the testimony of two witnesses to the same overt act, or on confession in open court.

Sec. 23. RIGHT TO KEEP AND BEAR ARMS. Every citizen shall have the right to keep and bear arms in the lawful defense of himself or the State; but the Legislature shall have power, by law, to regulate the wearing of arms, with a view to prevent crime.

Sec. 24. MILITARY SUBORDINATE TO CIVIL AUTHORITY. The military shall at all times be subordinate to the civil authority.

Sec. 25. QUARTERING SOLDIERS IN HOUSES. No soldier shall in time of peace be quartered in the house of any citizen without the consent of the owner, nor in time of war but in a manner prescribed by law.

Sec. 26. PERPETUITIES AND MONOPOLIES; PRIMOGENITURE OR ENTAILMENTS. Perpetuities and monopolies are contrary to the genius of a free government, and shall never be allowed, nor shall the law of primogeniture or entailments ever be in force in this State.

Sec. 27. RIGHT OF ASSEMBLY; PETITION FOR REDRESS OF GRIEVANCES. The citizens shall have the right, in a peaceable manner, to assemble together for their common good; and apply to those invested with the powers of government for redress of grievances or other purposes, by petition, address or remonstrance.

Sec. 28. SUPENSION OF LAWS. No power of suspending laws in this State shall be exercised except by the Legislature.

Sec. 29. PROVISIONS OF BILL OF RIGHTS EXCEPTED FROM POWERS OF GOVERNMENT; TO FOREVER REMAIN INVIOLATE. To guard against transgressions of the high powers herein delegated, we declare that everything in this "Bill of Rights" is excepted out of the general powers of government, and shall forever remain inviolate, and all laws contrary thereto, or to the following provisions, shall be void.

Sec. 30. RIGHTS OF CRIME VICTIMS.

(a) A crime victim has the following rights:

(1) the right to be treated with fairness and with respect for the victim's dignity and privacy throughout the criminal justice process; and

(2) the right to be reasonably protected from the accused throughout the criminal justice process.

(b) On the request of a crime victim, the crime victim has the following rights:

(1) the right to notification of court proceedings;

(2) the right to be present at all public court proceedings related to the offense, unless the victim is to testify and the court determines that the victim's testimony would be materially affected if the victim hears other testimony at the trial;

(3) the right to confer with a representative of the prosecutor's office;

(4) the right to restitution; and

(5) the right to information about the conviction, sentence, imprisonment, and release of the accused.

(c) The legislature may enact laws to define the term "victim" and to enforce these and other rights of crime victims.

(d) The state, through its prosecuting attorney, has the right to enforce the rights of crime victims.

(e) The legislature may enact laws to provide that a judge, attorney for the state, peace officer, or law enforcement agency is not liable for a failure or inability to provide a right enumerated in this section. The failure or inability of any person to provide a right or service enumerated in this section may not be used by a defendant in a criminal case as a ground for appeal or post-conviction writ of habeas corpus. A victim or guardian or legal representative of a victim has standing to enforce the rights enumerated in this section but does not have standing to participate as a party in a criminal proceeding or to contest the disposition of any charge. (Added Nov. 7, 1989.)

APPENDIX B
ADDRESSES OF STATE CRIMINAL JUSTICE AGENCIES, BOARDS, COMMISSIONS, DEPARTMENTS, AND LEGISLATIVE COMMITTEES

Alcoholic Beverage Commission
  5806 Mesa Drive
  P.O. Box 13127
  Austin, TX 78711-3127

Attorney General
  209 West 14th & Colorado Sts.
  P.O. Box 12548
  Austin, TX 78711-2548

Board of Criminal Justice
  Price Daniel Building
  209 West 14th Street
  P.O. Box 13084
  Austin, TX 78711-3084

Board of Pardons and Paroles
  8610 Shoal Creek Blvd.
  P.O. Box 13401
  Austin, TX 78711-3401

Commission on Alcohol and
    Drug Abuse
  9001 IH 35 North
  Suite 105
  Austin, TX 78753-5233

Commission on Jail Standards
  300 West 15th Street
  Suite 503
  P.O. Box 12985
  Austin, TX 78701

Commission on Judicial Conduct
  200 West 15th Street
  Suite 415
  P.O. Box 12265
  Austin, TX 789711

Council on Offenders with
    Mental Impairments
  8610 Shoal Creek Blvd.
  Austin, TX 78757

Council on Sex Offender Treatment
  Tom C. Clark State Office
  Suite 103
  205 West 14th Street
  P.O. Box 12546
  Austin, TX 78711-2546

Court of Criminal Appeals
  Supreme Court Building
  Room 106
  201 West 14th Street
  P.O. Box 12308
  Austin, TX 78711

Criminal Justice Policy Council
  Tom C. Clark State Office Bldg.
  7th Floor
  205 West 14th Street
  P.O. Box 13332
  Austin, TX 78711-3332

Department of Criminal Justice
  Price Daniel Building
  14th and Lavaca Streets
  P.O. Box 13084
  Austin, TX 78711-3084

  • Community Justice
      Assistance Division
    P.O. Box 13084
    Austin, TX 78711

- Institutional Division
  Spur 59
  P.O. Box 99
  Huntsville, TX 77342-0099

- Pardons and Paroles Division
  8610 Shoal Creek Blvd.
  P.O. Box 13401
  Austin, TX 78711-3401

- State Jail Division
  Price Daniel Bldg.
  Suite 400
  P.O. Box 13084
  Austin, TX 78711-3084

Department of Public Safety
5805 North Lamar Blvd.
P.O. Box 4087
Austin, TX 78773-0001

Judicial Districts Board
c/o Office of Court
    Administration
P.O. Box 12066
Austin, TX 78711-2066

Juvenile Probation Commission
4900 North Lamar Blvd.
5th Floor East
P.O. Box 13547
Austin, TX 78711-3547

Law Enforcement Officer
    Standards and Education
    Commission
6330 U.S. Highway 290 East
Suite 200
Austin, TX 78723

Legislative Committees:

- Senate Standing Committees
  State Capitol Building
  100 East 11th Street
  P.O. Box 12068
  Austin, TX 78711-2068
  - Criminal Justice
  - Jurisprudence

- House of Representatives
  State Capitol Building
  100 East 11th Street
  P.O. Box 2910
  Austin, TX 78768-2910
  - Corrections
  - Criminal Jurisprudence
  - Judicial Affairs
  - Juvenile Justice and
    Family Issues
  - Public Safety

Office of Court Administration of
    the Texas Judicial System
Tom C. Clark State Office Bldg.
205 West 14th Street
P.O. Box 12066
Austin, TX 78711-2066

Parks and Wildlife Department
Law Enforcement Division
4200 Smith School Road
Austin, TX 78744

State Bar of Texas
1414 Colorado Street
Texas Law Center
P.O. Box 12487
Austin, TX 78711

State Prosecuting Attorney
  Price Daniel Sr. Building
  Room 202
  209 West 14th Street
  P.O. Box 12405
  Austin, TX 78711

Supreme Court of Texas
  Supreme Court Building
  Room 104
  201 West 14th Street
  P.O. Box 12248
  Austin, TX 78711

Texas Judicial Council
  Tom C. Clark State Office Bldg.
  Suite 600
  P.O. Box 12066
  Austin, TX 78711-2066

Texas Youth Commission
  4900 North Lamar Blvd.
  P.O. Box 4260
  Austin, TX 78765

APPENDIX C
TEXAS CRIMINAL JUSTICE SYSTEM
WEB SITES

Texas Law

Texas and Local Government
http://www.texinet.net/texasgov.htm

This site functions as a general directory that allows the user to link to a wide variety of homepages related to state and local government agencies in Texas, including those that deal with crime and the administration of criminal justice.

The Texas Senate
http://www.senate.state.tx/us/welcome.htm

This page is an extremely valuable resource for anyone interested in the administration of criminal justice in Texas, because it allows the user to stay current with proposed legislative changes as well as senate bills that have become law. The site provides links to a diverse range of subjects, including information regarding the lieutenant governor, senate committee assignments, and the upcoming calendar of events. The site also allows a user to link directly to the Texas House of Representatives.

The Texas House of Representatives
http://www.house.state.tx.us/

This site is very similar to the homepage of the Texas Senate, and provides valuable insights on current criminal justice-related issues that the Texas House of Representatives is dealing with. The site also contains committee assignments and links to the homepages of members of the Texas House of Representatives.

Office of the Attorney General
http://www.oag.state.tx.us/index.html

This web site has numerous links to a wide range of information, including the text of opinions issued by the Texas attorney general, and current information about consumer protection and the Texas victim compensation program.

Texas Municipal Courts Education Center
http://www.tmcec.com/
> This site allows the browser to access the texts of legal opinions released by the Texas attorney general, and read past as well as current editions of the attorney general's newsletter.

Texas Law Pipeline
http://www.sbot.org/pipe/tx_refer.html
> This is a very interesting site that contains a diverse body of information related to Texas law and government. The page contains a complete text of the Texas Constitution, Texas Penal Code, and other administrative and regulatory statutes. This page also contains a very large number of links which allow the user to connect directly the Texas Senate (to read the text of new bills) and the Texas Court of Criminal Appeals (where one will find posted the text of recently written opinions).

Texas Law Enforcement

Texas Department of Public Safety
http://www.txdps.state.tx.us/
> This site is hosted by the Texas Department of Public Safety, and provides a wide range of important information about the organization, its mission, and the programs and services it provides. Additionally, the page has links to Department of Public Safety press releases, driver's license information, and current weather reports.

Texas Rangers Division
http://www.txdps.state.tx.us/rangers/index.htm
> The is a very interesting and valuable web site that gives a general historical overview of the Texas Rangers, and sets forth the requirements one must meet before becoming a Ranger.

Texas Department of Public Safety Officers Association
http://www.kdi.com/~dpsoa/index.htm
> This site provides an historical overview of the organization and describes its mission and membership.

Texas Highway Patrol Association
http://www.thpa.org/

This is a very unique, interesting, and valuable internet site sponsored by the Texas Highway Patrol Association, an independent organization formed by the men and women who are employed as troopers with the Texas Department of Public Safety. The page contains a diverse range of information, including updates on their legislative lobbying activities and information about educational scholarships for the children of slain and disabled officers. One of the more unique aspects of this page is its link to the association's electronic Hall of Fame, where one may read accounts of the lives of past and present Texas Department of Public Safety troopers. Additionally, the site also contains a driving simulator which puts visitors to the homepage behind the wheel of a patrol vehicle and gives them a firsthand glimpse of what an actual officer faces each day.

Texas Law Enforcement Fugitive Sites
http://www.ghg.net/patterson/LINKS.html

This site is sponsored by the fugitive apprehension squad of the Texas Department of Public Safety. The main purpose of the page is to widely broadcast information to aid in the apprehension of criminal fugitives. The page has links to the major Texas cities of Dallas and El Paso, as well as Harris County, and provides a list of the top five most wanted fugitives from each area. Upon selecting one of the locations you can view photographs of the wanted criminals, along with their names and the charge for which they are wanted. More detailed information about the fugitive can be acquired by linking directly to the original mug shot. Additionally, the site also has crime stopper links to both Brazos and Tarrent counties, where one may review unsolved crimes that date back as far as 1995, and submit anonymous tips.

Texas K-9 Police Association
http://txk9cop.metronet.com/index_2.html

This site was formed to support and advance the valuable work that is performed by police dogs in Texas. The page contains the training standards and certification requirements for police canines and their handlers.

Texas Women in Law Enforcement
http://www.anet-dfe.com/~twlenfc/index.htm

This organization was founded in 1988 with the purpose of advancing the public's recognition of the valuable role women play in Texas law enforcement. The site contains useful information about law enforcement employment opportunities for women and their contributions to furthering good police-community relations.

Combined Law Enforcement Association of Texas
http://www.NeoSoft.com/~cleat/

This statewide police association was established in 1976 to represent the men and women who were employed as peace officers in Texas. With its 16,000 members, it is by far the largest police organization in Texas. The site describes the mission of the organization and its current activities with respect to lobbying activities in the state legislature and their support of pro-police candidates in state and local political campaigns.

Texas Conference of Police and Sheriffs
http://www.tcops.org/

This site is dedicated to promoting the interests and welfare of Texas law enforcement officers. The page contains timely commentary and observation on economic, political, and social issues affecting police officers in Texas.

The Blues
http://www.thebluesnews.com

This is a very interesting and valuable web site for anyone interested in current news and issues that affect the law enforcement profession in Texas. The page allows anyone interested in Texas law enforcement to read past and current editions of *The Blues*, Texas' largest independent police publication (with over 15,000 subscribers). This on-line edition is updated monthly.

The Cop Shop
http://www.neurotech.net/~Cop_Shop/index.html

This interesting site is hosted and maintained by police officers, and is a valuable source of information. The complete texts of the Texas Constitution as well as the current Texas Penal Code may be accessed. Visitors to this page who are in need of some comic relief may browse topic "America's Dumbest Criminals." This page also provides the user with links to other local and federal law enforcement homepages, as well as description and locations of several law enforcement museums.

Bill Blackwood Law Enforcement Management Institute of Texas
http://www.shsu.edu/~lemit/

This impressive site describes the history, mission, operation, and curriculum offered by the Bill Blackwood Law Enforcement Management Institute of Texas. The institute, which is located in the George Beto Criminal Justice Center at Sam Houston State University, in Huntsville, Texas, is today the largest, most prestigious, and comprehensive statewide police executive and management education program in the United States.

Law Enforcement Related Links
http://web2.airmail.net/rja658/links.htm

This site has an alphabetical listing of links to other relevant Texas law enforcement homepages. The site also contains valuable links to federal law enforcement agencies, such as the Federal Bureau of Investigation and the Drug Enforcement Agency. The page also provides synopses of interesting research and statistical data.

Texas Court System

Texas Court of Criminal Appeals
http://www.cca.courts.statetx.us

This impressive site describes the structure and function of the Texas Court of Criminal Appeals. In addition this Internet page provides no cost access to the court's published opinions in a downloadable format. *The Texas Judicial System Procedure and Rules* is also available from this site as well as a *Judges Portrait* and biographies.

Texas Judicial System
http://www.courts.state.tx.us/overview.html

This site is a very valuable resource for anyone interested in the structure and function of the Texas court system. The well written and well organized page explains the adversarial process of liability adjudication in Texas courts, and contains a brief narrative regarding the qualification and selection of judges.

Texas Center for the Judiciary, Inc.
http://www.yourhonor.com/

The Texas Center for the Judiciary is the primary provider of specialized judicial education and training opportunities for Texas judges at the appellate, district, and county court at law levels.

This web page was created to publicize the topics and conference locations of upcoming judicial seminars. Additionally, the site contains links to other valuable web pages that are devoted to issues of law and justice.

U.S. Court of Appeals, Fifth Circuit
http://www.ca5.uscourts.gov
Because Texas is part of the Fifth Circuit of the United States Court of Appeals, this site is very interesting and beneficial. The page allows the user to view the Fifth Circuit's docket. Additionally, the page provides very detailed instructions on the proper ways to prepare and submit a brief to the Fifth Circuit, as well as offering assistance on how to prepare an oral argument. This site is very valuable to anyone interested in the federal court system, because the page is written in clear and concise language.

Crime Prevention and Victims' Rights

Texas Crime Prevention Association
http://www.tcpa.org/
This nonprofit organization is made up of 700 members that include law enforcement officers, crime prevention specialists, private security professionals, and private citizens who are dedicated to increasing awareness about crime prevention. The association works toward preventing crime through citizen involvement which will inevitably lead to safer neighborhoods. The page provides general suggestions for the prevention of crime, information on crime prevention resources, and crime prevention education and training opportunities. The site also contains recent press releases pertaining to crime prevention and the association's calendar of upcoming events.

Law Enforcement Helping Crime Victims
http://www.oag.state.tx.us/WEBSITE/NEWS/LEGALMAT/9702cvc.htm
This site is hosted by the Office of the Texas Attorney General, and is a very valuable and informative page for anyone interested in the rights of crime victims and the Texas Crime Victims Compensation Fund. The page provides information not only about crime victims' rights, services, and criminal justice resources, but also describes how the services and resources may be obtained.

Texans for Equal Justice
http://www.flex.net/~judge/
This web page is sponsored by Texans for Equal Justice, a private crime victim advocacy organization. Texans for Equal Justice was established in 1993 by citizens concerned about senseless violent crime and recidivist criminal offenders. The page contains information which is intended to educate individuals about the criminal justice system, the rights of crime victims, and legislative changes relating to the administration of criminal justice.

Texas Prisons and Jails

Texas Department of Criminal Justice Home Page
http://www.tdcj.state.tx.us/
This site provides a very valuable and succinct overview of the Texas Department of Criminal Justice and the four divisions that comprise the department: the Institutional Division (which manages and operates prisons and other facilities of confinement for adult felony offenders); the Parole Division (which oversees the reintegration of felons into society after their release from prison); the Community Justice Assistance Division (which is responsible for the general oversight of the probation function); and, the State Jail Division (which operates the facilities of incarceration for offenders who have been convicted of non-violent felony crimes).

Texas Commission on Jail Standards
http://isadore.tsl.state.tx.us/tVx/TCJS
This web page provides a short history of the Texas Commission on Jail Standards and an overview of the standards for the operation of county jails in Texas as well as the programmatic initiatives for their inspection.

Texas Corrections Association
http://www.ccsi.com/~asmi/GROUPS/TCA/tca.html
The Texas Corrections Association is a statewide organization of individuals, agencies, and institutions involved with the adult and juvenile justice system in Texas. The page provides a forum for discussions and gives the browser an opportunity to read past as well as current editions of the association's bimonthly publication titled *Journal of Corrections*. The site also has a useful calendar of events and information on a wide variety of membership options.

Texas Prisoner Fact Sheet

http://www.dfw.net/~acludatx/prisfact.html

This site contains interesting and valuable statistics concerning the operation of the Texas prison system. The data are well organized and displayed.

Texas Parole and Probation

A History of Parole, Mandatory Supervision and Good Time

http://www.tcdla.com/voice1996/Oct/PAROLE1.HTML

This very valuable and informative site traces the legislative history of Articles 42.12 and 42.18 of the *Texas Code of Criminal Procedure*, and how legislative changes have affected parole, mandatory supervision and the awarding of good time in Texas. The page was created with a view toward helping attorneys with plea negotiations for their clients.

Texas Probation Association Homepage

http://cust.iamerica.net/cscdadm

The Texas Probation Association was formed in 1974 with the intent of further developing the field by promoting continuing education, professional standards, and the free exchange of ideas and viewpoints. The page contains valuable information on a wide variety of topics related to the practice of probation in Texas.

Correctional Management Institute of Texas

http://www.shsu.edu/!icc_www/program/cmit/

The Correctional Management Institute of Texas was established in 1994 to provide professional training and leadership skills for adult and juvenile probation officers working in Texas courts. The institute's mission statement, training schedule, and publications can be viewed from this site.

Texas Juvenile Justice System

Texas Youth Commission
http://www.tyc.state.tx.us/index.html
> The Texas Youth Commission created this web site for the purpose of educating the general public about the importance of maintaining an effective and efficient system of juvenile administration. The page contains useful information about the mission of the Texas Youth Commission, as well as flow charts depicting the operation of the Texas juvenile justice system, and a variety of discussions about topics relevant to the problem of juvenile crime and delinquency.

Rules of the Judicial District Courts of Harris County Texas; Juvenile Trial Division
http://www2.co.harris.tx.us/~hcdc/juvrules.html
> This is a unique and extremely informative site that both attorneys and laymen will find useful. The page contains the complete text of the rules that govern the Juvenile Trial Division in Harris County. The information details the procedural guidelines employed in the Juvenile Trial Division of the Harris County District Courts to ensure that juvenile cases will be resolved in a fair, just, and efficient manner.

Gaining Ground
http://www.window.texas.gov/comptrol/tprgg/ggjustce.html
> This site contains excerpts, commentary, and observations on a publication titled *Behind the Walls: Price and Performance of the Texas Department of Criminal Justice*, which was produced by the Texas Comptroller's Office. The page contains interesting discussion about the perceived causes for the drop in the rate of violent crimes in Texas since 1991. The page advocates the importance of a strong juvenile justice system, and the important contributions to the administration of criminal justice in Texas made by both the Texas Youth Commission and the Texas Juvenile Probation Commission.

Improve Delivery of Parole Services for Juvenile Offenders
http://www.window.texas.gov/comptrol/tprgg/psc09gga.txt
> This web page discusses suggested improvements that the Texas Youth Commission could adopt and implement in order to improve the delivery of correctional and rehabilitation services to juveniles who have been adjudicated delinquent and are at risk of further involvement in criminal behavior.

General Links to U.S. Criminal Justice Related Sites

Jail.Net; The Global Corrections Resource
http://www.jailnet.net

This site is a valuable resource for obtaining information regarding prisoners and prisons in each of the fifty states. The user is provided with a menu of states to select from, and once a selection has been made, a wide variety of statistical data are displayed.

National Center for Juvenile Justice
http://www.ncjj.org/

This site is sponsored by the research division of the National Council of Juvenile and Family Court Judges. The page provides an overview of the center, its mission, and its activities.

The Justice Home Page
http://microsoft.com/industry/justice/default.htm

This site is the homepage of a bimonthly electronic publication that includes articles and commentary on a wide range of topics related to the administration of criminal justice. Past and current articles on topics such as national and state crime trends, the use of expert testimony in criminal trials, law enforcement case studies, emerging technologies with criminal justice application, and recent United States Supreme Court Decisions are available to the interested user. The page also allows the user to make internet searches.

Legist's Legal Links
http://www.legist.com/law-links/dictionaries.htm

This site contains links to dozens of other law related pages, both state and federal, and contains an on-line dictionary of legal terms.

National Criminal Justice Reference Service
http://www.ncjrs.org

This is a very valuable page for initiating literature searches and for receiving timely information about new research and publications relating to all aspects of crime and the administration of criminal justice.

★ GLOSSARY

The nuances of commonly accepted legal terms may differ slightly from state to state. Every effort has been made to craft the definitions of terms used in this book to conform with standard legal usage in Texas law.

absolute liability offense: A criminal act to which *mens rea* (mental state) is irrelevant.

acquitted (acquittal): A judgment of a court based on the verdict of a jury that the defendant is "not guilty" of the offense.

actus reus: The requisite criminal act accompanying the *mens rea* resulting in criminal culpability.

adjudication: The formal process in which a final judicial determination or decision is made.

adjudication hearing: A juvenile court fact finding hearing which determines whether or not a youth engaged in delinquent conduct.

affiant: A person who makes and swears to the truth of a written statement.

affidavit: A written statement sworn to or affirmed before a person with authority to witness the oath.

affirmative act: The commission of a crime by engaging in a specifically prohibited behavior.

affirmative defense: In pleading, a matter asserted by the defendant, which attacks the State's right to prosecute as opposed to attacking the truth of the criminal allegations.

aftercare: A parole system for juveniles operated by the Texas Youth Commission.

age of reason: The minimum age required by law to possess the requisite mental culpability for criminal responsibility. Texas law holds that children over the age of ten who engage in prohibited conduct may be held criminally responsible.

alcalde de crimen: The executive officer of the *ayuntamiento*'s *alcalde*

363

mayor, who functioned in the dual capacity of director of police and judge.

alcalde mayor: The president of the Mexican colonial governing body known as the *ayuntamiento*. The position is referred to in some archival documents as the *justicia mayor*.

alcalde ordinare: The officer responsible for matters relating to the administration of civil law in the *ayuntamiento* system.

alguacil mayor: The chief law enforcement officer under the Mexican colonial *ayuntamiento* system.

appeal: An application to, or a proceeding in, a court with appellate jurisdiction to review the finding of a lower court.

appeal bond: A written instrument of debt which allows a criminal defendant to remain free after conviction while his or her case is being appealed. The defendant deposits cash with the county or pays a fee, generally ten percent of the total, to have a surety guarantee the defendant will appear in court and surrender to authorities if so ordered. Under Texas law, appeal bonds are available to defendants convicted of any offense, as long as their sentence is 15 years or less.

arraignment: The criminal proceeding following grand jury indictment in which the accused is brought before a judge to be informed of the charges against him, appointed counsel, and allowed to enter a plea (i.e., not guilty, *nolo contendere*, or guilty).

arrest: The process in which a person is taken into custody by law enforcement for the purpose of bringing him before court so that he may be formally charged with an offense. The exercise of dominion and control over an individual by agents of the executive branch of government because of an alleged violation of law.

attachment: A written legal command issued by a magistrate ordering law enforcement to bring before the court a person guilty of contempt.

ayuntamiento: The principal governing body of Mexican colonial municipalities and surrounding rural areas that was responsible for the management of all civil as well as criminal affairs.

bail: To give security to procure the release of a person being held for an offense and to ensure the person's future appearance. The security required by the judge and given by the accused to ensure that the accused appears before the proper court at the scheduled time and place to answer the charges brought against him.

bail bond: A written instrument of debt made by a person in custody or by a surety to secure the release of an individual from jail. A surety promises to pay the amount of the bail bond should the individual fail to appear before the court when ordered.

bailiff: A sheriff's deputy or court officer who keeps order in a courtroom.

beyond a reasonable doubt: The burden of proof required to secure a criminal conviction (doubt based on reason and common sense after a careful and impartial consideration of all the evidence in the case). It is the kind of doubt that would make a reasonable person hesitate to act in the most important of his or her own affairs.

bifurcated trial: The division of criminal trial into two distinctive phases—a guilt phase and a punishment phase.

Bill Blackwood Law Enforcement Management Institute of Texas: A training center located at Sam Houston State University in Huntsville, Texas, with a legislative mandate to impart advanced leadership and management skills to police executives.

bill of attainder: An unconstitutional form of legislative action which singles out an individual or group for punishment without trial.

booking: The clerical or inventory process by which the police make an administrative record of the suspect's arrest.

boot camp: A sentencing alternative for young, first time adult offenders, that utilizes a regimented military style supervision strategy along with other intervention programs.

burden of proof: The legal requirement that the State bring forward evidence to prove guilt. Defendants are not required to prove that they are innocent. The burden of proof in criminal cases is "beyond a reasonable doubt." When the defendant asserts an "affirmative defense," he or she has the burden of proving the defense by a "preponderance of the evidence." The "preponderance" standard is the standard utilized in most civil cases.

Capital Offender Program (COP): A specialized form of correctional treatment located at Giddings State School which requires youth to reenact their crimes while role-playing both the perpetrator and the victim.

case law: Law based on judicial precedent (court decisions) rather than legislative statutes or common law. The word "precedent" is sometimes used instead of case law.

causation: A necessary link between a wrongful act and resulting damages which are essential to establishing criminal liability.

certification hearing: The legal procedure in which the juvenile court waives jurisdiction and the youth is transferred to the appropriate criminal court for criminal proceedings as an adult.

certification of questions: The procedure by which a federal court abstains from answering or addressing a question of state law until the highest court in the state has had the opportunity to rule on the certified question.

challenge the array: A challenge by either prosecutor or defense lawyer to the pool of potential jurors alleging that the panel was selected through a process which is legally corrupt or motivated by racism. A successful challenge to the array results in the dismissal of the current panel and the selection of a new panel of prospective jurors.

challenge for cause: The right of the prosecutor and defense lawyer to ask that the judge excuse potential jurors due to a specific legal ground, such as prejudice, unwillingness to enforce the law, or ineligibility due to disqualification.

chief justice: The senior judge of an appellate jurisdiction court which has three or more judges sitting together.

child under Texas law: a person who is (1) ten years of age or older and under seventeen years of age; or (2) seventeen years of age or older and under 18 years of age who is alleged or found to have engaged in delinquent conduct, or conduct indicating a need for supervision as a result of acts committed before the age of 17.

chronic serious offender: A youth whose Texas Youth Commission classifying offense is a felony in each of at least three separate and distinct due process hearings, where the second felony was committed after the disposition of the first felony and the third felony was committed after the disposition of the second.

civil law: The branch of law pertaining to protecting private rights and remedying wrongs committed against individuals (e.g., contracts, torts, real property).

Code A: thematic compilation of statutes, such as the traffic code, family code, and penal code.

codify (codification): The process of systematically collecting and arranging laws into a specific or particular form, e.g., when the legislature incorporates a particular aspect of a court decision into statutory law.

collateral attack: A separate and new lawsuit which attempts to defer the judgment of the trial courts on new grounds not raised in the direct appeal. In the context of criminal cases, the most common means of collateral attack is through a writ of habeas corpus.

comes stabuli: In Norman England, the chief law enforcement officer at the local or village level. The *comes stabuli* was the forerunner of the modern constable.

Common Law: Law deriving from usage and custom rather than statute. Before the American Revolution, English common law provided the legal foundation in American colonies. Though the common law has for the most part been replaced by the statutory law, it still plays an active role in the legal system. Since courts are ultimately called upon to construe and apply the common law it may be modified by judges to reflect the needs of society, as well as the facts and circumstances of a particular case.

community-based programs: Juvenile rehabilitation measures employed by the Texas Youth Commission which do not utilize institutionalization.

Community Justice Assistance Division (CJAD): One of the four divisions that comprise the Texas Department of Criminal Justice.

Formerly the Texas Adult Probation Commission, CJAD is responsible for (1) the general oversight of the adult probation function, (2) establishing standards for probation programs, facilities, and services, (3) distributing state money for the operation of local probation programs, and (4) providing technical assistance to the 120 local probation departments throughout the state.

community supervision: Formerly referred to as probation, community supervision is a type of sentence which may be ordered for either misdemeanor or felony offenses and is generally imposed in lieu of a jail or prison sentence.

Community Supervision and Corrections Departments (CSCD): Formerly referred to as adult probation departments, CSCDs comprise 120 local governmental agencies in Texas, generally based in a county or small group of counties, and are responsible for the oversight of adults placed on probation by the courts.

complaint: The sworn, written document that charges someone with committing a crime.

concurrent jurisdiction: When two or more courts have authority to hear the same type of case.

concurrently (concurrent): Running together, as concurrent prison sentences are served at the same time, which differs from consecutive sentences which are served one after another.

conduct indicating a need for supervision (CINS): Classification of juvenile behavior by the Texas Family Code; covers five distinct non-criminal or status offenses and less serious law violations.

constable: A precinct police officer, elected to four-year terms, who serves principally in the capacity of executive officer of a justice of the peace court.

constitution: A system of basic laws and principles by which a nation or state is governed.

constitutional law: The branch of law that involves the interpretation and application of the fundamental laws stated in the U.S. Constitution and the constitutions of each state.

contempt: Intentional disobedience from a known court order which may result in a fine or imprisonment.

contraband: Items that are illegal to possess, produce, import, or export.

Contract Care: The Texas Youth Commission's specialized juvenile parole program.

controlled substance dealer: A juvenile or adult whose classifying offense is any felony grade offense defined as a manufacture or delivery offense under the Texas Controlled Substance Act, Chapter 481, Health and Safety Code.

corporation: A business organized under state laws, considered for legal purposes to a non-human legal entity.

county: A geographical subdivision of a state made for political, administrative, and judicial purposes.

court administrator: Court personnel responsible for coordinating and scheduling matters before the court.

court clerk: Court personnel responsible for maintaining the files on all cases which come before the court and often administering the oath to witnesses.

court of record: Courts whose proceedings are permanently recorded and which have the power to fine and imprison for contempt.

crime index: The sum of seven index offenses used to measure the extent, fluctuation, and distribution of crime.

crime rate: The number of offenses per 100,000 population. To calculate a crime rate, divide the population of any given geographical area by 100,000 and then divide the number of reported offenses by that product.

criminal law: The branch of law which defines which public wrongs are crimes and accordingly assigns punishments.

criminal negligence: A culpable mental state in which the accused should be aware that his acts (or failure to act) might have dangerous consequences (i.e., inattentive risk taking).

cross-examination: The questioning of the opposition's witness in order to test the truth and accuracy of their testimony given on direct examination.

culpability: Criminally blameworthy; acting intentionally, knowingly, recklessly or with criminal negligence.

defense: Any fact or argument of law which exonerates a person from criminal prosecution.

deferred adjudication: The decision of a court to delay the imposition of penalty, subject to the future conduct of the defendant. Compliance with the terms prescribed by the court may result in no further penalty being imposed.

deliberation: The process of weighing and examining the reasons for and against a contemplated act or course of conduct, or a choice of acts or means.

delinquent conduct: Conduct other than a traffic offense which violates a penal law of the state of Texas and is punishable by imprisonment or by confinement in jail; or a violation of a reasonable and lawful order which was entered by a juvenile court. In general, a violation of the Texas Penal Code or a violation of the terms of juvenile probation.

***de novo* proceeding:** New trial which tries a matter as if it had not been heard before.

deputy: An official legally authorized to act for another person; the term is used most frequently in connection with the law enforcement offices of county sheriff and precinct constable.

determinate sentence: A blended sentencing system for the most serious juvenile offenders that provides the possibility of the juvenile's transfer at age 18 from the Texas Youth Commission to the adult system to complete their sentence at the Institutional Division of the Texas Department of Criminal Justice.

deterrent: Anything which impedes or has a tendency to prevent. The deterrence theory states that the main purpose of punishment is to prevent crime; the knowledge that severe punishment will follow commission of a crime is the most effective way to discourage potential criminals from committing crimes.

direct examination: The examination of a witness by the party who called him to the stand.

discretionary review: A form of appellate review which is not a matter of right but only occurs at the discretion of the appellate court.

disposition hearing: A juvenile court hearing held subsequent to the adjudication hearing only if the youth is in need of rehabilitation or the protection of the public requires that such as disposition be made.

District A: Subdivision of a geographical area made for political, administrative, or judicial purposes.

Docket A: List of cases scheduled for trial or appeal, or a brief record of court proceedings.

double jeopardy: The 5th Amendment of the United States Constitution protects an accused from both multiple prosecutions for the same offense and multiple punishments for the same crime.

duress: Unlawful threats of harm or other pressure used to force someone to act against his will. An act performed under duress relieves a person from the normal legal effect or consequences of his or her actions.

electronic monitoring: The use of an electronic device placed on a probationer or a parolee to monitor his location and activities at a given location and at a specified time in the physical absence of a probation or parole officer. Electronic monitoring is typically used in conjunction with non-residential supervision programs to enhance supervision.

***en banc* hearing:** In full bench. The term refers to situations where all qualified judges of an appellate court take part in a hearing.

enhancement: The use of a prior conviction to increase the punishment range of a new conviction.

entrapment: The action by police or other government officers of inducing a person to commit a crime he had not contemplated nor would have committed if not for the inducement. The mere act of furnishing an opportunity for criminal conduct to occur, where criminal intent is already present, is not entrapment.

enumerated offense: A specific grouping of designated crimes, generally listed due to the nature of the seriousness of the conduct.

evidence: The means by which an alleged fact is either proven or disproven. Any type of proof legally presented at trial to persuade the court or jury as to the truth of the matter in question. The most frequently encountered types of evidence in any criminal or civil trial are witness testimony, physical objects, and documents.

***ex post facto* law:** A law passed after the occurrence of a fact or commission of an act, which retrospectively changes the legal consequences of the act. The U.S. Constitution and a majority of state constitutions (including that of Texas) expressly prohibit such laws.

examining trial: A pretrial hearing for determining if sufficient evidence of guilt justifies further criminal proceedings. An indictment eliminates the defendant's right to an examining trial.

***exclusionary rule*:** Legal prohibitions against prosecution using evidence illegally searched or seized. Such determinations are often made by a court in pretrial hearing.

exclusive jurisdiction: The power which a specified court has, effectively barring all other courts from litigating specified matters.

felony: A crime that is potentially punishable upon conviction by incarceration for more than one year. A capital felony is punishable by either life imprisonment or by death.

field services: Services provided by local juvenile probation offices to delinquent youths residing in the community.

firearm offender: A youth whose Texas Youth Commission classifying offense involved a finding by the juvenile court or a Texas Youth Commission hearing examiner that the youth possessed a firearm during the offense. Classifying offenses for this classification are not limited to offenses specified in Chapter 46 of the Texas Penal Code.

forfeiture of bonds and recognizance: The result of failing to perform a condition as set forth in a bail bond, such as failing to appear at trial.

"Four corners" rule: A rule pertaining to the validity of warrants. For an arrest warrant to be valid it is critical that the basis for probable cause be stated within the four corners of the paper on which the affidavit is printed.

"Franks" hearing: A pretrial hearing for the specific purpose of challenging the veracity of the affiant, the information contained in the affidavit, and the existence of probable cause for arrest.

fruit of the poisonous tree: The doctrine that evidence seized illegally is considered "tainted" and cannot be used against a suspect.

fruits and instrumentalities: Tools used to effectuate a particular crime and the proceeds of the crime ("loot").

functus officio: A Latin term denoting the invalidity of a warrant by operation of law.

fundamental rights: Those rights which have their source in, and are explicitly or implicitly guaranteed by, the federal constitution.

guardianship: A person legally responsible for managing the legal affairs of an individual who is unable to manage his or her own affairs (by reason of age or mental infirmity).

general defenses: General defenses "justify" conduct that would otherwise be illegal (e.g., self-defense). If successful at trial, a general defense entirely insulates the accused from criminal responsibility. It is the burden of the prosecution to disprove general defenses "beyond a reasonable doubt." If the prosecution fails to disprove a general defense, the accused must be found guilty.

general jurisdiction in law and equity: A court which has the authority to hear cases both civil and criminal.

general offender: A youth who is not eligible for any other Texas Youth Commission classification.

"good faith" rule: An exception to the exclusionary rule which allows evidence obtained subsequent a faulty warrant to be admitted at trial. This rule recognizes that officers who have acted with objective good faith have a right to rely upon the issuing magistrate's determination that substantial basis existed for finding probable cause.

grand jury (grand jury review): A body of persons who have been selected according to law and sworn to hear the evidence against an accused person and determine whether there is sufficient evidence to bring the accused to trial.

guilty: An admission by the defendant that the charges brought by the State are true.

hearsay: Testimony given by a witness who relates not what he knows personally but what has been said by others. Since the truthfulness of such statements rely on individuals not present in court, it is inadmissible as evidence.

hung jury: A jury that after long deliberation is irreconcilably divided, or hopelessly deadlocked to the point that it is unable to reach any verdict.

inchoate offenses: The crimes of solicitation, conspiracy, and attempt.

indeterminate sentence: A sentencing practice that commits a youth to the Texas Youth Commission for an indefinite period of time, not to exceed his or her 21st birthday.

index crime: The foundation of the Uniform Crime Report, consisting of the seven following offenses: murder, rape, robbery, aggravated assault, burglary, larceny-motor vehicle theft, and arson.

indictment: A formal charging instrument returned by a grand jury based on evidence presented by State prosecutors.

inferior courts: A collective term used to refer to the justice and municipal courts, which denotes that their location is at the bottom of the judicial hierarchy.

information: A written statement filed and presented on behalf of the State by the district or county attorney, charging the defendant with an offense. As the functional equivalent of a grand jury indictment, an information is the process by which the State prosecutes misdemeanors. It is also used by criminal defendants accused of felonies who wish to avoid the drawn out process of grand jury indictment.

injunction: An equitable remedy in which the court orders a party to perform or to desist from a particular act.

insanity: An affirmative defense to criminal charges that relieves the accused of criminal responsibility. If the defense is raised it is the burden of the accused to prove that at the time of the crime he had a severe mental disease or defect that caused him to be unable to appreciate the criminality of his actions.

Institutional Division (ID): One of the four divisions that comprise the Texas Department of Criminal Justice, ID manages and operates the Texas prison system. Formerly known as the Texas Department of Corrections.

institutional programs: Texas Youth Commission programs that incorporate the use of incarceration or detention of serious juvenile offenders.

intake: A procedure in which the juvenile courts screen cases. After reviewing the case to determine if sufficient probable cause exists, the county intake officer decides whether to place the child on informal probation, file a formal petition with the court, or dispose of the referral.

Intensive Supervision Parole (ISP): A program that supervises parolees who are at a high risk of violating one or more conditions of their release on parole. The program requires a minimum of one contact per week and a more intensive level of parole supervision.

intentionally: A culpable mental state in which the accused is purposely committing an offense.

interlocutory order: A decree which does not determine a cause of action but which resolves an intervening matter which must be resolved before final adjudication.

Intermediate Sanction Facility (ISF): A facility used for the short-term incarceration of parole and mandatory supervision violators operated by and under the jurisdiction of the Parole Division.

Interstate Compact on Juveniles (ICJ): A national network which allows states to communicate with each other in the instance that a parolee or probationer moves from one state to another. The Texas Youth Commission administers the ICJ for the state of Texas.

intervening factor: An event or impeding occurrence which negates the causation element of an offense.

intoxication: The loss of normal mental or physical abilities caused by the consumption of alcohol or drugs.

jail: A facility constructed and financed by county government and operated by the county sheriff for holding pretrial detainees and incarcerating offenders convicted of misdemeanor offenses.

judges: Elected public officers who preside over courts of law.

judicial district: One of the circuits or precincts into which a state is commonly divided.

judiciary: A collective term referring to the systems of courts, its judges, and other court officers and personnel.

jurisdiction: The legal and geographical range of a court's authority.

jury: The group of citizens who must determine whether a defendant is guilty or not guilty. If requested by the defendant, the jury may also set punishment. A felony jury has 12 members and a misdemeanor jury has 6 members. Texas requires jury decisions to be unanimous.

jury charge: Instructions from the court to the jury. Without commenting on how much weight the jury should give particular evidence and testimony, the jury charge sets forth the applicable law in the case, explains the issues the jury must determine, provides guidelines for deliberating a verdict, and contains forms for recording the jury's verdict.

justice of the peace: A judicial officer of the inferior courts having jurisdiction as set forth by statute over minor civil and criminal matters.

juvenile board: Local panel generally composed of the district, county, and statutory judges of the locality. Responsible for overseeing and managing local juvenile probation and detention services.

knowingly: A culpable mental state in which the accused is consciously aware that he is committing an offense.

law: A body of rules or standards of conduct created by an authoritative body for the purpose of maintaining order and insuring compliance with particular norms.

legislature: The lawmaking body of the state. In Texas the legislature is composed of the House of Representatives and the Senate.

lynch: To put to death by mob action without legal sanction; many times the end result of the work of a vigilance committee.

lynch law: The punishment of suspected or actual crimes, usually by death, and without resort to due process of law.

magistrate: A public officer with specific executive or judicial powers.

mandatory supervision: A type of release from prison for restricted categories of convicts. Eligible convicts are released on mandatory supervision when their calendar time served and good time credits equal the length of their prison sentence, with no requirement for Board of Pardons and Paroles approval except for convicts who were convicted of committing offenses prior to 1 September 1996.

medical examiner: A public officer responsible for investigating all sudden, unexplained, unnatural, or suspicious deaths.

mens rea: An evil or guilty mind; the criminal intent required of a person committing an act which constitutes a crime.

mental health hearing: The procedure prior to an adjudication hearing in which the mental capacity of the youth is examined and recommendations are made by mental health professionals. Youths who are deemed incompetent are hospitalized by the Texas Department of Mental Health and Mental Retardation.

Mentally Retarded Offender Program (MROP): A program which allows mentally retarded convicts to be paroled under the supervision of a specially trained parole officer who can provide services to meet the special needs of these offenders.

mere evidence: Proof that a suspect committed a particular crime.

minimum length of stay (MLOS classification): The minimum period of time after being committed to the Texas Youth Commission that a youth must spend before he can be discharged or become eligible for parole supervision. The MLOS for offenders who receive a determinate sentence is based on the felony level of the offense and is set by the court. The MLOS for other criminal acts is determined by the most serious of the relevant offenses documented in the youth's record.

Miranda warnings: Warnings that peace officers are required to provide to a person they choose to question while in custody. Named after the landmark U.S. Supreme Court decision of *Miranda v. Arizona*, one's Miranda rights are based on the 5th Amendment protection against self-incrimination.

misdemeanor: A criminal offense punishable by a fine or imprisonment for less than one year.

mistake of fact: A general defense that justifies conduct on the basis that the defendant by mistake formed a reasonable belief about a matter of fact pertinent to the offense. However, the mistaken belief must negate the mental element (*mens rea*) required for committing the crime.

mistake of law: An incorrect judgment of the legal consequences of known facts. Since "ignorance of the law" is no excuse, mistakes of law are rarely utilized as a defense. However, where the accused relied on a "narrow class of official statements or interpretations of the law" (e.g., court opinions or agency regulations), mistakes of law may be submitted as an affirmative defense.

mistrial: A trial that is terminated without a verdict and declared invalid by the court because of some circumstance that creates a substantial irreconcilable prejudice.

mitigate: To lessen the punishment imposed by law.

municipal: Pertaining to a city.

municipal ordinance: A law or provision created by the legislative body of a city.

negative act: Failure to act in a way mandated by law. For example, failure to report abuse of a child or failure to file federal income tax returns.

new trial: A rehearing of a criminal case after a finding or verdict of guilty has been set aside by an appellate court due to specific legal grounds.

no bill: A grand jury's refusal to indict the accused. Sometimes called an ignoramus.

nolo contendere: A plea of no contest, which allows the defendant to avoid contesting the State's charges. It has the same legal implications as a guilty plea.

not guilty: A plea of not guilty contests the charges and challenges the state to prove them beyond a reasonable doubt.

omission: *see* negative act.

orientation and assessment (O&A): A procedure of combined medical, educational, and psychological testing, as well as information such as age, nature of offense, and length and degree of criminal activity, used in compiling a need and risk assessment for each entering youth institutionalized by the Texas Youth Commission.

original jurisdiction: Courts in which a case is first heard, usually in a trial.

outlawry: A process of old English law by which a defendant held in contempt was declared an outlaw. If for treason or felony, the defendant could be executed or imprisoned without a trial.

pardon: A form of executive clemency which absolves an individual from the legal consequences of his crime and conviction. There are several categories of pardon, including full pardons, conditional pardons, and pardons based on innocence.

parens patriae: A philosophy under which the State takes over the role of parent.

parole: The conditional release of an inmate from prison by the Board of Pardons and Paroles. The parolee serves the remainder of his sentence under the supervision of a parole officer in the community.

Parole Division (PD): One of the four divisions that comprise the Texas Department of Criminal Justice, PD oversees the reintegration of convicted felons into mainstream society after their early release from prison.

parole officer: An employee of the Parole Division of the Texas Department of Criminal Justice who is responsible for supervising convicts released from prison under parole or mandatory supervision.

parolee: A convicted felon who is released from incarceration in the Texas prison system prior to the completion of his sentence. A parolee reports on a regular basis to a parole officer, and must abide by specific conditions of release until the original sentence is completed.

Part I offenses: The first of two categories of index crimes established for crime reporting purposes. Part I offenses are by their nature more serious and occur more frequently. For Part I offenses, the reports of offenses committed are collected without regard to whether an arrest was made.

Part II offenses: The second of two categories established for crime reporting purposes. Collection of data relating to Part II offenses are limited to arrest information only.

penal: Pertaining to punishment or penalties.

peremptory challenge: Challenges to prospective jurors made without explanation. The only limitation on the use of peremptory challenges is that they may not be based on sex or race. In most misdemeanor cases, both the defense and prosecution have three peremptory challenges. In felony cases, not punishable by death, both sides have 10 peremptory challenges. In death penalty cases both sides have 15 peremptory challenges.

perjury: The legal offense of making a known false statement under oath in a legal proceeding which is material to the issue before the court.

personal bond: A written document in which an individual recognizes an obligation to behave in a defined manner in exchange for his or her release from jail.

plain view search (plain view doctrine): The rule that anything a police officer sees in plain view when he has a legal right to be where he is, is not the product of a search and is therefore admissible as evidence.

plea bargain: The negotiation of an agreement between the State, the judge, and the accused's attorney as to the charge(s) and sentence imposed if the accused pleads guilty.

police: Agents of the executive branch of government who are charged with the responsibility for maintaining order and enforcing law.

police power: The legitimate power of a state to pass laws, authorize the creation of law enforcement agencies, establish courts, and maintain prisons for the purposes of promoting the public peace, enforcing the law, and protecting the public. The police power is derived from the Tenth Amendment to the U.S. Constitution.

precedent: *see* case law.

precinct: A specific geographical area within a county.

pre-parole investigation (PPI): An investigation of a convict's parole release plan that takes into consideration the living arrangements, employment plans, and treatment and counseling programs which the convict will be involved in after his release on parole.

pre-parole transfer: The transfer of a convict who is within 180 days of parole eligibility, or who was denied parole on the first review, to a secure community based facility where he receives counseling and employment assistance prior to release on parole.

preponderance of evidence: The burden of proof utilized in civil trials which requires the party bringing the action to establish their case with 51% probability. In criminal trials, if an affirmative defense is raised by the defendant, the affirmative defense must satisfy the same standards of 51% probability.

pre-trial motion: An order of the court that governs the conduct of the trial. Generally, pre-trial motions are requested by either the defense or prosecution to fix the scope of the trial (e.g., what evidence is admissible, what particular witnesses can testify about, what issues can be raised, and what issues cannot be raised).

preventive detention: In setting the amount of bail, courts are allowed to consider the future safety of the victim, the victim's family, and the safety of the community.

prison: A State-financed and operated facility for the incarceration of convicted felons.

private law: Laws governing the relations between citizens (e.g., tort and contract law).

privileges: The right of certain individuals not to testify about certain matters.

probable cause: Sufficient evidence to reasonably believe that a suspect has committed or is committing a criminal act. The quantum of proof required by the Fourth Amendment to the United States Constitution for arrest.

probate: The legal process having to do with the administrations of wills and estates.

probation: A sentence imposed by the court which allows a convicted offender to serve a sentence in the community under the supervision of a probation officer. Probation is technically referred to today as community supervision.

proper predicate: Factual verification through sworn affidavit or testimony that evidence is accurate, genuine, and, in cases involving scientific proof, uncontaminated.

prosecutor: State attorney who instigates the prosecution of the accused and represents the interest of the state and its citizenry at trial.

public defender program: County-operated programs which provide legal representation to indigent defendants. Most public defender programs are located in large metropolitan areas.

public law: Laws governing the relationship between citizens and their government (e. g., criminal and constitutional law).

Public Safety Commission: A non-salaried, three-member commission appointed by the governor which oversees the operation of the Texas Department of Public Safety.

punishment: Any negative sanction imposed on an individual by legal authority, judgment, and sentence of the court for some crime or offense committed by him or her, or for omission of a legal duty; a deprivation of some legal rights excluding civil penalties such as forfeiture of interest.

question of fact: A disputed factual contention.

question of law: A disputed legal contention.

rebuttal: Evidence which defeats, refutes, or proves the contrary of a fact or presumption offered in evidence by the opposing party.

recidivism: The repetition of criminal behavior.

recklessly: A culpable mental state in which the accused is aware that his or her conduct could have dangerous consequences but chooses to ignore the risk (i.e., conscious risk taking).

referral: A recommendation by police agencies, parents, schools, victims, or probation officers that a youth should be entered into the juvenile justice system.

rehabilitation: The process whereby a convicted criminal offender loses the desire and intent to commit criminal acts and accepts the behavioral norms of society; the restoring or reinstatement of something to its former capacity or position.

relevance: Whether or not a particular piece of evidence makes an important issue at trial less likely to be true. Evidence must be relevant to be admissible.

res gestae: A Latin term meaning "things done." Statements or utterances made immediately and spontaneously upon arrest or during the commission of a crime. *Res gestae* statements are an exception to the hearsay rule.

resocialization: Correctional therapy for Texas Youth Commission juvenile offenders which entails correctional therapy, education, and work discipline training.

restitution: A condition of probation or deferred adjudication requiring offenders to compensate their victims for damages or to donate their time in community service.

restrictions: Court-imposed limitations on an individual's ability to exercise his or her freedom.

rights: Inherent power or privilege to freely act.

rule of witnesses: Commonly referred to simply as "the Rule," Texas law allows, with certain exceptions, either the prosecutor or defense lawyer to exclude all witnesses from the courtroom except when they are testifying.

rules: Principles or standards established by authority.

search and seizure: In a criminal investigation by law enforcement officials, the practice of searching persons or property and confiscating any items found that are relevant to the investigation; the search for and taking of persons and property as evidence of a crime.

search warrant: A written order, issued by a magistrate and directed to law enforcement, commanding the search of a specified premises for specified items subject to seizure.

self-incrimination: Any action or admission made by a person that implicates the person in the commission of a crime, either before or at trial.

Sex Offenders Treatment Program (SOTP): Specialized treatment for sex offenders provided by Texas Youth Commission and contract providers. The program is based on a cognitive-behavioral and relapse prevention model which not only focuses on correcting the offending behavior but also on the cognitive distortions ("thinking errors") that motivate criminal behavior.

sheriff: The chief law enforcement officer of counties in Texas. Elected to four-year terms of office, the sheriff is also statutorily responsible for the operation of the county jail.

shire reeve: In Norman, England, the chief law enforcement officer of a county, or reeve. The shire reeve was the forerunner of the modern American county sheriff.

shuffle: The right of either the defendant or the State that the order of the prospective juror list be randomly reorganized, resulting in a new sequential listing of prospective jurors.

small claims court: Courts established at the inferior court level which deal with civil claims involving small amounts of money.

Specialized Caseloads Program: The grouping of probationers by problem areas for supervision by a probation officer experienced and trained in that problem area. Specialized caseloads are usually limited to 40 probationers per probation officer.

State Jail Division (SJD): One of the four divisions that comprise the Texas Department of Criminal Justice, SJD operates facilities for the incarceration of offenders who have been convicted of non-violent felony offenses.

state jail felony: Certain offenses (primarily property offenses and low-level controlled substance offenses) committed after 1 September 1994 are classified as state jail felonies. A state jail sentence involves a mandatory term of community supervision, in some cases preceded by 60 to 365 days of confinement in a state jail facility. Confinement for the full term of a sentence may be ordered if the conditions of community supervision are violated. State jail sentences cannot exceed two years for one offense, but repeat offenders may receive overlapping state jail sentences not to exceed three years.

statutory law: A law created or codified by enactment of the legislature.

subpoena: A court order requiring a person to appear in court and give testimony. Individuals may be compelled to bring specified documents by issuance of a subpoena *duces tecum*.

surety: A third party who posts a bond for an accused (i.e., a bail bondsman).

technical violation: A violation of one or more of the conditions of a parole or mandatory release that does not involve the commission of a new criminal offense.

Texas Board of Criminal Justice: The nine-member board appointed by the governor which oversees the operation of the Texas Department of Criminal Justice. Its non-salaried members serve staggered six-year terms and are required by statute to meet at least once per calendar quarter.

Texas Board of Pardons and Paroles: An 18-member board with constitutional and statutory authority to approve or deny a parole release, to determine the rule and conditions of release, to revoke a releasee's parole or mandatory supervision, and to make executive clemency recommendations to the governor.

Texas Commission on Law Enforcement Officer Standards and Education: A policy-making body with the statutory responsibility for both creating and enforcing minimum qualifications for the selection, training, and certification of law enforcement officers in Texas.

Texas Department of Criminal Justice (TDCJ): The largest agency in Texas state government, TDCJ is responsible for the management and administration of the Texas prison system, state jails, probation, and parole, and consists of four major divisions: Institutional Division, State Jail Division, Parole Division, and the Community Justice Assistance Division.

Texas Department of Public Safety (DPS): The premier state law enforcement agency in Texas, whose responsibility is to preserve public order by enforcing state laws, providing for the prevention and detection of crime, and promoting and protecting the lives and property of Texans.

Texas Juvenile Probation Commission (TJPC): The state agency responsible for overseeing juvenile probation services of 160 local probation departments in all of Texas' 254 counties by providing training, technical assistance, supervision, and state funds.

Texas Rangers: The oldest state law enforcement organization in the United States, the Texas Rangers are today part of the Texas Department of Public Safety.

Texas Youth Commission (TYC): The state government agency with exclusive administrative control and oversight of the state's system of juvenile institutional incarceration and correction.

"The Rule": *see* rule of witness.

trial: Courtroom proceedings before a judge and jury to examine evidence and hear arguments so that questions of law and fact may be decided.

true bill: A grand jury's endorsement of the charge or charges filed against the accused that result in an indictment. At least nine votes are required to "true bill" a defendant in Texas.

Type A violent offender: A youth whose classifying offense is either the commission, attempted commission, conspiracy to commit, solicitation or solicitation of a minor to commit murder, capital murder, or sexual assault, and who has not been sentenced to commitment in the Texas Youth Commission.

Type B violent offender: A youth whose classifying offense is the commission, attempted commission, conspiracy to commit, solicitation or solicitation of a minor to commit one of the following enumerated offenses and has not be sentenced to commitment to the Texas Youth Commission: (1) manslaughter, (2) kidnapping, (3) aggravated kidnapping, (4) indecency with a child, (5) sexual assault, (6) aggravated sexual assault, (7) injury to a child, (8) injury to an elderly or disabled individual (1st degree only), (9) deadly conduct (felony only), (10) aiding suicide (felony only), (11) tampering with a consumer product (1st and 2nd degree only), (12) arson, (13) aggravated robbery, (14) burglary (only with intent to commit any other violent offense), (15) intoxication manslaughter, (16) intentionally participating with six or more persons in conduct at a Texas Youth Commission facility that endangers persons or property and substantially obstructs the performance of facility operation, (17) intentionally, knowingly assaulting or battering any Texas Youth Commission employee, agent, or volunteer.

unfounded offense: A criminal act reported to law enforcement authorities that, upon investigation, is found to be false or baseless.

Uniform Crime Reporting Program (UCR): The nationwide summary-based system for reporting crimes known to the police in a standardized fashion that allows for uniform comparisons of crime rates and trends.

uniform jurisdiction: The authority of a trial court to hear various types of cases without statutorily imposed limitations.

value ladder offenses: A subset of property offenses in which punishment is determined according to the worth of the property when it is taken (i.e., fair market value). The penalty increases with the value of the property stolen.

vehicle inventory: When a vehicle is either discovered abandoned or the owner is taken into custody, an inventory of the vehicle's contents (also known as an administrative search) may be conducted to protect the owner's property rights. Due to the administrative nature of such searches, vehicle inventories are not protected by the Fourth Amendment.

venire: A writ that summons prospective jurors.

venireman: A prospective juror.

verdict: The decision of a jury in a jury trial or a magistrate in a non-jury trial that the defendant is guilty or not guilty of the offense for which he or she had been tried.

vicarious liability: The liability of one person for the acts of another. Indirect legal responsibility. For example, the liability of the employer for the acts of an employee.

victim impact statement: A form used by law enforcement agencies, prosecutors, and other participants in the criminal justice system to record the impact of a crime on the victim. Victim impact statements are considered during sentencing proceedings and at all parole panel reviews.

vigilance committee: A group of citizens voluntarily organized to suppress and punish crimes summarily, especially under circumstances where the processes of established law appear inadequate to the task.

vigilante: A member of a vigilance committee.

violent crime: Technically refers to the index crimes of murder, forcible rape, robbery, and aggravated assault.

voir dire: French, meaning to "speak the truth." A process in which attorneys for the defense and prosecution are allowed to question the jurors and discover their individual biases and attitudes that may be legal grounds of dismissal.

voluntary: Acting without compulsion; intentional, or done by design.

warrant: Any number of writs issued by a magistrate that directs law enforcement officers to perform a specified act (generally, to search or seize a person, place, or thing) under the authority and protection of the law.

"wing span" rule: Legal rule holding that if an officer properly arrests a suspect, the officer may search the area within the suspect's immediate control (i.e., all the areas within the suspect's immediate reach).

writ: A written order issued by a judge authorizing and requiring that something be done outside the courtroom.

writ of certiorari: A writ issued by the high courts ordering some lower court to "forward up the record" of a case so that it may be reviewed.

writ of error: An order from an appellate court to a lower court to remedy an error which was incorporated into its final judgment.

writ of habeas corpus: A writ which challenges whether a person in the custody of legal authorities is being lawfully detained.

writ of mandamus: A court order which requires a public official or corporation to act in a specific manner to ensure compliance with the law.

INDEX

383